The Most Beautiful Natural Wonders

The Most Beautiful Natural Wonders

© 2008 Rebo International, b.v., Lisse, Netherlands

This edition reprinted in 2009.

This publication was compiled from a selection of the most interesting texts and photographs from titles published by Rebo Publishers, including *100 Wonders of the World*, *The 100 Most Beautiful National Parks of the World*, *100 Wonders of China*, and *100 Wonders of India*.

Authors: Winfried Maass, Nicolaus Neuman, Hans Oberländer, Jörn Voss, Anne Benthues (*100 Wonders of the World*)
Hanns-Joachim Neubert/ScienceCom, Winfried Maass (*The 100 Most Beautiful National Parks of the World*)
Nirad Grover, Malini Saigal, Malavika Chauhan, Rupin Dang, Hari Dang, Razia Grover, Sreelata Bhatia, Komilla Raote, Sudhir Sahi, Sanjay Singh Badnor, Dileep Prakash, Brinda Gill, Himanshu Joshi, Raaja Bhasin, Shonar Joshi, Yash Saxena, Nikhil Devasar, Devendra Chauhan, Karni Singh (*100 Wonders of India*), Wang Zhen, Liu Yanli, Li Linzhi, Hu Minyan, Sun Ping, Mei Sheng, Gao Xing, Zhang Qunxing, Liu Xiaotian, Wu Jiahao, Dao Zi (*100 Wonders of China*)

Translators: Stephen Challacombe, based on a translation by Dr. John N. Kraay (*100 Wonders of the World*); Susan Ghanouni and Rae Walter for First Edition Translations Ltd., Cambridge, England (*The 100 Most Beautiful National Parks of the World*)

Layout and typesetting: A. R. Garamond, Prague, Czech Republic
Cover design: Studio Element, Prague, Czech Republic

ISBN 978 90 366 2453 4

All rights reserved. No part of this book may be reproduced, stored in a retrieval system, or in any form or by any means electronic, mechanical, photocopying, recording, or otherwise, without the prior written permission of the copyright holder.

Key

 Natural wonders

 Mountains and peaks

 Water, in all its forms

 Fauna

 Flora

 Traces of civilization

 Nominated for the new 7 wonders

Foreword

Dear readers,

Our planet is incredibly beautiful–abundant and rich in varied scenery of all kinds. In the modern world, however, inundated with technology, life moves at breakneck speed, and we tend to forget the natural beauty surrounding us. Mother Earth provides rivers, brooks, streams, and the water of life. It's solely up to us to decide whether to guide the conservation of Earth's flora and fauna and help them to thrive; after all, the Earth is our most precious possession.

If we want to protect something, we must first appreciate it. This philosophy lies behind the vote on the new seven natural wonders. On July 7, 2007, in Lisbon, Portugal, seven new wonders of the world were voted on, starting with a vote on the best of Earth's natural wonders. Dozens of locations were nominated and this book reveals them, along with others of the most beautiful and fascinating wonders of our planet.

The book is divided into five sections. The first section presents the world's greatest natural wonders and invites you to explore, for example, sand dunes in France, rich chalk formations in Turkey, and the mysterious volcanic landscapes of Iceland. The next section of the book catalogues amazing mountains and peaks. Climb up the highest slopes in the world in Nepal, discover dormant volcanoes in Chile, and marvel at granite landscapes in the U.S. The book's third section will stun you, with its illustrations of the strong and thunderous waterfalls of India, China, and the U.S.

Among these natural wonders, the book does not neglect the flora and fauna of each location. You'll ride the Rio Negro, branch of the Amazon, and lose yourself in the dangerous swamps and moors of Great Britain. Within these pages, you'll find pandas draped in trees, enormous herds of migrating zebras and gnus traversing Africa, and fierce Komodo dragons and reptiles. Lovers of plants will enjoy the colorful blooms in India's Valley of Flowers, and the giant sequoias and redwoods of California will astound readers. Finally, the book chronicles the footsteps of the civilizations which first called these landscapes home. In this last section, you'll travel to exquisite rock temples in China, Greek monasteries, and even below the earth, where prehistoric-era paintings are hidden.

We hope your journey with this book will be full of breathtaking vistas and adventures through the most beautiful natural landscapes.

The Publisher

Contents

FOREWORD	5

NATURAL WONDERS
EUROPE
Great Britain
Giant's Causeway: black organ pipes — 10
Iceland
Iceland's geysers — 12
Finland
Finland's island kingdom — 14
France
The Pyla Dune: Europe's largest shifting dune — 16
Germany
Limestone rocks on Rügen — 18
Lithuania
The Courland Spit: the Baltic Sahara — 20

ASIA
Turkey
Göreme National Park: tufa paradise — 22
The beauty of Pamukkale — 24
India
Mysterious Rupkund Lake — 26
Amarnath Cave — 28
China
Quiantang tide, Zhejiang — 30
Shilin stone forest: fantastical rock formations — 32
Zhada clay forest, Tibet — 34
Crescent Moon Spring, Gansu — 36
Takelamagan Desert, Xinjiang — 38
Japan
On the floor of the Aso volcano — 40
On the peak of Mount Fuji — 42

Indonesia
Volcanic paradise in Java — 44

NORTH AMERICA
The U.S.
Geysers and hot springs in the Rocky Mountains — 46
Hawaii, land of volcanos — 48
The Grand Canyon — 50

SOUTH AMERICA
Ecuador
Cotopaxi: volcanic panorama — 52

AFRICA
Niger
Ténéré National Park: the Tuareg Desert — 54
The Sahara
Sahara, sea without water — 56

AUSTRALIA
Ayers Rock: Australia's red heart — 58

MOUNTAINS AND PEAKS
EUROPE
France
Mountains of the Cévennes — 60
The Czech Republic, Germany
The Elbe sandstone mountains — 62
Austria
Hohe Tauern National Park: the romantic eastern Tyrol — 64
Bulgaria
Pirin National Park: majestic fir trees — 66
Montenegro
The Durmitor massif — 68

ASIA
Nepal
Mount Everest: home of the gods — 70
India
Kachenjunga: sentinel of the eastern Himalayas — 72

Sri Lanka	
Sigiriya Mountain: King Kasyapa's rocky citadel	74
China	
Golden Stone Beach, Liaoning	76
Daocheng, Sichuan	78
The Yangtze River's three gorges	80
Hailuo Gully in Mount Gongga, Sichuan	82
Mount Changbaishan	84
Mount Huangshan	86
The source of Wuling, Hunan	88

NORTH AMERICA
The U.S.

Denali National Park	90
Yosemite National Park: El Capitan stands guard	92
Jasper National Park: Canada's alpine wilderness	94

SOUTH AMERICA
Venezuela

Canaima National Park	96
Peru	
Huascaran National Park	98
Chile	
Lauca National Park	100
Torres del Paine: at the end of the world	102

AFRICA
Tanzania

The craters of Kilimanjaro	104
South Africa	
Alpine landscapes on South Africa's plateau	106

WATER, IN ALL ITS FORMS
EUROPE
Great Britain

Northumberland: land of moors and peat bogs	108
The Lake District: high fells, brooding lakes	110
Dartmoor: the mists could swallow the world	112
Greenland	
Green hopes, white reality	114
The Netherlands	
The Waddenzee: sometimes sea, sometimes land	116
Germany	
Salt marshes and mud flats	118
Switzerland	
Glacial splendor in the Alps	120
Romania	
The Danube delta: islands in the stream	122
Croatia	
The Plitvice lakes	124
Russia	
The floodplains of the Volga	126

ASIA
Russia

The seals of Lake Baikal	128
Israel and Jordan	
The Dead Sea; the Sea of Lot	130
India	
The Rann of Kutch: a desert of many moods	132
Loktak Lake: floating stage of dancing deer	134
Chilika Lake: a fertile junction of waters	136
The Zanskar River: the land of white copper	138
The Brahmaputra: son of Brahma, the Creator	140
South Indian waterfalls: thunder and spray	142
China	
Lijiang River: passionate and dreamlike water	144
Hukou Falls, Shanxi	146
Luguhu Lake	148
Mapang Yumco, Tibet	150
Huangguoushu Waterfall	152
Japan	
Kushiro National Park: a paradise for wildlife	154
Vietnam	
Ha Long cliffs: land of rocks and water	156
Thailand	
Ang Thong National Park	158

NORTH AMERICA
The U.S.

The Everglades: river of grass	160

Niagara Falls: the "thundering water"	162
The Great Salt Lake: the American Dead Sea	164

SOUTH AMERICA
Brazil
Jau National Park: the forest of giant trees	166

Argentina
The Iguazu waterfalls: plummeting torrents	168
The Patagonian ice field	170

AFRICA
Zimbabwe
Victoria Falls: smoking thunder	172

Botswana
The Okavango Basin: river delta in the desert	174

FLORA AND FAUNA
EUROPE
The Svalbard Archipelago
Spitzbergen: sunbathing on the "Cold Coast"	176

Norway
Hardangervidda: the Vidda uplands	178

Sweden
The Saami herdsmen	180

France
The Luberon: vivid mountain landscape	182
The Camargue: the land of pink flamingos	184

Spain
Doñana National Park: in the shelter of the dunes	186
The Canary Islands	188

Portugal
The laurel forests of Madeira	190

Germany
The Luneberg heath: a kaleidoscope of colors	192
Berchtesgaden National Park: primeval forest setting	194

The Czech Republic and Germany
The Bavarian and Bohemian forests	196

The Czech Republic
The Krkonos Mountains: Krakonos's icy kingdom	198

Slovakia and Poland
Tatras National Park	200

Poland and Belarus
A forest undisturbed for almost 500 years	202

Hungary
Hortobágy National Park: the plains of the Puszta	204

Croatia
The underwater kingdom of the Kornati Islands	206

Italy
Abruzzo National Park: wolves of the south	208

ASIA
India
The Valley of Flowers	210
Assam: plantations for the perfect brew	212
Kaziranga National Park	214
Periyar: park of pachyderms	216
Chambal: blue-green river amid labyrinthine ravines	218
Bhitarkanika: where a million turtles nest	220
Gir National Park: roar of the Asiatic lion	222
Keoladeo Ghana National Park	224

Bangladesh
The Sundarbans: kingdom of the Bengal tiger	226

China
Kanas Nature Reserve, Xinjiang	228
Wolong: the pandas have all the bamboo they need	230

Indonesia
The Komodo Islands: the land of dragons	232

Malaysia
Taman Negara: walkways over the jungle	234

NORTH AMERICA
The U.S.
Sequoia National Park	236
Great Smoky Mountains National Park	238

Canada
Wood Buffalo National Park	240

SOUTH AMERICA
Costa Rica
Braulio Carrillo	242

Manuel Antonio National Park: the jungle and the coast	244
Ecuador	
The Galapagos: the land of ancient lizards	246
Peru	
Paracas National Park: paradise for sea lions	248
Brazil	
Pantanal: paradise in the swamps	250

AFRICA
Uganda
Queen Elizabeth National Park	252
Murchison National Park	254

Kenya
Masai Mara: land of the Masai	256
Tsavo National Park: the red soil of the savannah	258

Tanzania
The Serengeti: a land of lush grass	260
Ngorongoro Crater: the cradle of civilization	262

The Republic of Congo
The Okapi Reserve: forest giraffes of the Congo	264

Botswana
Chobe National Park	266

Namibia
Etosha National Park: spectacle of the salt flats	268

South Africa
Kruger National Park and Limpopo Park	270

Réunion Island (France)
Réunion: island of exotic plants	272

AUSTRALIA AND NEW ZEALAND
Australia
Fraser Island: an Aboriginal paradise	274
The Great Barrier Reef: the beauty of the coral	276

New Zealand
Mount Cook and Fjordland: the Southern fjords	278

TRACES OF CIVILIZATION
EUROPE
Stonehenge: sanctuary from the Stone Age	280

France
The Lascaux Caves' Stone-Age drawings	282

Greece
The Metéora Islands: floating monasteries	284

Italy
The cliffs of Cinque Terre	286
The fertile valleys of the Monti Lattari mountains	288

ASIA
Jordan
Petra: rock city of the Nabatean kings	290

India
Bhimbetka: mesolithic petroglyphs	292
Ellora's grand grottoes	294

China
Tai Shan National Park: the sacred mountain	296
Dunhuang Mogao Grottoes, Gansu	298
Longmen Grottoes, Henan	300
Yungang Grottoes, Shanxi	302
The Great Wall of China	304

NORTH AMERICA
The U.S.
The cliff dwellings of Mesa Verde	306

SOUTH AMERICA
Guatemala
Tikal: ruined rainforest city of the Mayas	308

Peru
Lake Titicaca: floating islands of reeds	310
Forgotten Machu Picchu	312
The mysterious giant pictures in Nazca	314

Brazil
Capivara: prehistoric treasure chamber	316

AUSTRALIA
Kakadu National Park	318
Photography credits	**320**

EUROPE

Black organ pipes

The lava pillars of the Giant's Causeway rise up from the Northern Irish coastline

Getting there:
Flights to Dublin airport. By road from Antrim and Ballymena to Ballycastle or Portrush

Where to stay:
At the historic Causeway Hotel in Giant's Causeway Park; all other categories of hotel in the surrounding towns. Bed-and-breakfast establishments available. Camping site

Climate:
Temperate Atlantic climate. Stormy weather in spring and autumn

Main attractions:
Port Reostan viewpoint; Organ, Giant's Eyes, Harp, Camel's Hump, and Chimney Tops (site of the Girona wreck); walk along the former hydro-electric tram tracks or to Dunseverick Castle

Even though Finn MacCumhail (also known as MacCool) was 50ft (15m) in height, he is one of the smaller giants in Irish mythology. According to legend, it was he who built this spectacular formation of basalt pillars that project out into the sea off the coast of Northern Ireland as a causeway designed to connect Ireland with the Scottish isle of Staffa. There are differing versions of the legend of the construction of the pillars. According to one, MacCumhail built it to save the woman he loved from getting her feet wet when he brought her over to Ireland. Another says he constructed them to enable him to do battle with a rival giant in Scotland, thus explaining the existence of similar pillars on Staffa.

These strange, five and seven-sided basalt pillars, have diameters of 12–20in (30–50cm) across and range up to 82ft (25m) in height. They form a tightly packed arrangement of black columns rising from the shoreline on the edge of the Antrim Plateau between Causeway Head and Benbane Head. They look as if they are reaching up from the seabed toward the 330ft (100m) high cliff tops. From above, they look like a piece of honeycomb, while viewed from the side they resemble steps leading down into the sea.

The Antrim Plateau extends over an area of 1,500 square miles (3,800km2) and is Europe's largest surviving lava plateau. It was formed 50 to 60 million years ago during the early Tertiary period when hot, molten lava erupted through fissures in the limestone landscape. The remains of some of these larger clefts in the limestone rock near the shore can still be seen today. There were three main periods of volcanic activity during which the lower, middle, and upper basalt layers were deposited. The Giant's Causeway columns originate from the middle lava emission, when five or six outpourings of molten rock flowed into the sea where it instantly solidified. The subsequent pressure between the lava flows compressed them into the angular columns we see today. There are around 40,000 such columns rising up from the sea around Giant's Causeway.

Giants' Eyes

Sixty thicker columns, all of equal height and size, soar upward in the formation known as Giants Organ. At Chimney Tops, erosion has separated the pillars into impressive, single chimney stacks.

The coast to the north of Port Ballantrae is peppered with fantastic

structures of this kind, created by lava, water, and weathering. Names like "The Harp," "Camel's Hump," "Amphitheater," or "Wishing Chair" encourage the imagination to run riot.

Erosion of the lower basalt layer, on which the columns stand, runs for approximately 3 1/4 miles (6km) along the coast in the form of a reddish band. The black cliffs, comprising innumerable bays and rocky promontories, end abruptly in a steep, luminous-white ridge of limestone. The round shapes, which have resulted in several places from erosion of the lower basalt layer, are known in Ireland as the Giants' Eyes.

During the seventeenth century, the Giant's Causeway became so popular that people came in droves to see it, often incurring the displeasure of local farmers and fishermen. It was not until 1897, following a lengthy legal battle, that local inhabitants were obliged to accept a road being built enabling people to visit this natural phenomenon on payment of a hefty admission fee. In 1961, however, Northern Ireland's National Trust association purchased the entire area and made it a protected area, at the same time abolishing all entry charges. Around 160 acres (0.7km2) of this breathtaking natural coastal spectacle now enjoys official protection. Thousands of visitors come here not only to marvel at the mighty pillars and steps, but also to enjoy the plant life and observe the animals.

Scree, grassland and heath

Over 200 species of plants make this strip of coastline a fascinating area for botanists. This biodiversity represents a whole range of different habitats, comprising seashore, cliffs, scree, grassland, scrub, and heath as well as marshland. Some of the rarer varieties found here include maidenhair spleenwort, hare's foot clover, wild garlic, and fescue grass.

Such a varied coastline is a paradise for birds and birdwatchers alike. In addition to a large number of songbirds in the hinterland, fulmars, petrels, cormorants, shags, redshanks, guillemots, and razorbills can all be seen along the coast.

Giant's Causeway is a breathtaking landscape. Apart from the unforgettable coastal scenery and basalt formations, not to mention the rich diversity of flora and fauna, walkers can stumble upon tiny fishermen's huts around little harbors tucked away in sheltered bays. The rocks of Giant's Causeway, however, have also been the undoing of several ships, most notably the "Girona," which ran aground here in October 1588 during a strong northwesterly gale with the loss of around 1,200 men. Only five souls survived and their descendants still live in the area. The "Girona" was a Spanish Armada galleon, which had rescued the crews of two other wrecked ships and was consequently heavily overloaded. Its fate was sealed when its rudder snapped.

View of the valley featuring the black pillars of Giant's Causeway (above)

The rocky coastline around Port Ballantra consists of cooled lava (below, left)

The eroded remains of once tall lava pillars (below, right)

EUROPE

Iceland's geysers

Route:
By air or water (from Hanstholm, Denmark) to Reykjavik, 50 mi. (80 km) to Haukadalur, 44 mi. (70 km) further to Hveravellir

Best time:
June—August

Further points of interest:
Falls at Gulfoss, Nature reserves Jökusárgljufur and Skaftafell, Hothouses in Hveravellir

The hot springs are an outstanding spectacle of nature

Some 65 million years ago the earth's crust ripped open between Greenland and Scandinavia. Magma, the glowing lava from deep within the planet was pushed up. The sea caused it to solidify into enormous blocks. Always higher rose the basalt mountains, until about 16 million years ago they emerged above the waves, hissing, smouldering and spewing volcanic islands. Iceland was born. Until the present day the tremendous pressures and movement of the earth crust that caused the fault and to which the island in the Atlantic Ocean owes both its hardships and its comforts, have not ceased their activity.

At the "Hot Spot"

Year after year the American and the Eurasian continents drifted apart, at a rate of ¾ in. (2 cm) annually. The glowing core breaks through the fault and so gives Iceland its amazing geological history.

Most fascinating is the earth spectacle in the theatre called the "Hot Spot," an area where the earth spews out great quantities of lava. The surprising thing is that the gigantic fire ovens are for the most part located under the mass of ice of the Vatnajökull glaciers, 3,204 mi.² (8,300 km²) of them, and thus the largest of Europe. To be sure, here you cannot see Iceland's active volcanoes spewing their lava, but dangerous they are nevertheless, as from time to time they demonstrate. Their enormous eruptions melt the glacier ice. Experts say that large parts of the fertile southwest of the island will ultimately be flooded and that the population must evacuate.

The volcanic activity has its advantageous aspects, too. The heat of the inner earth, so close to the surface in Iceland – groundwater temperatures at 3,280-ft. depth (1,000 m) is 536°F (280°C) – provide electricity and energy for factories, heat the homes and the greenhouses, and in capital Reykjavik even allow heated sidewalks, to keep them free from ice in winter time. In the "blue lagoon," the basin of a power station at Grindavik, the water has therapeutic powers and its temperature allows comfortable bathing. Finally, the glowing mass in Iceland's soil has still another positive side: the eruptions have become a tourist attraction. Especially the hot springs and Iceland's mighty geysers yearly draw thousands to the – for the most part – inaccessible island.

The thermal field of Haukadalur with its great geyser, about one hundred kilometres east of Reykjavik, is one of the most frequented natural monuments of Iceland, even if the springs seem to be tiring. No wonder, because they were already active in 1294. Since then, every sixty minutes the geyser blows steam up to sixty metres into the air. Nowadays it spouts water only rarely.

The springs of Strokkur

Visitors are catered to even better by the Strokkur geyser. Every ten minutes it spouts water and vapour 25 metres into the air. After the brief rain back down it the pool is almost still, except for a few wisps of vapor on the surface. And without any warning, the water suddenly begins to boil. Soon a vapor bubble grows larger, holds its own for a moment and then the water, shoots up. In the Islandic interior there are some 30 geysers, but few are as attractive as the Strokkur.

The thermal field of Haukadalur and its largest geyser, the Strokkur, is one of the major Icelandic tourist attractions. With regular intervals the Strokkur erupts into an enormous fountain of water and vapor. The water falls back and the basin is still again, as if nothing had happened. Only a few wisps of vapor play on the water surface. Without advance warning the water begins to boil, forms bubbles and, break through the surface.

EUROPE

Finland's island kingdom

Between the islands and the mainland is the largest archipelago in the world

Getting there:
Some islands are only accessible by private boat. Road or bus from Turku, as far as Kasnäs. Passenger vessels ply between the inhabited islands

Where to stay:
Camping permitted, except during the nesting season. Owner's permission must be sought before camping on private land. No other accommodation facilities except for an unlocked cabin on Konungskär. Hotels available outside the park boundaries

Climate:
July/August around 68°F (20°C) and dry. Temperatures always well below 32°F (0°C) in January, when the sea is frozen

Main attractions:
Boat trips; medieval churches: wooden church on Nötö, granite church on Nagu; lighthouses on Nötö and Bengtskär

Special tips:
Good navigational skills are necessary in view of the large areas of submerged rock

Despite their slender legs, elks are excellent swimmers and are found on several of the islands (above, left)

The Bengtskär lighthouse is a beacon to ships navigating their way between the islands (above, right)

Water and rocks, water and woodland: colorful flora decorating the shores of the Dragsfjord in the Turku Archipelago

The southern and southwestern coast of Finland is fringed with clusters of tiny islands and islets, the remnants of an ancient, slowly disintegrating section of the Baltic Shield. Between 2,300,000 and 10,000 years ago, Ice Age glaciers smoothed away the last traces of erosion and any veins of soft rock between the hard masses of granite, scouring the land surface bare and leaving behind a landscape of softly rounded humps.

When the ice melted, the land was initially inundated by a sea of freshwater, which built up between terminal moraines and the glacier. When the Baltic Shield rose, these numerous small hills were pushed up above the surface of the water.

Southwest of Turku, a group of islands stretching over a distance of 50 miles (80km) emerged from the Baltic, forming part of the world's largest archipelago, situated between the Åland Islands and the Finnish mainland. The rocky coastal cliffs on the mainland and the belt of tightly clustered, mainly forested islands lying just offshore form the inner archipelago. The islands and islets of the outer archipelago are often no more than bare rock, buffeted by the wind and sea.

Even so, the clefts in the rock bloom throughout the summer with chives, coastal chamomile, and common scurvy grass, while the sandy islands in the center of the Park are also populated by stonecrop and wild strawberries. Since the Baltic's saline content here is no more than five parts per thousand, the shores are also home to wild angelica and longwort, Dyer's woad, yellow toadflax, and fescue grass.

A thousand islands

Many of the people who once occupied these isolated islands and eked out a living from fishing and agriculture have departed. Nowadays, only about 1,200 remain — apart from the rash of holiday homes. This has changed a traditional culture that supported a unique bio-diversity. This natural and cultural landscape is now protected by a National Park and also forms part of an international biosphere reserve encompassing 1,620 square miles (4,200km2) and nearly 1,000 islands and islets.

The soil on some of the larger land masses is relatively fertile, thanks mainly to the veins of limestone that surface amidst the granite rocks. Farmers used to graze cattle in mixed woodland consisting of fir, spruce, and birch interspersed with oak, alder, ash, and aspen. This practice produced wooded meadows filled with colorful flowers such as buttercups, goldilocks buttercups, and heath pinks. Some of the flat and relatively stone-free meadows were mown. Even the lower tree branches could be used as winter fodder. This created areas of open terrain and a few of these lightly wooded meadows still survive even now.

Since the islands were abandoned, this traditional landscape is increasingly in danger of disappearing altogether as nature reclaims its own and the region becomes overgrown. There are a few dominant species, which tend to squeeze out all the others. The main culprits in this respect are the dark fir forests, which deprive flowering plants of adequate light. In an effort to preserve the individuality and diversity of this heritage landscape, some of the island inhabitants, supported by the park authorities, have begun reintroducing traditional farming methods.

Gray and ringed seals

Animal life is surprisingly abundant. Twenty-five different species of mammal have settled in this island kingdom. The majority of these are small rodents, although elks too have swum across the water to occupy the islands' woodland. Despite their thin legs, they are actually very good swimmers. Sometimes, gray seals and even Baltic ringed seals are sighted, a species that is teetering on the brink of extinction.

The islands are home to 132 different bird species and, during the breeding season, many of the islands are closed to visitors. Gulls, terns, eider ducks, and razorbills inhabit the bare rocks, not to mention the black guillemots with their white wing tips and bright red legs. Some endangered species, like the Caspian tern and scaup duck, also nest here undisturbed. The sea eagle is a success story in itself. These birds had almost disappeared from the region, but can now be seen circling majestically high in the sky.

EUROPE

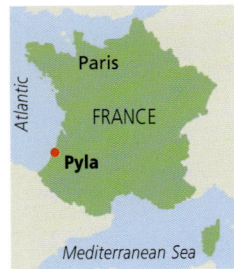

Europe's largest shifting dune

The Pyla Dune, sculpted by wind and waves, is a unique natural monument

Getting there:
Good roads, bus, and rail links from Bordeaux to Arcachon. Bordeaux airport

Where to stay:
The beaches of Aquitania are popular tourist destinations. Wide choice of holiday accommodation

Climate:
Around 45°F (7°C) in January; 77°F (25°C) in July

Main attractions:
Climbing to the top of Pyla Dune; paragliding; water sports

The power struggle between water, sand, and plants began some 15,000 years ago and it still dominates the Atlantic coastal landscape of Aquitania in southwest France. A perfectly even, smooth, sandy beach stretches 155 miles (250km) along the coast from the Gironde estuary to the Spanish border. For thousands of years sea currents have deposited sand along the coasts. The sand is blown into dunes by the wind, thereby creating a remarkable landscape between sea and land backed by a succession of enchanting lakes and ponds.

The most prominent natural feature along this breathtaking landscape of beach and constantly shifting dunes is undoubtedly the extraordinary Pyla Dune. It is nearly two miles (2.7km) in length and 1,650ft (500m) wide, stretching along the coast opposite Cap Ferret at the entrance to the Arcachon basin. Reaching a height of around 360ft (110m), it is the highest dune of its kind in Europe and has been placed under special protection as an outstanding natural phenomenon.

Each year, the dune moves about 13ft (4m) inland, slowly submerging the pines in the extensively forested hinterland and burying ancient huts used by resin collectors and pitch ovens, some of which are 400 years old.

On the seaward side of the dunes, there are some indications that the land now covered by the dune was once thickly forested. The oldest layers are around 4,000 years old, while the summit can be fairly accurately dated back to 1860. The dune passes through four so-called paleostrata, i.e., layers dating back to when the ground was forested and later when it was once part of a swamp area.

The silted-up bay

Pyla Dune is the product of one of the last active phases of dune formation in Aquitania. Between 1450 and 1750, when the winds were particularly strong during the so-called "Little Ice Age," two major dune systems gradually began to overlay each other. To begin with, marine currents off the coast began to build up a sandbank known as "Pile." This slowly extended toward the coast and eventually joined up with the shore during the sixteenth century. Further south, a new sandbank was meanwhile emerging from the sea, called "New Pile." During the eighteenth century, the Bay of Pilat was formed between "Old Pile" on the shore and "New Pile" in the sea. The sea winds continued to assail New Pile, driving its sand toward the coast, filling up the bay, and driving it onward to accumulate on the Pyla Dune. There were periods when the dune shifted up to 65ft (20m) inland each year.

In 1855, Pyla Dune was only 115ft (35m) tall. In only 150 years, it has tripled its height. Nowadays, the wind is taking its toll on the Arguin sandbank, adding further layers to Pyla Dune. The island that is left during the ebb tide measures 2.5 miles (4 km) in length and 1.25 miles (2 km) wide. It is a conservation area, narrowing into the Bay of Arcachon. Wind and waves continue to assault it and its shape is constantly changing. The region is not only a popular destination for water sports enthusiasts, but is also home to one of Europe's largest tern colonies.

During the course of history, Pyla Dune has been known by a succession of different names. For a time, it was called "Le Sabloney," followed by "Les Grands Tucs" or "La Grave." Today, it is generally known as the Pyla Dune, although its older name of "Pilat" is still quite common. The latter derives from its first recorded mention in 1484, when it was initially referred to as "Lous Pilat," until eventually shortened to simply Pilat in 1556.

Several paths lead along the ridge of the dune. The ascent is well worth it, however, as there are magnificent views from its summit across the vast horizons of the Atlantic Ocean and the Arguin sandbank on one side and panoramic vistas across the green pine forests of the Landes de Gascogne regional park in the hinterland.

The hinterland was once a vast, sandy swamp that dried up in summer to become a steppe landscape, supporting very little other than some sheep grazing. Following a directive by Napoleon in 1801, the region was drained and thousands of square miles were planted with trees, predominantly a species of pine that tolerates hot, sandy conditions. This measure was intended to stop the advance of the dunes and at the same time introduce what was, at the time, a lucrative resin industry. Today, the vast forested area behind the dunes provides a network of cool, shady paths.

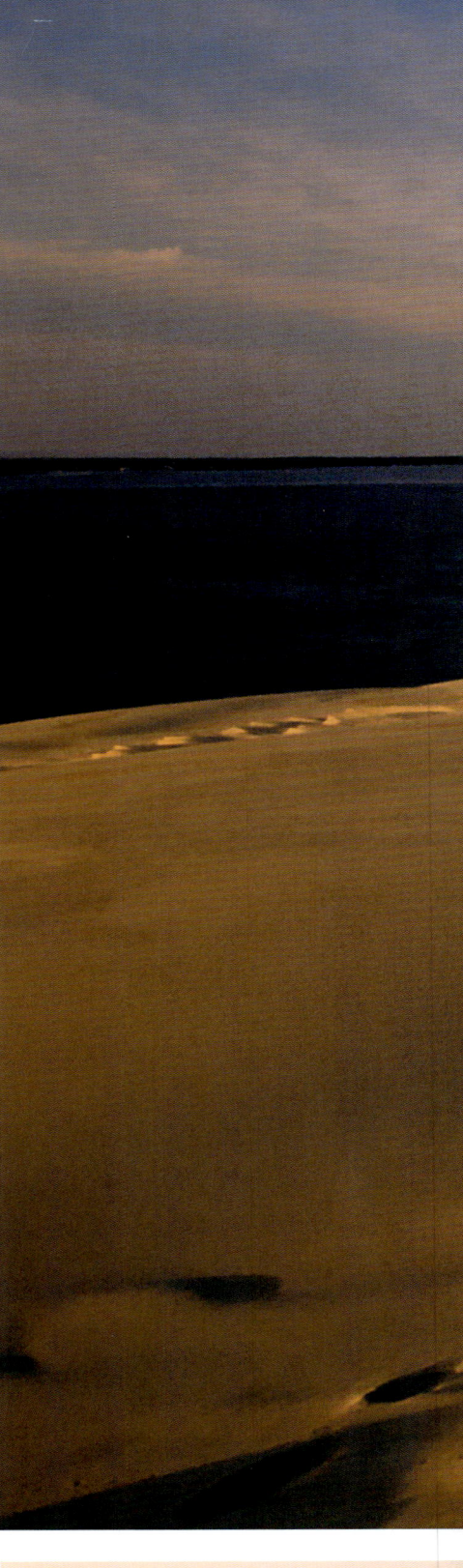

Two views of the magnificent Pyla Dune: View over the sandy expanses of the ridge to the sea beyond, with the pine forests in the background (above).

View along the shore toward the slopes of Pyla Dune and the Bay of Arcachon beyond (below)

EUROPE

Limestone rocks on Rügen

The King's Chair and the white cliffs inspired painters and poets

Route:
E 22/ B 96 from Stralsund to Sasznitz, from there 4 mi. (7 km) to Hagen; Train to Sasznits, from there walking route to Subbenkammer.

Accommodation:
Panorama Hotel Lohme (northwest of the Stubbenkammer) Gastronomics Waldhalle (near the Wissower Klinken)

Further points of interest:
Fishing village Vitt at Cape Arkona; hunting castle Granitz near Binz; Maria church in Bergen; Putbus

The image of a landscape: brightly blue, the Baltic Sea reflects the sunlight, green shimmering leaves on the beeches that overhang the banks, chalk white rock coast. Carved by cliffs, niches and deep channels the walls plunge down or rise at acute angles and take on wonderful contours and the peaks, many of which are named, are like mountains. The Stubbenkammer on the Isle of Rügen is one of the finest areas on the Baltic coast. This sea inspired poets, and painters like Gaspar David Friedrich found their model there. Much-travelled scientist Wilhelm von Humboldt was moved to say: "Nowhere does one encounter a simpler and nobler panorama."

Protected as nature reserve

The most famous rock mass of the Stubbenkammer is the 384-foot (117 m) high King's Chair. Annually, some 300,000 to 400,000 visitors climb the narrow stairway to the small platform that was built more than 300 years ago. They are rewarded with a marvellous panorama of the limestone cliffs and the sea. To the south are the Wissower Klinken, it is said that Caspar David Friedrich painted this and called his work "Chalk Cliffs of Rügen," but this is not true, for the artist painted a rock formation northwest of the King's Chair.

To protect the coastline, the Jasmund nature reserve was established in 1990. Its 7,413 acres (3,000 ha) include 4,942 acres (2,000 ha) of forest, left as much as possible in its natural state, about 1,235 acres (500 ha) of the Baltic and about 1,235 acres (500 ha) of limestone cliffs, morass and grassland.

At various locations between the King's Chair and Sasznitz one can leave the high road and climb down steep stairways to the beach. Walking on the beach is an arduous affair because of the many rocks. But it is from this flat perspective that the majesty of the chalk cliffs is most fully appreciated. And the bands of flintstone bulbs that run along the cliffs like a string of pearls can be seen from this perspective alone.

These flintstone phenomena are due to small organisms the skeletons of which dissolved in the chalky mud. These cliffs are of organic origin themselves. Some 80 million years ago, during the Mesozoic era, the earth atmosphere warmed up and enormous glacier masses melted and flooded all of Northern Europe. The sea was filled with starfish, mussels, corals, algae and plankton – their chalky scales, skeletons and armor dropped to the sea bottom. In the course of millions of years they combined with

other sediments into chalk cliffs up to 1,640 ft. (500 m) high.

During the next era of the history of the earth, in the Tertiary period, the sea had withdrawn to the point that the present Baltic became dry land. 800,000 to one million years ago (the Pleistocene epoch) thick glaciers flowed down from Scandinavia southwards three times and formed the surface of Rügen, though not yet of the cliffs.

The cliffs are the product of changing pressures and movement of the earth crust. During the Pleistocene

epoch the layers of limestone split and rose or dropped, and so obstructed the advancing glaciers. The glaciers in turn let go of the granite boulders they had transported from the Scandinavian mountains – some of them 21,888 ft.³ (600 m³) in volume and weighing up to 1792 tons.

When the glaciers withdrew, the changes caused over 100,000 years were not only due to the rise and fall of the sea. Humans, too, intervened in the course of nature. From the middle of the nineteenth century Rügen limestone is a desirable material, among other things for the production of paints, dishes and toothpaste.

From the steep coast one is offered a marvellous panorama of the Baltic and the Cliffs of Wissower Klinken (above). Enormous boulders and dead tree trunks make a stroll on Stubnitz beach less than easy-going (left). Only at the very edges one can truly get an impression of the total majesty of the limestone cliffs, the layers that in the course of millions of years originated from the chalky skeletons, scales and armor of minute organisms.

EUROPE

The Baltic Sahara

The Courland Spit belongs partly to Lithuania and partly to Russia

Getting there:
Short ferry crossing from Klaipeda. By car or bus from Kaliningrad. Airport at Palanga near Klaipeda

Where to stay:
Wide choice of hotel accommodation in the holiday resorts of Nida and Juodkranté

Climate:
Around 63°F (17°C) in July, with winter temperatures rarely dropping below 12°F (-6°C). Best time to visit between May and September

Main attractions:
Nida: Thomas Mann's house, Museum of Amber, sculptures on the Hexenberg in Juodkranté

The lagoon stretches between the Courland Spit and the mainland (right)

Some parts of the sand spit are protected areas. Wooden houses, like these pictured here in Nida, are typical of the region (below, left)

Even today, these great dunes are still being driven eastward by the wind (below, right)

The shifting sand dunes buried 14 villages before the people living in the area stopped the relentless forward march of the dunes by planting pines, European beach grass, and thyme - all of which acted as windbreaks against the constant sea winds and stabilized the sand with their roots. This 112-mile (180km) spit of land off the Lithuanian coast was populated by a deciduous forest of oak, lime, elm, and birch before the Knights of the Teutonic Order arrived on the scene during the thirteenth century, felling this ancient forest and sparking the relentless erosion of this sand spit separating the Courland Lagoon from the Baltic Sea.

Westerly gales regularly deposit vast quantities of sand in the lagoon and the sand mountains shrink by around three feet each year. Parnidzio Kopa, or the Great Dune, near Nida, in particular, becomes visibly smaller with each passing year.

The Courland Spit is located half in Russia's Kalingrad territory and half in Lithuania. Most of the Lithuanian side is a fascinating and scenic National Park, measuring altogether 102 square miles (265 km^2). Around 50 square miles (125 km^2) comprise the underwater kingdom at the bottom of the Baltic, while 16 square miles (42 km^2) of Park preserve life in the lagoon.

Shifting dunes and pyramids of sand

The chain of dunes that make up the "Lithuanian Sahara" stretches for just over 4 miles (7km), running in a southerly line from Nida to the Russian frontier. These shifting dunes have created a picturesque landscape of elegant waves, grooves, and steep slopes, with softly undulating contours that end abruptly in a sheer, sharp drop. From the summit of the Great Dune, there are panoramic views from which to appreciate the breathtaking color contrasts between the dazzling white sands, green forests, and shimmering blues and grays of the lagoon. At 170ft (52m), it is one of the highest shifting dunes in Europe.

Around Juodkranté, a few, steep-sided, pyramid-shaped dunes have managed to survive. These are unique formations that once stretched right across the sand spit in several places. From the top of the 130ft (40m) high Schafsberg, outstanding vistas extend across the lagoon, sand spit, and Baltic Sea. A few significant remnants of original forest have also survived in the area, including some impressive 200-year-old oaks and pines. These small, dense pockets of ancient forest are home to ermine and elk, while ospreys nest deep in the interior.

This peninsula was formed around 13,000 years ago, when the last Ice Age glaciers retreated. Deep underwater currents transporting sand from south to north collided with submarine ridges on the sea floor, blocking their flow and causing a build-up of sand. This sand barrier grew in height until it eventually broke the surface of the Baltic Sea around 5,000 years ago. A sand dune developed that drifted steadily from north to south, gradually forming this spit of land that is still moving slowly eastwards.

Over 60 miles (100km) of sandy beach

This eastwards shift continues to this day. Its progress can best be observed from the summit of the Vecekrugas Dune near Pervalka. This elevation, with its pine-clad slopes rising to a height of over 220ft (67m), is the highest in the National Park.

At its widest point, the Courland Spit is only 2.5 miles (4km) wide. Its western shore is lined with over 60 miles (100km) of idyllic and uninterrupted beach bordering on the Baltic, 165ft (50m) wide in places. Hidden in the fine, white sand are precious pieces of amber, petrified lumps of prehistoric resin from long-vanished, prehistoric pine trees. Where the beach meets the foothills of the dunes, the shifting sands are home to some rare species of plants including vetch and sea holly. Numerous sandy paths wind through the shady pine and birch forests that carpet these great dunes, helping to anchor them in place.

ASIA

Tufa paradise

The bizarre lava landscape of Göreme National Park, in Cappadocia, is a geological rarity

Getting there:
Nearest airport: Kayseri
Good road access from Nevsehir to Ürgüp

Where to stay:
All categories of hotel available in Nevsehir, Ürgüp, and Kayseri

Climate:
Around 73°F (23°C) May to September; average around 32–34°F (0–1°C) December to January, snow in January and February

Main attractions:
Devrent and Catalkaya valleys; Eustathios, Kilise, and Elmali churches; Ürgüp

The high valley landscape of Cappadocia between Nevsehír and Kayseri in Turkey is dominated by the silhouetted peaks of the mighty Hasan and Akdag volcanoes, not to mention Mount Erciyes, which towers to a height of over 13,000 ft (4,000m). Between two and five million years ago, these volcanoes paved the way for one of the most bizarre, yet beautiful, land formations on the planet. Past eruptions covered the area with soft tufa lava, which hardened into a mighty layer thousands of feet thick extending over an area of nearly 4,000 square miles (10,000 km²) in the Kizilirmak basin. During subsequent eruptions one to two million years ago, this was in turn covered by a thin, solid layer of basaltic lava.

Central Turkey's harsh continental climate with its hot, dry summers and frosty, snowy winters has eroded this volcanic material to form spectacularly bizarre sculptures and fantastic rock formations.

Thousands of conical peaks, mushroom-shaped rock formations, chimney-like pillars, and towers strain skyward in an almost surreal kaleidoscope of colors, ranging from brilliant red to shades of yellowy-brown or greenish-gray. These tufa obelisks and pillars, some of which reach a height of 130ft (40m), are crowned with basalt caps that slow down the process of erosion. Each rocky outcrop promises a brand new vista of different shapes, with every valley holding a fresh set of surprises such as the fairy chimneys in Devrent valley, north of Ürgüp, or the original toadstool formations in Catalkaya valley.

Then man arrived on the scene. The first caves were excavated around 4,000 BC, but it was during the early days of Christianity that the first monks and nuns found their way to this beautiful landscape. Such surroundings were ideally suited to inward contemplation, an ascetic way of life, and prayer. Far removed from the Persian wars and incursions by other invaders, this rocky valley also provided a sanctuary for those seeking to escape persecution and destruction, with the result that primitive monks' chambers and hermitages soon sprang up alongside the simple peasant homes.

Cave dwellings and rock monasteries

These cave dwellings were soon followed by extensive monastery complexes. The region probably reached its cultural peak around AD 400, when a period of extremely intensive excavation work began on the orders of Bishop Basileio of Kayseri. The monks carved entire monasteries, including churches, sleeping quarters, and churches, out of the tufa rock walls high above the ground and tunneled entire underground cities out of the soft rock. All the hallmarks of Byzantine sacred architecture are in evidence here — even huge, cruciform, domed basilica churches. The walls are decorated with frescoes depicting the life of Jesus. Today, these sumptuously decorated cave walls are still potent reminders of the richness and overwhelming beauty of Byzantine fresco painting.

The Kara Kilise, or "dark church," is particularly well-preserved. This is due to its having been buried — probably during the eleventh century — throughout the Islamic iconoclastic period, thereby managing to escape the destruction of Christian symbols. Having had virtually no exposure to natural light, the brilliantly colored frescoes have retained their original vibrancy against a background of midnight blue.

Abandoned in the twentieth century

The Göreme cave settlement was abandoned around 1923–1924. In the mid 1980s, a National Park was established covering around 40 square miles (96 km²) of this fantastic landscape. It was also designated a protected area in recognition of its status as one of the rare examples of a site combining outstanding natural beauty and interest with cultural heritage value. People form an important part of the scene as well, with around 20,000 farmers and artisans living within the Park. The local population is traditionally dependent upon agriculture, including viniculture and fruit growing, and pottery, the weaving of rugs and carpets, and dyeing skills. Tourism also grew to become an important source of income during the eighties. Göreme Park now attracts around 600,000 visitors each year, captivating them with its surreal landscape. The flora and fauna are typical of a heritage site. Uncultivated areas are populated by sandalwood, leadwort and thrift. The ancient volcanoes encircle the valley to such an extent, however, that many species have evolved individually since the volcanic eruptions hundreds of thousands of years ago. Biologists have identified 110 species of plants unique to the rocky landscape of Göreme National Park.

Many of the conical tufa hills have been carved into rock dwellings (above)

The National Park covers an area of nearly 4,000 square miles (10,000 km²) (below, right)

The obelisks are crowned with rock "caps" that protect them from erosion (below, left)

ASIA

The beauty of Pamukkale

In Turkey, hot springs created nature's art

Route:
149 mi. (240 km) south of Izmir, via the E87

Best time:
May – June, September

Accommodation:
Pamukkale Hotel (with thermal bath, not for hotel guests only)

Further points of interest:
Ancient city Aphrodisias

In central Turkey the mercury rises above 104°F (40°C) on many a summer day. All the more surprising that in Denizli province a mountain range has a broad area of glacier ice. The blinding white crust reminds the Turks themselves of a ripened cotton field and according call this wonder of nature Pamukkale – the cotton castle.

Plateaus of calcium down to the valley

The white magic is caused by hot springs, the water containing much calcium and carbon dioxide, dripping and flowing down in countless gullies to the valley 295 ft. (90 m) below. As the water cools calcium is deposited and form a white precipitation of chalky flakes. Over thousands of years, thick layers of calcium deposit formed a kind of stepped terracing reaching down to the valley.

The thermal ponds, supplied with mud by the springs, and the large warm water basins on the terraces were early understood to have healing powers. This probably played a role in the establishment, second century BC, of the city Hieropolis. Its residents used the warm water in a Roman bathhouse. Perhaps already then bathers bought souvenirs, branches, leaves and pebbles covered with a layer of Pamukkale calcium.

A less pleasant natural phenomenon in the vicinity of the hot springs was described by Greek geographer Strabo in the first century after Christ. In his 17-tome *Geographica* he mentions a cave producing poisonous fumes, fenced in so that none would inhale the harmful gas. Strabo had also heard of the neutered priests who served the fertility goddess Cybele. Into the cave they lowered sacrificial animals that suffocated immediately. The eunuchs themselves were reputedly immune to the fumes and so demonstrated their holiness.

Necropolis for craftsmen

In later ages Hieropolis fell prey to earthquakes and plunder. Part of the ancient buildings disappeared under a thick layer of pebble and flake. In the 1880s German archaeologists began excavation, and after a spell of some decades this was continued by Italians. Near an old bathing pond a thermal building was exposed, dating from the 2nd century. It is now the Pamukkale Museum. Not far from the poison cave Plutonium, described by Strabo, archaeologists found the ruins of an Apollo temple.

Among the objects from the classical period are the remains of an eight-cornered structure built in the 5th century as monument to the apostle Philippus, who it is assumed died a martyr in Hieropolis, an amphitheatre with a frieze with mythological designs and one of the largest ancient necropoli, the grave inscriptions of which refer to weavers, dyers and other craftsmen.

In recent years Pamukkale has become a significant Turkish tourist attraction. Numerous tourist coaches halt here and often the white terraces are thronged with people. Guests who can afford a longer stay encounter comfortable hotels with their own thermal baths. Physicians recommend the steaming springs when the complaint is rheumatism. The greater the volume of water diverted to the hotel baths or the supply conduits, the less is left for further deposits on the famous terraces – and slowly but surely the snow turns to muddy brown.

In the course of thousands of years, the thermal springs deposited calcium, a stepped layer of 295 ft. (90 m) depth. Bathing in the warm water basin nearby is medically beneficial. Ancient buildings of the old city Hieropolis were covered or closed in by the snowy chalk.

ASIA

Mysterious Rupkund Lake

Hundreds of human skeletons remain intact in its waters

State and capital:
Uttarakhand, Dehradun (176 mi./284 km to Mundoli roadhead)

Convenient access:
Road to Mundoli or a few miles further to Lohajang, thereafter trek. Rail to Haridwar, Rishikesh, air to Dehradun

Accommodation:
None on trek or at Lake; camping en-route

Best season:
April-May, August-September

Also worth seeing:
Day treks to Homkund, Bekhaltal Lakes; serious mountaineering on Trishul

Rupkund is not a classical high-altitude lake. In fact, more than a lake, it is a tarn, a small pond-like presence not particularly beautiful to look at. And it would not have attracted more than passing attention if in 1942 a forest guard had not stumbled upon it and its contents: a large number of human skeletons with personal belongings like leather shoes, etc. Today, the lake is a destination for hundreds of trekkers, not just out of macabre curiosity, but also for the challeng-ing yet spectacular Himalayan terrain one has to traverse on the way.

Lying nearly 15,748 ft. (4,800 m) above sea level, below the right flank of the majestic Trishul peak in the Garhwal Himalayas, Rupkund is not an easy place to reach. It takes at least four days of trekking over slippery trails through thick jungles, meadows, and rocky ground to get there. The walk starts from the head village of Lohajang and winds easily in the initial part through cultivated fields, oak and pine forest, up to the Wan village (at an altitude of 8,202 ft./ 2,500 m). From here a steep ascent through spruce and rhododendron woods takes one above the tree line onto a beautiful spread of bugyals (high-altitude meadows). The next stopover is at Bedni, an enchanting meadow, lush with plants, flowers and lichens in summer. A small lake here reflects Nanda Ghungti and Trishul peaks. The last halt before Rupkund is at cold and windy Bhagguwasa, hemmed in by huge mountain walls. On the final two-mile (3 km) trudge to Rupkund, one comes across the rare brahma kamal (literally "lotus of the Creator"; a member of the daisy family) wildflower, which is held sacred by the local people and offered at almost all village temples in the higher reaches of the Western Himalayas.

Swept away by a deadly avalanche

The last step of the climb brings you to an edge of a crater within which lies the mysterious water body. Recessed in so dark, bleak a place that the sun shines on it only for a couple of hours—that too on a rare clear day—Rupkund remains frozen for most part of the year, and this is why its hoard of skeletons has survived in almost perfect condition. Several scientific expeditions have been made to the site, though nothing certain has been established regarding the presence of the grim remains, much above the highest permanently inhabitable point in the Himalayas. Various theories propose that they are remains of soldiers, pilgrims, or Chinese travellers. The theory fa-

voured by many, including the local people, is that of Swami Pravana Nand, who worked in the region for a number of years. According to him, the Raja of Kannauj undertook a pilgrimage to Homkund Lake, which lies beyond the Trishul spur above Rupkund. When the group was passing above the lake, the weather took a turn for the worse and an avalanche swept away and buried the entire team. The story seems plausible as the drop from Juerigali, a ledge above the lake over which the trail passes, is a vertical 984 ft. (300 m).

So pristine is the condition of the bodies that on some bones, shreds of flesh can still be seen. Later, in 2004, a team of Indian and European scientists retrieved jewellery and other vital clues. DNA tests on the bodies revealed that there were two groups of people, a short group (probably local porters) and a taller group who were closely related.

Above: Though the numbers have not been completely ascertained, it is believed that a group of 300 to 600 people once perished at the enigmatic Lake, a pilgrimage and trekking destination. Radio carbon dating of the bones found fixed the time period in the ninth century.

ASIA

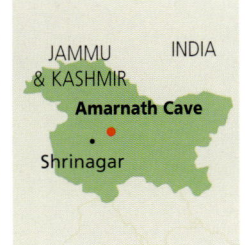

A stalagmite of staggering proportions
The cone of ice in Amarnath Cave waxes and wanes with the moon

State and capital:
Jammu & Kashmir, Srinagar 87 mi. (141 km)

Convenient access:
Road to Baltal, Chandanwari, air to Srinagar (heli-services up to Amarnath), rail to Udhampur, Jammu

Accommodation:
Tents during trek and at Amarnath

Also worth seeing:
Pahalgam, 28 mi. (45 km) SW (walk starts from here), Sonamarg, 9 mi. (14 km) from Baltal

The legend goes that Shiva, the Destroyer of the Hindu Trinity, on being constantly nagged by his consort Parvati, agreed to narrate the secrets of immortality and creation of the universe. Seeking a place where no one could eavesdrop, the God forsook his ride, Nandi the Bull, at Pahalgam or Bailgaon (Bull village), released the moon from his hair at Chandanwari (chanda means moon), shed the garland of Sheshnag the snake at its namesake place, departed from his son Ganesha at Mahaganesh Parvat (mountain) and at Panjtarni quit the five elements he was master of, that is, earth, water, air, fire and sky. With his wife Parvati, he finally reached Amarnath Cave, and to ensure that no one dare listen to the posterity mantra, he created Kalagini (the Ring of Fire) which ensured the area was devoid of life. Finally, sitting on a deer skin rug with Parvati, he narrated the immortal secret not knowing that there were two pigeon eggs under the mat. The mantra registered with the unborn birds and it is said that ever since they hatched, they have had eternal life. Many visitors today report seeing a pair of white pigeons near the cave.

Tucked away at the farther end of the Lidder valley, the mouth of the huge hemispherical hollow is 147 ft. (45 m) wide and 89 ft. (27 m) high. Extending 59 ft. (18 m) into a rugged cliff face of white Mesozoic dolomite, the cave tapers down to a width and height of 30 and 15 ft., or 9 and 4.5 meters respectively, at its deep end. The object of reverence within is a massive shivaling (phallus symbol identified with Shiva) made of ice. The deity is actually a stalagmite, which waxes and wanes with the phases of the moon—on the full moon day of August it attains a maximum height of 14 ft. (4.25 m)—and is formed out of water seeping down in sub-zero conditions from Ramkund Lake directly above the cave. Beside it are similar formations identified as Parvati and Ganesh.

A sage, a mendicant and a silver mace
Located in the Greater Himalayas, with no road leading to it, Amarnath is physically tough to reach and there is more than one fable relating to its discovery. According to the first, the Cave emerged when the ancient Sage Kashyapa drained the then underwater valley of Kashmir through a number of rivers and rivulets. Subsequently, Bhrigu, another of Hinduism's scriptural sages, on a visit to the Himalayas discovered the holy Cave. The more widely accepted story, however, credits the find to a Muslim shepherd named Buta Mallik who happened to meet a mendicant while on the pastures. The mendicant gave him a sack of coal and upon reaching home he discovered that the sack, in fact, contained gold. Overjoyed, Mallik rushed back to thank his benefactor but on the spot of their meeting discovered the Cave, which became a place of pilgrimage ever since. To date, a percentage of the donations made by pilgrims are given to the descendants of Mallik, and the remaining to the trust which manages the shrine. The shepherd community is also the guardian of the shrine and the pathway leading to it. A ceremonial five-day trek called the chhari yatra for the seasonal opening of the Cave is led by the head priest who belongs to the village of Ganeshpuri and is supposed to be a descendant of the priest who accompanied Mallik on his discovery of the shrine. Presently kept at Srinagar at the venue of the Dashnavi Akhara (sect), the chhari is a silver mace believed to have been handed over by Shiva to Kashyapa as a symbol of shakti (power) with the command that it be carried to Amarnath every year.

Top: The ice lingam of Shiva inside the cave.
Facing page: Located in the Greater Himalayas, with no road leading to it, Amarnath is physically tough to reach.

ASIA

Qiantang tide, Zhejiang

A natural aquatic wonder of the world

Location:
On the southern border of Hangzhou Jiaxin Plain, 75 miles (120km) west of Shanghai, and 38 miles (60km) east of Hangzhou.

Climate:
There is a northern subtropical and moist climate. It is temperate, with a clear contrast among the seasons. The annual temperature average is 60.6 °F (15.9 °C).

Special interest:
August 18th of the lunar calendar is the best time to watch the famous tide.

Main attractions:
Watching Tide Park in Yanguan township, Haining, Chanshan Dam-watching Tide Pavilion, the Big Dent, and the Dragon Head of Babao.

It is said that watching the Qiantang Tide began in the Tang dynasty and was in vogue in the Song dynasty. In the centuries that followed, it became a custom. Every year on August 10th of the lunar calendar, people hold ceremonies of various kinds to honor the god of the tide, pray for peace, and set forth their hopes for a better future.

A good place to watch Qiantang Tide is at Yanguan township in Haining county, Jiaxing city. Though this is just a small place, here tourists can appreciate the Thread Tide, the Clashing Tide, and the Returning Tide. It is said that the returning tide swells up to 39 ft (12m) high.

Nearly one thousand years ago, people set up the Zhenhai Pagoda in Yanguan township. They did so in the hope of suppressing the tide god.

The ancient Qiantang River flowed into the sea at Guanshan, now in Fuyang county. At that time the tide was not as great as it is now. The Yangtze River flows down from the north, carrying mud and sand all the way from its upper streams. These are deposited at the river's estuary and form sandbars. The waves of the sea are now held up by the sandbars, but they continue to be pushed forward by the waves that are behind them. In this way the head of the waves swells up, forming a great tide. Under the effects of the phases of the moon, the tide runs in a even more dramatic way, arriving near Yanguan with its head sometimes more than 10 ft (3m) high.

The Qiantang River has two big recurrent tides. At these times the magnificent surges of the water last for three to five days. The big tide usually appears in the first two or three days after the first or the fifteenth day of the lunar calendar.

Fall is the season that produces the biggest tide. The maritime climate, the influence of oceanic currents, and the high rainfall and typhoons at this time of the year make the tide fiercer than ever.

When the tide reaches you, you can imagine that you see hordes of troops and horses charging forward and galloping, sweeping over the raised banks, splashing in all directions. It is as if fireworks are exploding in the sky. The roaring and turbulent waves, full of power and grandeur – like a giant wall towering over you – make a deep impression that never fully fades away over the following years.

On August 18th every year, there is sure to be a big tide. Tourists swarm to Yanguan township to experience the excitement. The most renowned places for watching Qiantang Tide are Changshan Dam, the Big Dent, the Dragon Head of Babao, and Xiaoshan.

A pavilion for watching the tide is set up on the Changsha Dam, where you can see the tidal bore approaching. The Big Dent is the place to watch the soul-stirring "Crossing Tide," which is caused by the sand of the riverbed here. At the Dragon Head of Babao, there is a reef protruding from the sea wall, and you can stand here to watch the "Furious Billows," terrifying and stormy, seeming to shake heaven and earth. In Xiaoshan, you can experience the Thread Tide, the imposing Returning Tide, the Boat-Challenging Tide, the Tide between Tides, and the fierce Tide from the Rear. Tide Watching Park is a good place to watch the evening tide. It presents a different view, but the grandeur and astonishment is the same. In the supreme stillness and tranquility of night, you can hear the roar, as if numerous horses are running and rolling.

Beside playing its part in the Qiantang Tide, the sea wall is also an important component of the Qiantang Tide culture. In ancient times, for those living along the river the Qiantang Tide was a disaster that ruined their crops and their houses. People tried to ward off the threat, but the gigantic force of the tide made it nearly impossible to control it. Local people devised various ways to contain it in their struggle against the Qiantang Tide. One impressive creation was the Fish Scale Sea Wall. It was unprecedented anywhere else in the world. People placed piles 16 ft (5m) long in the bank to form a foundation. The walls, which at the bottom have a width of 13 ft (4m) and the top 5ft (1.4m), were made with stone bars, each laid upon another to form from 18 to 23 layers. They were glued together with a mixture of glutinous steamed rice and lime. Finally, they were locked with iron buckles. The Qiantang Tide Sea Wall, extending along the river and winding like the Great Wall, has been a spectacular sight ever since.

The sea wall on the northern bank of Qiantang River is a great feat of architectural engineering of ancient China. It enjoys equal popularity with the Great Wall, and it is listed as one

of four great ancient constructions, offering to the world an outstanding example of the ingenuity of early people.

The Tide Watching Site in Yanguan township of Haining county. It is best to watch Qiantang Tide around the mid-autumn festival every year (above)

The Anta Pagoda at the Tide Watching Site in Yanguan towship of Haining county (below)

ASIA

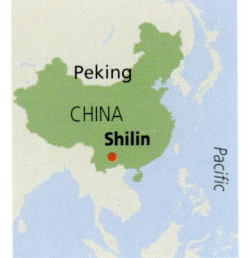

Fantastical rock formations

Shilin Stone Forest, in the Chinese province of Yunnan, is famous for its fairy-tale scenery

Getting there:
Bus service from Kunming

Where to stay:
Wide choice of hotels in Kunming; hotel within the Park

Climate:
Mean annual temperature around 59°F (15°C) with high humidity. Very little seasonal fluctuation

Main attractions:
Liziqing; Naigu; Zhiyundon (underground); Lake Changhu; Dadieshui waterfall

Myths and legends surround the stone figures in Liziqing Stone Forest (right)

Some limestone pillars can reach up to 100ft (30m) in height (below, left)

Some of the scenery in this natural garden is strongly reminiscent of a Chinese ink drawing (below, right)

Around 55 miles (90km) southeast of Kunming, the capital of Yunnan province in China, nature has created a truly fantastical limestone landscape, known as the Shilin Stone Forest. An amazing landscape of extraordinary limestone rock formations covers an area of 135 square miles (350km2) and stretches as far as the eye can see is. Wind and rain have eroded the rock to form three-feet-high mushroom shapes, petrified waves, teeth, and even animal figures out of the soft limestone. Spectacular cave systems have been carved out by subterranean rivers that appear above ground in the form of thundering waterfalls or tranquil lakes.

This whole region was still at the bottom of the sea 270 million years ago. Organisms with calcareous shells, including corals, built their intricate homes on a thick layer of sandstone that gradually became overlain with a layer of limestone three feet thick. As the sea retreated from the area over the course of millions of years, the undulating limestone plateau that had previously formed the seabed now rose 5,600–6,600ft (1,700–2,000m) above sea level. Weather and climate immediately set to work eroding the soft stone and sculpting these 100ft (30m) high pillars of rock into bizarre pinnacles, often resembling the shapes of plants or animals. They have been given a variety of imaginative names, such as "Phoenix smoothing its wings," "Rhinoceros looking at the moon," and the "ten-thousand-year-old mushroom." These rocky columns stand so close to one another that the effect is like walking through a maze of trees.

Smaller pinnacles, barely higher than 30ft (9m), populate the higher areas, while giant columns, obelisks, and ridges up to 100ft (30m) in height rise up out of the valleys. In the heart of this fairyland setting is the Liziqing Stone Forest, covering an area of 6 square miles (16km2) and encompassing more than 100 smaller rock formations. Stone Age and Bronze Age settlers have left large numbers of rock drawings in the area, depicting scenes from their everyday existence.

Gateway to the underworld

Naigu Stone Forest, 5 miles (8km) further north, covers an area of some 3 square miles (8 km2) and incorporates several cave openings leading into an underground world, where erosion has fashioned an amazing collection of strange rock formations.

There is even a subterranean stone forest, known as the Zhiyundon forest, covering an area of one square mile (three square kilometers) and extending nearly 330ft (100m) into the earth through a series of vast caves. The Qifeng cave system, through which a river has carved out a channel, is subject to such substantial differences in air pressure between August and November that a strong wind sweeps through its underground passages every thirty minutes.

There are more than 80 lakes in this stone forest region, created when the cave ceilings weakened and collapsed. The largest of these is Lake Changhu. It lies at an altitude of 6,257ft (1,907m), is 3 miles (5km) in length and nearly 1,000ft (300m) across. Stalactites and stalagmites can be seen beneath its crystal-clear waters, which descend to depths of 100ft (30m). The remains of columns that once supported this former cave now poke above the water in the form of four small, densely forested islands.

Nine subterranean river systems have so far been explored, including the Baijang River, which plunges 300ft (90m) down into the Nanpanjiang River, just southwest of Liziqing Stone Forest near the 100ft (30m) wide Dadieshui waterfall. This is one of the highest waterfalls in China. The surrounding landscape forms some of the most spectacular scenery in the entire stone forest.

Flora

Large expanses of the stone forest have been landscaped in the manner of a garden with pathways and lawns to make it more accessible to the streams of visitors. In some parts, however, the original vegetation has been left to its own devices. This consists mainly of subtropical trees such as the cluster-leaved oak, Chinese and Mason pine and Nepal alder.

ASIA

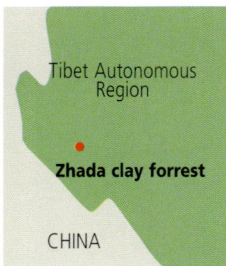

Zhada clay forest, Tibet

A creative work made by wind and water

Location:
Zhada Clay Forest is located in Zhada county in Ngari prefecture, on the west of the Tibet Autonomous Region.

Climate:
The annual average temperature of Ngari is 66°F (19°C). At more than 16,405ft (5000m) above sea level, the temperature here varies greatly.

Special interest:
Zhada Clay Forest features unique landforms with majestic clay pillars

Main attractions:
Zhada Clay Forest, Tholing Monastery, the ruins of the Guge kingdom, and more.

The splendid effects of the sun in Zhada county of the Ngari prefecture have become legendary. In the myriad rays of the sun the famous clay forest is particularly stunning. Endowed with life and vigor by glowing clouds at sunset, the clay pillars in their different shapes shine against the highland in a fascinating light.

Under the influence of mountain-forming movements in ancient times, the clay forest was formed when sediments deposited by lakes and rivers were exposed to erosion by water. Standing straight, steep, and majestic, these clay "trees" are in various fascinating shapes, some much taller than others. The clay forest of Zhada appears magical and gorgeous, made by the inspired and delicate touch of nature.

If you climb over the Kangdese Mountains, you will be struck dumb with amazement by the sight of the clay forest in its unparalleled magnificence. It looks splendid when seen from afar and exquisite on closer scrutiny.

Clay pillars are scattered everywhere on the slopes around the county seat of Zhada. You can take a walk from the town to the clay forest, and will find that you are offered scenes similar to those of the Great Canyon. The clay forest in Maoci Valley is considered the most spectacular of all. The castle-like clay pillars cover a huge area.

It is no wonder that people resorted to legends for an interpretation of what they could see here. A long time ago, it is said, there used to be a vast ocean where presentday Zhada stands. Under the blue sky, there was nothing but wind and water. Gradually, the clay forest began to emerge from under the sea. Though this is only a legend, it contains some elements of the truth. According to scientific research, in the area where the clay forest now stands there used to be a lake which was approaching 200 square miles (500 square kilometers) in area. The mountain-forming movements that created the Himalayas resulted in an uplifting of the lake's basin and a reduction in the water level. The clay forest was formed by the effects of erosion, which scoured and sculpted the clay from the basin into all manner of shapes of different heights. Erosion continued for tens of thousands of years, adding more delicate details to the clay pillars – as if they were touched by a stroke of genius.

Rainbow over Zhada Clay Forest (above, left)

Zhada Clay Forest under magical light (above, right)

Everything is still in Zhada Clay Forest, except souls floating in sunlight, along with clouds (center, right)

The magnificent scenery of Zhada Clay Forest (below, right)

ASIA

Crescent Moon Spring, Gansu

A bright pearl and a crescent moon in the desert

Location:
Located on the northern side of the ringing sand hills, 3 mi. (5km) south of Dunhuang city in Gansu province.

Climate:
There is a temperate and continental climate, with an annual average temperature of 48.7°F (9.3°C). Rainfall is poor, and there is a big temperature difference between night and day.

Special interest:
The area is renowned for its desert wonders.

Crescent Moon Spring is located on the northern slope of Ringing Sand Hill (Mingsha Hill), 3 miles (5 km) south of Dunhuang city in Gansu province. It is 984 ft (300m) long from east to west, 164 ft (50m) wide from south to north, and 16 ft (5m) deep. It has the appearance of a crescent moon, hence the name of the spring. Crescent Moon Spring used to be a section of the Danghe River. Owing to a change in its course, a bend of the river gradually became a separate pool.

On its north and south sides are the tall sand hills, each named Ringing Sand Hill. The hills have not acquired this name because they can produce sounds on their own. It is because when people slide down the sand hills, the sliding action makes a ringing sound. Because of the special configuration of the sand hills and the unique topography around, the wind – when blowing down the low-lying land – forms exceptional air currents as they bring the sand along and sweep by the spring. The spring is constantly supplemented by the undercurrent of the Danghe River, and therefore the spring water maintains a dynamic balance. As a result of all this, over the past thousand years the spring has brimmed over with water and coexisted with the sand hills. It never dries up, even in long droughts, and it never overflows in rainy days either. The water is forever limpid and bluish. People have given this area the name of Limpid Crescent Moon Spring at Dawn.

An ancient poet once wrote, "In the shape of a crescent moon, You offer a mirror to us. The wind can never bring sand to you, A tranquil life accompanies us forever." Through the ages, tourists have been fascinated by the beauty of Crescent Moon Spring.

It is said that a long, long time ago, the area around Dunhuang was the Great Gobi Desert. Then there were no ringing sand hills – and no Crescent Moon Spring, either.

One year there was a prolonged drought. All the crops and all the plants withered and died. People were terribly thirsty, and they cried and cried. When the beautiful and kind-hearted White Cloud Fairy Maiden was passing by, she heard their heart-rending cries. She felt pity for the sufferings of the people, and her uncontrollable tears rolled down from heaven as she went by. They at once became limpid springs which rescued the people from their disaster. The people felt deeply grateful to her and they built a temple to worship the White Cloud Fairy Maiden. This aroused the anger of the Big Sand Immortal in the Divine Sand Temple. He used his magic power to throw down the sand piles, with the intention of burying the spring in them. But the White Cloud Fairy Maiden, with the help of the moon, which she borrowed from the moon goddess, determined to fight against the Big Sand Immortal. The day when all this happened was the fifth day of the Chinese calendar, when the crescent moon shone in the sky in favor of the White Cloud Fairy Maiden, who converted herself into a cool and transparent pool from which the people could drink and irrigate the land. The Big Sand Immortal used more witchcraft in order to vanquish his opponent. When she discovered this, the moon goddess became very angry. She denounced the Big Sand Immortal as being impertinent and bullying. With a gentle stroke of the wide sleeve of her gown, she produced a gale, sending the drifting sand up to the hill's top. The Big Sand Immortal roared at this like thunder, which caused the ringing of the sand hills.

The spring water, so cool, so limpid, and so sweet, has been lying quietly in the embrace of the sand hills for thousands of years. Though there has been frequent harassment by the fierce wind and ominous sand, the bluish spring is still there, and the murmuring water is still there. It is just like the eyes of a rare beauty, lucid, charming, and passionate – or the lips of a maiden, so mysterious, so soft, and so seductive – or more likely a slice of Hami melon, jade green, crystal, and sweet.

By the Crescent Moon Spring, the poplar trees stand gracefully, and the weeping willows dance with the wind. There you can smell the fragrant flowers of the narrow-leaved oleaster, and see the swaying groves of reed and the hovering wild birds.

The Crescent Moon Spring abounds in fish. They are called Iron Back fish, and they are said to cure some intractable diseases. There is also a species of grass called Seven Star grass. It is said that if someone eats the fish and the grass, they will live for ever. The Crescent Moon Spring is therefore also a medicinal spring.

The marvelous scenery of Crescent Moon Spring and Ringing Sand Hill (Mingsha Hill) (below, left)

Sand-skiing at Ringing Sand Hill (Mingsha Hill) (above)

Camel caravan at Ringing Sand Hill (Mingsha Hill) (below)

ASIA

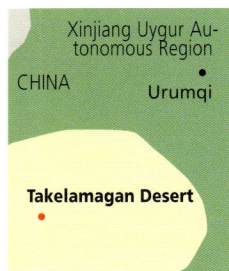

Takelamagan Desert, Xinjiang

The sound of the camel bell in the desert

Location:
Situated in the center of the Talimu basin, Xinjiang Uygur Autonomous Region, covers an area of 130,347 square miles (337,600 square kilometers). It is about 625 miles (1000km) from east to west and about 250 miles (400km) from north to south.

Climate:
The golden season for crossing the Takelamagan Desert is during the 20 days or so between late October and mid-November, as the leaves of the Populus diversifolia in the Talimu basin turn to gold. Visitors will gain a rich and colorful personal experience by walking along the Hetian River.

Special interest:
Large moving dunes may be as high as 984 ft (300m), and there are complex and varied types of dunes, some shaped like giant dragons resting on the sand.

Main attractions:
The Takelamagan boasts a magnificent history and culture based on the ancient Silk Road, which runs across the southern end.

The Takelamagan Desert is situated in the center of the Talimu basin of Xinjiang Uygur Autonomous Region (right)

Camel caravan in the Takelamagan Desert (above, right)

Ruins of ancient Milan city, in the Takelamagan Desert (far right)

Situated in the center of the Talimu basin of Xinjiang Uygur Autonomous Region, the Takelamagan Desert covers an area of 130,347 square miles (337,600 square kilometers), and is about 625 miles (1000km) from east to west and about 250 miles (400km) from north to south. The desert, dubbed "a place of no return" or "the sea of death" by the local Uygur people, now ranks as the second largest in the world and has fostered lots of legends and wonderful sights.

Once upon a time, the local people longed for the melting snow from Mount Tianshan and Mount Kunlun to be used to irrigate the arid Talimu basin. A kind-hearted god, who had two treasures to hand – a golden ax and a golden key – was moved by the sincere wish of the locals and decided to give the ax to the Kazaks and the key to the Uygurs. Originally it was intended to have Mount Aertai cleft by the ax in order to draw its clean water out, and to open up the precious deposits of the Talimu basin by using the key. Unfortunately, the golden key was lost by Magesha, the god's youngest daughter, and the god was so furious that he locked her up in the Talimu basin. From then on, the basin's center became the Takelamagan Desert, and it has remained so.

A desert is usually both enchanting and awesome. On the one hand, it can create a magnificent scene, as in a beautiful sunset. On the other hand, people may be frightened by the fact that a village can be buried under sand dunes overnight, and thus disappear with the wind. For travelers, choosing desert means choosing a challenge, and at the same time it also entails enjoying victory and devoting effort to a cause. It has nothing to do with anything soft and gentle, and only when standing on the type of land that is part of it could you really appreciate its breadth and awesome features.

After all, the desert has its own special way of expressing life – a river, a grove of Populus diversifolia trees perhaps. To the Takelamagan Desert, the Hetian River is its eyes and the Populus diversifolia trees its beard.

The Hetian River is the only river that has any life in the Takelamagan Desert. It originates on Mount Kunlun, winds down southward via the two towns of Hetian and Muyu, and then turns north into the depths of the Takelamagan, eventually vanishing into the boundless desert. All year round, the Hetian River looks like a river only when the snowfall from Mount Kunlun melts in summer. Sometimes it is affected by flooding even in such a dry area as the Takelamagan. Nevertheless, the Hetian River will run dry as soon as summer slips by.

It is the Hetian River that makes it possible for explorers and backpackers to experience walking on foot through the whole of the Takelamagan. Prior to the construction of the cross-desert highway, 90 percent of the journey across had been performed along this very river.

The Populus diversifolia groves of Takelamagan, planted in its desert park, are about 50 miles (80km) away from Taixian county and located in the core area of Talimu's Populus Diversifolia Reserve. The park features a variety of colors: green trees, clear blue river, and clear blue sky – just like a colorful Chinese ink and wash painting. When fall comes, the color will vary from yellowish green at the beginning to golden yellow later on. Looking into the distance from high ground, you will notice that the Talimu River is running tortuously nearby to form numerous branches, among which are some scattered lakes surrounded by the Populus diversifolia groves. They stretch out along the river and into the far horizon. The view is spectacular.

ASIA

On the floor of the Aso volcano

The collapse of the Aso crater, on the Japanese island of Kyushu, created the largest caldera on earth

Getting there:
Take the Minami-Aso train from Tateno Station to Takamori. By car or bus from Tateno and Beppu. Airport at Kumamoto

Where to stay:
Minami-Aso Vacationland Hotel and campsites. Further hotels in the vicinity

Climate:
Cool, but sunny, in summer; snow on higher ground in winter

Main attractions:
Naka summit (by cable car); Taka; Neko; Miyamakirishima and Senui-kyou gorges; Koga-no-taki waterfall

Cultural attractions:
The Avenue of 100 Cherry Trees near Takamori-Toge; Kuju flower gardens; mountain climbing

Steam still billows up from the Aso crater, the world's largest active caldera, situated at the heart of Kyushu Island in southern Japan. A caldera is the saucer-shaped depression formed when a volcano collapses and the outer walls of the volcanic cone are left standing. Aso extends over some 70 miles (110km), stretching 17 miles (27km) from north to south and 10 miles (16km) from east to west.

The lava that the volcano has spit out over the past 30 million years has created the island of Kyushu. Four gigantic explosions have occurred over the past 300,000 years, the last of which occurred around 90,000 years ago. This was one of the most powerful eruptions in geological history and signaled the end of Aso. Forty cubic miles (160 km^2) of lava poured out over central Kyushu, a volume so vast that the magma chamber beneath the volcano collapsed under the sheer weight of it. The ash cloud from Aso deposited a 6in (15cm) thick shroud over the island of Hokkaido, 1,050 miles (1,700km) away in northern Japan. The collapsed crater gradually filled with water, forming a giant lake. In time, however, five new volcanic cones have gradually emerged from the caldera basin. These are strung out in a line along an east-west axis across the center of the caldera. The volcanic peaks of Kishima, Eboshi, Naka, Taka, and Neko form the incredibly spectacular, lunar-like landscape of Aso Gogaku. The bizarre shapes left by the once molten rock as it solidified around the crater rims have a unique and eerie beauty.

Countless picturesque waterfalls cascade over the rocks to the valley below, many of which consist of hot, steaming water. Sensui-kyou, one of Aso's most enchanting gorges, is a refuge for a rare alpine plant, the Kyushu alpine rose, a small, pink species of rhododendron.

Taka, now extinct, is the highest of the five volcanoes, rising to a height of 5,226ft (1,593m). Naka, on the other hand, is still active. This 4,340ft (1,323m) high volcanic cone frequently emits black clouds of pungent and sulfurous gasses, sometimes to the accompaniment of rumblings from deep within the earth. A cable car ascends to a viewpoint from which visitors can peer over the rim of the crater and look down into the swirling chasm below. To protect visitors from sudden ash emissions, thick-walled concrete bunkers have been built in which they can take cover in the event of an eruption.

Traditional pasture farming

An overhead view sweeps across an unexpectedly charming landscape within the caldera. Lush green fields and meadows extend right up to the

edge of the crater on the horizon. The gently undulating terrain is dotted with peacefully grazing cattle and horses. The cars on the roads look tiny, as do the three villages and three small towns, which now accommodate around 100,000 people. Near the village of Tateno, rain and wind have eroded the caldera's crater wall to such an extent that it collapsed between 30,000 and 50,000 years ago, releasing the volume of water that once formed the crater lake and allowing it to drain away to the sea.

The Aso caldera has been populated since time immemorial. In early March, the farming community burns the dry winter grass to eliminate pests. They have followed this practice for centuries and nature has learned to adapt itself to this annual burning procedure by evolving a unique variety of meadow vegetation.

Nowadays, the entire Aso region forms part of the Aso-Kuju National Park, which extends over an area of 280 square miles (727km2) and was established not only to protect the magnificent natural scenery, but also to preserve traditional farming methods.

The park also comprises the mighty Kuju volcanic group, all with summits in excess of 4,950ft (1,500m). The highest of these is Mount Kuju itself, at 5,876ft (1,791m), the highest elevation on Kyushu. Plumes of white smoke occasionally billow out of Iwo, one of the craters. Kuyu lies along the same volcanic belt as Aso. The area is dotted with numerous hot springs, bubbling up from beneath the earth's surface. Beppu, Chojabaru, Yu-no-Tani, and Uchino-Maki are spa resorts popular with visitors seeking health cures or simply relaxation in the natural, hot spring baths.

The Kuju uplands are regarded as one of the last natural paradises left in Japan. From the base of these mountains, the slopes rise gently and gracefully upward to a high plateau. Here, too, the luxuriant meadows are grazed by cattle and horses. Higher up, the volcanic slopes support a rich diversity of flora and fauna. These mountains are particularly famed for their displays of wild azaleas, which bloom here during the summer in a dazzling riot of color.

Individual volcanic peaks, such as the extinct Taka, rear up from the flat plain within the Aso crater (above)

This large expanse of land at the bottom of the crater has been populated since prehistoric times. Farmers have cultivated the land in terraces in some areas (below, left)

ASIA

On the peak of Mount Fuji

Route:
Odakyu railway from Tokyo to Yumoto, mountain rail from there to Hakone-To-zan

Best time:
October – December

Further points of interest:
Sulphur caves, Lake Ashi

Japan's tallest mountain is a place of pilgrimage with a rich tradition

It is the most frequent motif of the Japanese landscape painter. With special watercolor drawings, based more on understatement than emphasis, a few diagonal lines upwards, a brief flat stroke and a line plunging towards the depths reveal the contours of the object of worship. Its symmetric beauty and its in Japan unsurpassed height 12,388 ft. (3,776 m) have made of Fuji-san or Fujiyama a holy mountain and Japan's emblem.

Even if its peak is covered with white caps of snow, Fuji-san is a volcano which from time to time does erupt. The main crater is 492 to 656 ft. (150–200 m) deep at a diameter of 1,968 ft. (600 m). During the most recent eruption of the Fuji in 1707, a 5-inch (12 cm) layer of ashes descended 56 mi. (90 km) away in the city of Edo, present Tokyo.

The crater mountain inspires not only painting artists; it plays an important role in Japanese poetry as well. The balance of its contours is praised in song, as is its top as it pierces the clouds, which it frequently does, and poets speak of the magic of the landscape below, place of primeaval forest and the five mountain-mirroring Fuji lakes. While nature was threatened by always expanding human settlement, recently the Fuji-Hakone-Isu Reserve enjoys special governmental protection.

An image of purity

Like the Olympus of the ancient Greeks, so the Fuji-san had an aura of divinity in former times. Could the gods find a more fitting place to dwell than on this mighty throne? The Fuji is holy, also for the most important Japanese religion, Shintoism, which fuses the worship of ancestors and of nature. And so it is a long tradition in Shintoism to climb the mountain as pilgrim, wearing white gloves and sandals made of straw.

Japanese Buddhists revere Fuji-san too. In the 13th century Buddhist samurai and guru Nichiren called upon his fellow faithful to found a 'sanctuary of true Buddhism' at the foot of Mount Fuji. A Buddhist organisation, the Soka Gakke Society, responded to this samurai's invitation in the 1960s and built the Sho-Hondo temples. Their modern concrete construction, praised as the largest temple in the world, is located in the temple district of Taisekiji, slightly raised to afford a fine view of the holy mountain.

On the sharply inclining paths singing Shinto pilgrims and other devout travellers are an exotic minority, though. It has long since become a popular sport in Japan to climb the mythical mountain at least one, preferable more often, during one's lifetime. On some summer weekends some 30,000 people, children and entire families armed with picnic baskets labor their upward way. The total number of annual mountain visitors is estimated at half a million.

In contrast with the Shinto pilgrims, who begin their climb from the prescribed foot of the mountain, the crowds find easier ways to reach Fuji-san's top. Buses park at the 7,545 ft. (2300 m) point, from where one can reach the crater after a walk of a mere five to seven hours.

Devout pilgrims (left) in a light precession pass the Shinto shrines (lower left) on their way to the top of the Fiji-san or Fujiyama, which rises 12,388 ft. (3,776 m) above the lakes of the Fiji-Hakone-Isu reserve.

ASIA

Volcanic paradise in Java

The Bromo-Tengger-Semeru National Park protects the unique natural landscape around the extinct Tengger volcano

Getting there:
By car from Malang via Tumpang through approximately 12 ½ miles (20km) of picturesque mountain scenery from Probolinggo to Ngadisari. Steep road from Ngadisari to Cemoro Lawang on the edge of the Tengger crater

Where to stay:
Simple guesthouse in Ngadisari at the park entrance. Thirty-bed hotel on the slopes of the Tengger Caldera ring near Cemaralawang. Numerous campsites available

Climate:
Monsoon climate with warm rainy season between December and March. Daily temperatures around 64°F (18°C), falling to 37–39°F (3–4°C) at night

Main attractions:
Bromo; the sand sea; viewpoint from Penanjakan; the crater lakes of Pani, Regulo, and Kumbolo; tropical rain forest around Lake Darungan

Special tips:
Special permission required to climb Mahameru issued by the National Park office in Malang. If visiting the Semeru volcano, be wary of toxic gasses and hot lava

Millions of years ago, the gigantic Tengger volcano in the volcanic region of East Java collapsed upon itself when the magma chamber in the earth's crust emptied beneath it. Java's largest and most impressive caldera measuring around 6 miles (10km) across remained. The high plateau has still not settled down, however, and five new volcanic cones have erupted here at heights of 6,500ft (2,000m).

Towering in the south, outside the 165–1,650ft (50–500m) high caldera, is the massive cone of the Semeru crater. Rising to a height of 12,000ft (3,676m), it is Java's highest mountain. It is also the most active, as evidenced by the thick plume of steam that rises every eight minutes from its interior and floats away across the tropical blue sky as a light white cloud. Lush, green, and dense tropical vegetation covers the lower half of the slopes, while above 8,000ft (2,400m) this gives way to sparsely covered, sub-alpine pine forest. Nothing grows at the highest elevation: the top of the cone is covered with ash and stones.

Sacred mountain of the Hindus

Bromo-Tengger-Semuru National Park comprises almost 225 square miles (580km2) of this volcanic region, which extends some 25 miles (40km) from north to south and over 12 1/2 miles (20km) from east to west.

In the center of the circular Tengger Caldera, surrounded by sheer precipices ranging from 165–1,650ft (50–500m) in height, are the symmetrical cones of the two volcanoes Bromo and Batok. Batok is dormant whereas Bromo continues to spew clouds of steam into the atmosphere. Bromo is also a sacred mountain to the Hindus, who retreated to this area when Indonesia was being converted to Islam. Each October, thousands of the faithful make the pilgrimage to take part in the Yadnya-Kasada ceremony, a type of thanksgiving festival. They celebrate the event in a small temple complex on the barren plateau.

A series of 140 steps leads up to the rim of the crater, where the pungent smell of sulfur makes breathing difficult. Thick steam rises from the vents in the 2,000–2,600ft (600–800m) wide crater. But the view into the fiery depths below and across the Tengger Caldera to Semeru in the background is breathtaking. The part of the caldera south of the Bromo crater is a green savannah filled with undulating grasslands. To the north is a sea of sand, a featureless moon landscape of lava and ash, poured onto the Tengger crater ring by the Bromo volcano.

Although sparse and unvarying within the Tengger crater itself, the plant life along its outer periphery, and indeed throughout the entire mountain massif, is amazingly varied due to the dramatic differences in elevation within this volcanic landscape. Biologists have identified 1,025 different species of plants, including 226 orchids and 260 used locally for medicinal purposes.

Depending on their elevation, the extensive forested areas provide three different habitats. The lower zone up to 5,000ft (1,500m) is colonized by primeval tropical rainforest with a large diversity of species. The dense leaf canopy of ancient trees protects the lower reaches of this jungle environment. Its branches are festooned with various species of lianas, forming an impenetrable thicket.

Above this, at a height of 5,000–8,000ft (1,500–2,400m), is a band of secondary forest consisting of pioneer plants, which cannot flourish in the half-light beneath the tropical rainforest canopy. These are mainly kangaroo trees, a species of birch and acacias.

Edelweiss occasionally blooms here

The sub-alpine zone above 8,000ft (2,400m) consists of pine trees, which diminish in size as the elevation increases. Meanwhile, the forest floor is home to a type of blueberry and even occasional edelweiss.

There is little wildlife in the park. The 22 species found here include red deer, wild boar, porcupines and also cheetahs. But the animals were apparently hunted so zealously before the National Park was established in 1982 that their numbers have never recovered.

Arguably the most spectacular view across this unique volcanic landscape is from the summit of Penanjakan.

The blunt volcanic cones in the Bromo region were created by violent eruptions within the earth (above)

Toxic sulfurous fumes bubble up from inside the volcano (below, left)

Away from the crater, the mountain slopes are covered with deciduous forest (below, right)

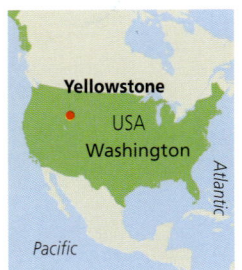

NORTH AMERICA

Geysers and hot springs in the Rocky Mountains

Yellowstone Park offers a glimpse of the prehistoric past

Getting there:
Interstate Highway 90; at Livingstone, go south on Highway 89 for about 50 miles (80km). Airports at Cody and Jackson; Bozeman and Billings; Idaho Falls. From June to September, also at West Yellowstone to and from Salt Lake City. Buses from Bozeman

Where to stay:
Historic hotels; Wild West style lodges; cabins; camping sites within and outside the Park

Climate:
Mountain climate: Average January temperature 10°F (-12°C); average July temperature 55°F (13°C)

Main attractions:
Old Faithful; Grand Prismatic Spring; Mammoth Hot Springs; Yellowstone Grand Canyon; Norris Geyser Basin; Madison Museum

Special tips:
Snowmobiles available in winter

Paradise for nature and animals alike: The sinter terraces of Mammoth Hot Springs (opposite, above left)

Bison and Wapiti deer are two of the animal species found in Yellowstone National Park (opposite, below left and above right)

Grand Prismatic Springs owes its shimmering colors to the presence of bacteria and algae (opposite, below right)

The eruption of a geyser is always a fascinating sight

Long ago, 630,000 million years to be precise, a massive magma chamber exploded beneath this region. The area involved surrounds the point of contact of what are now the three North American states of Wyoming, Montana, and Idaho. The pressure building up under the earth's crust was finally released in a sudden eruption, creating a crater, measuring 28 mi. (45 km) in width and 47 mi. (75 km) in length. This crater, now forms the heart of Yellowstone National Park.

Subterranean activity began pushing the southern segment of the Rocky Mountains upward 65 million years ago and fresh lava flows were still spilling out over the landscape as recently as 40 million years ago. Entire forests were buried by falling ash which petrified over the course of millions of years and now provides the visitor with a glimpse of what the world looked like in its infancy.

Yellowstone is located above a so-called "Hot Spot," an area where the layer of the earth's crust above the molten earth's mantle is only a few kilometers thick. Surface water seeps down through the cracks and fissures, becoming super-heated until it either erupts as a geyser, blasting a jet of water several feet into the air, bubbles up out of the ground as a hot spring, or else is ejected in the form of fumaroles, plumes of hot steam from deep within the earth with temperatures heated to 280°F (138°C). Yellowstone harbors the most intense of natural geothermal activity anywhere in the world. There are some 10,000 or so of these hot springs in Yellowstone and more than 300 geysers spouting columns of water into the air.

When Old Faithful blows

The most famous of the geysers is Old Faithful. Since time immemorial, it has been blasting jets of hot water 100ft (30m) into the air at regular intervals of 35 to 120 minutes. These eruptions can last anything between 90 seconds and 5 minutes. The longer an eruption lasts, the longer it will be before the next one. Old Faithful's neighbor, the Giantess, on the other hand, takes six to eight months to recover between eruptions.

The shallow lake formed by the Grand Prismatic Hot Springs shimmers with every conceivable hue. An assortment of brightly-colored bacteria and algae have established themselves on its bottom, surviving on the substances that hot spring water brings to the surface from the depths of the earth. Biologists are still puzzled as to how these organisms manage to survive in such super-heated temperatures.

Mammoth Hot Springs produces water with an extremely high calcium concentrate that has built up, over the course of thousands of years, unusual terraces of sinter, which have spread like soft vanilla ice cream.

Yellowstone Lake was hollowed out by glacial movement during the last Ice Age. Its waters have carved out Yellowstone's own version of the Grand Canyon in the form of a gorge measuring 800–1,220ft (240–370m) in depth and exposing a colorful range of rock strata within the steep walls.

This huge witch's cauldron of bubbling activity has long been a source of fascination to Americans, so much so that the whole area, stretching across an area of 3,500 square miles (9,000km2), was designated a National Park as long ago as 1872, becoming the first official conservation park of its kind in the world.

Haven for deer

Apart from providing an opportunity to observe these stunning spectacles of geothermal activity, the Park also supports one of the richest concentrations of plant and animal life anywhere in the United States and is a designated biosphere reserve. Unfortunately, Yellowstone is one of a long list of North American national parks that number among the world's most endangered nature conservation areas. Outside the Park's boundaries, various enterprises are poised to pounce on its reserves of mineral resources, such as gold and oil, or are waiting for an opportunity to tap this natural source of heat for use in power stations.

Eighty percent of the National Park is covered by pristine pine forest and is home to more than one thousand, often insignificant, species of plant, such as the Agrostis rossae, a genus of grass that is found only in Yellowstone Park.

Surrounded by giant peaks soaring to heights of up to 13,200ft (4,000m), Yellowstone is the only place left where herds of wild bison are once again free to roam. These animals, which were hunted to the verge of extinction towards the end of the nineteenth century, have now recovered in number to around 2,000. The animal population of Yellowstone includes examples of every species of wildlife found in the Rocky Mountains.

NORTH AMERICA

Hawaii, the land of volcanos

On closer inspection, the archipelago has the highest mountains in the world

Route:
Flight from Oahu over Honolulu or direct from San Francisco, Los Angeles, Vancouver to Hilo on Hawaii

Best time:
The whole year through (high season is Christmas)

Accommodation:
Chalet Kilauea, Carson's Volcano Cottage, Volcano House (all on Hawaii's volcano nature reservation) Also worth seeing is the Jaggar Museum

From the plane the 1,497 mi. (2,400 km) long chain of Hawaiian islands look like a long wound, sunk with crusts around the edges and red in the middle, in the endless blue Pacific Ocean. Only when descending are you aware of the fact that an exotic colour of green is the most dominant colour of the islands, interrupted by black lava, fiery volcano craters and - on the main island - by snow covered mountain tops.

Platform for observatories

The eight larger and 26 smaller islands of the archipelago, with their mountains, foaming cliffs and scenic sandbanks rose approximately 30 million years ago out of the sea. Fluid lava from the center of the earth made a way to the surface, lava masses flowed over one another and smoking craters broke through the water level of the ocean. The Hawaiian islands are mainly formed from above sea level mountain tops from an under water volcano or a group of volcanos.

The people who live on the main island Hawaii, of which the island group derives its name from, brag not justly about having the highest mountain in the world, the giant volcano Mauna Kea. From top to bottom it is 3,362 ft. (10,205 m) long, of which the largest part - 19,685 ft. (6,000 m) - is under sea level. It must of been unheard-of forces, which flung these basalt monster upwards, and whose last eruption was 15000 years ago, but which today is considered by vulcanologist to be non-active. On its top, which is covered by snow for several months of the year, the US and a number of other countries have placed their most modern observatories, because nowhere else in the world is it possible to observe the universe as well as on top of Mauna Kea, where the earth's atmosphere is 97% free of water particles.

Of the approximately 40 other smaller volcanos on the group of islands, many are still active today. Only Kilauea, also on the main island, has erupted more than fifty times in the last decennia. The scorched mountain walls drop almost perpendicularly 492 ft. (150 m) downwards, where they hit the solidified lava crust, a thin stone skin over a infernal glow. Walks in the craters are the island's biggest attraction. Although in many places a thick mist lessens visibility or suddenly tourists find themselves staring straight into the fiery mouth of a crater, these excursions are considered to be relatively safe. This is because if an eruption is impending, it is usually felt beforehand.

Polynesians sailed past the islands

The volcanic activities are closely watched from a special observatory on the brim of Kilauea. It is a seismographic center, from where all underground movements over a wide area can be registered and judged. Even a non-visible volcano, Loihi, in the southern part of the island group,

Three views of Hawaii: burning lava, fertile volcano earth and, right, a helicopter above the smoking Pu-Cu crater

is under continuous supervision. Its crater walls lie approximately 3,116 ft. (950 m) under the water's surface, which however does not stop it from posing great problems for the Hawaiians in the very near future.

The islands first inhabitants were the Polynesians, who sailed to the islands around 700 AD, and found the islands with their fertile volcanic bases and rain forest growth mountains to be a good domicile. These days the fiery archipelago, of which the four thousand mountain tops are nearly all covered with snow, does not only attract volcanologists and astronomers, but also many tourists.

NORTH AMERICA

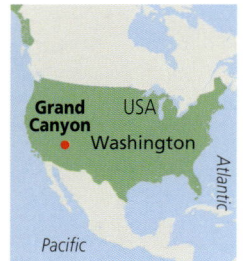

The Grand Canyon
The Colorado River offers a glimpse into the history of the earth

Route:
Flights from Los Angeles and Las Vegas to Grand Canyon. Via road from Flagstaff, Arizona 80 mi. (130 km) over Arizona 64 to the north

Best time:
South Rim closed from October through to May. Extreme ground heat in the high summer season

Accommodation:
Grand Canyon National Park Lodges

Also worth seeing:
Canyon regions National Park in Moab, Utah

The Grand Canyon is 217 miles (350 km) from another world. In 1898 the Scottish writer John Muir wrote about the Grand Canyon: "Its architecture is so unworldly, it is as if one has landed on an extinct place on another planet. A play of nature, wonderful, bizarre, huge. Unbelievable colors, dramatic contrasts, the intense aromas of nature, the deadly silence."

For more than 10 million years, the Colorado river has swept its way through stone and bares the earth's history. We can thank the river and the fact that there is very little rainfall in Arizona for this wonderful natural spectacle. If it rained more often, then the beautiful colors of the stone walls would have been washed away.

A deep gorge
The miracle of the Grand Canyon is not impressive from a distance, until one nears the edge of the canyon and looks into its depth, looks into a stair form landscape of rocks of all different glowing red colors, which is a surprising contrast to the ponderosa pine forest.

As if with a scalpel, the current has exposed the earth's crust and allowed us a glimpse into the millions of years old earth's history. But it is not only this geophysical relic from a distant past which attracts the people. The present is also impressive: the Canyon - geographically seen close to Silezie - is a gorge which is more than 5,905 ft. (1800 m). The Colorado which formed it, flows at a speed of 12 mph (19 km/h) per hour through 160 rapids to the valley. At this enormous speed it transports 40,000 tons of loam per day, in front of the forming of the Clen Canyon as much as 700,000 tons. On the floor of the Canyon summer temperatures reach 113°F (45°C), as high as in the Mexican desert, whilst above the Canyon the temperature is a pleasant 75°F (24°C).

The Spanish, under Francisco de Coronado, were in 1540 the first fair-skinned people to observe the gorge, the home of the Hopi indians. Approximately 30,000 people daily visit the view points grouped around the gorge in ring roads and where there are many possibilities to climb down into the gorge. One of the most popular holiday photos is Hopi Point, a protruding mountain platform, from where you can cast a glance from west to east.

Today, about 500 Havasupai indians, "the people of the green water", live far down on the floor of the gorge. The tribe came to this place of safety in the 12th century. The attraction of this difficult-to-reach reservation is the three waterfalls, from which the indians got their name, due to the falling emerald green water. In the course of their history they have been able to fight off all "attacks" on their gorge. In 1889 a rail road was going to be laid on their ground; in 1950 there were plans to build a christian chapel with a lift on one of the mountain walls; in 1961 a building company wanted to build an 18 floor hotel on the south wall. The people of the green water resigned themselves to the fact - no wonder after living for 800 years on the floor of the Grand Canyon.

The steep walls of the Grand Canyon are lit in glowing colors as if the sun is shining on them. In the stone groves made by the Colorado, one gets a glimpse of the earth's history (opposite)

Viewpoint over the Canyon

SOUTH AMERICA

Volcanic panorama

The National Park surrounding Cotopaxi, in Ecuador, provides a habitat for many alpine flowers verging on extinction

Getting there:
By road or bus from Quito to Machachi; railway station at Aloag

Where to stay:
Camping; José Ribas mountain cabin

Climate:
Daytime temperatures around 45°F (7°C), falling to 32°F (0°C) at night. Permafrost on the summits

Main attractions:
Hiking; mountain climbing; bird and wildlife-watching; El Boliche; stone ruins of pre-Columbian cultures and Inca civilization

The sight of the clouds above Cotopaxi glowing red at night, reflecting the fire within the volcanic crater, is a truly breathtaking spectacle. The conical summit of this perfectly shaped volcano, the most active in the world, is almost invariably hidden behind clouds. Its textbook symmetry is marred only by another, smaller cone, known as the Cabeza del Inca.

The volcano, which rises to a height of 19,350ft (5,897m), has a long history of destruction. It has seldom remained dormant for longer than 15 years at a stretch. It caused the greatest disaster in 1877 when an eruption dislodged masses of ice and snow from its summit, triggering an avalanche that wiped the town of Latacunga off the map.

The vast expanse of open grassland from which the volcano dramatically rises has frequently been devastated by earthquakes or buried under layers of ash and lava. The entire cone consists of alternating layers of dark lava flows and paler layers of ash. At the bottom of its crater, which is 1,200ft (366m) deep, is a cauldron of boiling, bubbling lava which periodically emits huge plumes of steam and gasses.

Cotopaxi's outer, older crater rim stretches about 2,300ft (700m) from north to south and more than 1,640ft (500m) from west to east. Its external flanks are covered with a deep layer of snow.

For a very long time, this mountain refused to be conquered. The first person to attempt its ascent was Alexander von Humboldt in 1802. He failed, as did many others who followed him. It was not until 28 November 1872 that Wilhelm Reiss, a German scientist and explorer, finally succeeded in reaching the summit.

Nowadays, Cotopaxi, situated just 37 miles (60km) from Quito, is a popular destination for mountain climbing expeditions, accompanied by experienced local guides. The José Ribas cabin, located at an altitude of around 15,750ft (4,800m) on the volcano's northeastern flank, provides climbers with overnight accommodation and an opportunity to become acclimatized to the thinner air at these high altitudes. From this high vantage point, there are absolutely stunning views stretching from the glittering lake in Limpiopungo valley to the magnificent and awe-inspiring volcanic scenery of the Andes mountains beyond.

Picturesque lakes

The 14 mile (23km) base of Mount Cotopaxi is situated at the heart of the 130 square miles (334km2) of Cotopaxi National Park. The Park also incorporates Mount Rumiñahui, 15,460ft (4,712m) in height, and the smaller volcanoes of Pasochoa and Sincholagua. This delightful nature park, dotted with lakes and criss-crossed with rivers of melted ice, is Ecuador's most popular conservation area. Even so, human beings, other than vistors, are relatively scarce and any that are encountered are most likely to be Quichua Indians, the native inhabitants of this region and direct descendants of the Incas.

The Park's broad valleys, all at least 11,200ft (3,400m) above sea level, support vegetation typical of barren high-alpine terrain, including a variety of grasses, romerillo, a plant resembling St. John's Wort, Quichuar lilac and heather. This high-altitude region is also an ideal habitat for the extremely rare and heavily protected Chuquiragua, a prickly, orange-flowering species of aster. The native Indians used this plant as a cure for stomach and intestinal problems. There are also a few dwindling areas of woodland, which still support populations of gnarled quinoa trees. The forested areas on the southwest flank of Mount Rumiñahui are also home to the Andean alchemilla, a type of lady's mantle.

Llamas

Blue and white miniature lupins bloom at higher altitudes and patches of gentians and club moss peep from between bare boulders and grow on scree beds. Sometimes, a waft of heavily scented valerian or loricaria may be carried on the breeze. From the recreation area at El Boliche, a network of hiking trails leads through a unique pine forest that was planted as an experiment in 1928 and has blended successfully into the rest of this mountain environment.

The snow-covered summit of Cotopaxi towers majestically above the high plateau of the Andes (below)

Extensive snowfields blanket the upper slopes of the volcano all year round (above)

AFRICA

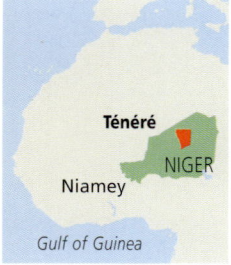

The Tuareg desert

Ténéré National Park in Niger lies in the middle of the Sahara

Getting there:
Flights from Niamey to Agadez; bush taxis; lifts in trucks. Landing strips for light aircraft within the National Park

Where to stay:
Camping in the bush in tents or under the stars; two basic rest houses in Iférouane

Climate:
Hot all year: around 86°F (30°C), rising to 122°F (50°C) between March and June

Main attractions:
Trip through the sea of sand dunes in the Ténéré desert; rock pictures; dinosaurs' graveyard south of the Aër massif

Special tips:
Taking a guide with you reduces the risk of armed attacks

Caravan traveling through the desert (right)

The desert sands stretch for hundreds of miles (below, right)

Rock pictures in the Aïr mountains (below, left)

Ténéré, this vast expanse of sand, gravel, and stones in the central Sahara, is bounded by the Tibesti, Hoggar, and Aïr mountain ranges and referred to by the Tuareg nomads as the "empty land." Endless miles of seemingly flat, barren desert stretch into the distance, where the wind has sculpted some of the Sahara's most beautiful dunes out of a "sea of sand." To the west, where their progress is halted by the forbidding Aïr massif around Arakao and Temet, their soft, almost erotically curving shapes tower upwards to heights of around 1,000ft (300m).

The Aïr massif rises out of the desert plain in the west like one single, mountainous mass, punctuated by individual peaks towering up into the sky, their improbable shapes sculpted by thousands of years of erosion by wind and sand. The unmistakable outline of Mont Greboun in the north, for example, rises to a height of 6,560ft (2,000m). Note also the shimmering blue, cobalt-rich Montagnes Bleues mountains.

Relics of the Mediterranean

The desert is truly alive. Here, and in the Aïr mountains, biologists have identified 350 different varieties of plants, 40 different mammals, 165 different types of birds, and 18 reptiles, including many endangered species. The National Park, created to protect this unique natural environment, encompasses half the Aër massif.

The desert is shifting above an ancient metamorphic plate, formed around 500 million years ago. It became a sea bed 280 to 300 million years ago and later supported a wet, tropical rainforest.

The Aïr mountains were created when volcanoes erupted from the plains 65 million years ago, forming one of the largest volcanic ring systems in the world. It comprises nine individual massifs, measuring up to 50 miles (80km) across and stretches 340 miles (550km) from the former sultanate of Agadez to the Algerian border. Arguably the most spectacular of these is the Arakao caldera, encircled by giant sand dunes in the northeast of the massif.

The plants found in these gray-black mountains and sandy plains grow around the oases, or burst into life in the event of one of the region's infrequent rain showers. They are relics of Sudanese and Mediterranean species, from which they have been separated for thousands of years. Zachun trees and horizontally growing Arak trees, the nearest relatives of which are found in the Sudan, are two such examples. Acacias and tamarisks grow in the mountain valleys, while the moister regions above 3,300ft (1,000m) also support various varieties of fig, similar to those found in Mediterranean regions. Above 4,950ft (1,500m), the wild olive, an internationally endangered species, has also managed to establish itself.

Similarly, any animals living here were separated from their ancestors thousands of years ago. These include relatively large numbers of endangered hoofed animals that have managed to survive the hazards of hunting, poaching, and growing tourism. The population of the rare Addax or Mendes antelope, similar to a red deer in size with long, slender corkscrew

horns, has increased from just 15 animals in the late 1970s to around 100 today. The 12,000 Dorcas gazelles are likewise more numerous following the creation of the nature reserve and several successive years of rainfall.

Protected area for antelopes

At the heart of the National Park is a large protected area, closed to visitors, which provides an undisturbed sanctuary for the rare Mendes antelopes, as well as around 70 olive baboons and 500 Patas monkeys. This special reserve extends over some 5,000 square miles (13,000km2).

Reminders of the region's prehistoric occupants can be seen in the dinosaurs' graveyard along the road to Bilm, which skirts the southern side of the Aïr mountains. Along this 95-mile (150km) stretch of road are the fossilized remains of numerous dinosaurs, whose bones have survived in the desert sand for thousands of years.

AFRICA

Sahara, sea without water

The desert covers almost one-third of Africa and keeps growing

Route:
From Fès. By coach to Erfoud (2 days, 264 mi./425 km) or flight from Casablanca to Fès and Er-Rachida and on to Erfoud (50 mi./80 km). From here 33 mi./53 km to Oasis Merzounga, at the Erg Chebbi.

Best time:
March–April, October–November

Accommodation:
Les Dunes d'Or in Merzounga

Further points of interest:
Rissani: mausoleum of the predecessors of the ruling Alaouit dynasty.

In the beginning was the Earth, the Bible says, and the earth was "void and without form." It may well that a few millions years hence the earth will be desert again, for the arid regions keep expanding. The largest of them is the Sahara, an enormous ocean of sand and rolling rock.

Measuring at least three and a half million square miles (9 million km^2), the Sahara stretches from the Red Sea, the Moroccan Atlantic coast and the Mediterranean to the Sahel zone – nearly one-third of Africa. But the desert is not everywhere the same. Only part of it consists of sand dunes; there are rocky canyons as in the Algerian Tassili mountains, endlessly varying plains of eroding stones, volcanic craters and very small green islands, the oases.

Once, waves rolled here

The impression of void and formlessness, to refer to the Bible again, is strongest in the flat pebblestone deserts, which the Arabs call Regs. A carpet of wind-and-storm-weathered gravel reaches to the horizon.

The Sahara has not always been like this. Earth's history plunged the Sahara from one extreme to the other. Four hundred million years ago, for example, the Sahara was a sea that emptied itself when tectonic forces lifted the floor. In the south of Morocco traces can be found of this oceanic past. Fossils of a former cefalopod (inkfish) and the remains of a sun-bleached coral reef. A mere 170 million years ago forest covered much of the present desert. In those days North Africa hosted herds of great dinosaurs. In South Morocco footprints of more than 3$^1/_3$ feet (1 m) long have been found in the fossilized deposits of a former river.

As the seas advanced and receded thick layers of salt, sand, deposit, pebbles and skeletons were left behind. During the last ice-age, some 10,000 to 25,000 years ago, the Sahara was a savannah landscape. The people of the Stone Age hunted gazelle, giraffe and elephant, using celts (axes held in the fist) and spears. About 7,000 years ago, cattle-growing tribes grazed the Sahara with their enormous herds, as rock drawings on the smooth walls of Tassli desert mountain range tell us.

In the course of time, grazing land in North Africa shrunk. Lack of rain and rising temperatures turned the green savannah into a dry steppe and into desert next. Even so, the Sahara still harbours animals. Close to the watering holes gazelle and mouflon move about. In the desert, lightning-quick "sandfish" – lizards – hunt insects. There are scorpions, snakes and cavia-like Goendis, called Okaokao by the Arabs. At dusk, desert mice of various kinds dare to leave their holes.

The people who live in the desert keep trying to make use of the great water reservoirs below the Sahara. Every 164 to 328 ft. (50–100 m) a well is drilled to the layers holding water and the moisture is led, via underground conduits, to Foggaras, articifical oases. This ingenious irrigation reclaims some 39 square miles (100 km^2) per year. However, at the southern edge of the Sahara alone the desert devours 965 square miles (2,500 km^2) of fertile land annually.

Allah could not have given a greater gift to the Bedouins than the camel. These desert animals can remain without water for a week – as long as they are well-watered first.

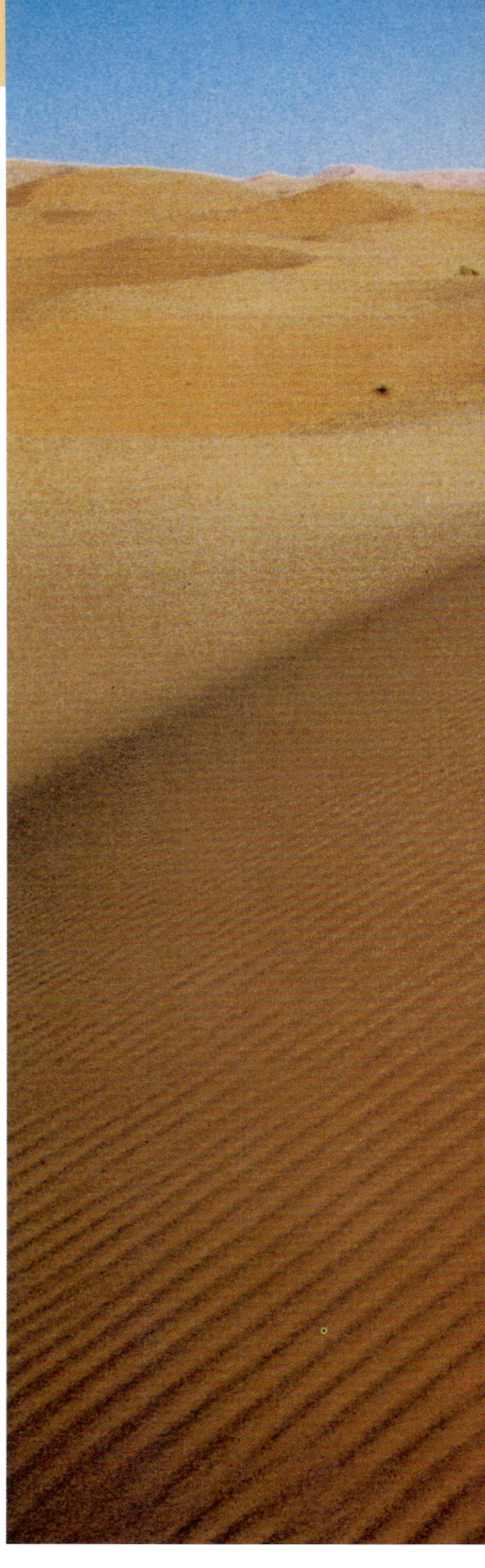

Sand dunes like these in the Algerian Sahara move on slowly, pushed by the wind, travelling 33 to 66 feet (10–20 m) per year. Algerians call these sand dunes "ergs." Typically Saharan, too, are the eroding mountains, slowly sinking into their own debris.

AUSTRALIA

Route:
International flights to Darwin, local flights to Alice Springs. From Alice Springs 264 mi. (425 km) via Stuart Highway/Lancaster Highway.

Best time:
April – October

Other points of interest:
Kata Tjuta (Olgas) and King's Canyon

Australia's red heart

To the Aborignes, Ayers Rock is a holy place

In the unbroken light from the horizon sunset, it seems as if in the middle of the Australian desert a giant statue of glowing lava lies supine. In the late evening hours, Ayers Rock, the holy mountain of the fifth continent, radiates its reddest red. Almost 1½ miles (2.5 km) wide and 1,148 ft. (350 m) high, the sandstone monolith southeast of Alice Springs is the world's largest isolated mass of rock.

Its origin dates back to 600 million years ago, when in the heart of Australia eroded mountains hardened into an enormous red mass of sandstone that, 400 million years later, was pushed half-way up from the sub-soil. The pressure created a new mountain massive, Ayers Rock, its walls weathered smooth. In similar ways began, 19 miles (30 km) southwestward, the 36 cone-shaped rock domes of the violet-blue Olga Range.

The name "Ayers Rock" commemorates a former Australian premier; the name Olga, too, reminds one of former English-speaking people. The Aborigines, the original inhabitants of Australia, have been using different names as long as they can remember. The red mass of rock is Uluru to them, which means "place casting shadow." And the Aboriginal name for the Olgas is Tjuta, "many heads." In the tradition of myths told by the original Australians, The Uluru and the Kta Tjuta, now part of the Uluru reserve, are the holiest places of the continent. It is said spirits created them at the beginning of things, these and other mountains, and rivers and people, animals and plants. The spirits named them in their song, calling all to life.

The Aboriginals have a "dream time" legend about an ancestor who with great pleasure fashioned a large sand dune into a sleeping whale – the later Uluru.

In the caves and crevices of the Uluru (Ayers Rock) the Loritja and Pitjantjatjara tribes long ago painted their murals, depicting archers, lancers, mighty horned heads, feathers and leaves. The oldest drawings are linear and geometric. Some caves are considered holy places, forbidden for tribal women and young men who have not yet participated in the initiation rites.

The pools at the foot of the mountain, too, are holy places. It is the domain of rainbow snake Ungud, the Mother of all living things, who provides the rains and ensures that women are fertile. In an annual cultic rite during the rainy season, the Murals depicting the creator snake must be retouched or repainted. Ungud's benevolent influence must not be interrupted.

Aboriginals and government long waged a juridical battle about closure of the Uluru reserve to tourists. The original inhabitants, who see themselves as the rightful owners of the land and guardians of the holy places, did not allow construction of tourist accommodation in the vici-

nity of the red mountain until, in 1985, the government confirmed their ownership and concluded a 99-year rental agreement.

In the midst of the Central Australian desert, nature heaved aloft an enormous sandstone monolith. Ayers Rock, 1,148 feet (350 m) high, is the largest monolith of the world.

EUROPE

Mountains of the Cévennes

Cévennes National Park is a region of remarkable scenery

Getting there:
Highway A7 near Loriol/Privas. D104 to Lablachère, continuing along the D104A and D901 to Villefort on the northern edge of the Cévennes National Park. Railway station in Ales. Airports in Montpellier and Rodez

Where to stay:
Numerous camping sites available. Wide choice of hotel accommodation and private rooms in villages within the Park

Climate:
Between 64° and 70°F (18° and 21°C) in July, with frost in January and lots of snow and storms

Main attractions:
Walking, wildlife, and bird watching; Cirque de Navacelles on the River Hérault; Saint Pierre des Tripiers cave with its prehistoric finds; Dargilan and Aven Armand caves; the Tarn Gorge; cliffs at Nimes le Vieux near Veygalier

Situated in the southernmost part of France's Massif Central is one of Europe's most spectacular mountain landscapes, namely, the dramatically chiseled yet relatively modest mountains of the Cévennes. In reality, this is not a single chain of mountains, but a combination of several mountain groups, wooded hills, extremely dry limestone plateaus and deep gorges, through which some of the Languedoc's main rivers flow toward the Atlantic or into the Mediterranean. This unique landscape with its unusually rich diversity of species and long history of human settlement is protected within a National Park, which extends over 1,250 square miles (3,230km2) and is simultaneously a significant international biosphere reserve. It is the only national park in France that does not lie in high mountain terrain.

Not only are its habitats exposed to a mixture of oceanic, continental, and Mediterranean climatic influences, but the ground is composed of three distinct types of soil, each of which has produced a different landscape supporting an individual diversity of flora.

There are the granite massifs, for example, consisting of erosion-resistant hard rock, namely the Montagne du Bougès Mountains as well as Mont Aigoual and Mont Lozère, the highest peaks in the Cévennes, which rise 5,300ft (1,600m) in height. Their slopes are covered with wet areas of heath and interspersed with remnants of ancient beech forests.

The extensive limestone plateaus form one of the most impressive and unusual landscapes in the Cévennes. The Grand Causses, as they are known, are famous for bizarre rock formations — typical examples of which can be seen in the Tarn and Jonte valleys and in their spectacular caves.

New species of sweet chestnut

The largest plateau is the Causse Méjean, a harsh, arid area covering 130 square miles (330km2) around 3,300ft (1,000m) above sea level. There is very little precipitation here and the winters are extremely cold and bitter. In spring, however, the steppe-like meadows erupt into a colorful carpet consisting of masses of different flower varieties.

Just a few miles north are a series of valleys, cut in schist and known as the Gardon Valleys. These present a rugged landscape with a milder climate supporting some agriculture, such as the cultivation of sweet chestnut plantations which grow in the thin soils.

Sweet chestnuts have been an important source of food for man and his beasts since time immemorial. In days gone by, around 200 different varieties of chestnut have grown in the Cévennes region, each with its own distinct qualities in terms of size and flavor. Chestnut blight decimated vast areas of woodland starting in 1870. During the 1950s, another fungal disease introduced from America destroyed yet more chestnut trees. Meanwhile, the few farmers who remain within the National Park are once more cultivating the old stands of chestnut as well as planting new varieties. Even so, the old, neglected chestnut groves still have an ecological role to play in providing nest-ho-

les for nuthatches and green and spotted woodpeckers as well as feeding grounds for deer and wild boar.

Farmers leave the area

The Cévennes area is now regarded as one of the least populated regions in France. As farmers moved away from the region, agricultural areas dwindled, allowing heath land, steppes, and mixed beech and pine forests and oak woods to reclaim the land. This has attracted many animals back to the region, including the black woodpecker, eagle owls, Egyptian vultures and gray herons, as well as mammals such as otters. Around 90 different species of mammal and approximately 200 varieties of breeding birds inhabit the National Park. Red deer, roe deer, mufflon sheep, beavers, capercaillie, and black vultures have been successfully introduced to the area, as well as griffon vultures.

Griffon vultures virtually disappeared by 1940. In 1985, five pairs were released into the wild and by 1999 their numbers in their colony near Le Truel had increased to 180 pairs. These spectacular birds, standing three feet tall with a wingspan of 8ft (2.5m), can no longer find enough food to sustain their numbers and are therefore feed off leftover animal carcasses and offal. The large herds of sheep and cattle that once grazed the Causses and regularly lost occasional animals over the steep-sided gorges are now considerably smaller than they used to be. In any case, dead animals are no longer left lying in the open, but are transported away for disposal.

The Cévennes landscape's biological significance would not be so marked were it not for man's influence. During the Copper Stone Age, hunters and gatherers roamed the Causses uplands, leaving evidence of their existence in numerous places in the form of menhirs and dolmen, some of which are difficult to distinguish among the rock masses.

At the heart of the National Park is a high limestone plateau with vegetation adapted to the arid soils (right)

Lower down, the scrubby terrain is occasionally dotted with ancient landmarks (left)

EUROPE

White battlements

The rock formations of the Elbe sandstone mountains are protected

Getting there:
By car from Dresden via the B 172, or from Prague via the E 55 from Lovosice, along the left or right bank of the Elbe. Scheduled flights also fly direct to Dresden

Where to stay:
Numerous guesthouses and hotels are available in the Czech part of the National Park, and even more in the German section.

Climate:
Pleasant climate from early spring until November. Even winter days can be mild if the weather is clear

Main attractions:
Neurathen Fortress
Königstein Fortress

Special tips:
A paddle-steamer trip from Dresden to Bad Schandau is an unforgettable experience

Artists of the Romantic Period captured it all on canvas: slim pinnacles of rock, flat-topped crags, and ravines reminiscent of North American canyons; veils of mist revealing the outline of a cross on a mountain summit; stone bridges, sculpted by nature and spanning dark gorges. The Elbe sandstone mountains, which lie half in Germany and half in the Czech Republic, comprise some of Europe's most picturesque scenery. The key areas of this region are under stringent protection, as part of the Národni Park Ceské Svycarsko in northern Bohemia and the Switzerland National Park, situated south of Dresden.

This upland region was created by subterranean forces around 90 million years ago, when part of earth's crust, once an ocean bed, was pushed upwards 1,650ft (500m). Sand and chalk from the bottom of the sea bed formed a high sandstone plateau, through which the Elbe and its turbulent torrents carved dramatic gorges over the millennia. Only occasional areas of harder rock were able to withstand the effects of water erosion, frequently producing a fascinating array of rock formations. The tops of the numerous flat-topped hills are the last remnants of the original, now deeply fissured, single sandstone plateau.

The largest sandstone bridge

If you follow the course of the Elbe as far as Usti nad Labem, you can see the gradual transition from the rounded domes of the central Bohemian mountains to the more rugged formations that form part of the Elbe sandstone range.

The rock walls along the eastern bank suddenly rise almost vertically next to the bizarrely beautiful Schreckenstein fortress, which inspired Richard Wagner's opera "Tannhäuser." A few miles further, the distinctive contours of the two highest table mountains of this sandstone plateau become visible in the west: the 2,383ft (726m) high Decinsky Sneznik (Hohe Schneeberg) mountain and Germany's Grosser Zschirnstein of 1,845ft (562m).

East of the Elbe, not far from Hrensko, ancient river torrents have created what is undoubtedly the largest sandstone bridge in Europe, namely the Pravcická brána, or Prebisch Gate. Around 53ft (16m) or so above ground level, the natural rock formation arches across a gap of 100ft (30m) from one cliff to another. In the early nineteenth century, it had become such a popular tourist attraction that a hostelry was opened at its base and it now forms one of the sights along the Eisenach-Budapest European hiking trail.

At the border town of Schmilka, the B 1172, which runs parallel to the Elbe, follows a stretch of the so-called "German Dream Route." Right from the outset, sheer rock walls bordering narrow strips of river bank reflect the power and persistence with which the Elbe has cut a path through the sandstone. This dramatic wilderness is known for its characteristic,

rectangular rock formations sculpted by ancient forces. Paddle steamers from Dresden deposit hordes of visitors at Bad Schandau on the right bank of the Elbe.

The Kirnitschtal Railway takes visitors up into the fantastic mountain landscape, popularized by Caspar David Friedrich's paintings. A 100-year old lift also transports hikers 165ft (50m) up to the Ostrau district, an ideal starting point for walks.

Further north, a breathtakingly beautiful walk starts from Rathen up to the 13th century Neurathen Fortress, continuing across the fortified bridge to the famous Bastei Viewpoint, 625ft (190m) above the Elbe. Far below on the right are the tiny-looking rooftops of the town of Wehlen. To the south, around the next bend in the river, is the 1,362ft (415m) high Lilienstein mountain, the most frequently painted and most photographed table mountain in Saxony's "little Switzerland."

Königstein Fortress

Directly opposite is Königstein Fortress, its mighty walls encircling a flat-topped crag 1,180ft (360m) above sea level. Bohemian and Saxon kings began building the fortress around AD

1200. Centuries later, the fortress served as an escape-proof prison. August the Strong imprisoned Johann Friedrich Böttger, the porcelain manufacturer, in Königstein for his failure to produce artificial gold and Emperor Wilhelm had August Bebel, the workers' leader, incarcerated here.

Not far from Pirna, the Elbsandstein Mountains drop away to the flatter terrain of Dresden's Elbe valley landscape. To the west, the view extends towards the Erz mountains while, to the east, the horizon stretches as far as the Lausitzer mountains.

Looking down into the gorge from the viewing platform at Neurathen Fortress (above)

Erosion has rounded off the tops of some of the rock formations (center, left)

Near Hrensko in the Czech Republic, the narrow gorge is navigable by boat (below, right)

EUROPE

The romantic eastern Tyrol

Hohe Tauern National Park is designed to protect the Grossglockner and Hochalpenstrasse region

Getting there:
Grossglockner high alpine road between Lienz and Kitzbühel; Tauern railway between Spittal and Schwarzach

Where to stay:
Well developed holiday area with a wide selection of accommodation

Climate:
Average annual temperature is 41°F (5°C) with heavy snow in winter

Main attractions:
Grossglockner; Pasterze; Krimml Waterfall; hiking; winter sports

The Grossglockner, at 12,470ft (3,800m), is Austria's highest mountain and the majestic heart of Hohe Tauern National Park. This mountain range in southern Austria forms part of the main central alpine ridge in the Eastern Alps. Its impressive succession of steep, awe-inspiring summits, including the Hochalmspitze at 11,025ft (3,360m), the Ankogel at 10,670ft (3,252m), and the Mittlerer Bärenkopf at 11,010ft (3,356m), extends for more than 60 miles (100km) between the Zillteral Alps and Italy in the west and the Katschberg Pass in the east. The Park safeguards some breathtakingly beautiful alpine scenery featuring rugged mountains, vast expanses of glacier, gentle mountain meadows, and rushing water falls.

At the base of the Grossglockner is the glistening, white ice tongue of the Pasterze Glacier, the largest of its kind in the Eastern Alps, stretching over a distance of 5 miles (8km) and measuring 3 miles (5km) across.

The Kriml Waterfall at the foot of Gerlos Pass is yet another unforgettable sight. More than 8,800 gallons (40,000 liters) of water per second tumble over its precipice, to plummet 1,215ft (370m) below into the forested Salzach valley basin in a series of three cascades.

Dazzling display of flowers

The National Park is a region of incomparable beauty, in which the wild, primeval landscape and the centuries-old cultural traditions of mountain farmers complement each other perfectly. The Park is home to 10,000 different species of plant and animal life. A large proportion of these are found in the valley meadows, which are constantly being mown and in the mountain pastures where the livestock grazes all summer long. The mown grass provides a rich habitat for bearded bell-flowers, blue wolf's bane, globe flowers, alpine asters, leopard's bane, orchids, and countless other plants. In spring and summer, the sloping meadows are carpeted with a truly dazzling display of colorful blooms.

Their original habitats are thickly forested valleys, which become less dense as the altitude increases, gravel-covered glacial moraines, and bare, sometimes snow-covered, summits. After the last Ice Age 10,000 years ago, the half-mile thick covering of ice receded from the Alps, and the area became populated by different types of plant from Siberia, the cold Central Asiatic steppes, the Arctic, and southern Europe. It is a harsh terrain, in which only certain, specially adapted species can survive. Many of them are at the limits of their existence since not only do they have to withstand a cold climate with temperatures averaging 41°F (5°C), but also incessant winds, high UV radiation, and winter snows several feet thick. High up along the fringes of the tree line, it is mainly only larches that survive, although an occasional, rare Swiss stone pine may be found. (The Swiss pine is a species of fir tree that only blooms once every six to ten years, grows very slowly, and can live for a thousand years.) The gray scree and gravel of glacial moraines and bare rock is highlighted here and

The dazzling display of flowers in the meadows of eastern Tyrol is unsurpassed (above)

The rugged slopes of the Tauern Mountains give way to gentler woodland in the valleys (below, right)

The Hochalpenstrasse (high alpine road), which traverses the Grossglocker region, winds its way in a series of numerous hairpin bends up to an altitude of 8,200ft (2,500m) at the top of the pass (below, left)

there by bright splashes of glacier crowsfoot buttercup and the alpine marguerite.

The dense forests still shelter an occasional, extremely shy brown bear, which stands eight feet (2½ m) tall. It is exceedingly rare for these creatures to leave the thick woods and wander out into the high, treeless mountaintops. Lynx, fox, wolves,

64

and badgers are also still found in this alpine region.

A landscape sculpted by rivers of ice

Fortunately, the marmot population is increasing again. These cute, mountain mammals, which grow to 20 in (50cm) in length and live in underground burrows, warn each other of danger by whistling. By 1800, they had completely vanished from the Hohe Tauern after being hunted for their fur and fat. Over the past century, they have been re-introduced into the area and have become a common sight once more.

The Hohe Tauern Mountains were formed 75 to 35 million years ago on the bed of the Thethys Sea, an ocean-sized precursor of the Mediterranean.

EUROPE

Majestic fir trees

Pirin National Park, in southern Bulgaria, is the last refuge for many European animals

Getting there:
Trains from Sofia to Septemvri; from there by narrow-gauge railway to Bansko. By car along Route E 73

Where to stay:
Small hotels; hunting cabins; private accommodation in villages around the Park

Climate:
Long, cold winters in higher regions, with snow for five to eight months of the year

Main attractions:
Vihren cabin and climb to the summit

Bulgaria is home to southeast Europe's highest mountain chains, stretching virtually untouched right across the country. Situated just 75 miles (1.20km) south of Bulgaria's busy capital city, Sofia, is one of the country's most impressive ranges: the Pirin massif. It is the second highest in the land, characterized by majestic, jagged peaks and sheer rock walls. Numerous sparkling lakes hollowed out by glaciers nestle in deep valleys. Silver ribbons of surging rivers wind their way through the valleys, fed even during the summer months by water melting from snow on the summits. They plummet from valley to valley in a succession of countless, breathtakingly beautiful cascades.

Pirin is part of Bulgaria's southern chain of mountains, incorporating both the Rodopi and Rila ranges. Forty-five of Pirin's peaks exceed 8,500ft (2,600m), most of them resembling three-sided pyramids or multi-sided structures with sharp, jagged edges. They are remnants of a 25-million-year old plateau that disintegrated when the mountains were forced upward into folds approximately 10 million years ago. Vihren, at 9,565ft (2,915m), is the highest and the second highest peak in Bulgaria. Its northern aspect consists of an almost sheer 1,500ft (450m) rock face, which can be seen for miles around.

Pirin People's Park, as Bulgaria's National Park is commonly known, protects the high-lying regions between the Strouma and Mesta rivers. It covers an area of around 155 square miles (400km2) and is a designated world heritage site.

Karst limestone regions

Although the mountains mostly consist of granite and slate, a remarkable karst limestone area also exists between the twin peaks of Vihren and Kaminitza as well as in the central sections of the Park, abounding in karst caves and overhangs. Near to the summit, there are several patches of areas of snow that have never thawed completely, even in summer. These are the early stages of new glaciers, which are form slowly over the years as the snow partially thaws, refreezes, then acquires a fresh, additional layer. As yet, these incipient glaciers measure only a few thousand square yards in area and are just a few yards thick.

Thanks to its remote location, the Pirin mountain massif is an ideal refuge for rare plants and animals. Whereas dense, mixed, broad-leaved and coniferous woodland extends around the base of the mountains, the precipitous slopes are covered with dark fir forests and interspersed with an occasional granite or dazzling white, limestone cliff. Along the tree line is a broad band of mighty, wind-

swept Bosnian pines. These trees grow nowhere else on earth. The Baiouvi-Doupki-Djindjiritsa Reserve is home to stands of 250 to 300-year-old trees that have been placed under special protection. These include what is probably Pirin's oldest tree specimen, the 1,200-year-old Baikousheva's Mura, a particularly impressive white fir.

The tree line here starts at just 6,600ft (2,000m), as a result of tree-felling in the past. Only in a few places does it extend any higher to around 7,200–7,600ft (2,200–2,300m). Above the tree line are glorious alpine meadows, full of different varieties of plants nestling between rocky cliffs, scree, and bare rock. A profusion of flowers, a combination of alpine, Balkan, and Mediterranean varieties, transform the bare, grass-covered terrain into a dazzling sea of color, particularly in summer. Peonies, alpine azaleas, yellow globeflowers, spring gentian, forget-me-nots, poppies, and crocus form a strikingly beautiful, floral carpet that is unequalled in its diversity anywhere in Bulgaria.

Well-marked trails

Glowing, red Pirin poppies peep from among the rocks, while delicate edelweiss flowers are occasionally glimpsed among the scree. Around 70 of the plants found here are unique to Bulgaria. Many of these are glacier varieties, survivors of geologically ancient times provided with a last refuge by these mountains.

The Park is also home to many species of animal, particularly invertebrates, which are endemic to this region. The dark forests surrounding the lower lakes have, since prehistoric times, been the haunt of numerous wolves, brown bears, and lynx, magnificent creatures pushed to the brink of extinction elsewhere in Europe. Eagles, falcons, and kites circle overhead, while quail, partridge, and pheasant can be heard rustling through the undergrowth.

Despite the remoteness of this mountain location and the dearth of visitors that make their way to the magnificent and matchless landscape, there are nevertheless many well-marked paths and cross-country ski trails, most of which are not at all difficult and lead to several idyllically situated hostels offering overnight accommodation. At 6,400ft (1,950m), the Vihren cabin is only a two or three day hike from the summit, but is also accessible by car.

Well-run mountain hostels, such as this one on the slopes of Mount Vihren, help make the National Park accessible to visitors (above, right)

Tree trunks are used to bridge the many mountain streams (below, left)

EUROPE

The mountains of Montenegro

The Durmitor massif is not only a National Park, but also a biosphere reserve

Getting there:
Zabljak can be reached from the road running between Sarajevo (Bosnia-Hercegovina) and Podgorica. By road or bus from Mojkovac (railway station). Summer helicopter flights from coastal resorts

Where to stay:
Zabljak is an up-and-coming holiday resort with several new hotels

Climate:
In July, 68°–84°F (20°–29°C); cooler at higher altitudes. Around 50°F (10°C) in winter, with frost and snow at higher altitudes

Main attractions:
Mountain climbing; hiking; white-water rapid trips; skiing. Ddjurdjevica Tara Bridge with views over the Tara gorge; Tmora with views across the valleys and villages; ice caves above Zabljak

Special tips:
The National Park can be explored only on foot

Traversed by some of Europe's deepest gorges, the sheer, jagged limestone peaks of the mighty Durmitor massif tower in the northeastern corner of Montenegro almost seem to touch the sky. Some of them are pointed pinnacles, while others resemble vaulted domes. Deep grooves have been carved out of the summits of Mount Savin Kuk and Mount Sljeme, while the pin-point summit of Uvita Greda is scored like a screw and that of Obla Glava rounded. The peak of Medvjed appears dramatically white against the green forests and the Crvena Greda shimmers in a variety of different colors depending on the sun's position. A total of 15 majestic mountain peaks dominate the 125 square miles (320km2) of Durmitor National Park. The highest of these is Bobotov Kuk at 8,275ft (2,522m).

Ice Age glaciers have carved deep valleys out of this mountain massif, leaving behind a legacy of 16 breathtakingly beautiful, tranquil glacier lakes dotted throughout this rugged karst mountain range. They gleam like eyes, sparkling amid the depths of the dark forests. Some of them benefit from special protection, while others exhibit some unusual features. For instance, the National Park's largest lake, Crno Jezero, simultaneously feeds two different rivers, the Tara and Komarnica, otherwise known as the Piva River. Water flows out of the lake into the River Tara, while water also simultaneously seeps through cracks in the lake bed, flowing through the Durmitor massif via an underwater drainage system and feeding the Komarnica River.

Mighty, rushing torrents such as the Tara, one of Europe's last wild and untamed rivers, have carved dramatic ravines in the soft rock. At the bottom of Europe's deepest canyon, nearly 4,300ft (1,300m) in depth, the Tara River swirls and surges around giant boulders before crashing into the valley below in a series of breathtaking cascades.

Rivers, lakes, dry karst landscape

This spectacular National Park is a designated world heritage site and part of a large, international biosphere reserve, covering an area of nearly 700 square miles (1,800km2). Rivers, lakes, dry karst, and dramatic differences in altitude within a comparatively small area have all contributed to form a wide range of habitats and climates. The Durmitor Mountains are influenced by two climatic zones, namely the Mediterranean and alpine. This unique combination of environmental conditions accounts for the exceptional diversity of species occurring in this spectacular landscape.

Dense, deciduous forests grow throughout the valleys and along the rivers. The high plateaus support alpine heath land dotted with sub-arctic vegetation, while the wetter areas are covered with marshes. Impenetrable Mediterranean pine forests cling to the steep slopes, while the bare summits of the sub-alpine zone are covered with small beech and dwarf pines. The gently rising scree slopes in the foothills of the mountains are interspersed with numerous

untouched alpine meadows, which explode into a stunning array of colorful flowers in summer. Along the fringes of the Tara valley, the last stretches of unspoiled black pine forest grow in soil that would more typically support beech woods.

Eagles in the sky

Brown bears, gray wolves, wild boar, wild cats, and chamois still roam these forests. These shy creatures are rarely glimpsed by visitors. Various species of eagle circle overhead, soaring on the thermals above the mountains, while black grouse and rock partridge can be heard rustling through the bushes or grassy undergrowth. More than 130 different bird varieties populate these silent forests or build their nests in the shelter of rocky, inaccessible crags.

From the holiday resort of Zabljak on the Park's northeastern border, this majestic natural landscape, a kind now rarely seen in Europe, can be explored by means of a network of some 1,250 miles (2,000km) of marked trails.

The foothills of the Durmitor massif with its mighty mountain ridges, where farmers graze their sheep, resemble alpine pastures (above)

The mountain forests reveal occasional glimpses of glistening lakes (below, left)

View into a valley near Lake Skutari (below, right)

ASIA

Home of the gods

Mount Everest is the world's tallest mountain

Route:
Mountain flights: one-hour flights from Katmandu. Flight Katmandu-Lukla, 10-day hike to viewpoint top Kala Pattar to Mount Everest base camp

Best time:
October – December

Further points of interest:
Thyangpoche Monastery and temple in Katmandu valley

On their way to the top of Mount Everest, (above) mountain climbers kept being embattled by heavy snowstorms. The first successful ascent of this giant situated between Hindu nation Nepal and Tibet occurred on May 29, 1953, when New Zealander Edmund Hillary and his sherpa Tenzing Norgay reached the peak. Reinhold Messner and his partner Peter Habeler reached the top in 1978 as the first to do without oxygen equipment. The small photograph shows Mount Everest in the glow of evening light. The Tibetans call the mountain Chomolungma, the White Goddess.

Tibetans tell us that the highest mountain in the world is best recognized by its "prayer flag." This is how they describe the veil of ice crystals that on most days swirl wind-driven around the top of Mount Everest. If the veil does not appear it is difficult to identify the famous giant of snow among the 8,000 other peaks on the border of Hindu kingdom Nepal and ancient Tibet. Enough errors have been made regarding Mount Everest, which, according to the latest measurements, attains an altitude of 29,107 ft. (8,872 m).

Long before people were aware that the mountain existed, the people in Tibet worshipped the mountain (called Chomolungma) as the holy abode of goddess Tseringma. And the people of Nepal, who declared their part of the mountain as reserve, refer to Sagarmatha "whose top reaches the heavens." Its Western name refers to British artillery officer and geodetic surveyor Sir George Everest. In the middle of the 19th century his trigonometric researches determined that the peak he had listed as Number XV rose above every other Himalayas mountain.

Scientific expeditions always did have great problems to find the trigonometrically calculated highest mountain peak of the world among the snowcaps of the eastern Himalayas. Early in the 20th century Western encyclopedias still identified Mount Everest with the Nepal peak Gaurisankar. This misconception was due to reports by a German explorer, Hermann von Schlaginweit. It was he who on a journey to Nepal had mistakenly taken the Gaurisanker — a "mere" 23,441–foot (7,145-m) hill for Mount Everest – perhaps because he was unaware of the "prayer flag."

Assaults on the top

In the 1920s British and Swiss mountain climbers did find the right mountain, but could not reach the top. After numerous failed attempts had been made, New Zealander Edmund Hillary and his Nepalese sherpa Tenzing Norgay were successful. They hoisted three small flags on the Everest, representing the colors of Great Britain, Nepal and the United Nations.

In the decade following, more than one hundred other mountain climbers reached the peak. In 1978, Reinhold Messner from South Tirol and his partner Peter Habeler were the first to complete a climb without oxygen equipment. Two years later, Messner repeated this feat singlehanded.

Although all climbed the same mountain, its precise altitude is a bone of contention. The first measurements were made in the middle of the 19th century and came to 29,002 ft. (8,840 m) later a height of 29,160 ft. (8,888 m) was given and since 1954 the altitude has been set at 29,028 ft (8,848m). In 1987 the Mount Everest was dethroned as the tallest by an American satellite measurement by the astronomer Professor George Wallerstein, who indicated that Himalaya-top K2 was 36 ft. (11 m) higher.

The old ranking was restored a few months later by Italian Professor Ardito Desio. On the basis of various electronic satellite measurements the K2 stood at 28,267 ft. (8,616 m) and Mount Everest at a new peak altitude of 29,107 ft. (8,872 m). But this figure has no enduring value either. Scientific measurements show that annually, Mount Everest grows about 7 inches (18 cm).

ASIA

Sentinel of the eastern Himalayas

Kanchenjunga remains one of the lesser-climbed 26,000-foot peaks

State and capital:
Sikkim, Gangtok (80 mi./130 km)

Convenient access:
Road to Yuksum, air to Bagdogra, Gangtok, rail to New Jalpaiguri

Accommodation:
Budget to mid-range at Yuksum; forest rest-houses and camping in Park.

Best season:
April to June, September to November. Largely snowbound from December to February

Also see:
Barsey Rhododendron Sanctuary, S, Maenam Wildlife Sanctuary, SE, Buddhist monasteries, 20-35 km S

Whether it is because the mountain is actually composed of five peaks, or because of the five Buddhist treasures of gold, silver, precious stones, grain and holy scriptures believed to be concealed amongst its pinnacles or, as wildlife enthusiasts would have it, due to the presence of five exotic species of flora and fauna—rhododendron, blood pheasant, the lammergeyer vulture, Sikkim's state animal, the red panda, and the phantasmal snow leopard—translated, Kanchenjunga, also spelled as Khangchendzonga, means "The Five Treasures of Snow." While Mt. Everest is well known and an imposing mountain in its own right and K2 is fierce and remote, Kanchenjunga is a beautiful peak when seen from any direction. Rising to 28,166 ft. (8,585 m), it is the highest mountain in India and the third highest in the world, after Everest and K2.

Rhododendrons and the red panda

It was Sir Joseph Dalton Hooker, the 19th century British botanist and explorer, who first highlighted the area's rich biodiversity to the world, estimating that on its higher altitudes, the mountainous terrain of the Kingdom of Sikkim harbored the entire alpine flora of Europe and North America combined. In 1977, India declared part around the peak, upwards in altitude from 6,003 ft. (1,830 m), as a National Park, thus protecting its immense natural wealth. This is most vivid in spring with the abundant display of flowering shrubs, dwarf rhododendrons, primulas, irises and numerous other wildflowers on high-altitude meadows, slopes of juniper, pristine forests and the banks of glacial flows. In addition, the Park hosts a wide array of rare Himalayan wildlife including the retiring snow leopard. Easier but not commonly seen are the leopard, black bear, blue sheep and barking deer. The furry arboreal red panda, of course, is a bonus. Various species of thrushes, sunbirds, finches, pheasants and raptors inhabit the mountainscapes. Just as the wildlife in the upper reaches is unique, the features of the lower forests are as fascinating: trees laden with bunches of flowering orchids, yellow-backed sunbirds on forest blooms, gurgling streams, energetic waterfalls cascading into limpid pools, swinging bridges and infuriating leeches.

Sunrise at Dzongri

Three of Kanchenjunga's peaks border the Indian state of Sikkim and the Taplejung district of Nepal, while two lie entirely in Nepal. Most visitors approach the Park from the Sikkimese town of Yuksum, the old capital. Here, on the directions of the venerated Buddhist Saint Padmasambhava, the first king of Sikkim was consecrated under a massive 400-year-old pine tree. The two to three days long trek passes through Bakhim or Tsokha, along the Rathong River in its initial stretches, with wonderful pano-ramas of soaring finials, glaciers and torrents. From the camping grounds at Dzongri 12,762 ft. (3,890 m), 15.5 miles (25 km) from Yuksum, one gets magical sunrise views of the mountain, as well as the peaks of Siniolchu, Pauhunri, Kabru and Rathong, framed by Buddhist prayer flags. Seasoned trekkers can venture further, to Goechala, which offers even better views. With the tree-line far below, yak herders tend to their large herds beyond the Dzongri plain, and the peaceful isolation is broken with the distant tinkle of yak bells, the occasional scream of a chough or an accentor, amidst the fragrance of dwarf rhododendron in the clear mountain air.

After four preceding unsuccessful expeditions, Kanchenjunga was finally climbed in 1955 by the British mountaineers Joe Brown and George Band. Out of respect to the religious sentiments of the Sikkimese people, who hold the mountain sacred, the duo stopped a few metres short of the summit, without actually stepping onto it. Pierre Beghin made the first successful solo ascent without oxygen in 1983, and in 1998, Ginette Harrison became the first woman to reach the top.

Right: Because of its difficult accessibility and tight restrictions on climbing expeditions, the inner sanctum of Kanchenjunga remains largely untouched and spared of the attendant litter that sometimes mars other popular Himalayan base camps.

Kachenjunga (above)

ASIA

King Kasyapa's rocky citadel

Sigiriya Mountain in Sri Lanka is one of the world's great cultural treasures

Getting there:
By road or bus from Colombo to Sigiriya

Where to stay:
Hotels, guesthouses, lodges in Sigiriya, Habarana, or Kandalama

Climate:
Humid, tropical climate

Main attractions:
Climb up Sigiriya mountain; tour of the palace gardens as well as boulder and water gardens; museum

Situated in the heart of Sri Lanka, a mighty, reddish-brown rock monolith rears 660ft (200m) out of the dark expanse of lush green jungle vegetation, interspersed with lighter patches of rice fields and glittering lakes. Long ago, the powerful ruler Kasyapa built the fortress for himself over a period of just seven years. It comprises an extraordinary system of steps, passageways, and walls within which he immured himself along with his followers, concubines, and treasures until his suicide in 495 AD.

The drama began over 1,500 years ago in Anuradhapura, the ancient capital of Sri Lanka. Kasyapa, the power-hungry son of King Dhatusena, overthrew his own father and had him chained naked to a rock face, leaving him to die. His half-brother, Moggallana, Dhatusena's legitimate heir, fled to India. From then on, Kasyapa lived in constant fear of his half-brother's return and transferred his residence in 477 AD to this huge rocky monolith surrounded by jungle. He converted it into a unique fortified palace with enchanting gardens and created a veritable work of art that has now been dignified with world heritage site status.

The entrance to this cliff-top citadel was originally guarded by the giant figure of a lion looking north carved partly out of rock and partly built of bricks and decorated with stucco work. The lion has not withstood the centuries well and only his paws remain today. The entrance to the palace once led up through the lion's gaping mouth to the main precinct, which covered 13,000 square feet (1,200m2) on this cliff-top plateau.

Erotic frescoes

Half way up the path to this hilltop palace, the staircase runs along the so-called Mirror Wall to a spiral staircase winding up to the dizzy heights above. The bricks of this wall used to be polished with egg-white and honey to such a high finish that they gleamed with a mirror-like shine. Well into the twelfth century and long after this rocky eyrie was abandoned, monks and visitors were still inspired to add hundreds of inscriptions and writings of their own to the Mirror Wall, some of which are acknowledged to be among the earliest examples of Singhalese poetry.

On reaching the top of this spiral staircase, the present-day visitor encounters around 20 captivating, erotic rock frescoes depicting bare-bosomed beauties of the fifth century. There were originally 500 such frescoes covering the rock face.

Having finally climbed the 1,860 steps leading up to the summit, the remains of the palace are visible scattered about the plateau. Kasyapa designed the palace so that its east wall would rise straight up from the vertical cliff wall. The remains of a carefully laid out kitchen garden can also still be seen on the western side, complete with a small pond and cisterns.

Breathtaking, panoramic views extend not only across the vast expanse of Sri Lanka's jungle plains, but also embrace the spacious and artistically designed layout of the palace, with its symmetrically planned gardens around the base of the cliff. The water gardens are a particularly impressive feature. They are based on a cleverly designed system, built over

several levels and incorporating water courses, retaining basins, underground terracotta pipes, and cooling systems. The miniature water gardens, separated from the main water gardens by a wall, once contained numerous pavilions, shady courtyards, refreshing bathing pools, and cisterns. As a finishing touch, King Kasyapa also added pebbles to some of the waterways in order to recreate the sound of natural running water and other jungle noises.

Water from an artificial lake

The heart of the main water gardens is a central island surrounded by water, linked to the main precinct by a system of causeways radiating from the center. The garden was supplied with water from Lake Sigiri Maha Weva, an artificial reservoir created by a 7-mile (12km) dam situated immediately behind this rocky fortress to the south.

The asymmetrical boulder garden is situated higher up the rocky plateau. The area is full of narrow twisting paths, winding between giant natural boulders as well as the remains of the Audience Hall with its 16ft (5m) long throne hewn out of rock. Almost every boulder once sheltered a brick or timber building.

In 495 AD, Kasyapa's worst fears became reality when his half-brother Moggallana returned from India with his own army. Deserted by his own followers, Kasyapa committed suicide and his luxurious citadel gradually disintegrated until British game hunters happened across it in 1828.

Sigiriya Mountain is a huge monolith of reddish-brown rock rearing up out of the surrounding jungle.
Its plateau once housed a fortified palace, surrounded by ornamental water gardens and a natural boulder garden (above)

Erotic frescoes are reminders of those bygone days

This memorable scenery is further enhanced by traditionally robed monks (below, left)

75

ASIA

Golden Stone Beach, China

A huge collection of rare and precious stones

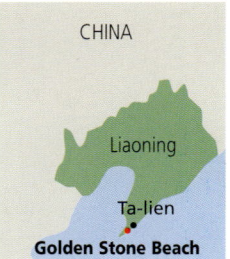

Location:
The Stone Beach is located on the shores of the Yellow Sea, 31 miles (50km) from Dalian.

Climate:
It is neither too cold in winter nor too hot in summer here. There is an annual average temperature of about 50°F (10°C), with four seasons.

Special interest:
The best summer resort in the northeast, this area includes the eastern peninsula, the western peninsula, the valley between them, and the swimming beach. The Stone Hall is the biggest home for the rare stones to be seen here, and is known today as the Garden of Precious Stones.

Main attractions:
The Rare Stone Hall, the Golden Stone Park, the Jinshi Waxworks of World-famous Figures, the Flower World, and the swimming beach.

Extending 5 miles (8km) on the eastern peninsula at Dalian and surrounded by the sea on three sides, the Golden Beach Stone bears witness to a major part of the earth's long geological evolution history, from 700 million to 300 million years ago.

This is praised as the most important site for rare stones in China, and in the Stone Hall here you can see nearly a thousand specimens of over two hundred varieties, among them Langhua stone, Boshanwen stone, and Kunlun Caiyue stone, which are the most valued kinds in the country.

Each stone on the beach is more precious than gold since it is the only one of its kind across the land and is rarely seen in the rest of the world as well. Geologists claim that each one will never be produced again.

These unusual stones seem to "bloom" and "sing," in that they show up in a variety of colors and give off sounds as the tidal waves come and go. Known as the garden of grotesque stones, this beach features an extensive area of pink and yellow stones. They look like golden roses in full bloom, row upon row of them. The pink stones are actually piled up fossils of seaweed that flourished 700 million years ago.

Covering an area of more than 10,765 square feet (1000 square meters) and made up of over a hundred huge and unique rocks, the Rose Stone Garden turns into a riot of flowers against the blue sea when the waves approach.

Discovered in 1996, the Golden Stone Garden extends for more than 107,640 square feet (10,000 square meters). Every stone looks golden, especially in sunshine.

One unique type of stone to be seen here is called a Guilie (turtle-splitting) stone because its pattern looks like the cracks on a turtle shell, combined with a lattice effect. On its outer surface this stone is patterned in green, while inside it is red. Praised as the best of the golden stones, it is even said to be the most outstanding stone in the world – after making a tour of inspection in this area, many eminent geologists have come to agree that the biggest and most beautiful examples of Guilie stone are displayed on the Golden Stone Beach in Dalian. They have claimed that it is a treasure not only in China, but also throughout the whole world.

On the beach there are nearly a hundred scenic places that are the result of geological processes that took place millions of years ago. They feature the sea-eroded coast, with caves and pillars revealing a huge variety of bizarre forms. For instance, one rock looks like an elephant drinking water, while another seems to represent the flying roc of The Arabian Nights.

There are a number of other amusing animal representations. One rock is just like a tiger scrambling for food, a second seems to be a monkey watching the sea, and yet another a dinosaur swallowing the sea. Everything to be seen on the beach is vivid and exciting. There are estimated to be more than three hundred dramatic rock formations to be seen here.

Situated east of the town of Dalian, covering an area of about 1,400,000 square feet (130,000 square meters), the Golden Stone Park also is known as the Stone Forest of the Sea, the Natural Geological Museum, the Fixed Animal World, and the Magic Sculpture Garden.

The Golden Stone Beach in Dalian, which has witnessed the long history of the geological evolution of the earth for 700 million years. (right)

The best beach for a vacation in northern China, the Golden Stone Beach is on a peninsula surrounded by the sea on three sides

ASIA

Daocheng, Sichuan

The soul of Shangri-la in Sichuan

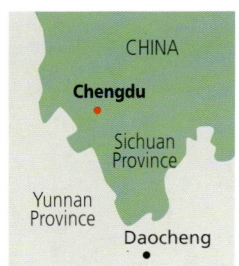

Location:
Situated on the south of the Ganzi Tibetan Autonomous Prefecture in the southwest rim of Sichuan, the county of Daocheng is 500 miles (800km) away from Chengdu, the capital.

Climate:
At an altitude of 12,303 ft (3750m), Daocheng receives a great deal of sunshine. Its low temperature is intensified by the drastic temperature range within a single day. Daocheng experiences its rainy season from June to August and has its winter from November to March. The best touring seasons are from April to May and from September to October.

Special interest:
The area boasts a great variety of fauna and flora, and charming natural scenery. The Yading Nature Reserve in the county of Daocheng is well maintained and regarded as land untouched by humans.

Main attractions:
Yading Nature Reserve, Chonggu Temple, Tibetan villages, magic peaks in Daocheng, and the Pearl Lake.

There is neither sorrow nor pain. There is only the singing of birds. This is where the immortals live.

Were this true, it would be said of Daocheng in Sichuan province.

Joseph Rock, the explorer, noticed three snow-capped mountains when he toured Lijiang in Yunnan in 1926. After consulting the local people, he found out that they were called "Nianqingonggarisonggongbu" in the Tibetan language. That was what is known as the Daocheng scenic area today. In the following four years, Rock explored the mountains with the help of local Tibetan officials. His words and pictures were published in *National Geographic* in June, 1931, and they made a big stir.

Daocheng had scarcely been visited since ancient times, for it is tucked away in the hinterland, inaccessible to the outside world. Its local people have had a loving heart toward life and nature, hoping to maintain the local religious culture, which holds that any form of life should be protected. This belief has made Daocheng one of the regions in China that boasts the best preserved primitive vegetation, and is also one of the last unpolluted territories.

Since Rock's time, many tourists have been amazed by the splendid landscape of Daocheng – after they have soothed away the numerous obstacles they met on the way there.

In 2002 a road to Daocheng was completed, and this has made the scenic area accessible to the rest of the world. Photographers have been busy exploiting the enchanting natural scenery, the primitive local customs, and the mysterious cultural relics.

The Daocheng Plateau is composed of Gongga Mountain and Haizi Mountain. Situated in the north and south respectively, the two mountains account for one third of the whole area, which stretches from north to south, and from west to east, in terms of geographical features. High mountains follow one after another, presenting a dramatic view. There are three principal rivers, called the Daocheng River, the Chitu River, and the Dongyi River, and all of them empty into the Jinshajiang River.

Originating at the foot of Haishan Mountain, the Daocheng River runs over 75.6 miles (121km). The Dongyi River, which comes from Echu Mountain, extends as far as 69 miles (111km). The county of Daocheng has nearly 30,000 people, over 96 percent of whom are Tibetan. The rest are Han, Naxi, and Yi.

The Yading Nature Reserve is regarded as the last Shangri-la. When you ride a horse from Yading village to the Chonggu Temple, you may spot a Tibetan village hidden in the flowers and among the extensive crops. You will come across the fathomless primitive forest, through which a jingling creek merrily runs. In addition, colorful lakes change their aspect from time to time. The snow-capped magic peak stands out, with the green forest extending around its slope and foot.

If you want to experience how friendly and kind the local people are, drop in at a household in the Tibetan village. The hospitality of the people there may make you reluctant to leave.

The famous scenery of the "Sea of Red Grass" in Shangri-La (above)

Yangfangyong ice peak (bottom, left)

Sparkling stream under the blue sky, with white clouds above (bottom, right)

ASIA

The Yangtze River's three gorges

Majestic gorges in Sichuan, Chongqing, and Hubei

Location:
The Yangtze River Three Gorges is the general term for Qutang Gorge, Wuxia Gorge, and Xiling Gorge. It starts in the west at Baidi city, in Fengjie county of Chongqing province, and extends 6 miles (10km) to Nanjinguan, Yichang City in Hubei province. People usually refer it to it as the Big Three Gorges.

Climate:
There is a moist subtropical climate, obviously influenced by the topographical features. The annual average temperature is 65 °F (18.4 °C), coldest in January when the average temperature is 44.78 °F (7.10 °C) and hottest in July, with an average temperature of 84.74°F (29.30°C).

Special interest:
The Yangtze River Three Gorges is the most attractive section of the landscape gallery along the Yangtze River.

Main attractions:
Besides the Three Gorges, Ghost City in Fengdu and the so-called Small Three Gorges are also worth a visit.

The Qutang Gorge (left)

The elegant Wushan Mountain in the clouds (above, left)

The Quyuan Temple at Zigui (below, center)

As the saying goes, "Qutang Gorge is stately, while Wuxia is elegant and Xiling risky."

Since ancient times, the countryside around the Yangtze River Three Gorges has been known as "Four Hundred Li Art Gallery." Here is a continuous view of landscapes, impressive and ever changing, a combination of vigor and charm.

The Yangtze River Gorges start at Baidi city, Fengjie county in Chongqing, and extend 121 miles (193km), arrogantly extending to Nanjinguan, Yichang city, in Hubei province. During its course, it crosses the Wushan mountain range that runs from south to north and passes through numerous deep valleys with torrents sweeping down uncontrollably.

When traveling downstream by boat, with sheer precipices on both sides sliding by and roaring water like galloping horses under their feet, travelers may experience some fear, but only the boatmen who have worked on the river for many years can fully understand the risk involved. A boatman's song that circulates around Xiling Gorge – which is characterized by roaring torrents and numerous reefs and shoals – goes like this:

"Terrible it is when the boat is traveling past Xiling George; Sweating all over with every tune, Courage called up with every tune."

When you hear this song, you realize the challenge involved in undertaking the Yangtze River voyage.

Of the Three Gorges, the Wuxia Gorge is the quietest section. It has 12 peaks, one of which is Shennu peak. On the north bank, a stone pillar stands high, with giant and lofty peaks gathering and acting as escorts all around, and clouds and mists veiling and unveiling the scene by day and night. This is the Shennu (Fairy Girl) peak. It is said that the Fairy Girl meets the king of Chu at Gaotang, and during that time there are clouds in the morning and rain in the evening. The story adds glamor to the mystery of the scenery. Three Gorges has three singular features: the Overhanging Tombs, the Plank Roads along the Cliffs, and the stone carvings. These are the essence of the culture of the Three Gorges.

The Plank Roads were built on the cliffs along the Qutang Gorge. There are two kinds of plank roads: wooden ones and stone ones. To construct the former, workmen fixed wooded pegs into the cliff, then laid wooden boards on them. For the latter, they dug roads directly along the cliffs. Many people sacrificed their lives to build the roads.

The Overhanging Tombs are said to have connections with the Ba people who used to live in the Three Gorges areas. They were descended from the Tibeto-Burman people. Coming from Hanshui and the upper streams of the Yellow River, moving continuously to the east and west of the Yangtze River and known for their strength and bravery, they played an active part in the history of this area during the sixteenth century BC. They planted paddy rice and wheat along both banks and they created a civilization as brilliant as that of the Yellow River. They disappeared into history, which is something of a mystery to anthropologists.

As well as the Ba, there was the Chu culture. Chu people practiced wizardry. The legend of the Wushan Fairy Girl was the natural development of this tradition. It seems to be the source of the mythological culture that features worship of maternity.

There are so many stories about the Yangtze River Gorges that have been passed down from generation to generation. An example is Qu Yuan, whose motherland was in the region of the Yangtze River. Wang Zhaojun, a famous beauty in the Han dynasty, once lived in the upper reaches of the Xiangxi River, at the west end of Xiling Gorge. A well on the northern bank of Qutang Gorge in Yufu county is called Baidi (White King) city, owing to the fact that white fog is forever rising from the well.

ASIA

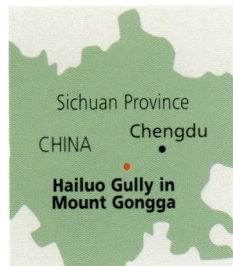

Hailuo Gully in Mount Gongga, Sichuan

A landscape filled with many wonders

Location:
Mount Gongga is located in Luding, Kangding, and Jiulong, the three counties of Ganzi Tibetan Autonomous Prefecture.

Climate:
The climatic conditions of the tropic, temperate, and frigid zones prevail. They are influenced by monsoons that come in from the ocean along the river gullies. Rainfall is abundant, and it is often cloudy and foggy. Weather conditions change rapidly.

Special interest:
This area boasts undulating mountains with snow-capped peaks, and there are a number of rare flora and fauna species as well as precious herbs.

Main attractions:
Glaciers, Muge Lake, Wuxu Sea, Renzhong Sea, Bawang Sea, Mount Paoma, Gongga Temple, Tagong Temple, and so on.

Hailuo Gully is an official scenic zone. The zone straddles Luding, Kangding, and Jiulong, the three counties of Ganzi Tibetan Autonomous Prefecture, and covers an area of 3,860 square miles (10,000 square kilometers). It consists of scenic places around Mount Gongga such as Hailuo Gully, Muge Lake, the Wuxu Sea, the southern slopes of Mount Gongga, and so on.

In Mount Gongga there are over ten alpine lakes, clear and pristine, at the foot of glaciers or deep in the forests. In the scenic zone a primitive ecological environment with diverse species of flora have been preserved – 4,880 distinct species have been identified. Over 20 fauna species are subject to first, second, or third level state protection. Besides this natural diversity, the temples of Tibetan Buddhism such as Gongga Temple and Tagong Temple open to the rich and extraordinary customs and culture of the Tibetan and Yi people.

Hailuo Gully is defined by three major features. First, there are the best views of the snow-capped peaks of Mount Gongga afforded at the Hailuo Gully, particularly the Golden peak and the Silver peak, both dazzling in the sunlight. Second, most of the glaciers in the world are located at a relatively higher altitude, but Hailuo Gully is known for its glaciers at relatively low altitudes – the lowest among glaciers of the same latitude. The lowest glacier in Hailuo Gully is only 9,350 ft (2850m) above sea level and extends 4 miles (6km) into the virgin forests, demonstrating that it is possible for glaciers and forests to coexist here. The cascading glaciers turn the serene gully into a crystal palace with huge ice caves and precipitous ice bridges. The third feature of Haihuo Gully is that hot springs with a temperature as high as 194°F (90°C) keep bubbling up from this world of ice and snow. Visitors can take a bath in a hot spring amid glaciers or swim in a pool of hot spring water.

Hailuo Gully also accommodates an icefall, 3,543 ft (1080m) high and 3,610 ft (1100m) wide. It is the largest in China and peerless in the world. It is ten times as big as the famous Huangguoshu Falls. When an avalanche occurs, ice and snow roll down, thundering and overwhelming. Glacier movements result in glacier arches and faults, and there are various grotesque ice forms to be seen – such as ice pagodas, bridges, mushrooms, city gates, and so on. Hailuo Gully provides different and equally splendid views on sunny days and in moonlit nights.

On the way to Hailuo Gully, visitors can make a brief trip to Mount Paoma (Running Horses) in the outskirts of Kangding county. Here, every year, the festival of Yufou (Bathing the Buddha) is observed on April 8th of the lunar calendar which, according to legend, is the birthday of Sakyamuni, the founder of Buddhism. During the festival, horsemen of all ethnic groups gather for activities like horse racing. It is an exciting and impressive event that will be appreciated fully by visitors.

The main ice peak of Hailuo Gully on Mount Gongga (center)

The virgin forests of Hailuo Gully, Mount Gongga (opposite)

The hot spring of No. 2 campsite of the scenic zone of Mount Gongga's Hailuo Gully (below, right)

ASIA

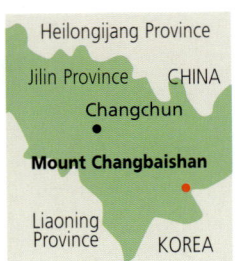

Mount Changbaishan

A dreamland of spectacular peaks and lakes

Location:
Changbaishan is located in Baishan city in the southeast of Jilin province.

Climate:
The winter is long and cold, while summer is short and cool. Weather conditions are unpredictable. The annual average temperature varies between 19.4°F (−7°C) and 37.4°F (3°C).

Special interest:
This is a state-level forest nature reserve with mixed mountain, forest, and river scenery, and it is rich in natural resources.

Main attractions:
Tianchi Lake, Changbai Waterfall, hot springs, Underground Forest, Heifeng Mouth (mouth of Black Wind), Grand Canyon, alpine ski fields, and so on.

"White Mountain and Black Water" is another name for northeast China. Black Water refers to the Black Dragon River and White Mountain stands for the Changbai mountain ranges in the three northeastern provinces of China. While the water in the Black Dragon River is not at all black, the mountain ranges are truly white. Mount Chanbaishan is white all year long, partly because of the pumice stones that cover its slopes. The whiteness is also often caused by snow, which covers the peaks for as long as nine months every year, wrapping the mountain in silver white and making it look pure and pristine.

It is said that the place where the mountain is now was an ocean hundreds of millions of years ago. Then volcanic eruptions occurred. In the process of thousands of changes, nature put in this place a huge mountain instead.

Changbaishan covers an area of 3,090 square miles (8000 square kilometers), with its main peak 9,019 ft. (2749m) above sea level, and it has altogether 16 peaks above 8,200 ft. (2500m). Those peaks are in various shapes, effectively forming a scroll of Chinese painting featuring stately and graceful, steep and sprawling peaks. Starting from the mountain foot, four landscape zones and different floral types were formed as the altitude rose from the temperate zone to the frigid zone, all described in the saying: "There are four seasons within a mountain and weather varies within a distance of ten li." Going up from the foot of the mountain, you would first come across coniferous forests with tall trees and thick shrubs. Gradually the conifers become smaller and disappear. As you climb above 6560 ft (2000m), you come to the lichen area, where only azaleas grow. If you are visiting in June, you will see enormous azaleas, bright and wild, in full bloom.

Changbaishan is a dormant volcano, and it is surrounded by more than a hundred other volcanoes. The largest crater is 8,530 ft. (2600m) above sea level, measuring 3 miles (5km) in diameter and 2,625 ft. (800m) in depth. According to historical data, it has erupted three times since the sixteenth century, and the latest eruption occurred over three hundred years ago. Trees turn the mountain luxuriantly green, and they even grow inside the crater where magma bubbled out, transforming it into an underground grove or a sea of forests on the valley floor of pines and cypresses in thick green. What would take your breath away is the King Korean pine near Tianchi Lake. It takes three people to stand with their arms stretched to embrace this 480-year-old pine that has witnessed the three volcanic eruptions. Having weathered natural disasters without withering away, this pine has become a living emblem of Changbaishan.

Tianchi Lake, Mount Changbaishan, in spring (below, right)

The snowscape of Mount Changbaishan (top)

White birch trees in fall on Mount Changbaishan (below, left)

The most famous scenic spot in Changbaishan is Tianchi Lake – a crater lake, blue and tranquil, that perches on top of the mountain as a result of the tumultuous volcanic activity. The lake is 7,182 ft. (2189m) above sea level, so high that from below it looks as if it is hanging up in the sky, hence its name of Tianchi Lake (Heavenly Lake). The lake is hemmed in by mountains like a hidden gem. The sun shows up now and then behind drifting clouds and shines through mists, brightening or dimming the peaks around the lake apparently as it wills. The lake covers an area of 3.86 square miles (10 square kilometers) and the deepest place measures 1,224 ft. (373m). The water in the lake is blue and clear all year round. Though strong winds are quite common on the mountain top, the tranquility of the lake is not at all disturbed and the unruffled water continues to reflect the peaks around. However, finding a fine day when this view is attainable does not come easily, owing to the capricious weather conditions caused by the high altitude. When it is sunny and clear at the foot of the mountain, you may come to the top only to find that it has turned to rain there, with clouds and mists all around, obscuring the lake and lending it a foggy yet beautiful grandeur.

While Tianchi Lake represents beauty in tranquility, the waterfalls in Changbaishan are symbols of power. Leaking from a gap on the north of Tianchi Lake, streams begin to form the Chencuo River on the cliffs above, 6,560 ft. (2000m) high. After flowing 4,100 ft. (1250m), the river gushes out from the mountain top and forms a waterfall over 197 ft. (60m) high. The cascading waterfall seems like a suspended river whose deafening roars may be heard miles away. The waterfall is considered the most spectacular sight in Changbaishan. Besides this one, a number of smaller waterfalls in various shapes have been formed around Tianchi. Among them, some are extensive and magnificent while others are smaller and more graceful.

A group of hot springs varying in size bring yet another surprise to visitors. Some are as big as a bowl while others are as small as a finger. These hot springs are scattered in an area of 10,800 square feet (1000 square meters) where spring water flows forth with a temperature up to 140°F (60°C).

ASIA

Mount Huangshan
The finest mountain in all of China

Location:
Mount Huangshan is located in the south of Anhui province, where it shares a border with Zhejiang province.

Climate:
Conditions are subtropical and monsoonal, with four distinct seasons: a warm spring, a pleasantly cool summer and fall, and a cold winter. The mean temperature in July is 69°F (20.7°C). It is quite cold in the mornings and at night up in the mountain.

Special interest:
The mountain has been proclaimed a site of scenic beauty and historic interest by the State Council, and was inscribed on the World Heritage List by UNESCO in 1990.

Main attractions:
Hot springs, the Human-shape Waterfall, the Paiyun Pavilion, the Shixin peak, the Welcoming Pine, the Lotus Flower peak, the Tiandu peak, the Yixian Tian, and the Nine Dragons Waterfall.

The footprints of Xu Xiake, the great traveler of the Ming dynasty, covered almost all the great mountains in China. Descending from Mount Huangshan, he proclaimed Huangshan to be the finest mountain of all, dwarfing even the Five Holy Mountains.

The four signature features of Mount Huangshan are its grotesquely shaped pines, its spectacular rocks, the sea of clouds, and the hot springs.

The Huangshan pines are considered remarkable for four reasons: the high places where they grow half a mile (800m) above sea level; their evolution from traditional Chinese pine species to Huangshan pines as they have adapted to Huangshan's unique geology and climate; the rocks including granite, in which they are rooted, sprout and grow; and the variety of ways in which they are shaped. Normally, pines grow upward. Huangshan pines, in contrast, are found growing downward. Since cliffs and rocks constitute the geology of Huangshan, these pines have to perch precipitously on the cliffs and break out of rocks, which gives rise to their extraordinary shapes as they grow sideways, lie flat, wind about, or suspend. Despite the adverse environment, Huangshan pines, when they do grow upward, assume an attractive appearance, with straight trunks, flat canopies, and layer upon layer of verdant green foliage. There is no such ting as ordinary-looking Huangshan pine. The ten most well-known Huangshan pines include the Welcoming Pine, the Farewell Pine, and the Phoenix Pine.

The rocks in Huangshan are spectacular too, with their odd shapes that can be taken for human beings, birds, animals, and so on. They attract attention also because they look very different from alternative perspectives. For example, when viewing the Tiandu peak from the Banshan Temple (a temple at the midpoint of the mountain), you might compare the rock on the peak to a rooster flapping its wings in readiness for flight. When ascending to the peak and turning around for another look at the rock, you may find the rock seems to turn into five old men with long fluttering robes. Oddly shaped rocks, over 1200 of which are individually named, may be found all over the mountain. At every turn, you come across a new view with imposing peaks and convoluted rocks, as if classical Chinese paintings were rolling out before your very eyes.

Almost every high mountain offers a view of a sea of clouds, and the one from Mount Huangshan is one of the most spectacular. More than two hundred days of the year are cloudy and foggy on Mount Huangshan. Peaks in Mount Huangshan rise high and low, interrupted only by clouds. Therefore, clouds can be seen almost everywhere on the mountain, with different views at different heights. The seething clouds between the peaks are turned into flickering waves in an upsurging sea. Visitors can feast their eyes on a spectacular sea of clouds, sometimes calm and tranquil, sometimes surging and sweeping, sometimes cascading all the way down, and sometimes lingering gently through the peaks. If the sun shines on the clouds, the whole scene becomes even more dazzling and glorious.

Hot springs are located at the foot of the Ziyun peak in Huangshan, the first stopover of the Mount Huangshan scenic site. The hot springs

maintain a temperature around 107.6°F (42°C). Apart from the springs, attractions include waterfalls, streams, and ponds, all of which provide visitors with various delights.

Mount Huangshan is miraculous. Seventy-two imposing peaks tower aloft in an area of 59 square miles (154 square kilometers), among which the three major peaks, Lotus Flower peak, Tiandu peak, and Guangming (Everbright) summit, are higher than 5900 ft (1800m). The mountain has many perilous roads, one of which leads up to the peak of Tiandu. To reach its summit, visitors have to take the Sky Ladder and walk through what is known

Beihai viewing platform, Mount Huangshan (main picture)

Huangshan pine tree (top, right)

Stone Monkey looking at the "Sea of Snow," Mount Huangshan (below, right)

86

as "The Back of a Crucian Carp." The Sky Ladder is the name for a flight of stone steps 1017 ft (310m) long, and the steps have a variety of dimensions. Some are so steep that they are almost vertical and climbers have to clutch the iron chains and climb up using their hands. The Back of a Crucian Carp is a rock 5807 ft (1770m) above sea level that is 33 ft (10m) in length and only 3 ft (1m) in width, and it has a slope of 85 degrees. Flanked by cliffs on both sides, the rock does indeed look like the back of a carp emerging now and then in the waves. Traversing this huge boulder is the only way through to the summit of Tiandu peak.

There are abundant scenic spots along the way up Mount Huangshan, such as the bamboo woods beside the Ciguang Pavilion, the tranquil Banshan Temple, Three Islands of Penglai, the North Sea, the Welcoming Pine of Yuping, the sea of clouds viewed from the Paiyun Pavilion, the sunset viewed from Qingliang platform, and so on. In a word, Mount Huangshan is the finest of all mountains.

ASIA

The source of Wuling, Hunan

Unique peaks and elegant waters in Zhangjiajie

Location:
Wulingyuan is located in the heart of the Wuling mountain range, within the jurisdiction of Zhangjiajie city, 237.5 miles (380km) from Changsha, the provincial capital.

Climate:
The area has a moderate climate, with an annual average temperature of 60.8°F (16°C) and a subtropical mountainous zone monsoon climate.

Special interest:
The scenery combines lofty peaks, winding rivulets, thick forests, deep caves, and waterfalls. These features are elegant, tranquil, wild, and also hazardous. The natural scenery here is listed as a World Natural Heritage site by UNESCO.

Main attractions:
Zhangjiajie National Forests Park, Emperor Mountain, Suoxi Valley, Yangjiajie Scenic District.

Emperor Mountain at Wulingyuan (top)

Yellow Stone Village, Zhangjiajie, Hunan province (below, left)

Gold Whip Stream, Zhangjiajie, Hunan province (below, right)

Zhangjiajie is a ready example of the dramatic changes in the world's geological history. People have just come to know Zhangjiajie in the last 20 years or so. In 1979 Wu Guanzhong, a famous oil painter, wrote a short essay awaking Zhangjiajie natives to its hidden beauty. The photographer Chen Fuli was stunned after visiting it in 1981, saying that the scenery was first rate.

When arriving at Zhangjiajie, seeing the mountains is likely to be a priority. Zhangjiajie is renowned for its peaks. They share grandeur with Taishan, grotesqueness with Huangshan, elegance with Lushan, and ruggedness with Huashan. You might say that all the mountain sights on earth are concentrated around here. A term used to refer to the sights is "2800 pillars," revealing something of the spectacular nature of the sights. With nearly three thousand grotesque peaks, running in an extraordinary continuous chain of thousands of mountains and forming a stone forest, among them there are more than two hundred summits above 2,625 ft (800m) high.

To enjoy the mountainous scenery, tourists have three angles of view. The Gold Whip Stream extends 4.7 miles (7.5km) and is a very beautiful canyon indeed. Following the stream, take the stone slab path that winds up into the distance to enjoy the beautiful sights, including the single log bridges, the old trees reaching into the sky, and so on. The Gold Whip Rock, an eyecatching landmark 984 ft (300m) high is as steep and smooth as if it had been split with an ax from above. The square pillar is certainly like a giant whip. Alongside the waters there are many more such peaks, such as Drunken Arahat, Treasure Lotus Lantern, Jade Bamboo shoot, and so on. The fascinating scene slides in and out of view with every step.

Straight ahead is Yellow Stone Village, which has an elevation of 3,280 ft (1000m). The sights here are not to be missed. The sightseeing platform is built on the summit of the rock, to which the only access is either through the front or the back entrance, for there are precipices on four sides that descend 984 ft (300m). From the platform, the peaks can be seen as stones in a raging sea, jumping tigers, or rolling dragons. The sea of clouds surging from halfway up the mountains to their tops is like hordes of troops and horses surging in every

direction. After rain, clouds and mists drown out the mountains, leaving lonely peaks standing here and there.

At the summit of the Emperor Mountain, look down. At an elevation of 3940 ft (1200m), you are overlooking the chains of mountains. The most extraordinary sights, beyond description, gather before your eyes. When looking upward, the mountains appear as a continuous chain. Looking down presents a different view, for now they are stalagmites, like forests, tall, graceful, and dignified. It is not possible to see the bottom of the valley owing to the clouds and mists lingering halfway down the mountainsides, and this may make you feel extremely giddy. It is strange that pines take root on the otherwise bare tops of the peaks. No wonder people say that the mountains of Zhangjiajie rewrite the concept of a mountain.

Strange stones call for water as a companion. The saying here is, "Eight hundred waters girdle three thousand peaks." To speak of eight hundred waters is no exaggeration. Take the Gold Whip Stream as representative. Here the pure green water flows throughout the year, even in long droughts, curving up and down, the glory of which pictures can never reveal. The red, white, and green pebbles at the bottom, the freely swimming rock fish, and the water all shimmer and gleam under the sunlight that filters down through the swaying woods. The numerous rivulets of this ancient ecosystem zigzag through the forests and link Gold Whip Stream, Flower Stream, Pipa Stream, and some of the other larger waterways, all of them reflecting the surrounding peaks and strange looking stones. When they meet gentle slopes, they become deep ponds or shallow pools. When they reach precipices, they transform into flying falls, some majestic and others charming. They set off the mountain sights and separate them from the world of mortals, giving you inspiration to become a hermit.

NORTH AMERICA

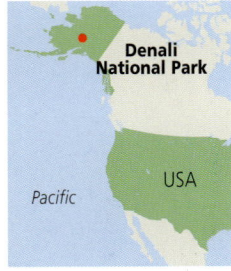

Among Alaska's mountain giants

Denali National Park, surrounding Mount McKinley, is one of the largest nature reserves in the world

Getting there:
Alaska Route 3 (George Parks Highway) passes the National Park. Alaska Railroad train station at the entrance to the Park. Airports in Anchorage and Fairbanks. The National Park's single road is only open to private vehicles within a 10 mile radius. Thereafter one must continue in one of the Park's own tourist buses, or else on foot or bicycle

Where to stay:
Choice of seven campsites. Maximum of 14 days' visit per year

Climate:
January: -4° to +14°F (-20° to -10°C); July: between 43° and 64°F (6° and 18°C)

Main attractions:
Hiking; bird and wildlife watching; white water trips on the Nenana River; Wonder Lake and Chilchukabena Lake

Special tips:
Special permits required for trails through the heart of the Park. Anyone wishing to climb Mount McKinley or Mount Foraker must book 60 days in advance. A fee will be charged for the permit.

Denali National Park in Alaska is a vast conservation area and biosphere reserve covering more than 9,300 square miles (24,000km2). It is home to North America's highest mountain, Mount McKinley, a steep-sided colossus rising 15,750ft (4,800m) below its snow and ice-covered summit. This imposing mountain, almost 20,350ft (6,200m) in height, crowns the 620 mile (1,000km) long Alaska Range, a crescent-shaped chain of mountains that acts as a buffer against the damp sea air blowing in from the Gulf of Alaska.

Gleaming white glacier tongues descend toward the valley from awe-inspiring mountain peaks. Their melted ice water feeds the multitude of dark, glacial rivers flowing through the broad valleys. Meanwhile, crystal-clear rivers and streams tumble down from the low, tundra-covered hills in the north of the Park, emptying into the mighty Yukon River or the Susitna River in the south. This tundra landscape is dotted with hundreds of sparkling lakes and tarns.

Granite grows faster

Deep within the earth, geological forces are still at work below the Alaska Range. More than 600 earthquakes per year testify to the fact that this mountain range is still being thrust upwards. Not only is the Mount McKinley granite massif increasingly resistant to erosion, but it grows three-hundredths of an inch each year. While Mount McKinley has only been rising for the past 65 million years or so, most of the other major mountains in the range, composed of softer sandstones and limestone, were formed 200 to 400 million years ago when Alaska was at the bottom of an ocean. They are consequently unable to keep pace with Mount McKinley' growth rate, as their comparatively soft rock, under constant attack from frost, thaws, and glaciers, is gradually being eroded.

Visitors to the Park remain oblivious to most of the earthquakes,

which usually occur directly underneath Mount McKinley. Generally speaking, these are relatively minor tremors occurring no more than 10 miles below the earth's surface. Only occasionally does the earthquake violently enough for visitors and buildings to feel tremors, which happens when the epicenter is at least 55–75 miles (89–120km) beneath Mount McKinley.

How the land bridge was formed

The pristine plant life preserved in Denali National Park is a unique combination of Asiatic and North American species. For most of the past two million years, Alaska was, after all, joined to Asia. Again and again, the land was separated from the southern part of North America by continental ice shields, thousands of feet deep. During the major Ice Ages, the bed of the Bering Sea also rose, forming a land bridge between Asia and America and providing yet another corridor for an exchange of flora and fauna. Denali National Park is consequently home to numerous species of plants that do not occur in the more southerly regions of North America.

Only plants that can withstand the long, bitterly cold winters and manage with just a short summer

growing season survive in this harsh landscape. Biologists have nevertheless identified more than 650 plant species and numerous varieties of mosses, lichens, fungi, and algae. Only a handful of tree species are able to survive in such extreme conditions. They are mostly found along the rivers, where the south-facing slopes support white and black spruce, paper birch, and quaking aspen. Many open areas are covered with heath vegetation and mosses. The north-facing slopes are underlain by deep beds of permafrost, but the thin layer of topsoil that manages to thaw each summer is enough to support forests of black spruce.

Cotton grass and dwarf vegetation

Apart from the heathers and mosses that populate the terrain, the region also contains sedges and grasses. The moist tundra slopes found at the foot of the mountains are covered with extensive meadows of cotton grass, interspersed with occasional dwarf shrubs, particularly alder and birch. The dry tundra area is carpeted by mats of mountain avens, grasses, and sedges. The National Park is home to 39 species of mammal, but most visitors are content to see the "Big Five," which can usually be spotted from the single road running through the park.

These include the massive moose, weighing in at 1,100lbs and often seen feeding on willows. Groups of caribou can sometimes be seen on the snow fields, trying to escape from the swarms of insects. Dall sheep peer down over the edge of precipitous cliffs, wolves roam the scant tundra vegetation and grizzly bears search the blueberry bushes for semi-ripe fruit.

One of the most unusual animals found in the Park is an inconspicuous little frog, measuring from just half an inch to three inches in size. This tiny wood frog is the only amphibian found in Alaska. With the advent of winter and the first frosts, the frog's liver produces glucose, a natural antifreeze that protects the body cells from damage. It then freezes solid into a small chunk of ice; it ceases to breathe and its heart stops beating. In this way, it is able to survive even laboratory temperatures of 10°F (-12°C).

At 20,335ft, (6,198 m) snow and ice-covered Mount McKinley is North America's highest mountain. It was first climbed in 1913 (above)

Autumn in Riley Creek, one of the main valleys in Mount McKinley region (above, left)

Deep, blue lakes present a picturesque contrast to the white, ice-covered slopes of the mountains (below, left)

The Alaskan moose is famed for its massive muzzle and hefty size (below, right)

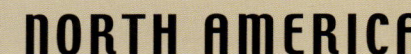

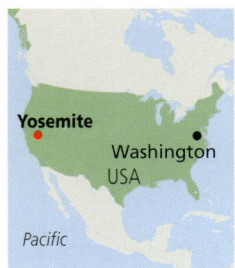

NORTH AMERICA

El Capitan stands guard

Yosemite National Park is the world's oldest protected granite mountain landscape

Getting there:
By car from Fresno; Merced; Modesto and Manteca; Lee Vining over the Tioga Pass. Airports: Fresno-Yosemite; San Francisco; Oakland; Sacramento. Bus links. Shuttle service within the Park

Where to stay:
Various categories of hotel in Yosemite Valley; cabins; camping near the Merced River

Climate:
From 25°–54°F (-4°–12°C) around 8,600ft (2,600m) and 46°–90°F (8°–32°C) under 5,000ft (1,525m)

Main attractions:
Yosemite Valley and waterfall; Nevada and Vernal Falls; Mariposa Grove (giant sequoia)

Olmsted Point offers panoramic views of Yosemite's granite mountains (above)

The vertical rock face of Half Dome is a challenge that climbers find hard to resist (below, left)

There are numerous waterfalls throughout the Park (below, right)

The ground squirrel is a rarity in the Park

The charming landscape of Yosemite Valley lies in the Sierra Nevada, approximately 160 miles (250km) from San Francisco. The valley is encircled by vertical rock walls of bare granite and huge mountains and its entrance is guarded by two mighty granite monoliths, El Capitan and Cathedral Rock, each rising to an impressive 6,600ft (2,000m). Winding its way like a silver ribbon through this gently sloping valley, carved out during the Ice Age to a depth of 3,000ft (914m), is the crystal-clear Merced Mountain River. Lying roughly in the middle of this 8 mile (13km) long valley is the largest waterfall in the United States, plunging over 2,400ft (730m) over three cascades.

Yosemite National Park abounds in waterfalls, although some of the most spectacular are often only accessible on foot, such as the magnificent 330ft (100m) high Vernal Falls and the 600ft (180m) high Nevada Falls. If you follow the one-and-a-half mile (two and a half kilometer) long Sierra Point trail from Happy Isles to Sierra Point, you will encounter three more waterfalls: the Illilouette and the Upper and Lower Yosemite Falls.

Formed in the Ice Age

One of the most impressive peaks here is the distinctive semi-circular peak of Half Dome Mountain. Its steep slopes provide an ideal summer training area where mountain climbers from all over the world can practice their skills. The most scenic view of this mountain is undoubtedly from Glacier Point, a 7,200ft (2,200m) high promontory, which juts out into the southeastern end of the valley. It is almost certainly the Park's most breathtaking viewpoint, providing an outstanding panorama of the high peaks of the Sierra Nevada and the valley more than 3,300ft (1,000m) below.

Yosemite National Park has the largest concentration of forests and lakes in the whole Sierra Nevada, encompassing 1,200 square miles (3,000km2) of spectacular granite mountain scenery shaped by the Ice Age. The area was placed under protection in 1864 and thus enjoys the status of being the oldest protected conservation area on earth, even though it was not inaugurated as an official National Park until 1890, 18 years after Yellowstone Park.

A grove of giant trees

This magnificent mountain scenery with its gentle valleys, tranquil mountain lakes, and rushing streams represents a unique environment. There are three sites where ancient giant sequoias have survived. In the southern part of the Park, Mariposa Grove alone boasts a group of 500 of these awesome giants, the oldest of which is nicknamed "Grizzly Giant." It has been growing on this spot for 2,700 years, during which time its girth has grown to 31ft (9.4m).

The dramatic differences in elevation within the Park, starting at around 1,300ft (395m) and rising to some 13,200ft (4,000m) above sea level, have created a diversity of 27 different habitats for plant and animal life, ranging from a chaparral-type scrub zone in the low-lying areas through meadow habitats and pine forests to, finally, barren alpine terrain at 12,900ft (3,900m). Biologists have so far identified 1,400 species of plant.

The emblem of the U.S.

The diversity of vegetation is equally matched by the variety of animal species. The Park is home to 74 types of mammal, the most common of which are little gray squirrels, marmots and guinea-pig sized pikas. Californian bighorn sheep are also sometimes visible on the crags, their horns crashing together in combat. By 1914, these had completely disappeared from the Park, but were successfully reintroduced in the middle of the 1980s. If you are very lucky, you might catch sight of a black bear or mountain lion on the fringes of the forest.

NORTH AMERICA

Canada's alpine wilderness

Jasper National Park, in the Rocky Mountains, spans several vegetation zones

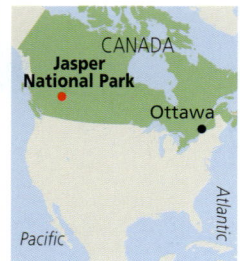

Getting there:
Yellowhead/Trans-Canada Highway 16 from Edmonton or Prince George. Airports in Edmonton, Calgary, and Vancouver. Rail and bus links from Edmonton and Vancouver to Jasper

Where to stay:
Campsites, several simple guesthouses, and individual hotels in all categories

Climate:
Temperatures range from 86°F (30°C) in July to -22°F (-30°C) in January. Average temperatures in the valleys: around 48°F (9°C) in July; 27°F (-3°C) in January

Main attractions:
Jasper Tramway to the mountain station on Whistlers with its superb panoramic views; drive along the Icefields Parkway; Athabasca Glacier (by special "Snow Coaches" bus trip or on foot); hikes along spectacular trails

Special tips:
Few roads are suitable for motor caravans. Keep well away from wild animals — at least 330ft (100m) from bears and 100ft (30m) from other wild animals

Yellowhead Highway between Edmonton and Prince George runs through the heart of Jasper National Park, Canada's largest mountain park. It extends over an area of 385 square miles (1,000km2) and together with Banff, Kootenay, Yoho and several other smaller parks, forms a world heritage site protecting around 8,900 square miles (23,000km2) of unique Rocky Mountain scenery.

Snow-covered, jagged peaks tower majestically 9,900ft (3,000m) above broad valleys while glistening tongues of glaciers separate the summits. Dark, untouched forests cloak the mountainsides up to the tree line, while tranquil ribbons of lake line the valleys fed by the rushing waters of sparkling silver streams.

Jasper, the small tourist resort at the center of the park, is the starting point for visitors. It is here that the Icefields Parkway branches off to the south. This panoramic road, punctuated with numerous viewpoints, was to enable visitors to appreciate the Park in all its glory.

Traversing Wilcox Pass in the south of Jasper National Park and crossing into Banff National Park, the road runs past the tongue of the Athabasca Glacier, which measures 3 1/2 miles (5.5km) in length and over half a mile (1km) across. It is the largest tongue of ice in the entire 125 square miles (325km2) of the Columbia Icefield, which is itself the biggest glacier area in the Rocky Mountains. The compacted ice of the Columbia Icefield stretches up to 1,150ft (350m) thick in places. Five of Canada's highest peaks, including Mount Columbia, surround this snowy expanse. Mount Columbia is the Park's highest mountain at 12,295ft (3,747m).

Rivers feeding two oceans

In addition to the Athabasca Glacier, seven other glaciers, including Dome, Kitchener, and Stutfield, descend from the Columbia Icefield. These feed three of the largest river systems in North America: the Mackenzie, which discharges into the North Polar Sea; the Nelson, which flows into Hudson Bay and thence into the Atlantic; and the Columbia, which empties in the Pacific. The Columbia Icefield has been receding since the eighteenth century, but its retreat seems to have slowed somewhat in recent times. To the east of the central mountain chain, a narrower road, running parallel to the Icefields Parkway, weaves its way through the spectacular Maligne Canyon. Overshadowed by steep, vertical cliffs, it winds past Medicine Lake with its many legends until it reaches the 14 mile (22km) long Maligne Lake.

Every autumn, a curious natural phenomenon occurs at Medicine Lake. When its main tributary, the Maligne River, turns to ice, the lake vanishes, its waters seeping away through the porous limestone bedrock which forms a singular subterranean drainage system.

When the road terminates, the visitor is greeted by the breathtaking sight of Canada's largest mountain lake, Maligne Lake, nestling against a backdrop of majestic, snowy, glacier-covered mountains. The sparkling water, plunging to a depth of 320ft (97m), is an unbelievable and almost impossible shade of shimmering turquoise.

The Rocky Mountains were formed 135 million years ago following the collision of two continental plates which pushed up a mountain chain stretching 2,800 miles (4,500km) along the western seaboard from Alaska to New Mexico with peaks rising to 13,125ft (4,000m) in places. Their upward movement ceased 65 million years ago, but hot springs still testify to powerful forces slumbering beneath this mighty fault zone.

High alpine fauna

Jasper National Park supports an incredible diversity of plant and animal life. The different habitats found in the various lower, sub-alpine, and alpine zones are populated by well over 1,200 species of plant and around 56 types of mammal. The most abundantly populated habitat is the sub-alpine region situated between 5,900–6,900ft (1,800–2,100m) in altitude. Dense forests consisting of Douglas firs, arolla, and lodgepole pine cover the slopes and high valleys, providing shelter for elk, moose, mule deer, white-tailed deer and mountain caribou as well as their predators in the shape of hungry wolves, grizzly and black bears, wolverines, Canadian lynx, and puma.

The Park's most delicate region is the alpine zone above 6,900ft (2,100m). The main vegetation here consists of hardy sedges, grasses, and small polar willows, which provide fodder for mountain goats, bighorn sheep, pikas, and marmots.

The Maligne Canyon leads to the turquoise-colored Maligne Lake, surrounded by rugged rock formations (above)

The black bear is one of the mammals found within the National Park (below, left)

SOUTH AMERICA

Venezuela's table mountains

Many areas of Canaima National Park remain unexplored

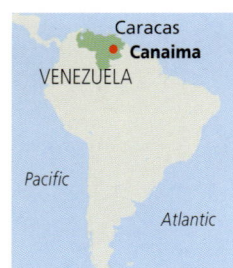

Getting there:
By air from Caracas, Bolívar, Puerto Ordaz, Porlamar, or Santa Elena to Canaima. Highway from Bolívar to Brasil bisects the southeastern corner of the National Park, with a turnoff to Kavanayen

Where to stay:
Several lodges in a range of price categories in Camp Canaima; good accommodation available at several mission stations; simple inns along the road from Bolívar

Climate:
Warm year-round temperatures of about 77°F (25°C). Dry season in the northwest section of the Park from December to April

Main attractions:
Camp Canaima with lagoon; Angel Waterfall; Roraima; Isla de la Orquídea (Orchid Island); Kamarata and Kavac (mission stations)

Special tips:
Any sites or attractions not directly on the road from Bolívar are only accessible by plane or helicopter, including Camp Canaima. No park management

In Venezuela's southeastern corner, the landscape is punctuated by gigantic table mountains (Tepui). Between 3,300ft–6,600ft (1,000m–2,000m) in height, their sheer rock walls rise dramatically from the plains of an endless expanse of tropical savannah. Innumerable waterfalls cascade over their precipices, plunging down to the steep, forested slopes far below, where millions of years of erosion debris have accumulated. Numerous rivers and streams have carved their way through the towering cliffs and cut a channel across the plains to the great Caroni River, which forms the western boundary of Canaima National Park. Its total area of 11,600 square miles (30,000km2) earns it a place among the ten largest national parks in the world.

It stretches from the uplands of La Gran Sabana and the eastern table mountains of the Roraima range to the mighty sandstone plateau of Chimantá and Auyántepui in the west, with the flat plains of the northwestern Canaima lowlands rolling away into the distance. The main settlement of Canaima is also situated in this western sector, on the shores of an enchanting lagoon. It is the main departure point for most of the excursions into the largely impenetrable wilderness. Even the idyllic hiking trails around the immediate vicinity of the Park's center are soon swallowed up in the overwhelming solitude and vastness of this incredible landscape. The curtain of water at the Sapo waterfall, for example, conceals a hidden trail. A small group of Pemón, a tribe native to the area, with a population of 10,000 live within the National Park.

The Guayana shield was formed during the Pre-Cambrian period. At that time, America and Africa were still part of what is though to have been the supercontinent of Gondwana, worn away by millions of years of wind and rain and eventually split into two sections, forming this uniquely spectacular landscape.

Solitude on the Tepui summits

The table mountains, or Tepui, as they are known, are composed of horizontal layers of colored sandstone, interspersed with seams of glittering quartz and agglomerates. The flat Tepui summits rise to heights of 6,600ft–8,900ft (2,000–2,700m) above sea-level. Their surfaces are scarred by gullies, narrow canyons, and sinkholes, some of which are several hundred yards deep. Some of these summits have almost certainly never been explored by man. One of the most picturesque of these table mountains, the heart-shaped Auyán-Tepui Massif, encircled by the Carrao and Akanán rivers, is in the north of the region. During the 1930s, an American bush pilot, James Crawford Angel, discovered a waterfall, nestled deep within a north-facing cleft in the rocks. This waterfall, which proved to be the highest in the world, was named after him. Angel Falls plunges a good 3,300ft (1km), creating a rainbow-colored cloud of spray visible for miles around in front of the cliff wall. This spot is only accessible by aircraft — or by a two-day boat trip or ten-day hike.

Moss and lichen reign supreme

The endless green savannah with its groves of Mauritia palms and impenetrable shrub lands is the result of centuries of forest burning by the indigenous people. Forested areas are really only found along rivers, in lateral valleys, gullies, and on the gentler slopes at the foot of the Tepui Mountains. Even in the less densely wooded bands of riverine forest, the trees are still in fierce competition with the large population of epiphytic plants and lianas.

The flat plateaus are at such high elevations and subject to such a harsh climate that, by and large, algae, ferns, mosses and lichen are the only species of vegetation which flourish here. Nevertheless, biologists have estimated that algae and ferns alone account for 3,000 to 5,000 separate species. Higher forms of plant life grow in more sheltered places. The region has a particularly high proportion of endemic plants, some 10 percent of which are exclusive to this massif and not found anywhere else on earth. Carnivorous plants and orchids in particular seem to thrive here and the Park is home to around 500 different varieties of orchid. Although not particularly abundant, the wildlife is relatively diverse.

Lagoon and waterfall in La Gran Sabana, with the table mountains or "Tepui," as the natives call them, in the distance (above)

Aerial view of a valley in the tropical rainforests of Guayana Mountains (below, left)

SOUTH AMERICA

Amid the high peaks of the Andes

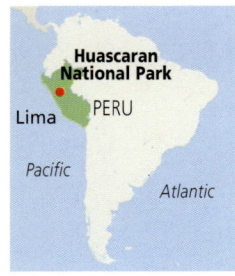

Huascaran National Park, in Peru, protects the extraordinary flora of the Cordilleras

Getting there:
Panamerican highway from Lima to Huaraz and then on to Callejon de Huaylas and Pativilca. Road up into the mountains to an altitude of 13,450ft (4,100m). Airport for charter flights

Where to stay:
Basic hotel accommodation; camping

Climate:
Mountain climate with warm, moist winds from the Amazon basin. Rainy season from December to May; dry period from May to October. Temperatures up to 77°F (25°C)

Main attractions:
Hiking; mountain-climbing; mountain-biking; climb to the top of Mount Huascaran; prehistoric ruins

Special tips:
Risk of high-altitude sickness

Some 170 million years ago, the Nazca Plate on the floor of the Pacific Ocean began to slide underneath the South American continent, pushing it upward. Over the course of millions of years, massive layers of rock were pushed into folds, rifts opened up and immense quantities of magma poured out from within the earth and overlaid the original rock. Just like the Himalayas, the Cordillera de los Andes is a chain of mountains that is still rising.

In Peru, the awe-inspiring mountains of the Andes Cordillera tower up into the tropical skies just 95 miles (150km) inland from the Pacific coast. The Cordillera Blanca, or "white mountains," situated beyond the wild, rushing torrents of the River Santa near Huaraz, is not only one of South America's foremost mountaineering regions, but its slopes and valleys are protected as part of the Huascaran National Park, one of the most breathtakingly beautiful high mountain ecosystems in the world.

Cotopaxi's outer, older crater rim, which stretches about 2,300ft (700m) from north to south and more than 1,640ft (500m) from west to east. Its external flanks are covered with a deep layer of snow.

For a very long time, this mountain refused to be conquered. The first person to attempt its ascent was Alexander von Humboldt in 1802. He failed, as did many others who followed him. It was not until 28 November 1872 that Wilhelm Reiss, a German scientist and explorer, finally succeeded in reaching the summit.

Nowadays, Cotopaxi, situated just 37 miles (60km) from Quito, is a popular destination for mountain climbing expeditions, accompanied by experienced local guides.

Over 600 glaciers

Twenty-six dazzlingly white mountain peaks rise to heights of more than 19,700ft (6,000m). Mighty walls of ice cover the steep rock faces surrounding the summits and some 660 glaciers descend towards the valleys, their melted ice water supplying at least 160 lakes. The region, which is a designated world heritage site, is also intersected by 41 rivers.

Situated in the Ancash province, Huascaran nature reserve extends across several provinces, including Recuay, Huaraz, Carhuaz, Yungay, Huaylas, Pomabamba and Mariscal Luzuriaga, Huari, Sihuas, and Bolognesi. It presents the visitor with a high-alpine landscape of indescribable beauty, full of cultural and natural treasures. The Park, which covers an area of 1,300 square miles (3,400km2), rises from an altitude of 8,200ft (2,500m) in the valley basins to the 22,200ft (6,768m) high summit of El Huascaran, the highest mountain in Peru.

Sheer walls consisting of thick bands of sediment, dating from the Calcareous and Jurassic periods, rise almost vertically. The rapid increase in height forces vegetation to adapt various ways and provides an explanation for the rich diversity of species found here – each of which has had to claim an individual niche for itself at various altitudes. Above the forests of gnarled quenual trees, which occur among the valleys and slopes, is a moist, sub-alpine habitat supporting Paramos vegetation, including a large number of grasses and shrubs in the higher areas, interspersed with an occasional low bush. Around the summit is the barren alpine tundra zone. Scientists have so far managed to identify about 800 plants from 104 species and 340 sub-species.

Orchids and bromeliads are particularly prevalent here under the tropical, high-altitude sun and have evolved into a large number of different species. The area is home to a unique alpine bromeliad, the puya raimondii, which bears the largest flower in the world, growing to a staggering 33ft (10m) in height. It can live to be than 100 years old.

Rare bloom

The mountain Indians claim that this extremely large-flowering species of puya only blooms once every 8 to 12 years. Adult plants of the same species not only bloom together during the same year, but also develop at the same speed. This helps optimize pollination and seed production.

This varied mountain landscape, where it is comparatively easy to climb one of the awesome 16,400ft (5,000m) peaks, is home to ten species of mammal, the most spectacular being the spectacled bear, puma, pampas

cat, white-tailed deer, vicunas, and Andean huemol. These rugged mountains are home to about 115 different bird varieties, including magnificent birds of prey such as the booted eagle and Gurney's eagle, not to mention the superb Andes condor. Like the plant life, some species grow to enormous sizes in this part of the world; for instance, the giant coot or the giant humming-bird native to Peru.

This region has been populated by man for many centuries. Spectacular ruins, such as those found in Gekosh, Chuchumpunta, Willcahuain-Huyllap-Pumacayan, and Hechkap-Jonkapampa, some of them dating back to pre-Inca times, testify to past cultures and long vanished civilizations.

The high valleys of the National Park are flanked by 26 mountain peaks, each higher than 19,700ft (6,000m). Huascaran is the highest of these (above)

SOUTH AMERICA

In the shelter of the precordillera

Lauca National Park in Chile lies at an altitude of 13,125 ft. (4,000 m) in the northern altiplano

Getting there:
By air via Santiago to Arica, then by bus to Parinacota

Where to stay:
Simple accommodation and camp sites within the National Park. Hotels in Arica

Climate:
Summer temperatures are between 54–68°F (12–20°C), dropping at night to 14°F (-10°C)

Main attractions:
Parinacota; the hot springs of Jurasi; Salar de Surire; hiking; mountain climbing on Payachata

Special tips:
Risk of high-altitude sickness as most of the Park is situated at a height of around 14,800ft (4,500m)

Lauca National Park in northern Chile runs some 100 miles (160km) along the Bolivian border. Sheltered in the lee of the precordillera, whose volcanic heights rise to over 19,500ft (6,000m) in places, the Park extends across the northeastern altiplano, a high plateau situated some 13,000ft (4,000m) above sea level between the cordillera ranges. This nature reserve covers an area of almost 540 square miles (1,400km2) and is home to most of the great diversity of species found in the Andes. This high Andean consists of an endless expanse of grasslands with deep ravines cutting into the plains. The scores of shallow, shimmering lakes contrast sharply with dark lava fields, such as those in the Cotacotani region. The area is dotted with dazzling white salt pans glittering in the harsh, high-altitude sun. Freshwater, saltwater, and brackish lakes glisten on the plateau and raging rivers crash down into the valleys below. The most important of these rivers is the Lauca, which flows from the Parinacota. It meanders through the southern part of the Park before its waters flow into the Coipasa salt deposit in Bolivia, where they evaporate leaving nothing behind but the salt washed down from the mountains.

Dormant twin volcanoes

At the heart of the national park, the spectacular heights of the Payachatas, dormant twin volcanoes, soar skyward. The two snow-covered summits of Pomerape and Parinacota are around 20,700ft (6,300m) in height. Glittering at the foot of this magnificent picture is Lake Chungara, covering an area of over 8 square miles (21km2). This lake is one of the most elevated in the world. Located at an altitude of 14,810ft (4,514m), it is a full 2,300ft (700m) higher than Lake Titicaca.

Lake Chungara is home to the 130 or so bird varieties that occur in the Park: flamingoes, silvery grebes, night herons, and crested ducks as well as the ostrich-like rheas and giant coots. High above, condors circle majestically as they have done for thousands of years.

Huge flocks of flamingoes gather periodically at Salar de Surire salt lake, which is situated in a remote spot on the Park's southern periphery. This lake shore also provides a habitat for the vicuÉa, an elegant species of llama that grows to a height of 51/4 ft (1.6m). Its wool is so greatly prized that it has been heavily hunted outside this conservation area and is consequently very scarce. Apart from these, alpacas are the only other mammals which have adapted to the lack of oxygen and extreme conditions of these altitudes of more than 13,000ft (4,000m).

The lower regions, however, are home to a further 30 species of mammal including wild guanacos and tarucas, which strut haughtily over the rocky landscape, while remaining on the alert for pumas. The Magellan fox hunts little vizcachas, Andean rabbits that are distantly related to chinchillas and guinea pigs.

Rare trees and shrubs

The vegetation, which grows between 12,500–13,800ft (3,800–4,200m), comprises a number of botanical rarities seldom found elsewhere. The hillsides support gnarled queÉoa trees, whose trunks constantly shed their reddish bark, which peels off in flaps. Thickets of low, green bushes grow between these isolated groups of trees.

Up to an altitude of 13,800ft (4,200m), the cliffs are thickly covered with llareta, an unusual species of light green bush that grows in hard compact cushions. It grows very slowly, only three quarters of an inch a year, but was once very widespread. Nowadays, it is found only in Chile, and the best examples can be seen in Lauca Park. Llareta was used by the Indians for domestic fuel, but the mines and saltpeter refineries, which burnt vast quantities of this unique bush, brought it to the verge of extinction.

The Park is inhabited by the Aymaran Indians who singlemindedly keep their ancient traditions alive. Archeological finds in the Las Cueva region are proof that they are the descendents of the hunters and gatherers that traveled across this plateau some 9,000 years ago.

The snow-covered peaks of extinct volcanoes rear up from the altiplano (opposite)

Undemanding cacti populate the endless steppes of the altiplano (above, right)

The native Indians keep herds of llamas, much prized for their wool (below, right)

SOUTH AMERICA

At the end of the world

Torres del Paine National Park, in southern Chile, is still turning its back on civilization

Getting there:
By road from Pintas Arena via Puerto Natales. Bus links available

Where to stay:
In lodges or at campsites within the Park. More expensive hotels along the boundary of the Park

Climate:
December/January: 50°–64°F (10°–18°C), maximum 73°–77°F (23°–25°C). June/July: 32°–46°F (0°–8°C)

Main attractions:
Extensive network of hiking trails lead to the most interesting parts of the Park. The paths are safe and, for the most part, not particularly difficult

Special tips:
Vehicles prohibited in the Park

Aerial view of the Torres Park lake district (opposite)

Melted ice from the Grey Glacier flows into an inland lake (below, center)

Multi-colored grasses rippling across the flat steppes (below, right)

Traces of branches of low-growing trees on the rocks

Torres del Paine epitomizes remote, faraway wilderness, the inaccessible end of the earth. Local people tell the story of Cai Cai, a wicked snake who caused a tidal wave to overwhelm Torres del Paine to eliminate an enemy tribe of warriors living there. After the flood waters had receded, Cai Cai seized the two biggest warriors and turned them into pillars of stone, the Cuernos del Paine, or "horns of stone." These pillars now dominate the Paine mountain massif, together with the Torres, three high, bare granite towers rising 7,385ft, 8,070ft, and 8,200ft (2,250m, 2,460m, and 2,500m) respectively.

Here in southern Chile just before the Andes plunge into the Pacific Ocean, a profusion of bizarre granite rock formations rear skywards, each of them over 6,600ft (2,000m) high. This must surely be one of the most beautiful and magnificent landscapes in all of Chile, supporting natural habitats that have remained untouched for thousands of years. These mountains were fortunately too inaccessible for European settlers and their vast herds of beef cattle.

Tongues of ice extend south from Campo del Hielo Sur, the Patagonian glacier and the world's largest single ice mass outside Antarctica.

The gradual demise of the glaciers

Despite their massive size and spectacular appearance, the Grey, Tyndall, and Balmaceda glaciers are mere remnants of what was once a vast system of ice-fields and glacial mountains. Like most other glaciers throughout the world, these too are gradually receding. Smoothly carved out, rounded valley bottoms and moraines below the lower edge of the glaciers testify how far these huge masses of ice extended only a few decades ago. Gigantic chunks can frequently be heard breaking off the Grey Glacier with a thunderous roar and plunging deep into the waters of the lake of the same name.

North of this glacier-filled, snowy mountain wilderness are the sparkling lakes known as Dickson, Paine, and Azule Lagune. To the south, are the finger lakes of Grey, Pohoe, and Nordenskjöld, while to the east is the Armarga Lagune.

The turquoise glacier water of the National Park's main river, the River Paine, springs in Lake Dickson from where it flows along the eastern flank of the massif before finally discharging into Lake Toro at the southern end of the Park. Along the way, it negotiates the various elevations in a series of three spectacular waterfalls: the Paine Waterfall, Salto Grande Waterfall, and Salto Chico Waterfall.

Sub-polar ecosystem

Torres del Paine National Park comprises more than 930 square miles (2,400km2) of extremely sensitive, but richly diverse, sub-polar habitat. Guanacos — smaller relatives of the camel that have become increasingly rare outside protected areas — are still fairly common here. The shy Patagonian red and gray foxes, on the other hand, remain hidden as they stalk the small Cuvier dormice or the European hares that were introduced into the country. As in all parts of the southern Andes, one must always beware of pumas.

The majority of the 106 species of birds, including numerous water birds and many endangered varieties, are generally found near the lakes and lagoons. Condors cruise above the mountain peaks, easily identified by their seven splayed primary feathers. Darwin rheas, a species related to the ostrich and equally under threat, inhabit the rocks and bushes alongside duck-sized Coscoroba swans with their spoon-shaped bills.

Striped woodpeckers, which can be spotted in the low-growing trees along Lake Nordenskjöld, have had to make a remarkable adjustment to the prevailing conditions: since there are no high trees available, they build their nests on the ground.

AFRICA

The craters of Kilimanjaro

Africa's highest mountain is capped with snow throughout the year

Route:
Direct flights from Europe to Kilimanjaro International Airport near Arusha (Tanzania), or via Nairobi (Kenya). Tourist support centre for Kilimanjaro tours is Moshi (Tanzania).

Best time:
December – March, July – October

Accommodation:
Kibo Hotel, Marangu

Further points of interest:
Arusha National Park
Ngorongoro National Park

The two German missionaries Johannes Rebmann and Johann Ludwig Krapf were long told they were suffering from tropical madness. Although in the mid-nineteenth century they independently insisted that in Africa they had seen a great mountain covered with snow, their reports were greeted with hilarity in Europe. Snow in Africa? Surely the heat would soon take care of it!

Scientists divided into two camps. Geographers in London agreed that these clergymen, sent out by the Anglican Church Missionary Society, were mistaken. In Berlin, however, famous physicist Alexander von Humboldt was not at all skeptical about the idea of a tall, snow-covered mountain in East Africa. Soon thereafter, other Africa travellers confirmed the missionaries' observation. In 1848 Rebmann was the first European to see the Kilimanjaro; his colleague followed less than a year later.

Soaring a stupendous 19,340 ft. (5,895 m), Mount Kilimanjaro stands high above the flat East-African savannah. It is not only the highest mountain in Africa, but also arguably the mightiest free-standing elevation on earth. Africans named it "Kilimanjaro," the "shining white mountain." Above 16,404 ft. (5,895 m), the temperature is arctic and the summit is largely covered with ice and snow. Upon the first ascent of its face in 1889, geographer Hans Meyer and Ludwig Purtscheller christened the summit as "Emperor Wilhelm Summit."

Colonial powers Germany and England drew a straight line on the map to create an arbitrary border between German East Africa and the British colony Kenya. But for the Germans they drew a wide circle around the Kilimajaro – in exchange the British got the second highest mountain in Africa, Mount Kenya 17,040 ft./5,194 m. After the rise of the national states, the border was maintained, so that the Kilimanjaro now belongs to Tanzania.

Authors such as Isak Dinesin (*Out of Africa*), Ernst Hemingway (*Green Hills of Africa*) or Robert Ruark (*Safari*) visited the Kilimanjaro and wrote about their adventures on the black continent. And anyone who for the first time sees from afar the snow-capped top of the Kilimajaro rising above the Masai savannah will share their poetic experience. Often, however, the beauty and majesty of the mountain remains hidden in clouds.

A panoramic view of the Kilimanjaro's snow can be had from an aircraft. The three craters of the volcano loom black above the icy glacier. The top of the Kibo crater looks like a giant's eye. Its snow-surrounded black stack is the pupil, a ring formed by lava reminds one of eyelashes. From the depths of the stack hot sulphur vapours escape through the Kibo-eye, evidence that the crater, 19,340 ft. (5,895 m) up, is not yet quite extinguished – in contrast to the other two, the Mawenzi at 16,860 ft. (5139 m) and the Shira at 12,998 ft. (3,962 m).

Gillman's Point is the goal

Tourists, led by native mountain guides, can climb the Kilimanjaro along various routes. Up to a line at about 7,545 ft. (2,300 m) different kinds of

tropical fruits, rice, maize, coffee, vegetables and herbs are cultivated. Rain forest occurs in the misty zone, between 6,560 and 9,840 ft. (2000 - 3000 m). The great trees are draped with lianas and braids; orchids bloom on bare wood. The next 3,200 ft. (1,000 m) are covered with fields of heather and the Kilimanjaro swamp areas. Between 13,123 and 16,404 ft. (4,000-5,000 m), a desert-like climate prevails. Here the temperature varies greatly.

Most travellers go for Gillman's Point at the edge of the Kibo crater, 18,657 ft. (5,685 m) above sea-level. It is said that from this point no sunset is more enchanting than in Africa. The absolute summit of the Kilimajaro is up another 688 ft. (210 m), now called the Uhuru "freedom" Peak.

In the nature reserve at the foot of the snow-covered Kilimanjaro live many species of wildlife, including giraffe. At the same time the savannah surrounding the volcano has been recultivated into pasture for the Masai herds of cattle. In Amboseli National Park at the Kenyan side there are large troops of wild buffalo and elephant. Characteristic of the savannah landscape are the umbrella acacias with their broad, shady crowns.

AFRICA

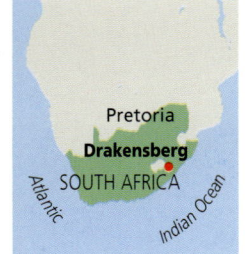

Alpine landscapes on South Africa's plateau
The Drakensberg and Royal Natal parks flourish

Getting there:
Johannesburg is South Africa's main airport; some airlines also fly to Durban. From the airport, by hire car, comfortable buses, or group taxis to the perimeter of the Park

Where to stay:
All categories of cabins, chalets, and lodges within the Park; camping sites also available

Climate:
Warm, but rainy in December and January. June and July night frosts in elevated places. Best time to visit: Spring flowers in September-October

Main attractions:
Giant's Castle; tour through Royal Natal National Park, visiting the Amphitheater, Cathedral Peak, Garden Castle, and Tal Bushman's Nek

A mighty mountain chain, 620 miles (1,000km) in length and forming a series of deep geological folds, forms the eastern boundary of South Africa's vast high plateau area, where it drops away steeply to the low-lying coastal region. The alpine section of this escarpment, which lies some 9,850ft (3,000m) above sea level, is located in the province of KwaZulu-Natal, along the eastern border of the Kingdom of Lesotho. From the main highway between Johannesburg and Durban, 15 access roads lead into the Park, where the visitor can choose accommodation ranging from cabins and lodges to tents and even caves.

Deeply fissured mountains rise steeply to towering summits, sheer rock faces of black basalt loom over light-colored sandstone, unspoilt river valleys, and rocky ravines. Such natural scenery presents a breathtakingly stunning panorama. Raging mountain torrents have carved deep gorges out of the terrain, cascades of water crash their way down through narrow canyons, and mushroom-shaped peaks sprout up in the midst of sweeping valleys. This entire area is protected by a combination of the Royal Natal National Park, the Drakensberg/Ukhahlamba Park, three additional nature reserves, a wildlife reserve, and six state-administered forests.

In the far north of the Park is the so-called "Amphitheater," a 5 mile (8km) long and 1,650ft (500m) high vertical rock face, which rises out of the Royal Natal high plateau. It is here that the Tugela River plunges down through a series of five cascades into the valley some 2,800ft (850m) below. The Tugela is just one of eight rivers that spring from the nearby 10,768ft (3,282m) high Mont-aux-Sources.

Record numbers of plant species

This imposing mountain massif sports a wide variety of vegetation and an impressive diversity of fauna, which have established themselves in a variety of different, and occasionally extremely rare, habitats: dark stretches of woodland, dry and exposed grassland, impenetrable bush thickets, and lush green pastures as well as the rolling hills of the high plateau, which explode into a sea of color when the flowers burst into bloom each spring.

The extraordinary variations in landscape, the climate fluctuations relative to the different altitudes, ranging from below 32°F (0°C) to 95°F (35°C), the basalt or sandstone bedrock, and the wet or dry environments contribute to create a profusion of vegetation. So far, 2,153 species of plants have been recorded, 109 of which are internationally endangered species. Almost 30 percent are only indigenous to this area, a concentration of species unparalleled anywhere else in the world.

The wildlife is equally diverse: 48 different types of mammals, 299 species of birds, including numerous rarities such as the black vulture and bearded vulture, 48 different types of reptiles and 26 species of amphibians have their home here. These also include a number of endemic species, such as the gray reebok, a species of waterbuck, between 1,500-2,000 of which still roam the high plateau.

Long extinct animals have also left their mark here in places where the sandstone is visible beneath the basalt. This sandstone was formed in prehistoric times, when reptiles roamed the region and left their fossilized footprints etched forever in the ground. For tens of thousands of years, this magnificent, yet inaccessible, mountain region has been inhabited by man. Wind and water have carved numerous caves and overhangs out of the soft sandstone and it is here that the San people left one of the largest and loveliest collections of rock drawings found anywhere south of the Sahara. They are remarkably well-preserved and depict, in great detail, both the animals of their time as well as their fellow man, thus shedding a little light on a way of life and religious beliefs that disappeared 150 years ago. Many of these caves are no longer featured on tourist maps in order to protect them from further damage by visitors.

"Bourke's Luck Potholes" rock formations in the Drakensberg mountains of East Transvaal (left)

Aerial view of the Berlin Falls cliffs in the Drakensberg mountains (above, right)

View of the "Amphitheater" in Royal Natal Park, a sheer rock wall measuring 5 miles (8km) in length and 1,650ft (500m) in height (opposite)

EUROPE

Land of moors and peat bogs

Northumberland National Park, in northeast England, is a unique nature reserve

Getting there:
By motorway from Newcastle, Carlisle, and Edinburgh. Train stations in Newcastle and Carlisle have connecting bus links to most places in the National Park. Regular shuttle bus service along Hadrian's Wall

Where to stay:
Large choice of all categories of accommodation in and around the National Park

Climate:
Damp, temperate, northern climate. Cool in the Cheviot Hills

Main attractions:
Hadrian's Wall; Simonside; Yeavering Bell; Thirlwall Castle; Harbottle Castle. Hiking in the northern sector

The far northeastern corner of England is a landscape of uninterrupted horizons, tranquility, and spectacular natural scenery. This landscape has known the influence of man for thousands of years and so far his efforts to preserve it have proved successful. Northumberland National Park extends over an area of some 400 square miles (1,000km2) from the Scottish border in the north to Hadrian's Wall in the south. It is intersected by the idyllic Rede and Coquet Rivers, whose waters teem with vast quantities of salmon while otters play along their banks.

Stretching along the border with Scotland are the majestic, gently-sloping Cheviot Hills, a mountainous massif consisting of ancient volcanoes. Over many thousands of years, wind, rain, snow, and ice have combined to erode them into soft, smoothly rounded hills, the highest of which is Cheviot itself, rising to a height of 2,675ft (815m). Despite its remoteness, this hilly region is inhabited and farmed mainly by sheep farmers who maintain the heath moorlands and watch over the wild flora and fauna, thus helping to preserve this unique landscape.

Toward the south, the Cheviots give way to the gentler slopes of Coquetdale and the Rede and North Tyne river valleys, their grassy slopes rolling away into the distance. Beyond the Park's boundaries, Kielder Forest, the largest man-made European forest, forms the backdrop to a scenic landscape of fields interspersed with small pockets of mixed woodland and intersected by numerous small tributaries and streams, flowing through the side valleys toward the major rivers.

During the fifteenth and sixteenth centuries, this border country next to Scotland formed a buffer between two warring nations. The region is full of medieval fortresses and strongholds that were once the heavily fortified domains of pugnacious landowners.

Today, an idyllic and peaceful landscape, harmoniously shared between man and nature, greets the visitor. A healthy balance between conservation and tree-felling has been struck in the small forests. This approach is working so well that the rare red squirrel, driven from its traditional habitats elsewhere in England by the larger gray squirrel, has successfully found a home here.

The northern outpost of the Roman Empire

Hadrian's Wall is the most important Roman structure in England. This famous Wall, built by Roman Emperor Hadrian in AD 122, is more than just the route leading hikers through the magnificent and dramatic landscape in the southern part of the National Park. It has been placed under international protection because of its Roman origins and its watch towers, roads and settlements provide excellent examples of how the ancient Romans organized their occupied territory. The 75 mile (120km) long military fortification, running from east to west, has bisected this barren countryside for the past 2,000 years, at one time defining the northernmost frontier of the Roman Empire.

The legionaries built this defense barrier on a hard ridge of volcanic outflow known as Whin Sill, which drops away steeply on its northern side, making the fortification unassailable. Following the Romans' departure from Britain around AD 400, much of the Wall was carted off and used in the construction of other buildings, such as Thirlwall Castle near Greenhead. Even today, the area is not without its military connections. A large army training area separates the northern part of this nature reserve from the southern sector.

A protective blanket of turf

Northumberland National Park is a protected sanctuary for many species of flora and fauna, most of which have adapted to the specific types of environment found here. Although fairly common within the Park itself, some species are very rare elsewhere in Britain and Europe.

Ancient forests, for example, have become extremely scarce in the United Kingdom, even though they once covered the entire country. Nowadays, only a few small pockets of such forest are left, even in Northumberland National Park. The presence of the wood anemone indicates that forest has covered a particular area for hundreds of years. This plant is not found in younger woodlands, but is present in many parts of the National Park.

Castles and fortified strongholds are frequent sights in this border country (above, right)

Large flocks of sheep are still helping to keep this idyllic moor and heath landscape intact (bellow, right)

Hadrian's Wall was built in AD 122 by the Roman army. Substantial sections of this ancient defense barrier are still standing

EUROPE

High fells, brooding lakes

The Lake District in northwest England: a varied landscape in the British Isles

Getting there:
Direct train link from Manchester airport. M6 motorway. Coach link from Hull ferry terminal

Where to stay:
Hotels, guesthouses, self-catering cottages, bed and breakfast establishments, and camping sites

Climate:
January around 43°F (6°C), August around 73°F (23°C). October to March frequent rainfall. August is a relatively dry month

Main attractions:
Hiking; Ullswater and Langdale (rock carvings); Cunsey Beck (smithy); houses where famous English artists and poets lived

Special tips:
No fossil-collecting permitted

View of Scafell from Wasdale near Nether Beck (left)

Pine trees along the shores of Buttermere on an autumn day (above)

Bucolic landscape near Mill Brow, on the Brathay river (below, right)

Twilight descending on Derwentwater (below, center)

The Lake District in the northwest of England is one of the country's most popular tourist destinations and Lake Windermere is the largest of its many lakes. Its 865 square miles (2,240km2) were designated a national conservation area in 1951. It was established in order to testify to thousands of years of human habitation in the area and to safeguard various ancient habitats, which have dwindled dramatically throughout England.

This grandiose landscape of fells and mountains is so named because of the 60 or more lakes in the region. Many of the mighty mountains with their soft contours and bare summits rise to 2,300ft (700m) or more in height. Foremost among these are England's three highest peaks: Scafell Pike (3,210ft/978m), Sca Fell (3,195ft/974m), and Helvellyn (3,115ft/950m).

The lakes at the southern end of the National Park are surrounded by low, elongated fells, carved into softly rounded shapes by the glaciers of the last Ice Age. These glaciers cut ever deeper through the U-shaped trough of the major valleys, sheering off many of the side valleys. These so-called "hanging valleys" now end abruptly part way up the mountainside, their river tributaries plunging in spectacular waterfalls over the precipice into the main valleys below.

Recent discovery of prehistoric rock art

For centuries, its endless expanses of moorland and fells, unfathomable black lakes, and sinister forests have set the Lake District apart from the scenery found in southern and eastern England. Stone Age settlers began cutting down the forests on the coasts 5,000 years ago.

A few years ago, rock carvings were discovered in the Ullswater and Langdale valleys, bearing witness to prehistoric settlement during the Late Stone Age. The Ullswater finds show that these early settlers hollowed out different-sized depressions in the rock, connecting them with carved lines. The carvings found in the Langdale Valley consist of sets of concentric circles and spiral designs. These are the first such finds in England to be completely unconnected to any prehistoric stone circle, several of which also exist within the Lake District National Park. Similar carvings have also been found in southern Scotland and Ireland, a sure indication of the links between the two cultures either side of the Irish Sea. It is thought that the stone axe factories, frequent evidence of which can be found throughout the Lake District, date from this same period.

From AD 200-500, England was occupied by the Romans. It was they who built the first two roads through this inhospitable landscape. The Romans were followed by the Norman invaders, who began widespread tree-felling throughout the region in order to procure timber for their ships. The monks of the Cistercian monasteries at Furness and Byland continued with this policy, to provide grazing pastures for their flocks of sheep. Wool from these sheep was, after all, a lucrative form of trade. The last of the region's great forests disappeared when iron smelting got underway along the shores of various lakes and lead and copper mining began in the area. By 1870, it was clear that not all these industrial experiments were proving profitable and focus eventually shifted primarily to quarrying stone for slate and building requirements.

The forest authorities and many private landowners have gradually begun reforesting this mountain landscape, albeit with economically lucrative conifer plantations, a type of tree not indigenous to the region.

Despite this, many areas of deciduous woodland have been preserved in the Lake District. The mixed woodland is dominated by oak and ash and provides essential habitats for various species of plants and wildlife, such as the rare red squirrel that depends on these trees for its survival.

Grasses and weeds

Another important Lake District habitat is the grassy terrain carpeting the broad, flat valleys. Soil quality, nutrients, and climate all determine the type of grassland. Every bit of ground in each meadow nurtures a unique combination of grass and weed vegetation which, in turn, attracts certain specific varieties of butterflies and beetles. Despite needing regular mowing, these meadows are a breathtaking sight in spring and summer, with brilliantly colored butterflies flitting back and forth amidst a profusion of bright flowers.

Heather-clad slopes and vast expanses of moorland carpeted with dense, green moss lead up to the bare mountain summits. The views across the fells in late summer when the heather is in full bloom are spectacular. A little later in the year, the rust-red autumn foliage of the ubiquitous bracken is equally stunning.

EUROPE

The mists could swallow the world

Dartmoor National Park has many Stone Age and Bronze Age finds

Getting there:
By rail from London to Southwest England then bus. By car from Exeter to Easton, Chagford, Moretonhampstead, or North Bovey, from where narrow roads lead up into the heart of Dartmoor

Where to stay:
All categories of hotel available in Exeter, otherwise mainly bed-and-breakfast establishments and camping facilities within the Park itself

Climate:
Frequent rain and wind

Main attractions:
Hiking; Castle Drogo; Sir Francis Drake's house; Widecombe-in-the-Moor with the Cathedral of the Moor

Special tips:
Compass and up-to-date maps are essential

Dartmoor's deciduous woodlands provide a feast of color against the first frost (right)

A September day on Dartmoor. Numerous streams help soften the wild and lonely landscape (opposite)

The past and the present: stone bridges within the nature conservation area (above, center)

View of Widecombe-in-the-Moor (below, center)

A granite plateau, rising 1,650–2,000ft (500–600m) above sea-level, extends some 465 square miles (1,200km2) across the county of Devon in southern England. Much of it is covered by wide expanses of bleak and desolate moorland dotted with great, gray, granite rock formations, known as tors, rising out of the landscape like sculptures from some past age. The largest of these is Yes Tor, its summit rising to 2,065ft (629m) above sea-level.

Dartmoor's landscape can suddenly disappear behind an abruptly descending curtain of swirling mists, making the plateau resemble the ill-defined shadow of a large, slinking beast. Its moors have always fuelled the imagination of novelists, serving as an effective setting for innumerable tales of mystery and suspense. Dartmoor's forbidding atmosphere lent additional menace by the presence of Dartmoor Prison, built in the heart of the moor to house Napoleonic prisoners in 1806. The settlement of Princetown was built specifically to provide accommodation for the personnel of the prison and is still the main town in these inhospitable moorlands. The real core of Dartmoor, which was designated a National Park in 1951, is the high moorland known as Dartmoor Forest, covering 365 square miles (945km2). It is situated to the northeast of Plymouth and stretches from Tavistock and Okehampton in the west to Exeter in the east.

High moorland forest

Despite its inhospitable landscape and air of mystery, Dartmoor has, in fact, been inhabited by man for over 10,000 years. In its early days, this moorland plateau was thickly forested. During the Stone Age, between 8,000–4,000 BC, groups of hunter-gatherers began felling areas of forest to make it easier to hunt the wild animals that came to graze in the clearings. The first farm dwellings probably began to appear in the valleys sometime during the late Stone Age between 4,000–2,500 BC. By the middle of the Bronze Age, all the moorland forests had disappeared.

The National Park contains numerous prehistoric Bronze Age remnants dating from 1600–800 BC which testify to Dartmoor's ancient past. These include settlements, dwellings, burial mounds, and standing stones, as well as stone circles and solitary obelisks of religious significance.

Around 1700 BC, people began to cultivate fields and enclose pastureland with stone walls, some of which have survived until this day. Very little evidence of any other kind has survived to provide insight into life in prehistoric times, since any ceramics, bones, or metal artifacts have been destroyed by the acid soil that is typical of moorland areas.

The National Park protects a number of increasingly rare habitats. The two main areas comprise a substantial expanse of peat bog on the northern plateau and a similar, smaller area to the south. Both are ringed by a mixture of grass and heather moors, while the more sheltered valleys are populated with oak woodland. The craggy, exposed tors and roaring rivers surging through deep ravines also provide uniquely individual habitats, as do the cave systems and former stone quarries found in the limestone rock of southeast Dartmoor.

Prehistoric animal remains

Britain's largest selection of prehistoric animal remains, some of which are over 150,000 years old, were discovered in Dartmoor's limestone caves. Joint Mitnor Cave, for example, contains the prehistoric bones of hippopotamuses and straight-tusked elephants, as well as the fossilized remains of early wild boar, hyenas, and lions.

Most of Dartmoor is consists of what is known as blanket bog, one of the earth's increasingly rare landscapes, seldom found nowadays anywhere south of Dartmoor. The bogs themselves lie under a layer of turf at least 20in (50cm) deep and measuring 23ft (7m) thick in some places.

There is one other spectacular and even rarer area of peat bog within the National Park, namely the Tor Royal Bog, measuring 3 square miles (8km2), where the peaty ground bulges up like a dome arching above the surrounding moorland.

EUROPE

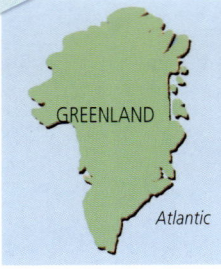

Green hopes, white reality

Greenland, the largest island on the globe, retains its primaeval, icy nature

Route:
Flight from Copenhagen to Kangerlussuaq (Sandre Stromfjord). From there local connections in Greenland with Grönlandsfly

Best time:
June—September (winter clothing necessary)

Accommodation:
Overnight accommodations are scarce, timely booking recommended

"Kalaallit Nunaat," human hand, the Greenland natives call their country, although humans are a scarce commodity on this largest island of the world. Only 57,000 people inhabit this autonomous part of the Kingdom of Denmark, the most southerly region of the Arctic. The name Greenland the island owes to a rapacious Viking, Eric the Red. More than a thousand years ago it was his PR show, in the hope of attracting colonists. And he indeed managed to get 400 persons to build settlements on the green island. Bringing wives and children, equipment and cattle, they followed the robber chieftain to his place of exile. In the summer of 986 their fourteen Viking prows reached Ericsfjord. Not far from Narssarssuarq, now a landing place for flights from Copenhagen, they founded their first large settlement in the inhospitable land.

From the Arctic icefields to Oslo the island measures 1700 mi. (2,735 km), of which only 10.5 mi. (17 km) are paved roads. More than four-fifths of Greenland is covered with a layer of ice 1.8 mi. (3 km) thick. White and cold like the North Pole – at least from the air. Only here and there basalt mountains burst through the icy surface and give the comforting feeling that here – unlike at the Pole – one has solid ground under one's feet.

The greens, free of ice, that Eric promised the colonists, is a mere strip land on the coastline. It is here that the Greenlanders live in small settlements – the countless fjords make mutual visiting a major undertaking. Only by air or water one can travel from the capital Nuuk (Godtháb) to the provincial town Ivittuut. In Nuuk lives one-fifth of all Greenlanders.

From Eskimo to Inuit

After the Vikings, the Danes took possession of the island in 1721 and soon ruled almost without a break, until in 1979, more than 250 years later, the colony achieved virtually complete autonomy. From then on the island prospered. It now has a freely elected parliament of 27 members and a government with six ministries. The Royal Greenland Business Association, which until recently controlled the entire island economy, was succeeded by the Greenland enterprise "Kalaallit Nuerfiat." Because of disagreements regarding the fishing quota, Greenland left the European Community by referendum. Cultural identity is a theme growing in importance. In consequence of this: Greenlanders do not wish to be called Eskimos, but Inuit, after their relatives in Canada, Alaska and Siberia. The blessings of Western civilisation – hospitals, radio stations, schools etc. – are welcome; the two American air bases are tolerated. Other than that the pole circle determines daily life in Greenland. In the north and east of the island the men in their kayaks still engage in traditional seal hunting – a basic need for people in this world of ice, as animal protectors are now acknowledging. Others live on fishing crab, trout and codfish, using very modern fishing vessels for the purpose. The main source of income of the Greenlanders is something that they have little use for, but is readily available: ice. Grandiose nature, mind-boggling geysers and up to 13,123-ft. (4,000 m)-high mountains lure increasing numbers of tourists to the island. They want to breathe the arctic air of Greenland, see musk oxen and arctic foxes, purchase native artefacts (made of rope) and enjoy Greenland's Smörrebröd. And when they return, tourists have learned the most important Greenland word: "imaga," meaning something like "maybe" and used especially when weather conditions prevent a flight back to the civilised world, as they frequently do. It happens so often, that all airports in Greenland have a stay-over hotel. The waiting record due to bad weather is set by an airport which is in use under all conditions, Kangerlussuaq (Sandre Stromfjord), where a group of tourists once had to wait three weeks before they could leave the island. Natives tell us, however, that this sort of thing occurs in winter only.

Four-fifths of Greenland is covered by a layer of ice

Enormous ice blocks, broken off from the north coast of Greenland, near the North Pole, a majestic spectacle of nature floating by Inuit huts. One can approach the white giants by a boat tour through the fjords.

EUROPE

Sometimes sea, sometimes land

The Waddenzee, between the West Friesian Islands and the Dutch coast, is a unique type of sea landscape

How to get there:
By road or train to Den Helder and Leeuwarden. Onward journey by ferry

Where to stay:
Wide choice of accommodation all along the coast and on the holiday islands of Texel, Vlieland, Terschelling, and Ameland

Climate:
Temperate, marine climate. Average January temperature: 35°F (1.7°C), average July temperature 63°F (17.2°C)

Main attractions:
Visits to the islands of Texel, Vlieland, Terschelling, and Ameland; Den Helder Ijsselmeer Dam; guided walk across the mudflats

Extending from Den Helder to the mouth of the River Ems on the coast of Holland is a landscape which alternates twice a day between sea and marshland. This sweeping, muddy coastal plain, known as the Waddenzee, is criss-crossed by islands, shallows, sand banks and creeks and is a designated biosphere reserve extending over some 965 square miles (2,500km2).

A chain of islands including Texel, Vlieland, Terschelling, Ameland, and Schiermonnikoog, curve gently around the Waddenzee. These West Friesian islands form a protective barrier, sheltering the wetlands against the onslaught of the North Sea. Over the past 10,000 years, an unparalleled landscape has evolved, supporting an ecosystem that could scarcely be more diverse or more delicately balanced. Every 12 hours and 25 minutes, the channels between these islands fill up or empty as the saline North Sea waters ebb and flow. These tides originate far out in the Atlantic. As the moon orbits the earth, its gravitational pull builds up a swell of water, drawing a giant wave along in its wake. Fingers of this massive wave thrust their way across the English Channel, pouring into the North Sea between Scotland and Norway. The two waves converge off the coasts of Holland, Germany, and Denmark. If the crests of these waves collide, the mudflats are flooded, but if the troughs collide, the ebb tide draws the water away.

Ever-changing dunes

The islands off the Dutch coast are relatively young. Wave action created the first sandbanks around 10,000 years ago after the end of the Ice Age. As soon as they were exposed above sea level, the wind was able to blow the sand into dunes. Sheltered from the sea on the side facing the mainland, salt marsh has managed to gain a foothold.

This landscape is in a constant state of flux, however, due to the action of the wind and the North Sea. Most of the dunes visible today are at most 600 to 900 years old. Sand is removed from the western ends of the islands and re-deposited at the eastern ends. Shallow areas are washed away, only to reappear elsewhere. Since the Middle Ages, man has also played a key role in shaping this environment, not least by constructing dikes, originally as a protection against unexpectedly high tides, and later as a means of creating new agricultural land.

These island dunes have, in the meantime, been stabilized by a dense cover of vegetation. The seaward side of the dunes has, in some cases, been sheltered by additional protective measures and man-made sea walls. These sea defenses have, however, thwarted the natural process of sand dune renewal. Nor can any wind-borne sand be added to the mud flats, a process that would once have helped firm up the mainland side of the dunes. The mature dunes, therefore, are being gradually depleted of their nutrients and the vegetation cover is becoming sparser and more fragile. Tourists trampling their way through this unique dune landscape after the end of World War Two caused so much damage to local vegetation that the wind was able to blow away entire stretches of dunes. In consequence, the area where great dunes once dominated the landscape has been transformed into an irregular, undulating landscape.

This amphibious landscape between the islands and the mainland is so highly productive from a biological point of view that it would be difficult to find its equal elsewhere. Not only are the mud flats well supplied with oxygen, but they are also well fed with large amounts of nutrients from freshwater from the Ijssel and Llauwers seas and Ems and Westerwoldse Aa Rivers, which produce huge quantities of tiny, microscopic plankton organisms. These, in turn, provide the necessary nutrients for innumerable creatures that are at home in the mud, such as soft-shelled clams, cockles, Baltic tellins, mussels, mud snails, lugworms, mud shrimps, and starfish. Many young fish can feast at low tide, undisturbed by larger predatory fish, in the shallow pools and channels left by the receding sea.

Stopover for migrating birds

Any creatures or fish that live in these mudflats are, in turn, prey to others, such as the common seal, the only mammal that lives here. Above all, however, they are a vital food supply for the two to three million migratory birds that stop here each spring and autumn to recharge their batteries in preparation for the next stage of their long flight. When the mudflats dry up, hikers can enjoy a much more intense encounter with this unique natural landscape. Trails through this muddy terrain, sometimes soft and oily, sometimes firm and sandy, open up a whole new world. Ameland and Schiermonnikoog can be reached at low tide after a three-hour hike. The other islands are separated from the mainland by fast flowing creeks. It is not advisable for the uninitiated, who may be unaware of these hidden and unpredictable hazards, to venture out alone onto these mudflats, nor should they stray far from the mainland or attempt to wade across creeks. Special guides are available to lead tourists safely across the muddy landscape, and acquaint them with the unparalleled flora and fauna that lies hidden just a few inches beneath the surface.

An area of lush, green salt marsh extends between the mudflats and the mainland and the landward side of the islands, providing a unique habitat for some highly individual plants, including glasswort, false spike grass, common salt marsh grass, and sea asters which have successfully adapted to saline soil.

Currents carry the water back out to sea, draining the mud flats (above)

Such as glasswort, have established themselves along the fringes of the mudflats (opposite)

A walk across the mudflats is an unforgettable experience for any tourist

EUROPE

Salt marshes and mud flats

The "Vorpommern Boddenlandschaft" National Park lies off the coast of Mecklenburg

Getting there:
By car from Rostock via Barth to the Zingst-Darß peninsula. To Hiddensee (vehicles prohibited) by boat from Schaprode on Rügen

Where to stay:
The National Park is a popular holiday area with a large choice of accommodation available

Climate:
Temperate central European climate with continental influences. Daily summertime temperatures around 68°F (20°C); often below 32°F (0°C) in winter; occasional drift ice

Main attractions:
"Bodden" landscape along the Darß-Zingst shores; dune landscape on Hiddensee Island. Autumn is the best time for watching the crane migrations

In spring and autumn, some 60,000 cranes en route to or from Scandinavia glide gracefully down to the strange and rugged coastal area between Rostock and the island of Rügen on Germany's Baltic coast. During this time, more than a third of Europe's entire population of these large, elegant birds with their long, slender necks feast on the rich pickings yielded by the salt marshes and sand banks, mud flats and shallow lagoons located in the transition zone between land and sea, before resuming their journey across the wide expanse of Baltic Sea or continental Europe.

The "Vorpommern Boddenlandschaft" National Park covers an area of 310 square miles (800km2) and comprises one of the last surviving natural landscapes in Europe. Not only is it a breeding ground for numerous species of rare water birds, but it is also a spawning ground for fish and a sanctuary for amphibians. The Park encompasses two extensive lagoon areas. To the west, the Darß-Zingst peninsula protects a chain of shallow inlets, or "Bodden," from the pounding Baltic seas. To the east, the island of Hiddensee forms an effective breakwater for Rügen Island. Fifty percent of the National Park lies underwater, forming part of the largest inland sea in the world. Over the course of thousands of years, numerous species of flora and fauna have managed to adapt to its low saline levels. Although the fish found in the Baltic are derived from species that also live in the open oceans, they have evolved as an individual subspecies, fundamentally different from their cousins in ordinary seawater habitats. The "Bodden" lagoons are home to creatures from two different environments. Mud snails, for example, which normally only occur in the open sea, co-exist with melon shells, which are traditionally freshwater creatures.

Steep cliffs, flat shorelines, coastal lakes, land spits, dunes, forest, marshland, salt marsh, and sand bars are all part of this diverse landscape, which provides plants and wildlife with a variety of habitats. Geologically speaking, this is a very young landscape, formed after the last Ice Age around 10,000 years ago. Once the weight of the glaciers lifted, the Scandinavian shield rose in the north and east, while the southern Baltic coast sank accordingly. Six thousand years ago, the North Sea gradually broke through into this giant inland sea left behind by the retreating glaciers. Water inundated the land, transforming the higher elevations into islands from which the sea continued to wrest substantial chunks, depositing them elsewhere as sand spits, sand bars, or peninsulas.

First shallows, then sand banks

The present "Bodden" lagoon landscape looks much as it did 4,000 years ago, yet it is still undergoing changes. Wave action and currents are still transporting sand from one place to another. The once individual islands of Darß and Zingst have gradually merged together, forming a peninsula. The island of Hiddensee is likewise linking up with Rügen. Currents are gradually removing the sand from the southern tip of Hiddensee, carrying it northward along the shoreline and depositing it at the northern tip of the island. Areas with shallow water eventually become sandbanks and ultimately small islands. Meanwhile, the wind whips the dry sand into dunes where salt-tolerating plants can establish themselves, stabilizing this new land with their roots. Finally, dwarf shrubs, juniper, and the first conifers appear, forming the sparse beginnings of a heath. Meager though this plant life may be, it nevertheless paves the way for the birch, beech, and oak that will eventually populate the area with dense, mixed woodland.

Non-tidal mudflats

The flat coastal areas, which are subject to periodic high-water flooding, sustain the salt marsh vegetation found along all Central European coasts. For some plants, such as sea lavender and sea wormwood, the water is not saline enough, making them something of a rarity. Other plant species, such as wild celery, salt marsh flat sedge and sea purslane, which

The reed beds along the shore and flat coastline are typical of the "Bodden" landscape (opposite)

One of the most popular harbors is Ahrenshoop on the western edge of the National Park (below, right)

Visitors can enjoy boat trips through the flat "Bodden" landscape in traditional fishing boats

once grew abundantly throughout the Baltic region, have dwindled dramatically. They have at last found refuge in the sheltered waters of the lagoons.

Although the Baltic Sea is not tidal, an extensive area of mud flats, known as the "Windwatt," still spreads across the wetlands. If the wind blows for several days from the same direction, the Baltic Sea builds up a large swell. Once the wind drops, this build-up of water falls back as a wave, flooding the low-lying sandy areas. The vagaries of the weather mean that it can also remain dry for weeks on end. As the sun dries up the residual water, salinity increases. If it rains, on the other hand, the salt is washed out. Only a few creatures, such as rag worms, can withstand such conditions. These species reproduce so successfully, however, that birds such as saw bills and sanderlings are able to eat their fill.

Below the steep cliffs, known as "Dornbusch," is a totally different type of mudflat. The cliffs that abound here overlook rocky mud flats. The large boulders found in this area are encrusted with bladder wrack and other large types of algae. This ecological niche provides an ideal feeding ground for birds such as the turnstone and sandpiper.

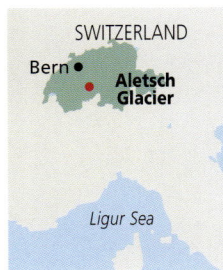

EUROPE

Glacial splendor in the Alps

The Aletsch National Park in central Switzerland safeguards Europe's largest glacier

Getting there:
By road from Interlaken to Lauterbrunnen or Grindelwald. From various locations between Naters and Fieschan on the road between the Simplon and Grimsel Pass. By the Jungfraujoch railway

Where to stay:
The entire area around the National Park is geared towards accommodating tourists

Climate:
Sub-oceanic climate on the northern side, sub-continental climate on the southern side. Average annual temperature on the Jungfraujoch is 47°F (8.5°C) and 48°F (9.1°C) at Brig

Main attractions:
Jungfraujoch viewpoint; guided walk across the Aletsch glacier; ecological center at Villa Cassel

Special tips:
Mountain climbing or skiing for experienced climbers/skiers only and at their own risk

Europe's largest glacier, the Aletsch Glacier, resembles a river of ice, winding its way down into the Massa valley from the heights of the Jungfrau massif in central Switzerland's southern alpine region. Its melted waters form the source of the River Massa, one of the headwaters of the Rhône. The glacier is more than 12 miles (20km) long and, at its highest point, the so-called Konkordiaplatz, this frozen mass towers to a height of 2,950ft (900m). It is here, some 9,200ft (2,800m) above sea level, that four mighty snowfields converge to supply the glacier with ice and snow, namely the Aletsch névé, the Jungfrau névé, the Eternal Snow névé, and the much smaller Grüneck névé. The valley end of the glacier, or glacier tongue, lies far below the tree line at 5,100ft (1,560m). This mighty glacier, which extends over an area of 34 square miles (87km2), dominates the entire 208 square miles (540km2) of the Jungfrau-Aletsch-Bietschhorn region, a world heritage site comprising what must surely be one of the most awe-inspiring mountain ranges anywhere in the Alps. Visitors have marveled at the mighty, rugged peaks of the Eiger, Mönch, Jungfrau, Aletschhorn, Fiescherhorn, Grünhorn, and Finsteraarhorn for centuries. Not one of these alpine giants measures any less than 13,000ft (4,000m) in height. Together they form the crest of a massive ridge of mountains, which, in turn, forms one of the largest watersheds in Europe. The steep, northern slopes supply the catchment area of the River Aar, a tributary of the Rhine, which flows into the North Sea. Water from the gentler, southern slopes discharges, via the Rhône, into the Mediterranean.

Textbook glacial activity

The approximately 27,000 million tons of ice comprising the Aletsch glacier is being propelled downwards under its own weight at the rate of some 650ft (200m) a year. Over the millennia, this sea of ice has transformed the surrounding alpine region into a unique landscape, leaving perfect, textbook evidence of the different features of glacial activity in its wake. For example, the U-shaped Lauterbrunnen Valley, scree fields, drumlins, and moraine fields, extends upward either side this river of ice to the 815 acres (3.3km2) of Aletschwald nature reserve.

A walk across this gigantic glacier, passing mysterious, shimmering turquoise crevasses in the ice and deep chasms, running with gurgling melted ice water, is a simply unforgettable experience. The glacier is melting faster than it is forming, however. Up to 2,800ft3 (80m3) of water can flow into the Massa gorge on a warm day. The glacier has been retreating since the mid-nineteenth century, currently at an average rate of 100ft (30m) per year, and as much as 300ft (90m) a year in the event of a hot summer. It is already nearly two miles shorter than it was 140 years ago.

It is, in fact, quite normal for alpine glaciers to fluctuate in size over the years. Aletsch glacier ice, for example, has left scrape marks on 3,000-year-old tree roots, indicating that the region was still forested at that time. According to medieval sources, the glacier was so huge in those days that this mass of slow-moving ice was actually threatening villages. Nevertheless, today's rate of the glacial retreat far exceeds natural climatic fluctuations.

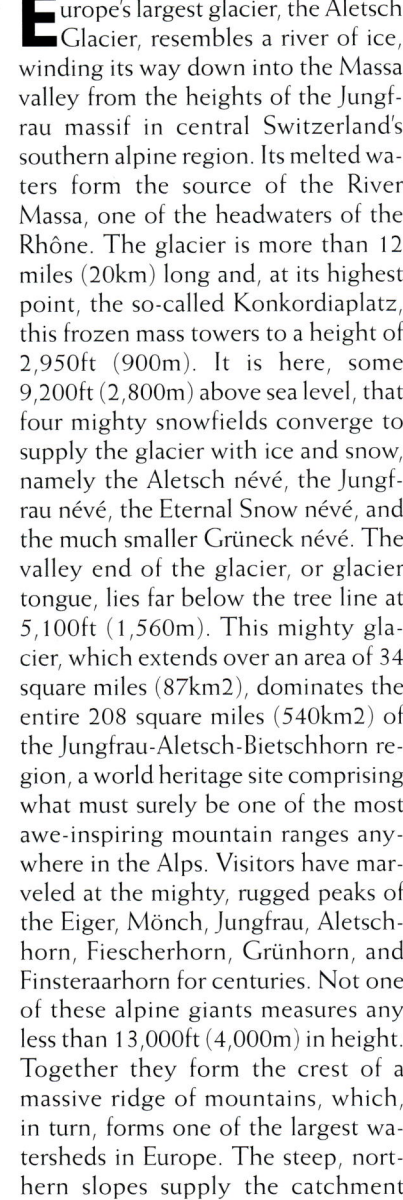

The fabled Aletsch forest

The moraines pushed aside by the glacier's advance and the drumlins left in its wake start off as barren, inhospitable scree fields. Within a short time, however, the terrain is soon covered with moss and lichen, followed by seed-grown plants. After around 25 years, the first bushes begin to sprout on terrain that was once glacial detritus. The areas that do not support trees are covered instead with alpine herbaceous perennials, such as blue wolf's bane or alpine blue sow thistle, while alpine rhododendron and alpine toadflax occur in drier soils. The dramatic elevation differences that occur in mountain regions and the changes that glaciers are constantly inflicting on the terrain result in a fascinating diversity of plant and wildlife habitats. Above the tree line, an incredible 529 different species of flowering plants and ferns have been recorded, each occupying their own ecological niche. At the altitudes of 3,000–4,300ft (900–1,300m), the low-lying northern slopes are populated with broad-leaved beeches. Since it is too dry for beeches to thrive on the southern side of the mountain range, this particular zone, with an altitude of 650ft (200m) higher, is populated mainly by pine trees.

The Aletsch glacier sliding down from the heights of the Jungfrau massif through the canyon formed by the sides of the Aletsch valley — view of this spectacular natural wonder from the Bettmeralp (above)

Lower down the valley, the glacier reaches the tree line (below, left)

Looking north towards the mountain chain, behind which the ice mass takes shape (below, right); a typical alpine meadow (center)

EUROPE

Islands in the stream

A unique natural landscape has evolved in the Danube estuary

Getting there:
By rail, bus, or road to Tulcea and from there by minor Route 222 as far as Mahmudia in the direction of Murighiol. Only waterways in the delta region itself.

Where to stay:
Campsites. Hotels as well as private rooms available in small villages. Houseboats

Climate:
Best time to visit is late spring to autumn. Summer temperatures around 75°F (24°C)

Main attractions:
Bird watching; canoe trips; fishing; old church at Leta; ancient Greek settlement and small museum on Lake Sinoe near Cetatea Istria; boat trips from Tulcea along the Sulina or Sfantu Gheorghe river

After journeying 1,771 miles (2,850km) through nine different countries, the Danube, Europe's second longest river, finally empties into a huge, flat, fan-shaped delta and into the Black Sea. The Danube delta extends across an area of 1,740 square miles (4,500km2) from Tulcea to the coast 50 miles (80km) away in the northeastern corner of Romania on its Ukrainian border. This unique landscape includes 110 square miles (280km2) of National Park and enjoys world heritage status.

The Danube splits into three arms as it approaches Tulcea. To the north, the Chilia Veche arm flows along the border, dividing yet again near Periprava and forming its own small delta. The central arm, known as the Sulina River, which has been partially straightened, flows straight into the sea. It is a main shipping route, carrying passengers and freight upriver to Austria and Germany. To the south, the Sfantu Gheorghe river arm meanders its way 70 miles (112km) to the small town of Sfantu Gheorghe, where it finally discharges into the Black Sea.

The Danube delta constitutes one of Europe's most significant wetlands and presents a landscape that is constantly changing. The result of the inexorable struggle between land and water is a constant succession of new islands, rivers, sandbanks, ponds, and marshes which wash away as soon as they are formed. The contours of the area alter from one year to the next and even from one season to another.

All three arms of the river carry enormous amounts of mud along with them, which they deposit as they approach the delta. Each year, the Danube delta deposits another 80–100ft (24–30m) into the sea. The Chilia arm carries the largest volume, 63 percent, of all the Danube's water of water. The Sulina arm carries around 16 percent. This fan-shaped delta area is peppered with a large number of lakes, some of which are overgrown with reeds or water lilies, not to mention hundreds of canals and inaccessible swamp areas.

Reed beds cover 660 square miles (1,700km2) of delta as far as the eye can see, possibly the largest single area of its kind anywhere in the world.

Explosive reed roots

The root system of these reeds forms the basis for a very unusual type of floating vegetation in the delta, known as plaurs. The decomposing organic material gives off a potent mix of gasses. Occasionally, these explode among the submarine thickets

of reed roots, blasting apart large sections of decaying vegetation to the surface to become floating islands. These in turn have become home to a unique ecosystem of plant life, even providing a foothold for trees. Plaurs can remain anchored to the sea bed or become floating islands that sometimes block the waterways.

The vast reed beds disguise the fact that the delta is actually home to an extremely rich diversity of bog and water plants, including white and yellow water lilies and floating ferns. Various carnivorous plants, such as bladderwort, commonly occur here. The strips of terra firma and sandbanks, or "Grinduris" as they are known, are generally covered in steppe grasses and dotted with patches of woodland.

Lianas and tamarisk

One such woodland area lies near Padura Letea. A unique environment has evolved here, which has been left undisturbed for centuries. The 500-year-old oaks, willows, elms, and lime trees are draped with lianas and interspersed with sub-tropical Mediterranean plants, such as tamarisk and whitethorn.

This vast labyrinth of ponds, rivers, canals, and marshes attracts millions of birds. Some 300 species occupy this amphibious landscape, 176 breed here. These latter include around 2,500 pairs of pygmy cormorants, more than 60 percent of the world's population of this rare bird. Alongside the cormorants are flocks of pink and Dalmatian pelicans, which can be seen flying across the horizon in spectacular formations if not strutting through the shallow waters in search of food.

Herons are likewise attracted to these floating islands and reed beds. Nearly every species of heron has been recorded here: gray, silver, the purple heron, night heron, and little egret to name but a few. Mute swans, graylag geese, teal duck and moorhens paddle contentedly over the open water and between 30 to 40 ospreys circle majestically in the skies above.

Reed fences help protect the villages in the Danube delta from flooding (above)

Local fishermen still use traditional fishing methods, such as the fish traps shown here (below, left)

Floating island or solid ground? Willows under water (below, right)

EUROPE

Over limestone ridges into the valley below

The Plitvice lakes in the heart of Croatia were created as the result of an unusual combination of natural circumstances

Getting there:
The main road between Zagreb and Dalmatia crosses the National Park near to the lakes. Express bus link between Karlovac and Zadar

Where to stay:
Several major hotel complexes on the Kozjak offer a wide choice of accommodation. Camping sites

Climate:
Midday temperatures in July around 75°F (24°C); in January around 37°F (3°C), with snow

Main attractions:
Hiking trails around the lakes, waterfalls, and karst caves. Cross-country skiing in winter. Climb up to the Ostri Medvjedak viewpoint

Special tips:
Do not leave the marked trails

Crystal-clear water plunges down from one lake into another through a series of foaming waterfalls. Almost hidden in the fine spray, the bare limestone crags separating the cascading water are carpeted with thick, bright green mats of moss, hanging like curtains from the glistening wet rocks. Incorporating the mighty slopes of Licka Pljesevica, Mala Kapela, and Medvedjak mountains, Plitvice National Park in Croatia was established as a conservation area to preserve this fascinating, foaming water landscape with its bizarre cliffs, grottoes, and dense, silent forests.

The 16 crystal-clear Plitvice lakes were formed as the result of the interaction between a number of unusual biological and chemical processes, which even now are continually altering the direction of water flow, reshaping the lakes, and creating new basins and cataracts. The 12 upper lakes in this karst basin are dammed by natural barriers formed by soft calcium carbonate deposits, which continually increase in height. Certain varieties of moss, as well as algae and water bacteria, extract calcium carbonate, or travertine, from the water and encrust it around their roots. By accumulating one layer on top of another, these organisms are gradually raising the height of the limestone barriers, which dam the river upstream and create a constantly changing succession of new cataracts, some of which have now reached 260ft (80m) in height. Travertines, extremely brittle and delicate calcium structures, continue to grow at the rate of approximately one-third of an inch a year. Occasionally, sections of these soft calcium barriers are broken off by the force of the water, which then finds fresh routes down to the nearest lake.

As the mosses get older

Young mosses are green and soft because they have not yet accumulated any travertine. After about a year, however, when they have encrusted the first calcium deposits around their roots, they become darker in color. Older moss is yellowish, completely covered in calcium, withered, and rock hard.

The biochemical relationship between minerals and organisms is extremely sensitive. Above all, the water must be extremely clean and pure. Even the tiniest amount of pollutant or even fertilizer is enough to destroy the delicate balance. Just below the bridge spanning the Korana River at the end of the park, where one can discern the beginnings of new lakes and cascades, the travertine build-up ends abruptly due to the large amount of organic material entering the river at this point. It is partly for this reason that visitors to the Park are asked to follow long wooden walkways around the lakes and waterfalls.

The four lower lakes were created in a completely different way. These were formed where karst caves collapsed. Much of the water in the upper lakes drains away through the porous limestone ground, hollowing out giant subterranean caves en route. Approximately 20 such caves exist near the lower lakes. When their ceilings collapse, the hole quickly fills with water and becomes a lake.

Hidden refuge for bears and wolves

Plitvice Park is constantly changing. Visitors will only get a snapshot impression at any given moment. The scene may look quite different in a several years' time. In just 35 years, for example, the water level in some of the lakes has risen by 20in (0.5m), resulting in some major changes to its outline and the contours of the cascades.

Although this large National Park covers 115 square miles (300km2), only a fraction is comprised of lakes and waterfalls. The dense, dark forests and surrounding karst landscape are also protected since without such extensive forested areas, the wind and weather would quickly erode the Dolomite cliffs. Boulders and gravel would accumulate in the lakes and destroy the fragile travertine cataracts.

The water plunges in a series of cascades from lake to lake. To avoid possible contamination, a system of wooden walkways renders the area accessible to visitors (opposite)

Young mosses seem to act as a water filter. They retain traces of calcium, encrusting this around their roots, and turn themselves into petrified plants (above, right)

There are many drowned trees among the lakes (above, left and below)

EUROPE

The floodplains of the Volga

The Volga delta is home to a unique, amphibious environment protected by the Astrahan Nature Park

Getting there:
To Astrahan: Airport. By rail from Pawelezer station in Moscow. By road from Volgograd and Elista. Volga ferry services from the Baltic and from Moscow (package trips)

Where to stay:
Hotel accommodation in Astrahan; cruise and club hotels in the river arms of the delta; campsite

Climate:
In July up to 113°F (45°C); in January as low as -40°F (-40°C)

Main attractions:
Ship and boat cruises and excursions from and to Astrahan; canoe trips; bird watching; fishing

Special tips:
Large areas of the Volga delta only accessible by boat

Vast fields of water plants carpet the waters of Astrahan National Park (above)

Surrounded by reed beds, the profusion of waterways in the delta are lined with white and French willows (below)

At the end of a journey of some 2,250 miles (3,600km), the waters of Europe's longest river, the Volga, deposit their mud content in a unique delta landscape of marshy river meadows on the northeastern shores of the Caspian Sea, the world's largest inland lake. The Volga delta measures almost 125 miles (200km) across. The town of Astrahan, which in the eighteenth century was a scattered community straddling 11 islands just off the coast, now lies 56 miles (90km) inland from the Caspian Sea. Extending over 7,300 square miles (19,000km2), an area roughly the size of Slovenia, this intricate network of lakes, ponds, and flowing streams with channels of saltwater, brackish water, and freshwater is dotted with innumerable islands and islets. On the mainland, deserted dry steppes and semi-deserts stretch far into the North Caspian interior.

Life in this amphibious kingdom is not only affected by the extremes of temperature, ranging from -40°F (-40°C) in winter to 113°F (45°C) in summer, but it is also affected by vast fluctuations in water level to which the Volga is subject. In spring, melted ice from the upper reaches of the river inundate many of the lower lying islands and vast tracts of the cattle-breeding areas in the north. At this time of year, water levels rise by an average of 5ft (1.5m), producing a landscape characterized by scores of shallow bays and lakes.

Rare species of willow

During the periods of low water in summer and autumn, new marshes emerge, only to be submerged again during autumn and winter flooding.

Along the coast is an area of 3,100 square miles (8,000km2), generally regarded as one of the world's most significant wetland areas. The numerous tributaries in the heart of the conservation area are lined with white and French willows. Tamarisk and red-leaved dewberry bushes thrive in the transition zone where these waterways give way to broad shallows, while the open expanses of still water are carpeted with various types of reeds, water lilies, water chestnuts, and flowering rushes. In the summer months, once the melted ice has drained away and water levels have dropped again, the delta puts on a breathtaking display of lotus flowers. Although the lotus flower is actually a tropical plant, vast surfaces are covered with their rich red blooms. The Volga delta marks the northernmost point of the lotus flower's range. Its leaves provide useful nests for whiskered terns, white-winged black terns, and black terns.

These nutritious mudflats of the Volga delta provide an ideal breeding ground and resting place for millions of water birds. Around 150 species reside here, including cormorants, glossy ibis, gray heron, and spoonbills, as well as ospreys and herring gulls. The balloon-shaped nests of tiny penduline tits dangle precariously from the outermost tree branches while waders converge on the sand and mud banks that are exposed during the summer months. This deserted delta area is one of a handful of sanctuaries remaining for the rare Dalmatian pelican and pygmy cormorant.

European otters, minks, and muskrats

Hoopoes, blue rollers, great gray shrike, and lesser gray shrike are the most common species populating the vast landscapes north of the delta, while demoiselle cranes rear their young in the dunes and dry steppes.

More than 30 types of mammal roam the islands or hunt for food in the water or along the shores, the most common being raccoons, wild boar, mink, and muskrats. The shy European fish otter and beaver also reside here as well as some of the rarer species include the Saiga antelope and European lynx.

All of these animals are largely dependent on the incredible abundance of fish available in the largest wetland area in Europe. The most common species are catfish, pike, and zander. When the spring floods arrive, many fish lay their eggs in the shallows. Even wild carp can sometimes be found in inundated areas. This is the season when the sturgeon set off from the Caspian Sea, heading for their breeding grounds in the upper reaches of the river. All too often, they fall victim to the nets of poachers wanting to exploit the valuable caviar market.

ASIA

 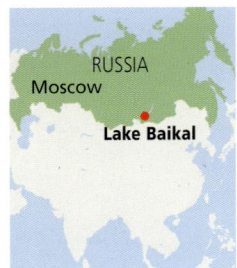

The seals of Lake Baikal

The National Park surrounding the world's largest freshwater lake is a refuge for many rare animals and plants

Getting there:
International airports at Irkutsk and Ulan Ude, with connecting flights to Moscow three times a week. The Trans-Siberian railway also stops in Irkutsk

Where to stay:
Baikal is a popular tourist destination. Several fairly basic hotels

Climate:
-13°F (-25°C) in winter, rising to 64°F (18°C) in summer

Main attractions:
Ivolginsky Dazan theatre and Buddhist temple in the capital of Ulan-Ude. Hot spa and thermal springs in the Schumak region. Flora and fauna in the Sajan mountains

View over the conservation area on the eastern shore of Lake Baikal with Barguziski National Park (above)

Many rivers, springing from the surrounding hills, empty into the lake (below, center)

These traditional, wooden houses are typical of the region (below, right)

Between the lake and the distant hills lies an expanse of steppe (below)

In eastern Siberia, surrounded by mountain ranges towering over 6,600ft (2,000m) in height, is Lake Baikal, which holds the largest volume of freshwater of any lake in the world. It contains approximately 5,518 cubic miles (23,000km2) of water, or 20 percent of the world's total freshwater reserves. Even to a depth of 130ft (40m), its waters are crystal-clear because they contain only half as many minerals as other lakes. The numerous rivers that tumble down from the steep, barren mountains in the west and east transport very few sediments into the lake.

Covering an area of 12,000 square miles (31,000km2), Lake Baikal is virtually the same size as Belgium, measuring 395 miles (636km) in length, yet only 50 miles (80km) wide. Twenty-five million years ago, the continental plates here began to shift, thereby creating the East Siberian rift system, a series of deep troughs. During the course of time, the 365 mountain rivers and streams filled up this system of troughs, which is drained by a single river, the Angara, in the south. Even now, the east and west shores are still drifting apart at the rate of approximately half to three-quarters of an inch a year, creating space for yet more water.

The lake bed is divided into three deeper basins. The northern basin is geologically younger. The mighty, underwater Akademiker ridge separates it from the two southerly depressions which are, in turn, separated by a barrier of sediment deposited by the Selenga River, the largest tributary to empty into the lake.

Lake Baikal, descending to depths of 5,370ft (1,637m), is the world's deepest and oldest inland lake. Not only is it of enormous geological significance, but it is unusual because it represents a veritable Aladdin's cave for ecologists and evolutionary biologists alike. For this reason, Lake Baikal has been designated a world heritage site.

Even the vegetation covering the slopes on either side of the lake varies considerably. The western side is populated by coniferous forest and mountain steppes, while the eastern slopes are covered with stone pine forests.

The home of the Barguzi sable

Along the northern shore, the western flanks of the Barguzinski mountains are covered with thick larch woods, interspersed with rhododendron thickets. This mountainous region around the 9,320ft (2,841m) summit of Mount Baikal gives way higher up to an alpine belt of lichen vegetation and barren mountain tundra, forming a protected area known as the Barguzinski National Park.

It is a remote and unique environment, in which around 40 types of mammal and more than 240 species of bird — including ospreys and capercaillies — can live virtually undisturbed by man. The forests are inhabited by large numbers of brown bears, wolves, foxes, otters, elk, Siberian roe deer, and white-tailed deer. The renowned Barzugi sable has also become a common sight once more after having been hunted almost to extinction on account of its thick pelt. Luckily, the area was declared a National Park in 1916. Since then, its numbers have recovered well.

Underwater wildlife paradise

The greatest and most surprising diversity of flora and fauna is to be found in the waters of Lake Baikal itself. So far, between 1,500 and 2,500 species of animal have been identified in the lake. Eighty percent of these are endemic, occurring here and nowhere else. The most famous of these are the rare Baikal ringed seals, one of the few species of freshwater seal in the world. It is possible that they made their way to Lake Baikal from the North Sea during the Ice Age along the Jenisej and Angara rivers, or perhaps they swam up the River Lena. Lake Baikal boasts a population of around 3,000 of these wonderfully graceful swimmers, although they are being placed increasingly at risk from environmental pollution and waste water draining into the lake from local timber factories.

One of the most surprising evolutionary processes to have occurred over the course of millions of years involves Lake Baikal's freshwater shrimps, of which there are more than 255 species and sub-species. They have adopted a variety of feeding methods in this unusual habitat. Some of them search for plankton in the open water, others populate the plant life growing in the bays, and yet others have transformed themselves into parasites.

ASIA

The Dead Sea; the Sea of Lot

In the lowest sea of the world, salt snuffs out all life

Route:
From Jerusalem 19 mi. (30 km) east, from Amman 22 mi. (35 km) southwest

Best time:
March – June, September – November

Accommodation:
Moriah Dead Sea resort

Other points of interest:
Masada, Qumran

Evaporating water deposits a crust of saline crystal on the shore.

Millions of years ago, water flowed into the lower places of a grave-like earth fault at the current boundary of Israel and Jordan, forming the Dead Sea, 50 mi. (80 km) long and up to 11 mi. (18 km) wide. Its surface lies at 1,312 ft. (400 m) below normal sea level and its bottom on the north side lies twice that deep.

Steep walls surround the shore

Most of us are familiar with photographs of bathers drifting on their backs in the Dead Sea, effortlessly floating, sometimes even reading a newspaper. Because of the extreme salinity of the water, almost 30 percent, you can't sink. But you can't very well swim in it, either. It is nearly impossible to crawl or to do the butterfly stroke.

The salts – mostly magnesium, sodium chloride and calcium chloride – render life in the Dead Sea impossible. The water contains only a few bacteria, such as nitro bacteria, sulphur bacteria and germs that break down cellulose. The shore, too, defined by a steep 1,968 ft. (600 m) scraggy mountain wall, is a dead desert. Part of the edges are encrusted with salt and only a few wadis, small valleys between the high walls, have temporary vegetation.

In Hebrew the Dead Sea is called *Yam Hamelach*, Salt Sea. One of the names used by Arabians is *Bahr Lut*, the Sea of Lot, named after Abraham's cousin who lived in Sodom. In antiquity the Greeks and Romans called it the asphalt sea, and from its depths arose a high-quality bitumen that can easily be recovered from the water surface. From about 150 years before Christ until the fall of the Romans in AD 68, a monastery of the Essenes, a Jewish faith community, stood on the northwestern shore. Excavating the ruined city, which included many caves, archaeologists in the middle of the 20th century chanced upon more than 400 manuscripts which proved of great significance for biblical scholarship. They are Hebrew, Aramaic and Greek texts on leather and parchment and a copper plate with inscriptions.

The Dead Sea receives it water from the Jordan and some smaller mountain basins, and has no affluent of its own. The extreme temperatures, in summer reaching to 115°F (46°C), enough of the water evaporates so that the influx of water – there is virtually no rain – does not affect salinity. Over time water is increasingly being taken from the Jordan for irrigation purposes. The water level of the Dead Sea will drop sharply in the near future. Accordingly, in Israel plans are made to prevent threatening drying up by building an open rock inlet to allow water from the Mediterranean to flow into the Dead Sea. It could at the same time be the site for a hydro-electric station.

One of the many features of this deepest landscape on earth is the unusually high amount of oxygen in the air. At the same time, because of the longer distance for sunrays, UV radiation is greatly filtered, so that one can sunbathe for longer periods which risking sunburn.

This aerial photograph shows the Dead Sea against the background of the Jewish mountain fortress Masada, whose 960 residents killed each other in 73 BC, so that they would not fall into the hands of the Roman enemy. At then northwestern shore of the Dead Sea archaeologists found a Essene monastery, destroyed by the Romans. It contained manuscripts from the time prior to the birth of Christ. The level of the Dead Sea (small photograph) is 1,312 ft. (400 m) below that of the great oceans.

ASIA

A desert of many moods

The Rann of Kutch is a salty marsh

State and capital:
Gujarat, Gandhinagar 178 mi. (286 km)

Convenient access:
Road to Rann, air, rail to Bhuj, Ahmedabad

Accommodation:
Budget to midrange at Bhuj

Best season:
November to March

Also worth seeing:
Dholavira, Mandvi

Villagers who live in mud houses on the edge of the desert say the Rann has a huge population of "whites," the spirits of men who never returned from the endless desolation. They watch out for them in the quivering mirages and the still night air, and while the eyes of the outsider squinting into the lifeless expanse may not sight these restless phantoms, they might notice the dust kicked up by a galloping herd of *gudhkur* (Asiatic wild asses) on the shimmering horizon. For the Rann of Kutch, flat and white, seemingly uninhabitable, is home to this chestnut brown beast not found anywhere else in the world.

Once the waters of the Arabian Sea lapped easily over this 20,077 square mile (52,000 km²) tract of land on the western coast of India, stretching from the edge of the great Thar Desert southward to the Little Rann and the Gulf of Kutch. First a geological upliftment cut off its seawater supply, so that by the time of Alexander the Great it existed as a vast navigable lake. Hundreds of years of silting and a few earthquakes later it had withered into a desert of varying moods. Now in March, it is a cracked salt flat, while in the searing heat of the long dry season, it becomes parched, with one of the highest annual evaporation rates in the region; temperatures, during this time, can reach 50 degrees Celsius. While the monsoon runs its course, from July to September, the Rann metamorphoses into a salt-clay desert covered by seawater; a shallow salt marsh, with patches of salt-free but sandy higher ground known as bets. Several rivers—the Bhambhan, Kankavati, Godhra and Umai from the south, the Rupen and Saraswati from the east, and the Banas from the north east—drain into it during this time. In August, the water is almost knee-high, but by winter it has evaporated, leaving behind salt crust.

The word rann comes from the Hindi word ran, meaning "salt marsh," or from the Sanskrit word ririna meaning "a waste." And yet this bleakness, devoid of clouds and movement harbours diverse life. The bets offer a foothold for trees, grass and scrub that provide shelter and food for animals. Three of these, Pung Bet, Vacha Bet and the Jhilandan Bet, are refuge for the wild ass. When it transforms into a marshland, the Rann is taken over by acres of flowering plants, and millions of tall, pink flamingoes, which fly in each year to nest and raise their young in "cities" of conical mud-nests, turning it into one of the largest flamingo breeding colonies of the world. Besides these, wolves, desert foxes, jac-

kals, the elusive caracal and desert cat are shadowy presences, and chinkara (gazelles), nilgai (India's largest antelopes), the elegant blackbuck (another Indian antelope) and hyena, tramp its sands. More than 200 avian species, including the lesser florican, houbara bustard, Dalmatian pelican and 13 species of lark live in the seasonal salt marshes. The coastal wetlands support over 40,000 birds. There are also smaller mammals, such as hares and honey badgers, and reptiles like the spiny-tailed lizard, monitor, red and common sand boa, saw-scaled viper, cobra, and the Indian rat snake. Uniquely, the Rann is a combination of desert and wetland habitats.

It is believed by genetic scientists that 60,000 years ago early humans from Africa migrated to Kutch. Today 18 different tribes, each with its own culture live in this region. Amongst these are Bharwad shep-herds, Rabari camel and cattle herders, Maldhar buffalo keepers, and Samra and Sindhi Muslim cameleers.

Above: Flamingoes feed in the shallow waters of the Rann. Below: The Asiatic wild ass once roamed the north-western plains of India from the Satluj to the Indus Rivers. At the Little Rann Sanctuary they number about 2,000. Able to survive on the sparse scrub, these strong beasts can weigh up to 542 lb. (240 kg) and attain gallop speeds of 43 mph (70 km/h) per hour.

ASIA

Floating stage of dancing deer

Loktak Lake provides a precarious prop for the nearly extinct sangai

State and capital:
Manipur, Imphal
30 mi. (48 km)

Convenient access:
Road to Loktak, air to Imphal, rail to Guwahati, Dimapur

Accommodation:
Budget to midrange at Imphal

Best season:
October to February
Also worth seeing: Bishnu Temple, Phubala

Below: Circular, floating phoomdi (vegetation) patches give the Lake its distinctive landscape. Facing page: Besides fishing from their boats, fisherfolk are often seen sitting on the phoomdis outside their huts, with nets.

The largest freshwater lake in north eastern India, Loktak is located at the centre of the state of Manipur. Designated a Wetland of International importance under the Ramsar Convention, Loktak is an integral part of the socio-cultural and economic fabric of the region.

Actually a complex monsoonal floodplain system, comprising several smaller lakes called "pats," which become one continuous sheet of water during the monsoon. Numerous rivers and streams flow into the Lake from the surrounding hills; the two main rivers are the Imphal and the Nambul. A rare ecosystem of floating grass and herb mats, known locally as phoomdis, covers the Lake surface. These masses of buoyant vegetation, soil and organic matter at various stages of growth and decomposition host numerous specialised species, besides being useful to the local people in many ways. Loktak is only about a meter deep and, originally, during dry seasons, phoomdis temporarily settled onto the lakebed drawing their nutrition from the soil. However, in recent times, forced maintenance of a higher water level does not allow the phoomdis to settle, thus reducing the thickness of the layer.

The aquatic vegetation of Loktak numbers over 230 species providing edible produce like the lotus and trapa. The largest single mass of phoomdis covers Loktak's 15 square miles (40 km^2) of its south-eastern corner, which has been declared the Keibul Lamjao National Park. The Park is the last natural refuge of the Manipur brow-antlered deer or the sangai, a sub-species of the Thamin or Eld's deer. Reported extinct in 1951 and then rediscovered, the sangai population is currently estimated at about 200. With their splayed-out hooves and horny pasterns, the sangai can balance on the shaking, unstable phoomdis. Also known as the "dancing deer" due to its listing gait on the floating mats, the sangai is a much loved creature in Manipuri folklore and dance tradition. The deer live in small herds, remain hidden during daylight and come out to feed at dawn and dusk. They can be viewed from boats or from viewing platforms provided in the Park. Amongst the 425 species of animals are otter, civet, wild boar, hog deer, Indian python, sambar and barking deer. The Lake provides refuge to at least 116 species of birds of which 21 migrate from north of the Himalayas.

Distinctive landscape

The Lake is a vital fish habitat and breeding ground for numerous migratory fish species. Outside the Park area, fisher folk build their huts on the phoomdis. They also use the phoomdis to concentrate fish into the mat's root zones, which they then surround with nets, making circular fish culture zones.

Over 120 square miles (312 km^2) in area, the huge water body regulates the local climate. It is also the main source of water for hydropower generation, irrigation of agricultural land and drinking water supply for the region. Over 100,000 people on and around the Lake depend on its fish produce—it yields about 1,653 tons of fish per year. Loktak's vegetation is used for building huts, weaving, fencing, extracting medicines, handicrafts, and rituals and ceremonies.

ASIA

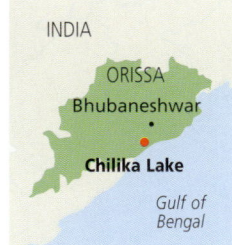

A fertile junction of waters

Chilika is the largest inland lake on the subcontinent

State and capital:
Orissa, Bhubaneshwar 62 mi. (100 km)

Convenient access:
Road to Lake, air to Bhubaneshwar, rail to Rambha, Balugaon

Accommodation:
Budget to mid-range

Best season:
November to March
Also worth seeing: Puri, Gopalpur on sea

It is said that many hundreds of years ago the pirate king Raktabahu arrived on the eastern coast of the Indian sub-continent, close to the estuary of the Mahanadi River, to ransack the rich city of Puri. His daunting fleet of fast ships anchored just over the horizon out of sight of the coast. But the Sea washed up the ship's refuse to the shore warning the townspeople, who then fled with all their possessions. Thus when Raktabahu set foot ashore he found a deserted city. Furious at what he saw as the Sea's betrayal, he attacked it with his entire army. The Sea initially gave way, and then surged back in anger, drowning the army and forming what is now known as Chilika Lake. Historically, Chilika has been integral to the economy and culture of coastal Orissa. A poem penned 400 years ago by the saint-poet Purshottam Das elaborates on Lord Krishna dancing on its shores with a local curd-seller girl, Maniki. Even today the village of Manikagauda (Gauda is the local cowherd caste) stands on Chilika's bank.

Biodiversity influenced by saline and fresh water

Located on coastal Orissa, Chilika is the largest inland lake on the Indian subcontinent. Forty miles (60 km) long and with an average width of 12 miles (20 km), the Lake was a part of the Bay of Bengal until a spit of sand grew between the sea and the open lagoon, leaving it connected to the former by a narrow mouth. This mouth is unstable, varying with time in both location and size. Often it gets completely blocked, whereupon it is dredged open, usually by local fisherfolk, whose livelihoods depend on maintaining a sea inflow into Chilika. Presently the sea is connected to the Lake by a 20-mile (32 km) long, narrow, outer channel near the village of Motto. However, due to Chilika's huge size, the influence of the sea is restricted to the zone closest to the open mouth. As a result of this constant movement of water, the Lake changes size in different seasons. During the monsoon, when fresh water pours in from the rivers it expands to over 444 square miles (1,150 km^2), whereas in the dry summer it shrinks to about 348 square miles (900 km^2).

As the junction of fresh and saline water bodies, the Lake is a unique ecosystem and a biodiversity hotspot. Animal and plant life, adapted to a range of conditions, includes over 220 fish species, numerous aquatic plant species, and about 720 land based plants in the immediate surroundings. The Indian Zoological Survey recorded over 800 types of fauna from the lake region, with a number of rare and endangered species like the Barakudia limbless skink, found

nowhere else in the world, estuarine turtles, numerous kinds of snakes, rodents, otters, bats, and sloth bears on the hills around Chilika. Once commonly seen following boats and playing near the Lake's mouth, the rare Irrawaddy dolphin is now sighted only occasionally. A huge migrant bird community, some from Central Asia, Russia, South East Asia and Ladakh, flies in to feed and breed in the fertile waters. A recent survey identified 205 avian species in the Chilika environs.

The continuous input of river silt has made Chilika very shallow, creating islands, many of which are inhabited by fishermen—more than 150,000 fisherfolk live in and around the lake—who scour the waters for mackerel, prawn and crab. Nalaban, a marshy island, is one of the largest. Completely submerged during the monsoon, it is a major feeding and roosting habitat during winter for over 100 species of migratory birds and has been declared a bird sanctuary.

Left: Chilika is fed by fresh water, which enters it from 52 rivulets and rivers, as well as by the sea; during high tide, the sea rushes in, while during low tide the waters recede. The Lake was one of the first Ramsar Sites (a wetland of international importance) to be declared by India in 1981.
Above: Fishermen at the mouth of the Lake.

ASIA

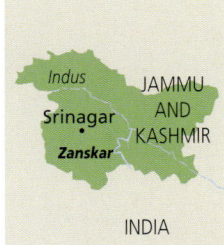

Land of White Copper
The Zanskar River forms valley on its way to the Indus

State and capital:
Jammu & Kashmir, Srinagar (277 mi./445 km to Padum)

Convenient access:
Road to Padum, air to Leh (295 mi./475 km to Padum), Srinagar

Accommodation:
Camping (with own equipment)

Best season:
July to early October (for driving, trekking, river journey), January-February for upriver trek

As you stand on top of the Pensi La Pass, at 14,501 ft. (4,420 m) above sea level, you can see Drung Dirung glacier's massive, fractured hunk on the south-west, from which drips the essence of the Stod, which later unites with the Tsarap to form the Zanskar River. The valley stretches below, expanding as it extends further, the fledgling stream running through it. It is an awesome sight, and one that not many people see, for Zanskar is one of the last frontiers of India—unmapped and unknown to the world until penetrated by 19th century British expeditions—contiguous to trans-Himalayan Ladakh, yet cut off from it except by way of high mountain passes and sneaking river valleys.

Hemmed in by mountain ranges

The traditional way in from the north is over the Pensi La by road and then one can either trek, or choose to ride the river on rafts and kayaks. The former is a classic 111-mile (180 km) journey for as the Zans-kar runs away eastward to seek the Indus, it rams through the heart of the Zanskar Mountain's, carving out a spectacular gorge. On its upper end, however, it is a shallow, rippling stream, chilled to a few degrees above freezing point, running through a beautiful landscape. On one side of the wide valley, the dark wall of the Greater Himalayas is riddled with waterfalls and glaciers, while on the other side, the pastel-colored Zanskar range is drier and sandier. Due to its glaciers amid ochre-hued mountains, Zanskar is also known as the Land of White Copper. Almost totally Buddhist, it is dotted with gompas (monasteries). These are hundreds of years old, and can mostly be reached only on foot. From the heights of Karsha gompa, one can gaze at the entire panorama of the Zanskar plains; Sani is thought to date to the second century; Dzonkhul was the retreat of solitude-seeking hermit masters; and Lingshed, the remotest of all, is accessible only by days of trekking into the heart of the Zanskar Mountains.

Through sheer rock walls

Fortified with the volume of the Tsarap, the Stod gains stature and turns northward. The mountains start closing in and the gorge looms ahead. Once in it, on a raft, one is in surreal isolation, totally removed from the outside world (which, to begin with, is itself considerably removed). Rock spires, in various shades of ochre, shoot up from the surface of the river to heights over 2,460 ft. (750 m); it is akin to sitting in the front row of a huge cinema hall, except that the panorama is all around, not just in the front. The staggering scale is put into pers-pective by a bobbing raft ahead, a tiny speck at the toe of a soaring mountainous mass. Triangular slopes of scree slide into the fluvium and vertical formations of rock rise from under it. No longer are there banks, just a blunt meeting of water and land. Far above, one might spy the ragged thread of a mule caravan making its perilous way along a groove in the cliff. At this stage, the river picks up speed and rapids start forming, and further on, the gorge opens out for about

1640 ft. (500 m) and then promptly reconverges, squeezing the effluence into a six-metre gap with sheer rock walls on both sides. Forced into the mouth of the narrow opening the water works up swirls and boils, riding up the walls. This is one of the most exciting sections of the river trip. Shortly thereafter, the walls recede to reveal a scenic spot by a waterfall. The gorge continues, as the River flows over a visually spellbinding section with an archetypal ochre Zanskar mountain rising behind. As it exits the gorge, it is joined by the Markha River, and the first signs of settlements appear; Chiling, on its banks, is a village of traditional goldsmiths and metal workers. Not much lower downstream, it joins the Indus as its largest tributary in India.

Top left: A frescoed wooden capital in Karsha monastery. Below: Gorge of the Zanskar. Facing page: The stream flows through the Zanskar Valley.

ASIA

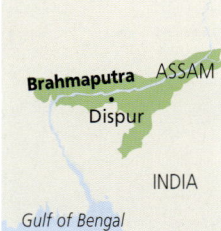

Son of Brahma, the Creator
The Brahmaputra is India's only "male" river

State and capital:
Arunachal Pradesh, Itanagar; Assam, Dispur

Convenient access:
Road to Tuting, Pasighat (AP), Tezpur, Guwahati, Dibrugarh and other towns (Assam), air to Itanagar (AP), Tezpur, Guwahati, Dibrugarh (Assam), rail to Dibrugarh, Guwahati

Accommodation:
Budget in AP; midrange in Dibrugarh, high-end in Guwahati

Best season:
November to March

A river that tracks 1,790 miles (2,880 km) through three countries, providing sustenance to people of three of the world's great religions—Buddhism, Hinduism and Islam—apart from ancient animistic faiths, has to have a plural identity. Thus, the glacial trickle of the Brahmaputra's source, near the legendary Mt. Kailash, in the Tibetan mountains, christened Tamchok Khambab or the Celestial Horse's Mouth becomes the Tsang Po (Great River) in eastern Tibet. Descending off the plateau, it storms into Arunachal Pradesh, in India's extreme northeast, as the Dihang or Siang.

Up to the 1930s, Arunachal Pradesh, known as an inaccessible and inhospitable land of leech-infested rainforests and unfriendly tribals, held attraction only for intrepid ethnologists and botanists. Cutting through its green tangle, the blue-green Siang pools and drops, forming massive rapids that offer one of the world's most exhilarating white-water trips. Over these restless waters, the sun-moon worshipping Adi tribals have thrown swinging rope bridges, sometimes with large gaps between foot planks. Hillocks of logs and mangled trees, torn out of the hillsides with powerful flash floods, are often found piled along the banks. More picturesquely, the forest breaks to create occasional pristine beaches, under the rocks of which live beetles eaten raw as a delicacy by the tribals.

Majuli is the largest island of silt

Already wide and deep for a mountain stream, the River breaks into the plains at Pasighat and enters Assam. Assuming its most famous identity—Brahmaputra, Son of the Creator—it rapidly acquires an immensity best appreciated from an aircraft over Dibrugarh or Guwahati, the gateways to this region. Below, the heavily braided, widespread course seems like many rivers and the vast swathes of silt are unending islands rather than mere sandbanks. This scale is not always evident while on a river ferry, for often the craft noses into channels to avoid treacherous shallows. From these sub-streams, what seems to be the River's true edge is actually a big island; beyond it, there is another channel, and another sandbank, sometimes up to a dozen such fluvial features. During the monsoon, of course, all of this is consumed and the River literally becomes a mind-boggling sea, making inroads kilometres inland, so that only a horizon of water is in sight. Because of the destruction caused, it is also referred to as the Sorrow of Assam.

Island formation reaches its zenith with Majuli, the world's largest riverine atoll. At 340 square miles (880 km^2), it is large enough to carry a population of people spread over 155 villages, and even boasts its own capital at Garmur. Majuli is especially visited for its monasteries. Established by the poet-philosopher Sankardeva in the 15th century as a seat of Hindu Vaishnavite learning, the institution of satra (monastery) is alive today in 22 centers scattered across the Island. These are rich repositories of traditional classical culture, including dance, music, art, and antique handicrafts.

Flowing past sanctuaries and historic towns

India's only "male" river nourishes a formidable ecology—22,239 square miles (56,700 km²) of tropical and sub-tropical moist, broad-leaved forests flourishing in its basin have been designated a distinct eco-region. Visible on misty, low hills in the distance, and often creeping right up to the banks, 12 of these tracts have been protected as sanctuaries and national parks. Beginning upstream with Dibru Saikhowa National Park—grazing ground of the feral horse—these include Pobha and Gorompani Wildlife Sanctuaries; Kaziranga and Nameri National Parks; Laokhuwa, Orang and Pobitora Wildlife Sanctuaries, and Manas National Park, a World Heritage Site.

Towns steeped in history pass by: at Tezpur is the 1,500-year-old Da Parbatia Temple, Assam's finest and oldest example of sculptural art; Guwahati is most famous for the Kamakhya shrine, an ancient tantric seat where the deity is a manifestation of Shakti.

*Left: The Brahmaputra or Siang in Arunachal Pradesh; the pool-drop character of the stream is clearly visible in this view.
Adi tribals of the Siang valley have a strong martial tradition. Their bamboo shields and helmets are strong enough to withstand the full-blooded blow of a dao.
Above: On the floodplains of Assam, the River meanders around huge islands of silt.*

ASIA

Thunder and spray

These South Indian waterfalls are a spectacle to behold

States and capitals:
Karnataka, Bengaluru; Tamil Nadu, Chennai

Convenient access:
Road to Hogenakkal, Jog, Sivasamudra, rail to Shimoga (Jog), Bengaluru (Sivasamudra, Hogenakkal), air to Mangalore (Jog), Bengaluru (Sivasamudra, Hogenakkal)

Accommodation:
Budget to midrange (Hogenakkal); Budget (Jog and Unchalli); none (Sivasamudra)

Best season:
July-August (for high water volume); otherwise November to March

Blessed with an immense network of rivers, India has its fair share of waterfalls. Contrary to what one would except, many of these are not on Himalayan streams but are created by rivers of the southern peninsula, flowing off the relatively low up-lands of the Eastern and Western Ghats. Some of the more notable ones are Hogenekkal, Jog, Siva-samudram and Unchalli Falls.

Hogenekkal Falls are situated at an isolated location at the confluence of the Chinar and Kaveri Rivers, with only a little village sharing the space. From its origins in the Kodagu region of Karnataka, the Kaveri makes its way to the neighbouring state of Tamil Nadu, weaving in and out of forests and open areas, finally tumbling down in a series of voluminous cataracts at the village of Hogenekkal—the name itself means "Smoky Rocks" after the misty spray created by the cascading water slamming onto the rocks below—near the town of Dharmapuri. With a drop of only 66 feet (20 m), this cataract may not be very high, but it is one of the most picturesque.

Besides standing aside and viewing them, one can journey up close to the base of the Falls. Before it crashes down in masses of white water, the Kaveri spreads over alternating shallow rocky land and deep stretches with strong currents, as it meanders around small islands interspersed with wooded tracts and unusually patterned boulders. Local boatmen take visitors in traditionally crafted circular coracles known as "parisals," which are essentially made of light wicker frames with buffalo hide stretched over to keep it waterproof. Everyone wades through the shallow segments of the river while the boatman carries the coracle over his shoulder, only to set it down once there is sufficient depth in the water for everyone to climb back on again. Initially, the coracle is taken near to the edge of the first of the two main waterfall levels accessible by boat. From here one can see the cascade from above and is within range of the sprays. The roar is thunderous and the views spectacular. If the river isn't in spate, the boatman may decide to take the passengers to the section below, bringing them as close as safety permits. As the proximity increases, so does the turbulence. Along the banks women sell freshly fried fish, masseurs with oils and powders offer their services under shady canopies, and village children dive into the waters for a price.

As the Kaveri approaches the forested hills and lush valleys surrounding the tiny island town of Sivasamudra in Karnataka, it segregates into two channels, which tumble as a series of cascades, 2,785 feet (849 m) wide and 295 feet (90 m) high. These are the Sivasamudram Falls near a group of ancient temples. Pristine but not easily accessible up close, the Falls widen to about 984 feet (300 m) during the monsoon.

The four streams of Jog Falls

In Shimoga district of Karnataka, the Sharavathi River creates the spectacular Jog Falls (830 ft./253 m at their highest), one of the highest in India. At the place it drops, the river splits itself into four separate streams, each of which has been named for their individual characteristics. They are Raja (King), for its serene countenance; Roarer, as it is the loudest section of the Falls; Rocket, owing to the huge volume of water that shoots out from a small opening; and Rani (Queen), named so for the twisting and turning trajectory that is taken to resemble the graceful movement associated with royalty.

Unchalli Falls, originally called Lushington Falls after the British Collector who discovered them in 1845, are the most difficult to get to. Plummeting 381 ft. (116 m) off the top end, they lie on the Aghanashini River, near the town of Sirsi, and are accessible only by a three-mile (km) trek.

The single-drop Jog Falls in the monsoon. At its peak in late monsoon, the Sharavathi River pushes water up to 120,000 cubic feet (3,400 cubic meters) per second down the cataract.

ASIA

Lijiang River
Passionate and dreamlike water

Location:
Lijiang lies between Guilin and Yangshuo, in Guangxi province.

Climate:
The area belongs to the mid-Asian tropical moist monsoon climate. It is temperate with plentiful rainfall. There is a saying about it: "Three winters without snow, four seasons with flowers throughout."

Special interest:
With its elegant mountains and charming waters, this is typical karst topography.

Main attractions:
Dragons playing with Water, the Gongs and Drums Yuanyang shoal, Elephant Trunk Hill, Paintings Hill, Jianshan carvings, and many more.

Scenery of Xingping, recognized as the most beautiful part of the Lijiang River (right)

Huangbu shoal (Yellow Cloth shoal), Lijiang River (below)

Sailing down the winding Lijiang River, you might suddenly think of the verses written by He Jingzhi, a modern poet of China: "Gods in clouds, Immortals in fogs, Divine posture of Mountains in Guilin! So passionate, and so dreamlike, You waters of Lijiang!" Xu Xiake, a traveler of the Ming dynasty, once took a journey from Guilin to Yangshuo. Greatly fascinated by what he saw, he said, "Here is a world of green lotus and jade bamboo." By boat, one can fully enjoy the graceful and touching landscape of Lijiang River.

Lijiang River is part of the Zhujiang water system, originating in the Cat Mountain (Maoer Shan) of Xinan county, to the north of Guilin city. Within the boundaries of Xinan county there is a canal that was dug in the Qing dynasty. The first one of its kind in China, it is called the Xinanling Canal. It is at this point that the Xiangjiang River runs northward, while the Lijiang runs southward. Called "the diverging point of Xiang and Li," the Lijiang River gets its name from this phenomenon. Li in Chinese also means "lucid" and "transparent." The Lijiang River is like a sparkling, sinuous jade band, there being shallows at every bend. Some have counted the number of shoals in the river from Guilin to Yangshuo. They amount to 3,605 in the 52 miles (83km) of waterway. The water at both ends of each shoal is shallow, producing a gurgling sound as it flows – like celestial music in a heavenly palace.

The visitor can take a boat down from Guilin to Yangshuo to enjoy the 52 miles (83km) of river landscape of Lijiang River. This is a typical area of karst topography. Here you can see the numerous ridges and peaks, and their reflections in the ever flowing blue water. It is like making your way through a hundred-mile (160 km) long spectacular art gallery. The reflections have their own special charm, hazy and swaying. The mountains in the water seem clear compared with the real ones, and it seems as though they flow together with the water. When tourists go boating on the ever winding Lijiang River, they can enjoy the landscape from different angles, each of which presents a picturesque scene. On arriving at the Zhulin scenic point, see along the precipices the stalactites hang down from above, gigantic as well as imposing, looking like dragons bending down and drinking the water. After that you come to Yangdi scenic point, and there you can see the lofty mountains and the floating clouds. Yangdi is a place that offers urbanites the opportunity to enjoy moments of leisure and to experience a carefree state of mind.

In the imposing mountainous chain, there is a set of eight peaks that very much resemble the Eight Immortals of ancient Chinese myth. Further on, there is another peak coming up, long and big, across the Lijiang River. It has the appearance of a carp, and on its back stands a small hill somewhat like a fin. Local people call it "Carp going against the River." Traveling along the Lijiang River, tourists not only appreciate the beautiful mountains, they also relish the roaring waterfalls, the flowing streams, the dangerous shoals, and the bamboo forests.

The Paintings Hill is a sheer cliff that features shades of different colors. Seen from a distance, the precipice seems to present a picture with faintly discernible horses. Tourists are invited to count the number of horses. It seems that no one is able to give the exact answer.

When traveling by boat along the Lijiang River, you will feel as if the scenery is sliding by too swiftly to allow you to catch sight of everything you want to see. Eventually you reach your destination, Yangshuo. As the old saying goes, "Guilin's landscapes are the finest under heaven, but Yangshuo's landscapes are even finer than Guilin's." From the Green Lotus peak (Bilian Feng), it's possible to get a bird's eye view of Lijiang River, embracing the Lijiang scenery. At Yangshuo, you seem to draw to a perfect stop on your journey. Halfway up the Green Lotus peak, there is a scenic path. Along this path, you can enjoy the unique landscape of Yangshuo, as well as the scattering of farmhouses and the ancient carvings on the precipices.

ASIA

Hukou Falls, Shanxi

The Yellow River rushes down from the sky

Location:
Hukou Falls are situated at the junction of Shanxi and Shaanxi provinces, about 138 miles (220km) from Ya-n'an.

Climate:
Shanxin has cold winters and hot summers. The best time to visit is from April to October. You need to be careful about windy and dusty weather and avoid becoming sunburned.

Special interest:
Hukou Falls, the greatest waterfall in the Yellow River, are second only to Huangguoshu Falls in Guizhou province.

Main attractions:
The roaring of the Yellow River at Hukou, and local customs and conditions.

"Do you not see the Yellow River come from the sky?" This is the first line of the lyrical poem by Li Bai (701–762 AD), a great Chinese poet of the Tang dynasty, who could not have written it without having been to the falls at Hukou Mountain. The Yellow River, known as the mother river of the Chinese nation, has remained the symbol of Chinese civilization and the national spirit.

The waterfalls at Hukou are cited as one of the national scenic areas. Going southward across the Central Shanxi Plain and passing through high mountains to Jixian county, you will find the Yellow River at the juncture of Shanxi and Shaanxi provinces. The Grand Shanxi–Shaanxi Gorge is the natural passage changing the Yellow River's east–west flow direction to a south–north one, which is a rare situation since almost all rivers in China flow eastward. The Yellow River, with its more than four thousand tributaries, originates in the plateau at Qinghai, and runs all the way across Sichuan province, Gansu province, and Ningxia Hui Autonomous Region down to Hekou town in Inner Mongolia. Blocked by Lvliang Mountain, the river turns abruptly to the south, roaring through the Grand Gorge into Hukou, where – owing to the sudden narrowing of the watercourse from over 884 ft (300m) to only 164 ft (50m) – it rushes 98 ft (30m) down below.

Legend has it that the formation of the falls is thanks to Yu the Great, who managed to tame the Yellow River from causing floods, by opening up the course at Hukou, Mengmen, and Longmen, and diverting the water to tributaries. That gave rise to a lot of traditional stories about Yu the Great, in whose honor many temples and shrines were set up.

Having seen the spectacular scene of the falls at Hukou, you will be aware of their remote antiquity, perhaps while cherishing lofty aspirations and becoming broad minded and in harmony with the great Yellow River, which Li Bai tells us comes from the sky.

Invitation To Wine

Do you not see the Yellow River come from the sky
Rushing into the sea and ne'er come back?
Do you not see the mirrors bright in chambers high
Grieve o'er your snow-white hair though once it was silk-black?
When hopes are won, oh! Drink your fill in high delight.
And never leave your wine-cup empty in moonlight!

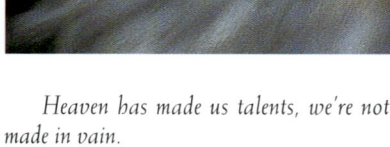

The Hukou Falls (center)

The Yellow River in force at Hukou Falls (opposite)

The impressive scenery of the river at Hukou Falls, like a stone trough

Heaven has made us talents, we're not made in vain.
A thousand gold coins spent, more will turn up again.
Kill a cow, cook a sheep and let us merry be.
And drink three hundred cupfuls of wine in high glee!
Dear friends of mine,
Cheer up, cheer up!
I invite you to wine.
Do not put down your cup!
I will sing you're a song, please hear,
O hear! Lend me a willing ear!
What difference will rare and costly dishes make?
I only want to get drunk and never to wake.
How many great men were forgotten through the ages?
But great drinkers are more famous than sober sages.
The Prince of Poets feast'd in his palace at will,
Drank wine at ten thousand a cask and laughed his fill.
A host should not complain of money he is shot,

To drink with you I will sell things of any sort.
My fur coat worth a thousand coins of gold
And my flower dappled horse may be sold
To buy good wine that we may drown the woes age old.

ASIA

Luguhu Lake

Where a matriarchal community exists

Location:
Luguhu Lake is situated in the Ninglang Yi Autonomous County, Yunnan province. It is at the juncture of Sichuan province and Yunnan province, on the Dianxibei Plateau.

Climate:
Luguhu Lake area is cool in summer and warm in winter, owing to the surrounding mountains and the big lake. Its annual average temperature is less than 68°F (20°C), with not a great deal of rainfall all the year round. The best touring seasons are spring and summer.

Features:
The Mosuo people are said to be the only group around Luguhu Lake who still live in a matriarchal community.

Highlights:
Luguhu Lake, the Mosuo people around the lake, three islands in the lake, the Yongning hot spring, and the Zhameishi Temple.

Situated in the northwest of Yunnan province and covering an area of 19 square miles (50 km2) with an average depth of 295 ft (90m), Luguhu Lake has very long, serpentine banks dotted with numerous islands. The area near the lake is remarkably different from the outside world, in that the local people maintain a matriarchal tradition to this day.

These people are called the Mosuo, and are perhaps the last matriarchal community in the world. There are many special customs among the Mosuo people. They are very different from other communities with regard to such things as clothing, food, housing, and transportation. One unique feature is that they still have primitive marriage rites called zouhun. These have added a somewhat mysterious luster and atmosphere to the region, which has long been regarded in the East as the Kingdom of Girls.

The kingdom is characterized by tenderness and love. The Mosuo attach the utmost respect and importance to mothers and girls. The most striking feature lies in the fact that a big family is built up and strengthened by maternal blood ties, not the usual paternal ones. It is the grandmother that presides over family affairs and has the final word in every important thing. What is more, the significant family members are the daughters, while sons are regarded as uncles to nephews and nieces. In addition, women are dominant in such aspects as farming and community affairs.

Perhaps the most interesting is the zouhun ("walking marriage"). A man and woman do not marry and live under the same roof. If a man is attracted to a girl, it is customary for him to walk to her house in the still of night, perhaps after making some overtures to her in advance, and have a heart-to-heart talk with her. If everything goes smoothly, he is allowed to stay overnight, leaving before daybreak.

In practice, both men and women attach a greet deal to love. They are free to continue their relationship or to continue on their own in that they live in their respective mothers' houses. However, once their relationship is settled, they remain loyal to each other. If their relationship produces a baby, the baby naturally belongs to the woman, who takes on the responsibility of caring for the child and bringing it up.

No matchmaker or parent is ever involved in these arrangements. In the community very few disputes occur. Villagers are friendly and kind hearted, and have a calm attitude toward people and things around.

In addition to the local customs, which make this ancient land charming and mysterious, the natural scenery is eyecatching.

In the Kingdom of Girls you can take a boat on the lake and visit the Mosuo villages nearby. The log cabins and the compound courtyards are worth touring. Besides, it gives you a good opportunity to observe zouhun in practice. You may consult the local people if you are interested in the folklore as well.

There is a village called Luoshui on the west bank of the lake. It is a typical scenic spot with a primitive landscape, and it is a must-see place, accessible thanks to easy transportation and its convenient location.

Another attraction is Yongning, 12.5 miles (20km) north of Luoshui village. There you may visit the Zhameishi Temple and the Yongning hot spring, where you have the chance to learn about the daily life, history, religion, culture, and folk art of these people.

A distant view of Luguhu Lake (above, right)

The spring scenery of Luguhu Lake

A unique local boat, just like an eating trough used by pigs (center)

A Mosuo woman standing by Luguhu Lake (far right)

148

ASIA

Mapang Yumco, Tibet

A forever invincible jade lake

Location:
Mapang Yumco is located within Burang county in Ngari district, at the foot of Kangdese peak, and has an area of more than 154 square miles (400 square kilometers).

Climate:
Ngari district is located in the west of Tibet, at an average elevation of 14,764 ft (4500m) above sea level. The weather in this rugged natural environment is variable.

Special interest:
Mapang Yumco is one of the highest freshwater lakes in the world.

Main attractions:
Pilgrims come to take a ritual walk round the holy lake, traveling clockwise. The perimeter of the holy lake is about 38 miles (60km), and this takes two days to complete.

Mapang Yumco is the name of a holy lake. It is at an elevation of 14,435 ft (4400m), and is one of the highest freshwater lakes in the world.

Mapang Yumco is located within Burang County, Ngari District, at the foot of Kangdese peak (Mansarovar), with an area of 154 square miles (400 square kilometers).

In the Tibetan language, "Mapang Yumco" means "forever invincible jade lake." The title can be traced back to the time of a famous religious war which happened near the lake in the eleventh century. The result was that the Gagyu Sect of Tibetan Buddhism defeated paganism decisively. The title of the lake reflects their overwhelming victory.

The vast, tranquil, and transparent lake is now deemed a holy lake by devotees of several of the world's religions, and it is one of the most renowned lakes in Asia. In many ancient Buddhist sutras the lake was referred to as "King of the Holy Lakes." And according to the earlier Bon religion, Mapang Yumco is the palace of a holy dragon that has a man's body and the head of either a snake or a horse. In many ancient murals, the lake is depicted as a fairy maiden with a girl's head and a fish's tail.

Mapang Yumco is encircled by snowy mountains on three sides. The mountains are precipitous, craggy, and dazzlingly white, while the water of the lake is so blue. The reason for the color is the unfathomable depth of the water. Some say it is as much as 253 ft (77m) deep. The snowy mountains around are just like white jade, setting off the beauty of the lake. The water is absolutely still, without any sound of wind whistling and not even tiny waves on the surface. The unique surroundings and stately atmosphere leave a lasting impression.

In Indian mythology, Mapang Yumco Lake was conceived in the mind by the great god Brahma. His son needed a lake to bathe in after adopting asceticism in the divine mountains. Usually followers of Hinduism would bathe in the lake during their ritual worship. Tibetans make a similar walk round the lake, but differ from the Hindus in that they prostrate themselves instead of bathing.

It is said that the water in this lake can remove the five sufferings of the human mind. These are greed, madness, anger, laziness, and envy. It can remove dirt from the body, too. Bathing in the lake can clean a person's body and soul, build up their health, remove annoyance, and prolong life. A lot of followers of Buddha, come here to worship and bathe some time during summer and fall every year. After bathing, they often take some "holy water" back with them to give to their friends as a gift.

According to the monk Xuan Zhuang of the Tang dynasty, in his *Journey to the West* – written after he made his pilgrimage to India to find the Buddhist sutras – this lake is the abode of the immortals, and is associated with the fairy mother goddess. It has four bathing places, with Lotus Bathing Gate in the east, Sweet Bathing Gate in the south, Dirt Removal Gate in the west, and Belief Bathing Gate in the north. It has consistently been held by Buddhist pilgrims that taking the opportunity to bathe in this lake brings great fortune in life. Buddhists believe that Mapang Yumco is the nectar bestowed to human beings by the great god Chakrasamvara, and that it can cleanse our bodies as well as removing all kinds of vexation, annoyance, and improper thoughts from our souls. Drinking the water of the lake can get rid of numerous diseases and keep our bodies healthy. If pilgrims make the ritual walk around this lake, they obtain boundless benefits.

Mapang Yumco, the holy lake (top right)

The Chuguogongba Pagoda (adjacent)

An old Tibetan man standing beside Mapang Yumco Lake, watching the sun rising in the east (center, right)

Mani Piles beside Mapang Yumco Lake (below, right)

Besides its unusual significance for pilgrims, Mapang Yumco – the King of all the Holy Lakes – is such an outstanding scenic place that no-one can pass by without being affected. Even though they may not pay attention to the fascinating myths and legends associated with it, on account of its rare and pure beauty travelers will effectively prostrate themselves before it and may even feel it appropriate to worship it after their long and arduous journey.

ASIA

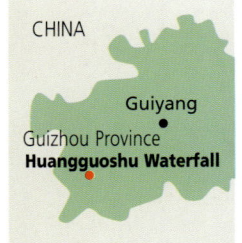

Huangguoshu Waterfall

Spectacular vistas

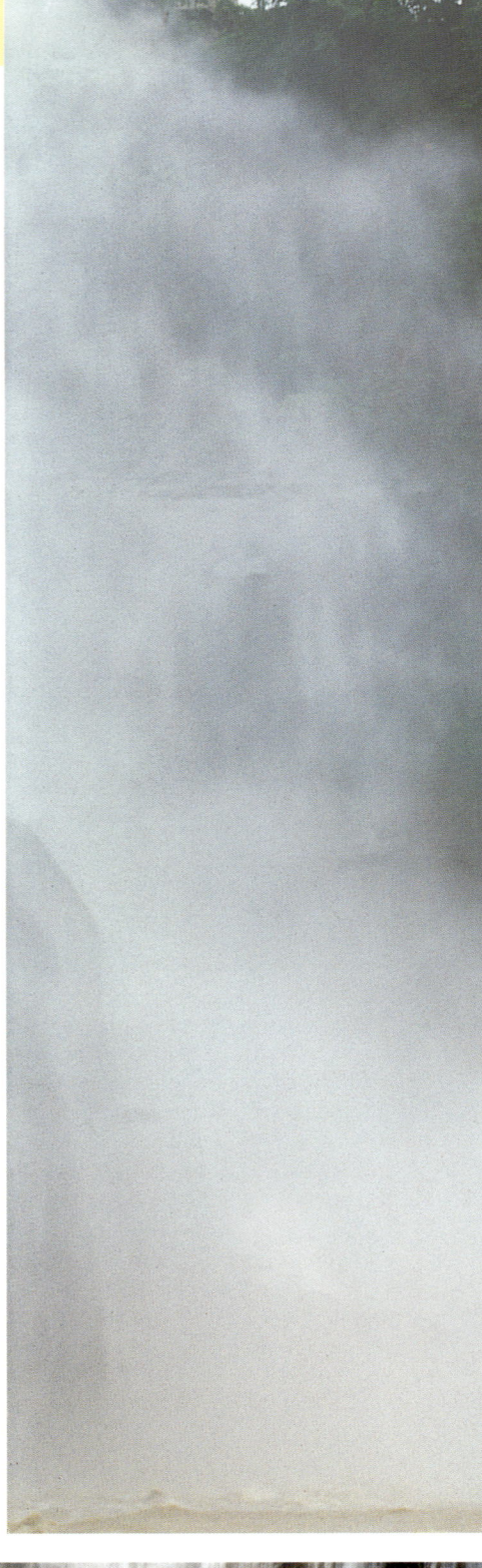

Location:
Huangguoshu Waterfall is located in Huangguoshu, in Zhenning Bouyei and Miao Nationalities Autonomous County, 28 miles (45km) southwest of Anshun city in Guizhou province. It is 94 miles (150km) from Guiyang, the capital of the province.

Climate:
The area has a subtropical climate, with a clear temperature contrast between the four seasons, but no extremes of cold in winter nor of heat in summer. There is plentiful rainfall.

Special interest:
There are dozens of waterfalls above and under ground, and the gorgeous Tianxing Garden to be seen.

Main attractions:
Waterfall cluster, Water Curtain Cave, Tianxing Bridge Stone Forest, Tianxing Cave, and many more.

As the legend goes, Huangguoshu Waterfall pours down directly from the Milky Way in the highest heavens.

The story is that while falling, the main part of the Milky Way becomes the major waterfall, the splashing parts are turned to a cluster of small waterfalls, and the stars falling together are changed into glittering stones, ponds, grasslands and trees, bridges and caves.

In Zhenning Bouyei and Miao Nationalities Autonomous County, 28 miles (45km) southwest of Anshun, the Baishui River rushes furiously all the way to Huangguoshu and suddenly breaks, creating this wonderful sight. Down the Rhinoceros Pool from high above, with thunderous roars that can be heard far away – as if the Yangtze River were truly being poured down from heaven – nature offers a masterpiece to the visitor. Huangguoshu Waterfall is traditionally compared to a white dragon. It dashes out from its heavenly palace, down to a deep pool resembling a rhinoceros that is leisurely enjoying its view of the moon. When the dragon runs into the rhinoceros, the latter becomes so angry that it stirs the water of the pool completely upside down and produces terrible howls. It offers kaleidoscopic views, causing confusion and fascination.

The original name of Huangguoshu Waterfall was Baishuiquan Waterfall. It has acquired its present name from the yellow fruit called the huangguo that grows here in abundance. With regard to geological features, this is typical karst topography.

A mountain building phase of ten thousand years ago created the rupture in the rocks that accounts for the local configuration. Presented here is a main fall that is 243 ft (74m) high and 266 ft (81m) wide, with dozens of other falls scattered around, some visible and others invisible. It is rare, both here in China and elsewhere in the world, to see such a concentrated cluster of waterfalls in one area. The falls have a plentiful supply of water all through the year, the average fall being 35,100 cubic feet (1000 cubic meters) per second at a speed of 56 ft (17m) per second. You can feel the tremendous momentum even from a distance. Even when you are as far as half a mile (1000m) away, and separated from the falls by the river and the forest, you are affected by it. As soon as you enter the gateway to the scenery, you hear the deafening roar, like continuous thunder. You will certainly feel excited, for you know that after taking a turn around the hill at the front and behind the thick forest, you will immediately begin to experience the wonders ahead of you. Here is revealed the power of nature that works wonders throughout the universe, and that for long ages peo-

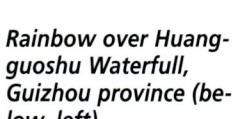

Rainbow over Huangguoshu Waterfull, Guizhou province (below, left)

The Longgong scenic area (above, right)

Huangguoshu Waterfall, like the Milky Way pouring down directly from the heavens (below, right)

152

ple have worshiped and marveled at. The surrounding air is so damp that it seems as if water is coming out of your hands, and you find that cool water beads are unexpectedly hanging down from your hair and your eyebrows.

Xu Xiake, a famous traveler of the Ming dynasty, once offered a splendid description of Huangguoshu Waterfall: "A giant cloth is flying down with stones like lotus leaves covering three caves, like curtains of silk and satin, splashing pearls and jade, glistening in a torrent of foam."

Huangguoshu Waterfall comprises three main scenic features: the waterfalls themselves, the Water Curtain Cave, and the Rhinoceros Pool. Every summer when the river floods, the abundant water crashes down with a sound like hordes of troops and horses marching forward, and the sound flows out to the surrounding area.

Then there is the extensive Water Curtain Cave, which seems to hide itself behind the waterfalls, with drapes of anonymous creeping and climbing plants hanging down over its entrance. Inside the cave, you can watch the waterfall sweeping down and you become aware of the dangers. The Water Curtain Cave is a limestone structure, and it lends great charm to the scene. Still another marvel is the Rhinoceros Pool. Here there are in fact two pools. The one on the left is 57 ft (17.5m) deep, and the one on the right is 50 ft (15.2m) deep. The snow-white water of the falls dashes down to the bottom of the two deep green pools, then rises up again angrily, scampering out through the deep valley like a multitude of silver snakes.

After coming out from the Water Curtain Cave and passing by the Rhinoceros Pool, you climb up the mountain slopes opposite and the mountain ranges and the fog-veiled green forests are before you, and the scale of your surroundings opens up your mind. On a fine day in summer, you can see rainbows appearing through the mist.

ASIA

A paradise for wildlife

Kushiro National Park, on Hokkaido Island, is home to the legendary red-crested cranes

Getting there:
The National Park extends from the suburbs of Kushiro. Road, bus, and rail links from Kushiro; airport at Kushiro

Where to stay:
Hotels in Kushiro; camping site within the Park near Takkobu Marsh

Climate:
Sub-arctic climate, mean annual temperature 41°–43°F (5°– to 6°C). Frequently foggy in summer; cold with some snow in winter

Main attractions:
Tsurui Observatory; Onnenai Visitor Center; Wildlife Center; Natural History Museum; Japanese Crane Conservation Area with winter feeding stations; observation areas at Hokuto, Hosooka, Kottaro Marsh (3), Sarubo between Lake Toro, and Shiratoro Marsh

Just 3 miles (5km) away from Kushiro, the island's capital, in the southeastern corner of Hokkaido in northern Japan, is an area of marshland that is home to the world's most significant population of red-crested cranes. These majestic white birds with black and gray trim on their faces and throats and their scarlet caps are on the list of internationally endangered species. Fortunately, however, their numbers are slowly recovering and 1,000 of them now live and breed in Kushiro National Park, an area of some 104 square miles (270km2). This represents one third of the world population of these birds. For centuries, red-crested cranes have been a national symbol of long life and prosperity, yet very few Japanese are actually likely ever to have seen one.

Eighty years ago, the "tancho," or "red crest," as the cranes were known in the Land of the Rising Sun, teetered on the verge of extinction. Towards the end of the nineteenth century, Hokkaido began developing rapidly into a heavily populated, industrial island. The cranes were thought to have vanished from the region, but in 1924 a hunter discovered one of these symbolic birds in the marshes. A thorough search ensued, resulting in a dozen of these spectacular birds being found in other remote parts of the marshes. This marked the start of an unprecedented rescue program to save these birds from extinction. Following some particularly severe snow storms in 1952, which left many of them on the brink of starvation, local residents undertook to feed the cranes with grain until they had recovered their strength. Each winter, 200 birds still visit the feeding grounds at the Tsurui crane observatory, where visitors are rewarded with a close-up view of these magnificent creatures.

The swamps of Kushiro Park also provide a refuge for many other species of bird. European sea eagles come here to breed and, in winter, the marshes provide a home for the Steller's sea eagle from Kamchatka and Sachalin. The rare Japanese fish owl also breeds in this protected area.

Lakes and swamps

Kushiro National Park, measuring some 70 square miles (180km2), protects Japan's largest marsh, the sweeping bends of the Kushiro River and its tributaries as it meanders across the plains at the foot of the Oakan and Meakan mountains. The Park encompasses Lake Toro, the Shirarutoro Marsh, Takkobu Swamp, and the surrounding low hills as well. Almost 30 square miles (80km2) of Japan's last remnant of surviving swampland have been placed under special protection as a significant wetland area.

In the center of this vast wetland environment are a few scattered areas of ancient high moorland and, to the east, three large, freshwater lakes. This seemingly endless expanse of wetland, populated by turf and mosses, reeds, and sedge, began forming 4,000 years ago while it was still a bay on the shores of the Pacific Ocean. Sea currents and waves created shallows and the constant winds continued the process by forming sand dunes, which eventually blocked off the bay from the sea altogether.

There are even alder woods growing around the hills. The rainwater runoff deposits considerable amounts of nutrients in these areas so that alders can grow to heights of around 32ft (10m) in some cases. By contrast, trees growing in the much poorer soils of the open moor reach 16ft (5m) in height at most. Usually, alders sprout several trees from a single root system. Once they have reached their optimum height they die, by which time some of the new shoots will have developed into trees themselves.

Unspoiled nature

For thousands of years, nature remained completely undisturbed on Hokkaido Island. It was not until 1870, when 537 Japanese immigrants came to settle in what is now the city of Kushiro, that the island began its rapid development. More than 2,000 different varieties of plant and animal life still exist in the region's marshes and waters, many of which are rare species.

The Siberian salamander, for example, which is fairly common in other parts of Asia, only occurs in Japan's Kushiro Marsh. It has only recently been discovered that this reptile's main distribution area actually lies just outside the Park's boundaries so that it is still at risk from agriculture and industry. Similarly, the region contains Japan's last remaining population of the mosaic damselfly, a wonderful species of dragonfly whose limited habitat is restricted to high moorland.

Low hills surround the moors and marshes of Takkobu area. Unusual grasses produce a colorful landscape

ASIA

Getting there:
Good roads from Hanoi to Halong. Bus and helicopter connections

Where to stay:
The town of Ha Long offers a wide choice of all types of accommodation

Climate:
Hot and humid tropical climate

Main attractions:
Boat trips on Halong Bay, including stops at some of the grottoes and floating villages

Land of rocks and water

A coastal bay National Park: Ha Long cliffs in Vietnam are a stunning natural spectacle

Possibly no other bay on earth presents as magnificent a sight as Halong Bay near Hong Gai, southeast of Hanoi on the Gulf of Tonkin. Halong Bay's tranquil waters are dotted with hundreds of islands and islets, jutting dramatically out of the sea to heights of 330–660ft (100–200m). The entire area is strewn with bizarre, jagged limestone rock formations, which have been sculpted into fantastic shapes by thousands of years of wind and weather erosion. These strange shapes are individually named: for example, the Pencil, the Saddle, the Junk Sail, the Bat, Fighting Cocks, the Turtle, the Buffalo, and many others are named after spirits. The majority of the 1,600 or possibly even 3,000 islands are uninhabitable, since their steep cliffs are impossible to climb. Along the water line, where the tides eat away at the limestone, deep grottoes have been hollowed out. The clefts, overhangs, and summits of these stone giants and rocky pillars are populated by green jungle plants. The larger islands, such as Ba Mun and Cat Ba, support undisturbed, pristine tropical rainforests. The area's inaccessibility has safeguarded a unique and rare ecosystem that remains largely untouched.

Bamboo-covered boats

The approximately 300 families in Ha Long National Park have lived here for generations, living on the water in bamboo-covered boats or, more recently, in floating houses. The largest of these floating villages is To Bo Nau, located right in the middle of the bay. These people are fishing folk, but some of them have learned how to breed all kinds of exotic marine life in cages beneath their houses: rock lobsters, for example, which they sell directly to the many passing tourist boats full of visitors from all over the world.

Although the bay has never been heavily populated, traces of the Hoa Binh culture were found in archeological remains discovered on Giap Khau Island (Hon Gai). During the Stone Age, this region was home to the Ha Long, a unique culture that had no equivalent on the mainland. Archeological evidence testifying to this was found on the islands of Tuan Chau, Ngoc Vung, Cai Dam, Dong Naim, and Cat Ba. Cave findings testify to an earlier culture, known as the Soi Nhu, which evolved in this area perhaps 25,000 years ago. These people were followed 7,000 to 5,000 years ago by the Cai Beo culture, which mastered the technique of pottery making and paved the way for the Ha Long. Evidence of their presence can sometimes be found on the beaches of isolated bays and in the limestone mountains. The early Ha Long people were still predominantly land dwellers, occupying the dry, flat land between the bizarre peaks of the limestone mountains until the sea rose and covered the region. Nowadays, Ha Long Bay is home to altogether 21 different ethnic groups.

Whenever a tropical cyclone threatens to blow in off the South China Sea, the boat folk seek refuge in the large grottoes and tunnels that the rain has gouged out of the soft rock. Many grottoes lead through to circular lakes nestled in the center of karst islands, snugly sheltered thanks to their steep vertical rock walls. These are saltwater lakes, which are connected to the sea by underwater tunnels.

Colliding tectonic plates

The most spectacular grotto of all is Hang Dau Go, which consists of three giant caverns in whose deeply fissured walls nature has carved a variety of bizarre shapes. Sung Sot is as big as a cathedral. Stalactites, several feet in length, hang from its ceiling, shimmering in a rainbow of colors thanks to the atmospheric lighting and throwing mysterious shadows onto the craggy walls.

This stunningly breathtaking scenery of rock and water owes its existence to one of the most spectacular geological events in the earth's history, which took place around 50 million years ago approximately 1,250 miles (2,000km) northwest of Vietnam. It was then that the Indian subcontinent, which had split away from the supercontinent of Gondwana some 100 million years previously, collided with the Asian continental plate. Not only did this thrust the seabed between India and Asia upward to form the 29,500ft (9,000m) high Himalayas, but it also ripped apart the earth's crust all over southeast Asia, including the 3,300ft (1km) thick limestone plate of Halong Bay.

For millions of years, the tropical monsoons, with the help of wind and heat, then set to work on the exposed rock. As sea levels rose following the last Ice Age 7,000 to 8,000 years ago, the ocean slowly began laying claim to this remarkable and distinctive landscape of limestone pillars.

Ha Long region has been inhabited by people living on houseboats since time immemorial (above)

The traditional-style, bamboo-covered boats are gradually being replaced by more comfortable, wooden boats (below)

ASIA

Home to troops of frolicking monkeys

Ang Thong National Park is a unique island reserve with its own coral reef

Getting there:
Wide choice of package tours. Independent travelers: bus and rail links from Bangkok to Chumpon. Airport in the northwest of Ko Samui. Daily boat trips to the Marine National Park or by kayak

Where to stay:
Included in package tours. Independent travelers: wide range of hotel accommodation available out of season. Cabins and tents bookable via the park authorities in the Marine National Park.

Climate:
December to February around 86°F (30°C); March to June around 104°F (40°C) and high humidity levels. Monsoon season with daily downpours from July to November

Main attractions:
Beaches; Samui Everest viewpoint; Na Muang, Hin Lat, and Big Buddha waterfalls; butterfly garden; snake farm; aquarium; tiger zoo. Secret Buddha garden; mummified monk. Marine National Park with Tham Bua Bok cave, Tale Nai saltwater lake, coral reef near Ko Sam Sao, Had Chan Charat Beach, and viewing platform

Special tips:
Four-wheel-drive vehicles recommended for trips into the island's interior. Many routes impassable during the monsoon season

Endless palm forests and dense jungle cling to the steep slopes and ravines at the heart of the island of Ko Samui, which covers an area of 95 square miles (250km2) in the Gulf of Thailand, 20 miles (30km) off the mainland. The highest elevation is Khao Phlu. Its summit, rising to 2,100ft (640m), is hidden by a thick canopy of tropical rain forest in which primeval ferns and banana trees are interspersed with splashes of bright red hibiscus blossoms. The innumerable streams that spring from Khao Phlu teem with colorful tropical freshwater fish, while the shady valleys below are populated by coffee bushes and rubber trees.

The bays, surrounded by bizarre rock formations sculpted out of the steep, limestone cliffs, are edged with miles and miles of idyllic, white, sandy beaches.

Beneath the palm trees

Like its neighboring islands, Ko Phangan and Ko Tao, Ko Samui Island was formed during the cold, rainy Pleiocene period around 10 million years ago. It was during this period that a limestone plateau was pushed up from the seabed and finally emerged above the surface of the ocean. Wind and rain gradually eroded this plateau, leaving behind strange, steep, rocky columns and islands.

Ko Samui is Thailand's third largest island and exactly represents the stereotypical island paradise. Eighty percent of the 40,000 Thailanders that live here earn their living from Western tourists, who come here in search of peace, recreation, and relaxation. However, the view across the green hills and blue sea is not marred by any hotel buildings because none of the buildings are higher than the tops of the palm trees.

The most spectacular beaches are found along the north and east coasts, the most popular of which are Chaweng and Lamai. Families tend to seek out the quieter beaches of Bophut and Mae Nam. Chaweng beach, which stretches for 4 miles (6km) along the coast, is considered the island's most beautiful beach.

Intrepid snorkelers are rewarded with a breathtaking glimpse of the colorful underwater world that surrounds a coral reef. The flora and fauna here are similar to that found on all Thailand's other reefs, although the colorful coral fish are not quite so common here.

South of Lamai Beach, nature has sculpted two extremely erotic male and female forms into the cliffs between the villages of Ban Hua Thanon and Ban Lamai, known as Hin Ta and Hin Yai, the phallus-like "Grandfather" and "Grandmother" rock formations. This area is a popular holiday destination, particularly for native holidaymakers.

Above the beach, a concrete road leads to two unusual waterfalls, the 60ft (18m) high Na Muang 1 and Na Muang 2, which plummet with a deafening roar through a series of cascades 260ft (80m) down into a lake which can only be reached from Na Muang 1 by way of a steep natural staircase of rock and tree roots. These spectacular cascades were formed as the result of calcium encrustations left by mosses that form a thick carpet over the damp cliffs and deposit calcium sediments in the water, thereby accumulating layer upon layer of porous, calcareous tufa, which creates an ever-increasing number of barriers and small terraces. These tufa formations grow about three-quarters of an inch to an inch (two to three centimeters) each year.

Emerald-green saltwater lake

One of the most scenic waterfalls, only 13ft (4m) in height, lies very close to the island's capital of Na Thon. It can be reached only via a steep path, winding through an enchanting, dense forest of giant trees, fern fronds, and intertwined lianas. This landscape offers a glimpse of how Ko Samui looked before coconut palms were planted here.

A two-hour boat ride away is a miniature, fairytale world, consisting of 40 uninhabited islands strung out to the west of Ko Samui and known as the Ang Thong Marine National Park. Weirdly shaped cliffs overgrown with dense jungle vegetation and umbrella trees tower up out of the calm, azure-blue sea to heights of 1,300ft (400m).

Ko Surin Island, off the coast of Thailand, is a holiday paradise for tourists (right)

The Ang Thong islands remain uninhabited (above, left)

Waterfalls beneath a canopy of palm fronds are a common sight (below, left)

NORTH AMERICA

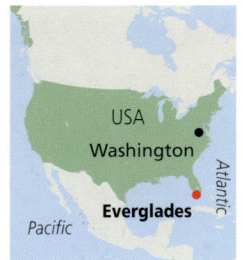

River of grass

The Everglades' landscape is a combination of mud flats, coastal prairie, and swampland

Getting there:
Nearest airports: Miami, Ft Lauderdale, and Ft Myers. The main entrance for motorists at Flamingo is well marked

Where to stay:
Three lodges, three camp sites, one camping ground out in the wilderness, accessible only by boat

Climate:
Rainy season from May to October with temperatures around 90°F (32°C). Hurricane season from June to November

Main attractions:
Boat (or canoe) trip from Flamingo, cable car trip from Shark Valley, hiking

Dense areas of saw grass grow in the swamps and flood lands (opposite)

An alligator (below, center) and two ibis (below, right) in search of food

A view across the wide expanse of arid coastal prairie (below, left)

The Indian name for the vast expanse of swamp known as the Everglades is "river of grass," an area where the waterways are filled with huge expanses of saw grass stretching as far as the eye can see. Flowing through this area of southern Florida, and unlikely to be noticed by any visitor, is one of the most unusual rivers on earth. It is 50–60 miles (80–100km) wide, but even during the summer rainy season measures no more than 12–36in (30–90cm) in depth.

The first spring thunderstorms signal the start of the rainy season in May and rainwater begins collecting in Lake Okeechobee in central Florida. This lake averages a depth of just 12ft (3.7m), yet covers an area of 730 square miles (1,900km2). After just a few days of rain, it overflows its banks, saturating the broad expanse of flood plains. In October, when the amount of rainfall decreases, the water level drops and during the dry months, the lake splits into numerous smaller lakes. The rhythm of the seasons and vast expanse of flood land have created several unique, yet extremely sensitive, habitats that the Everglades National Park in southern Florida, comprising an area of over 2,300 square miles (6,000km2), struggles to protect. However, as the National Park is not an island, immune from environmental influences, preservation is increasingly difficult. Fifty percent of the Everglades, an area that once covered the whole of southern Florida, has dried up, yet the burgeoning cities in the area are constantly increasing their demands for water. Flood protection systems installed on the tributaries feeding the National Park are intended to channel the river, yet it remains one of the most endangered natural oases on earth.

A variety of habitats

The Everglades are not simply a monotonous landscape of water and swamp that dries up for a couple of months each year. A range of totally different habitats co-exist here side by side, and yet are heavily dependent on one another. The water discharged by the "Sea of Grass" into Florida Bay, for example, is saline, producing an environment in which saw grass cannot grow. Instead, the seabed is carpeted with dense areas of seaweed, an essential nutrient in this part of the ecosystem. The tidal waters of the coastal lagoons and tributaries, however, are a combination of salt and freshwater, creating an ideal environment for dense thickets of red, black, and white mangroves. Their root systems provide nurseries for a variety of crabs and fish. Huge flocks of wading birds can also be seen on the mud flats at low water, searching for food.

Saline coastal prairie

Situated between the wading areas and the higher hinterland is the coastal prairie, a bone-dry area supporting plants that are capable of tolerating saline soil conditions. Only a few specialized desert plants thrive in the face of the extreme conditions here.

The saw grass has its main domain in the central section of this broad waterway, where the swamps are somewhat deeper and the water flows more quickly, if only at the rate of around 100ft (30m) a day.

The area is dotted with numerous islands, rising just one or two feet above the broad expanse of water, which support small areas of woodland including mahogany, swamp cypresses, royal palms, maple and fig trees and evergreen oaks. Further up, where the humidity level is higher beneath the dense tree canopy, there is a thriving population of ferns, orchids, and epiphytic plants.

The indigenous animal world rivals that of the plants in its variety and abundance. The Everglades National Park is the only place on earth where crocodiles and 20ft (6m) long alligators live side by side in peaceful harmony. Both of these creatures are number among the thirty-six endangered species in the Park.

NORTH AMERICA

The "thundering water"

The cliffs of Niagara Falls are a background for adventures

Route:
Flights to Buffalo/New York. Many daily line and Airbus flights from Toronto. Road links from Toronto and New York to Niagara Falls

Best time:
June to August

Accomodation:
Hotels and motels of all price classes. Book well in advance

Also worth seeing
Round trips with the "Maid of the Mist" ferry, Hovercraft over the Niagara river and helicopter trips

Forty-four million gallons (1.69 million liters) of water falls per minute over the 164-foot (50 m) high, hoof shaped cliffs of Niagara from Lake Eerie to Lake Ontario, which are linked to one another by the Niagara river. A heavy mist of water is always over the abyss and conceals the small ferry boat "Maid of the Mist," with which thousands of tourists, in brightly coloured rain clothing yearly observe the magnificent natural spectacle.

The Indians gave the world's most famous waterfalls the name "Thundering water." The waterfalls are situated on the border between the USA and Canada and is a Mecca for tourists, Dutch gold seekers and a magnet to those with suicide plans. The English writer Charles Dickens was very impressed by the tremendous power of the nature and wrote: "It was as if I had left the earth and cast a glance in heaven." His fellow countryman and colleague Oscar Wilde on the other hand, after regarding the flourishing marital tourism said: "The Niagara waterfalls are the biggest disappointment of American married life."

Ice from Lake Erie

There are very few who can free themselves from the spectacle. From far away one can already hear the noise of the falling water mass. When closer, one feels the ground vibrating. The Niagara waterfalls are very impressive at the beginning of spring, when the Niagara river transports its ice freight to the waterfalls from Lake Erie. Tens of thousands of ice floes fall cracking into the depths and form a great barrier of ice below.

The actual season starts in May. Each year some 13 million people visit the waterfalls, thirty-five thousand per day. They do not all come to look - some of them want to be seen. This is because the waterfalls are a spectacular stage for those who like to give a show. Many have attempted the waterfalls in a sailing boat. Others have tried to overpower the falls in boats and barrels. Just as, for example, Charles Stephens. The Englishman, father of eleven children, allowed himself to be tied to an oak barrel and be thrown over the waterfalls. The Niagara river only relinquished his arm, tied to the lid of the barrel.

Border struggle on the bank

In 1812 the United States declared war on England and therefore also on the Canadian province British North America, and they occupied the town on the Niagara peninsula and the bank regions of the Falls. It was not until two years later that Isaac Brock, governor of Upper Canada, was able to force the Americans to retreat. Still today there are a number of historical monuments on the western bank of the Niagara river, a reminder of this war, which bought about a sense of Canadian national feeling for the first time in the British colony.

It is no longer important to the border over steppers, who still today visit the Niagara waterfalls, if the thundering water falls on Canadian or American ground.

Directly on the shore lies the street from which the tourists can see the Niagara waterfalls spectacle (right). This part of the panorama (adjacent) shows the grandness of the landscape.

NORTH AMERICA

The American Dead Sea

Rain determines the size of the great Salt Lake

Route:
Flight to Salt Lake City from all states in America. San Francisco - Salt Lake City approximately 746 mi. (1200 km)

Best time:
April through to June, September through to November

Opening times:
Great Salt Lake City State Park on Antelope Island. Visitors center open daily 9-17 hr.

Also worth seeing:
Salt Lake City: Temple Square (entry only to Mormons), Pioneer Trail State Park.

The lake - 62 miles (100 km) long and nearly 31 miles (50 km) wide - covers a large area of the northern part of the state of Utah, but is only a fraction of the size of what it once was. The inland water was 19,305 square miles (50,000 km^2) and used to stretch far into Nevada and Idaho. The danger of the Dead Sea of America, "The Great Salt Lake," reducing even more in size is very real. This is due to the fact, that the inflow from Bear River, Weber River and Jordan River - all from the Wasatch mountains, and partly from the Rocky Mountains - is no longer sufficient to replenish the salt water.

In earlier times, the lake has been as deep as 984 ft. (300 m), but these days it's barely 16 ft. (5 m) deep. The changeable deposit and evaporation cause the sea level to decrease - about 24 inches (60 cm) per year. The rebound of this also effects the size of the Salt Lake. Due to its flat banks, the lake is considered to be a sensitive climate seismograph and even the slightest decrease in the water level has great consequences for the surface. This depth loss means a loss of 97 square miles (250 km^2) surface area. That is why, due to heavy rainfall the lake had a surface area of 2,316 square miles (6000 km^2) in the eighties, whilst the surface area shrunk to only 965 square miles (2,500 km^2) in the dry Sixties.

The Mormons, who colonized this area and made Salt Lake City the capital of their land and the State of Utah, have never really worried about the changing volume of their holy water. It was here that their prophet Brigham Young on the July 24th, 1847, was told by God how life should be lead in the holy state. Today the Mormons still live by the strict rules laid down by the founder of their religion and the "Temple complex" is still the center of the city, which now has a population of 160000.

On the dike road over the lake

From the beginning of the 20th century, the lake has posed a problem regarding the laying of the rail roads through America. For a long time it

was a roadblock for the great East-West route New York - Chicago - Omaha - Cheyenne - Ogden - San Francisco, a part of which in Utah, between Ogden and Lucin, pertains to the Pacific line. It was not until 1902 through to 1904 that the "Lucin Cutoff" was built, a dike railroad which runs 12 miles (20 km) across the lake.

In spite of the high salt level - which depending on the water level can be as high as 27 percent - there is life in the lake, not in the water but on the small islands. Bison and pelicans have found a place of refuge, away from the people. Since the fifties, large amounts of cooking salt - approximately 165,346 tons per year - is obtained from the lake. And in Grantsville, on the south bank, a flourishing industry now also produces chemical salt from the bottom of the lake.

From quite early on the lake offered other possibilities. The quiet, very flat beaches were used by the army as a testing area, during the development of new types of transport. These activities lured private car garages, which in turn resulted in the "Bonneville Speedway," a very flat endless race track, on which many speed records have been broken. The flat race track is marked with a black line and can - if there is no new record planned or heavy rainfall has blanked the beach - be used by anyone who wants to have a go. And that for a country in which speeding carries a heavy fine. Needless to say, the speedway is visited by thousands of car racers every year.

Salt Lake was once a very large lake, which stretched from Utah far into Idaho and Nevada. These days, the small amount of water which flows into the lake is not sufficient to compensate foor the evaporation of water. The salt industry (left) and car industry profit from this. The car industry can test new motors here and new speed records are regularly set on the flat banks.

165

SOUTH AMERICA

The forest of giant trees

Jau National Park protects a central area of tropical rainforest

Getting there:
Only accessible by boat along the Rio Negro from Manaus, via Novo Airčo to Foz de Jau (approx. 24 hours)

Where to stay:
On board special boats

Climate:
Tropical; temperatures between 72°–90°F (22°C–32°C). Rainy season between December and April

Main attractions:
Tropical flora and fauna; Indian craft work at the river ports; dolphin watching at Encontro das Águas.
In Manaus: Forest of Science and Mindú Park

Special tips:
Admission with the permission of the Brazilian Government only. Never venture into the jungle without a local guide, preferably an Indian

The Amazonian rainforests are the green lungs of our planet. Around 30 percent of the earth's surface is covered with forest, half of which lies in the Tropics. The rainforest bordering the Amazon River covers an area of 3,250,000 square miles (8,500,000km2), and is the largest single forest in the world.

The Amazon River winds its way for 4,000 miles (6,400km) through tropical South America. It was so named in 1541 by Francisco de Orellana, the first European to set foot here. He hit upon this name after observing female Indian warriors on its banks who reminded him of the Amazon women of Greek mythology.

The river is known by several names, however. In the Peruvian Andes, it is called the Maratón River (or Maranhčo in Portuguese). Until it merges with the Rio Negro, Brazilians refer to it as the Solmões River. Only then does it officially become the Amazon.

Unlike the whitish waters of the main river, the Rio Negro — literally "black river" — is very dark in color. For 1,550 miles (2,500km) between Columbia and Manau, it flows along a river bed channeled out of dense primeval forest and collects a great deal of plant detritus, such as leaves, roots, and fruit as well as sand or minerals, which explains its dark color.

The unique diversity of flora and fauna bordering both sides of this mighty river is protected by three huge national parks. One of these, the Jau National Park, lies some 145 miles (230km) upriver from Manaus. It spans the area between the Carabinani and Unini rivers, extending 155 miles (250km) into the rainforest itself.

Ideal habitat for epiphytes

The rainforest areas located on solid ground, or "terra firma," are home to giant trees that grow 100–200ft (30–60m) in height. The jungle is so dense and impenetrable here that most wildlife is restricted to the treetops. The rainforest does, however, support 180 different species of tree and plants per 2.5 acres (one hectare). In the Igapo region, which remains flooded for several months at a time, the river banks are lined with Mauritious palms and there is also a striking profusion of flora in the form of bromeliads and orchids. The region around the Rio Negro, where there is better water drainage, supports dense thickets of shrubs and trees in the Campinarana area.

There is still very little known about the 3,000 or so tree varieties found in the Amazon region. The consistent climate means that the trunks of these 200 to 250-year old trees do not produce growth rings. Some of them shed their leaves one by one during the year, while others lose them all in one go. These giant trees are frequently home to many epiphytes, particularly bromeliads, which are members of the orchid family. In order to get as close as possible to the light, they grow on branches, collecting droplets of the ever-present moisture in their funnel-shaped leaves. These leafy reservoirs constitute an ecosystem in themselves, supporting various varieties of fauna, especially frogs and insects, which in turn enrich the plants with their excreta.

Larger mammals, the most famous of which is the Amazon manatee, occasionally stray into this inhospitable region via the Rio Negro. These sizeable plant eaters differ from their marine cousins, the Dugongs, because they do not graze on plant life on the river bed, but feed on floating water plants. Consequently, the mouths of these slow-moving, extremely shy creatures are aimed upwards.

Adapted to an aquatic life

These former land animals have adapted well to an aquatic life. They can close up their nostrils and ears, pick up ultra sound, their neck is foreshortened, their front limbs have evolved into fins, and their rear limbs have reverted to tail fins. The Amazon manatee has poor eyesight, but excellent hearing, and can remain submerged for up to 16 minutes before needing to surface for air.

Biologists have identified more than 120 mammals, 470 bird varieties, 15 reptiles and 320 species of fish in Jau National Park, Brazil's largest conservation area. Ten types of turtle inhabit the muddy shores of the river and three varieties of caimans, giant otters, and numerous species of monkey, jaguar and ocelot roam unchecked over the 1,040 square miles (2,700km2) of Jau National Park, which was established to protect this dense, evergreen jungle.

Marshland along one of the Amazon's largest tributaries, the Rio Negro. A unique diversity of flora thrives beneath the canopy of these jungle giants (above)

The abundant rainforest wildlife also includes squirrel monkeys (below, left)

View of the forested banks of the Rio Negro (below, right)

SOUTH AMERICA

Getting there:
Airports at Foz do Iguaću, Ciudad del Este, and Puerto Iguazu. Buses from Foz do Iguaću and Puerto Iguazu

Where to stay:
All categories of hotel; youth hostels; camping sites in Puerto Iguazu, Foz do Iguaću, and along the routes to the National Parks

Climate:
December/January 79°F (26°C) to max 108°F (42°C). July 57°F (14°C), frequent mist. Best time to visit: August to November

Main attractions:
Hikes and boat trips on the Argentinean side; bird watching; various exhibitions in the park's visitor centers

Plummeting torrents

The waterfalls in the Brazilian-Argentinean nature reserve of Iguazu are among the most spectacular natural splendors in the world

The source of the Iguazu River rises at an altitude of 4,300ft (1,300m) in the Brazilian Serra do Mar mountain range not far from the Atlantic coast. No sooner has it emerged than it finds its direct route almost immediately blocked by the mountains themselves. Consequently, the Iguazu River, sections of which measure 1,650–4,950ft (500–1,500m) across, is obliged to wind its way more than 300 miles (500km) across the hinterland before discharging its waters into the Rio Paraná in the vicinity of Foz do Iguaću in Brazil, Ciudad del Este in Paraguay, and Puerto Iguazu in Argentina. It begins by hurling itself more than 230ft (70m) over the precipice of a mighty lava plateau extending 400,000 square miles (1,000,000km²) across Brazil, Paraguay, Argentina, and Uruguay, in what is one of the most magnificent waterfall spectacles on earth. This plateau of lava erupted 135 million years ago through cracks and fissures in the earth's surface, but no volcano ever formed here.

There is a stunning panoramic view from the Brazilian shore of the crescent-shaped waterfall. During the rainy season, 230,000ft³ (6,500m³) of water thunder over its 8,900ft³ (2.7km) lip, forming a roaring curtain of water, comprised of over 270 individual waterfalls. Great white clouds of mist rise up from this devil's cauldron of swirling water, producing numerous intersecting rainbows of spray in a unique spectacle of nature. During the dry season, the volume of water is a mere 10,600ft³ (300m²), roaring its way down in around 150 separate cascades.

Just before the Iguazu reaches the precipice, it broadens out to more than a mile across, splitting into numerous tributaries that encircle the equally numerous islands and islets. Chunks of lava, which have broken away from the precipice over the course of time, have meanwhile become islands and islets, dissecting the wildly raging waters at the base of the falls.

Around 20,000 years ago, the waterfall was situated at the confluence of the Iguazu and the Paraná. Over thousands of years, however, it has carved itself a 17 mile (28km) long, 260ft (80m) deep channel out of the soft lava rock.

Below the Falls, a bridge leads across into Argentina. On this side, it is possible to approach within touching distance of the waterfall, either through winding hiking trails along the bank or by way of bridges or boat trips to the islands both above and below the actual waterfall.

These waterfalls are situated at the heart of a National Park area, which straddles both Brazil and Argentina over an area of nearly 400 square miles (1,000km2) and is designed to protect this region's increasingly endangered primeval forest environment. Both Parks are part of mankind's natural heritage, preserving intact an area of almost pristine Paranaensic jungle, a type of primeval forest of which only 5 to 10 percent remains in Brazil and Paraguay.

Drenched by the cascades

The Park is a sub-tropical rainforest sporting an abundant diversity of species and several separate vegetation levels, starting with the high treetops 100ft (30m) above the ground, to the medium-sized trees and shrubs, and right down to the vegetation on the forest floor. One of the most beautiful trees is the jacaranda tree, which grows to a height of more than 130ft (40m) with a girth of around 5ft (1.6m). Dwarf palms are usually found growing in its shade. Altogether 2,000 different varieties of plant, including lianas, tree ferns, and numerous climbing plants, have been recorded here. More than 60 species of orchid and countless bromeliads are indigenous to this region.

The lion's share of the waterfall, encompassing one-and-a-quarter miles (two km) of this semi-circular spectacle, belongs to Argentina. The habitat that has evolved here reflects the constant humidity produced by the mists from the cascades. This relatively isolated biotope is also called kauri forest, after the Cupay tree, whose copper-colored buds unfurl into pendulous foliage. Lush Paspalum-Illoi grass flourishes between the boulders.

The fauna is equally diverse: biologists have recorded a total of 68 mammals, 422 birds, 38 reptiles, and 18 amphibians. Many of these are rare or even endangered species such as the giant otter, the La Plata otter, jaguar, ocelot, great anteater, lowland tapir, crab-eating raccoon, and South American coati. The bird life is particularly eye-catching and colorful.

Specially constructed footbridges lead to an island at the foot of the waterfalls (above)

The water plunges down in a series of cascades from the high volcanic plateau above (below, right)

Aerial photograph of the precipitous rock walls of the falls, bordered by primeval forest (below, left)

SOUTH AMERICA

The Patagonian ice field

Los Glaciares National Park in Argentina incorporates several climatic zones

Getting there:
Regular flights from Buenos Aires to Calafate. By car via Santa Cruz on National Route 3, or by bus via Rio Gallegos. Don't miss a drive along National Route 40 from Rio Gallegos or Esquel

Where to stay:
Hotels, guesthouses, cabins, apartments, camping sites

Climate:
Moderate climate, 37°–54°F (3°–12°C). Rainy season April to May

Main attractions:
Glaciers: Moreno (front edge of the glacier) and Viedma. Lakes: Argentino and Viedma. Mountains: Chaltén/Torre. Places to visit: Calafate, Chaltén. Glacier and forest hikes. Boat trip into the bays of Lake Argentino

Special tips:
Puma territory! Camp at least 165ft (50m) from the lakeside in case of swells caused by collapsing sections of glacier.

At 7.09 p.m. on March 14, 2004, watched by thousands of curious onlookers, an immense body of water burst through a 656ft (200m) high dam of pure, glittering ice, creating a mighty wave that traveled the 100 mile (160km) length of Lago Argentino in the west of the Argentina's Santa Cruz province.

During its advance, the Perito Moreno Glacier, one of the most imposing glaciers in the entire Andes, had pushed a tongue of ice across this narrow drainage arm of Lake Argentino, effectively blocking the channel and separating Rico Bay from the main part of the lake. Melted ice from the mighty glaciers in the Patagonian ice fields raised the water level in Rico Bay to 82ft (25m). The barrier of ice was eventually unable to withstand the growing pressure of water and a fracture appeared, creating a huge tunnel, which collapsed two days later with a thunderous roar, releasing the trapped volume of water.

The Moreno Glacier is just one of 47 icy giants within Los Glaciares National Park, an area covering around 1,740 square miles (4,500km2). It also encompasses two hundred or so smaller glaciers, each with areas of just over one square mile (3km2). Upsala and Viedma are the two largest glaciers in the park, each covering an area of approximately 230 square miles (600km2). Unlike most glaciers across the globe, Moreno Glacier is is actually increasing in volume.

The three-mile (5km) expanse of its front edge is an unforgettable sight. The ice presents a magical scene: every conceivable shade of blue and white glitters and shimmers, depending on the angle of the tropical sun. It creaks and groans like a living creature when a section of the glacier is in the process of breaking loose and dropping away into the lake. When this happens, the collapsing chunk of ice plunges deep into the lake, creating a huge swell before resurfacing and finally coming to rest as a gently bobbing iceberg.

220 miles (350km) of white wasteland

Fifty percent of the National Park encompasses the southern section of the snow-covered Andes Cordillera, between whose summits and ridges this vast Patagonian ice field, a surreal and strange-looking landscape covering some 5,400 square miles (14,000km2), has evolved. Towering on the northern horizon are the highest peaks in Los Glaciares National Park: Chaltén and Torre, rising to heights of 11,073ft and 10,262ft (3,375m and 3,128m) respectively.

This white wilderness, measuring nearly 220 miles (350km) in length, is the largest single body of ice anywhere in the world outside the Antarctic. Its existence so far north is explained by the fact that the Andes Mountain chain forces moisture-laden westerly winds off the Atlantic upwards into much colder air. Any precipitation consequently falls as snow, which is compressed under its own accumulative weight into ice. To the east, the Park stretches across a relatively ice-free, pre-Andean zone into the middle of Lake Argentino Basin, where it merges into the steppes of Patagonia.

Vegetation within the Park reflects these two distinct geographical zones. The mountain slopes support the so-called Patagonian-Magellan rainforest, populated by southern beech and cypress, interspersed with the bright colors of red or golden-yellow catafate bushes. The steppe landscape is dominated by a waving sea of tussock grass stretching as far as the eye can see, kept in constant movement by the relentless, often stormy, west winds. Beneath the boundless sky lie the gentle hills of Patagonia, left over from previous Ice Ages and sculpted by giant glaciers.

Forbidding landscape

No matter how forbidding and harsh this singularly beautiful and captivating landscape might seem, it has nevertheless been occupied by man since prehistoric times. The hunter-gatherers, who appeared after the Ice Age, depended mainly on guanacos, small South American camels, for their survival. They were followed by the Tehuelchia Indians, vestiges of whose culture can still be visited in 14 different archaeological sites within the park. Their successors were driven out and killed by new arrivals from Europe.

The advance of the ice giants — shown here near Santa Cruz — into the colorful vegetation zones (above)

Icebergs, broken loose from glaciers, floating off-shore (below, right)

The impressive rock faces found in the Chaltén Torre range represent an irresistible challenge to mountain climbers (below, left)

AFRICA

Victoria Falls: smoking thunder

At the Zambia-Zimbabwe border lies the Zambezi's unique panorama

Route:
International flights to Harare (Zimbabwe). Local flights to the Victoria Falls or, via Lusaka (Zambia) to Maramba/Livingstone

Best time:
May through September

Accommodation:
Victoria Falls Hotel

Further points of interest:
Lake Kariha, Hwange National Park, Matoba Hills National Park near Bulawayo

British explorer David Livingstone's description was lyrical: "This is the most marvellous sight I ever beheld in Africa," he jotted down in his notebook in November 1855 as he stood gazing from a river island the thundering mass of the Zambezi's waters cascading into a narrow gorge. Deep below, he saw two rainbows against the backdrop of a dense white cloud and, rising aloft "a column of vapour two or three hundred feet in height, the upper portion of which took on the color of dark smoke."

Traversing Africa from the Atlantic to the Pacific, the Englishman was the first European to reach the legendary Zambezi Falls, the largest of the continent. The sound of falling water was deafening to the point that natives, fearful of the mighty spirits at work, dared not draw near. Mosi oa Tunya, smoking thunder, was their name for this marvel of nature. From afar, Livingstone had already glimpsed five smoke-like pillars "as if wide reaches of savannah were being burnt off."

Falls in nine canyons

David Livingstone named the "smoking thunder" after his queen: Victoria Falls. Later, the city, a short ways from the falls, was named after him. Today, the map of Zambia refers to Livingstone by the African name "Maramba."

1,280 miles (2,060 km) in length, the Zambezi is the longest river in southern Africa. At the border between Zambia and Zimbabwe, (former Rhodesia), at the place described by Livingstone, its mass of water 1 mile (1.7 km) wide, drops some 361 feet (110 m) over a basalt edge into a narrow gorge linked up with nine more canyons. Geologically, these are former receiving basins for the cascading waters. The Victoria Falls as such consist of five falls – the east cataract, the rainbow falls, the horseshoe falls and the devil's cataract on the west side of the fault.

Since the days of Livingstone, the falls have retained most of their originality, except that in their vicinity luxury hotels like the Mosi-oa-Tunya Intercontinental were erected and a motorway leads almost up to the brink. Since 1904 a railway bridge crosses the Zambezi at a narrower section to connect Zambia and Zimbabwe. A picturesque jungle track in Zambia leads to Knife Edge, a slippery rock path between the first and the second canyon of the Victoria Falls.

Although the "pillars of smoke" as described by Livingstone are rarely visible nowadays, an enormous cloud of foam still hovers over the falls. This cloud reaches its highest point towards the end of the rainy season in April – some 84 million gallons (320 million liters) of water dropping every single minute. Afterwards the volume decreases for a time, to 48 million gallons (18 million liters) per minute at the end of the dry season.

An exceptionally lush vegetation, also described by Livingstone, still characterises the wide surroundings of the Zambezi falls. For 19 miles (30 km) around the continually rising foamy clouds cause a fine precipitation and allows a great wealth of plant life to flourish. All of this, including the falls, are now part of the Mosi-oa-Tunya National Park on the Zambia side and the Victoria Falls National Park on the Zimbabwe side.

Tourist centre in Zambia is the city of Livingstone (Maramba). The falls are at a distance of no more than four miles (7 km).

With deafening roaring, water cascades into a narrow gorge 360 ft. (110 m) deep and 164 ft. (50 m) wide. The rising clouds of foam cause a fine mist to descend in a radius of 19 miles (30 km)

Separating Zambia and Zimbabwe, the Zambezi becomes Mosi oa Tunya, smoking thunder

AFRICA

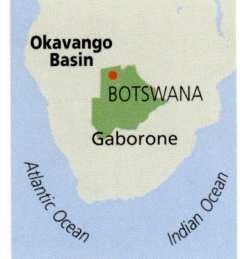

River delta in the desert

Botswana has declared the Okavango Basin and Moremi Reserve a conservation area

Getting there:
Mainly roads from Francistown, Windhoek, Bagani, or Livingstone/Kasane to Maun. Charter flights from Gabarone and Francistown. The delta area is accessible by light aircraft, canoe, or on foot. Only very experienced drivers of four wheel drive vehicles should venture onto the limited number of tracks in the Moremi reserve. Large choice of Safari tour operators in Maun. Apart from in Maun itself, no fuelling stations for hundreds of miles.

Where to stay:
Hotels and camping sites in Maun. Plenty of lodges and campsites in and around the delta, ranging from luxurious lodges to basic tent accommodation. Off-site camping is prohibited

Climate:
Dry season is from July to October. Most animals move into the delta from the Kalahari during this time. Wet season is November/December and is very hot and humid

Main attractions:
Moremi Game Reserve; lodge accommodation; guided canoe safaris; light aircraft flights over the delta

Originating in the highlands of Angola, a river known as the Cubango springs from the Bié Plateau south of Vila Nova. It flows generally southward before turning east, at which point it becomes the Okavango River, flowing along the border between Angola and Namibia. Measuring nearly 1,000 miles (1,600km) in length, it is the fourth longest river in southern Africa. It does not empty into the ocean, however, but discharges its waters into a vast delta in the middle of the Kalahari, one of the world's greatest deserts. The Okavanga Delta extends over an area of 6,600 square miles (17,000km2) and is unquestionably Africa's largest oasis situated in the middle of the parched wilderness of the Kalahari.

After crossing the narrow Caprivi Strip, the river gradually broadens, eventually dispersing its waters into a maze of lagoons and immense labyrinths of innumerable waterways connecting small, and sometimes not so small, islands of palm and savannah. The southern edge of this fan-shaped area of saturated sand and water is approximately 150 miles (240km) long.

Only three percent of the water that the river feeds into the plains flows out again. It accumulates instead in the southern swampland surrounding the diminutive Lake Ngami or continues for another 185 miles (300km) through the Kalahari Desert to Lake Xau on the Makgadikgadi Pan to the southeast. This small outflow is nevertheless sufficient to remove the salts that would otherwise be deposited when the water evaporates. Without this small outflow, the delta would be a lifeless salt pan.

The Kalahari was once a lake

The Okavango Delta is a remnant of a vast lake that once filled the Makgadikgadi Basin. Its waters and swamps covered a large part of the central Kalahari. It is probable that the Okavango, Chobe, Kwando, and upper Zambezi rivers converged at one time to form a single, mighty river that flowed through the central Kalahari across the Limpopo and into the Indian Ocean.

Each year, the Okavango deposits around two million tons of sand in the delta, creating sand bars that regularly block the river's natural flow. This forces it to keep switching directions, resulting in an ever-changing pattern of channels and waterways across the delta plain. Dense thickets of papyrus reeds, growing just a few inches under water, can also cause the channels to become blocked. Only a handful of waterways are deep enough to be navigable by canoe. The Okavango Delta is consequently an outstanding example of an ecosystem that has achieved an extremely dynamic, natural balance, while constantly changing. As a result, this island in a sea of arid desert supports a surprising variety of habitats and an abundance of plants and wildlife. For the great migratory animals of the Kalahari, the delta repre-

sents a natural, virtually trackless reserve and one huge watering hole.

Impenetrable papyrus thickets line the river and waterways cross the expanse of floodplains. Mopane woodland and palm trees surround the higher-lying islets, affording a shady refuge for the larger animals. Beyond the forest, the landscape unfolds to reveal the drier expanse of the savannah where elephants and antelope roam, trailed by lions, cheetahs, hyenas, and wild dogs. About 30 percent of all wild dogs, whose numbers are declining throughout Africa, are thought to live here. After dark, the hippopotamuses trample broad paths through the papyrus on their nightly forays. By day, these pathways enable the antelope to move from one island to another.

Water for the elephants

Altogether, a total of 1,060 species of plants and 32 large mammals have been recorded here. The area is also home to around 650 spectacular varieties of brilliantly colored birds, which flock here from all corners of equatorial Africa. These include storks, ibis, herons, cranes, and weaver birds.

In the eastern sector of the delta is the Moremi game reserve, an area covering 1,930 square miles (5,000km2) and comprising around 20 percent of the Okavango Delta. It is a combination of mopane woodland and acacia forest, floodplains, and lagoons.

It is the only area that visitors can penetrate without too much difficulty. Large herds of elephant congregate here particularly during the dry season, but the area is also a magnet for buffalo, giraffes, zebras, and all the other African animals that come to slake their thirst at the numerous pools.

This aerial photo of the Okavango Delta illustrates how quickly the river could change course on this floating bed of sand (above)

Pictured left is a colony of pelicans

EUROPE

Sunbathing on the "Cold Coast"

Spitzbergen is home to almost as many polar bears as people

Getting there:
Summer flights from Oslo via Tromsø, ships from Tromsø and Honningsvåg/Nordkap. Longyearbyen is a popular destination for cruise ships

Where to stay:
Several hotels and bed and breakfast establishments; accommodation available in former workers' quarters. Indoor heating is excessively warm.

Excursions and main attractions:
Svalbard museum in Longyearbyen; Spitzbergen cruise (1 week); easy one-day hike through the Advent valley (fossils, reindeer, flora). Tourists not admitted to Ny Ålesund

Clothing:
Warm clothing, waterproofs, sunglasses, stout shoes

Special tips:
Do not stray from inhabited settlements without a weapon or armed guide. No roads or tracks away from inhabited settlements. No formal emergency services

The first people who accidentally found their way here were Vikings, who stumbled upon Svalbard, the "cold coast," in 1194. They very quickly forgot about it again and it was not until 400 years later, in June 1594, that another ship approached the precipitously steep mountain peaks of the main island. On board were two Dutch explorers, Willem Barents and Jacob van Heemskerck, who named the island Spitzbergen.

It is the largest of Svalbard's nine major islands and comprises over half the archipelago's overall landmass of around 24,300 square miles (63,000km2). To the northeast, the region's highest mountain, Newtontoppen, rises to a height of 5,634ft (1,717m), standing out in dramatic relief between the other peaks.

Svalbard is home to three national parks, two nature reserves, two areas of plant conservation and 16 protected bird sites. Almost 50 percent of its entire area is consequently under protection and entry is either forbidden altogether or restricted to authorized trails.

A surprisingly mild climate

Despite their position on the Arctic Circle, the islands enjoy a mild climate. The west coasts remain ice-free from June to December, thanks to warm currents from the North Atlantic Drift, a northern extension of the Gulf Stream. In July, when the sun is shining and there is no breeze, temperatures can easily rise to 68°F (20°C), high enough to shed the weatherproof clothing and sunbathe. However, despite the midnight sun, which never sets here between April 21 and August 24, the mountaintops are often shrouded in cloud and the valleys frequently veiled in mist.

The ground remains frozen for most of the year, only thawing a little along the coast during the summer. During this period, the tundra becomes a carpet of mosses, lichen, ferns, grasses, and even 40 varieties of flowers bearing tiny, vividly colored blooms in spring and summer. Incredible though it may seem, biologists have even identified two unprepossessing tree species among the 170 different varieties of plant: a robust, weather-resistant arctic willow and a bushy miniature birch, which grows to a height of just 6in (15cm).

Spring witnesses the arrival of millions of birds, which migrate here from the south to breed. Svalbard boasts around 150 varieties of bird, including eider ducks, puffins, ptarmigans, barnacle geese and numerous species of gull. However, it is a little warm at this time for the estimated 3,000 polar bears, which prefer the feel of ice under their paws and consequently retreat to the polar ice floes in the north, thereby affording a brief respite to the numerous seals and sea dogs that are the polar bears' staple diet. This is also the season when herds of walrus begin to gather on the beaches to fish for eels and indulge in their courtship rituals beneath the midnight sun.

For the small, tough reindeer that live on Spitzbergen, summer is just one long picnic. No more strenuous scraping and digging to uncover tasty morsels of lichen beneath the snow. They become popular photo models for the brightly-clad tourists clutching shiny cameras in their gloved hands. They are obliging animals and often allow people to get within a few yards of them.

This is not so in the case of the blue or white arctic foxes, which slink away to seek cover among the rocks. Another animal that prefers to keep its distance is the almost prehistoric-looking musk ox, introduced from Greenland in 1929.

Port of call for cruise ships

These islands, whose majestic mountains provide a landscape of jagged outcrops and bizarre rock formations, constitute the highest elevations on a splinter of continent that has, for the past 600 million years, been drifting across all the climatic zones on earth at the rate of 11/4 in. (4.5cm) a year – and is still doing so.

Nowadays, around 3000 Norwegians and Russians, as well as an equivalent number of polar bears, inhabit the three settlements of Longyearbyen, Barentsburg, and Nyålesund. During the summer months, cruise ships disgorge around 60,000 tourists at Longyearbyen on the Advent fjord. The eastern shore of this fjord is a popular destination for day excursions into an unspoiled natural environment, where visitors frequently encounter unlikely reminders of earlier human activity in the region that have survived for centuries in this unpolluted and cold atmosphere.

The edge of a glacier where a section has broken away. Spitzbergen glaciers are constantly collapsing into the sea. These massive chunks of ice break away with a thunderous roar (above)

Magdalena fjord is accessible in summer from Trinity harbor (below center)

The seals are quite at home on drifting ice floes (bottom right)

For the small Spitzbergen reindeer, summer is just one long feast when lichen, their favorite diet, is easy to find (left)

EUROPE

The Vidda uplands

Hardangervidda, in Norway, is home to Europe's largest reindeer herd

Getting there:
Several highways lead along the National Park boundaries. The Oslo-Bergen line has several stops at the northern end of Hardangervidda. No trucks are permitted within the Park.

Where to stay:
Comfortable hotels in the towns and villages bordering Hardangervidda. Numerous overnight cabins located along the hiking trails (750 miles/1,200km of marked trails). Camping permitted

Climate:
Arctic; rarely exceeds 50°F (10°C) even in summer

Main attractions:
Nature center in Jvre Eidfjord; wildlife watching; hiking; fishing and hunting by special permit; Oddatal with its numerous waterfalls; Utne Hotel dating from 1722 and Kjeåsen mountain inn from around 1300; Stone Age settlements

Special tips:
Open fires, including camping stoves, prohibited within the Park from May 15 to September 15

In contrast to the mountain regions of Central Europe, Ice Age glaciers in Norway eroded the mountain peaks into broad, high plateaus and rounded domes. Extending across an area of almost 3,500 square miles (9,000km2), Hardangervidda in southern Norway is Europe's largest peneplain, an eroded, almost level plateau, roughly the same size as Cyprus. Approximately one-third of this plateau, which lies at an altitude of between 3,950–4,600ft (1,200–1,400m), has been awarded National Park status and placed under protection. Since the tree line in the central part of southern Norway stops at 3,300ft (1,000m), this wide expanse of high plateau, a gently undulating landscape of moor and marsh crisscrossed with streams, is typical Arctic tundra, known locally as "fjell."

Apart from occasional dwarf shrubs, which provide a habitat for blue-throats, winchats, meadow pipits, and reed buntings, the terrain is mainly covered with a dense carpet of lush grasses and lichens.

In the west, just before dropping abruptly away into the Sørf and Hardangerfjords, a few steep mountain ridges up to 5,600ft (1,700m) in height rise up from the plateau. During the tourist season, from June 1 to September 15, the magnificent Vøringsfoss waterfall plunges down into the fjord at the far end of the Måbødalen valley. Outside the tourist season, it supplies Norway's largest power station, the dynamo of which is housed 2,300ft (700m) deep within the mountain.

Hard, primeval rock
An unusual, dome-shaped mountain, Mount Hårteigen, rises from the flat center of the Vidda plateau to a height of 5,550ft (1,690m). It is a significant landmark in the region and its snow patches are visible for miles. Its rock is so hard that glaciers have been unable to erode it.

The hard bedrock in the southeast of Hardangervidda is the last vestige of a mountain landscape before it was eroded, eventually sinking into the sea a thousand million years ago. Limestone rocks in the northwest testify to the fact that they originally formed from deposits accumulating on the sea bed. Millions of years later, a large tectonic plate pushed the submerged mountains back up to the surface again. Mount Hårteigen and Mount Hardangerjøkulen are relicts of this mountain chain.

When the ice shield retreated after the last Ice Age 9,000 years ago, the Hardangervidda plateau was left free of ice, as were the summits of the surrounding mountains. The bare rocks were quickly covered with a dense carpet of lichen and, during the next 2,000 years, forests reclaimed the high plateau. Consequently, there was adequate food for reindeer, who were hunted by early settlers. Around 250 Stone Age dwellings dating from around 6300 BC have been discovered on the Vidda plateau, as well as numerous pits for trapping wild animals.

Glaciers on the high plateau
When the climate cooled again 2,000 to 3,000 years ago, a giant glacier formed on the 6,250ft (1,900m) high Hardangerjøkulen. By 1750, the mountain reached its peak. The forest vanished and the high plateau was abandoned by human settlers. Between 1930 and 1970, the Hardangerjøkulen glacier, like the rest of Norway's glaciers, retreated and a few rocky peaks, still buried under the ice at the dawn of the twentieth century, gradually became visible again. Although the surrounding mountains are ice-free, a 28 square mile (72km2) glacier still survives on Mount Hardangerjøkulen due to the high amount of precipitation from the southwest, nearly of all of which falls in this very spot.

In search of snowflakes
Higher levels of precipitation also mean much lusher vegetation during the summer months in the western part of Hardangervidda. This is the season that sees the arrival of Europe's largest reindeer herds in time for the females to calve in May. During this time, between 10,000 and 15,000 animals move across this high tundra region seeking even higher terrain in order to escape from the midges and mosquitoes. Herds of several thousand reindeer may be seen congregating near the few remaining areas of snow. They remain here until the autumn, when they return to the windy valleys of Ostvidda.

These huge herds of reindeer are accompanied by Arctic foxes, skulking among the rocks and crags. This National Park marks their southernmost distribution area in Europe.

Along Hardangervidda's western edge, the fjord's fingers penetrate deep into the surrounding terrain. Even during the summer months, the wide expanse of the Vidda plateau is never entirely free of snow and is often veiled in mists (above)

Patches of snow and barren, lichen-covered rocks are typical of the type of scenery found in parts of the Vidda (below)

EUROPE

The Saami herdsmen

Four major national parks protect the tundra in the Swedish sector of Lapland

Getting there:
The region is easy to reach by train, road, plane, or helicopter

Where to stay:
Hotels and cabins in Abisko. Padjelanta: overnight cabins along the trails. Camping permitted everywhere, but all litter must be removed

Climate:
Cool and damp in summer. In winter, -4° to -22°F (-20°C to -30°C)

Main attractions:
Abisko: Njulla summit, Torneträsk Sea; Padjelanta: flora and fauna, Lakes Vastenjaure and Virihaure; Stora Sjöfallet: Akka Massif, pine forest near Vietas, Teusadel Valley, Kierkau cliffs; Sarek: scenery and fauna

Special tips:
Some areas are off-limits during the early summer breeding season and have virtually no tourist infrastructure. The Saami have special rights with regard to use of motor vehicles in the tundra

A rugged, ice and snow-covered mountainous region in the west and large expanses of swampland, dense forest, sparkling lakes, and numerous rivers in the east comprise the largest single area of continuous primeval landscape in Europe. Extending into Sweden from beyond the Arctic Circle are four large national parks, two equally sizeable reserves, and three other conservation areas, all part of an area encompassing 3,630 square miles (9,400km2) that has been designated a natural world heritage site.

Above the tree line, the bleak, blustery heights of the steep mountains on the Norwegian border are mainly barren and strewn with bare boulders and rocks. Wherever the rocks are not covered by glaciers, the summit areas are populated with a few alpine heathers, mixed with various types of scrubby vegetation, grassy tussocks and sedges.

Between the treeless heights and vast pine forests that cover most of central Lapland is a belt of heath land with dense thickets of diminutive, windswept birch. This is an unusual type of vegetation to find along the tree line as, in other parts of the world, it is mainly pine trees that grow at this altitude. The only other area in the world where this type of birch forest occurs is on the Kamchatka peninsula in Siberia.

Padjelanta National Park comprises 766 square miles (1,984km2) of an elevated plain surrounding the large lakes of Vastenjaure and Virhaure. The park has an extremely rich diversity of flora and fauna. Despite its Nordic alpine character, its rolling plains, softly rounded mountain ridges and vast areas of water are unusually open and accessible.

Arctic foxes and wolverines

The limy soil of the National Park supports over 400 different plant species, quite impressive for this type of remote mountain landscape. The lush alpine meadows are home to scarce species such as potentilla hypartica, a type of cinquefoil, and creeping sandwort. Arctic foxes and wolverine stalk the undergrowth and snowy owls breed here undisturbed. Padjelanta also provides valuable grazing pastures for the semi-wild reindeer, driven here each summer by the Saami, Lapland's native inhabitants.

The two National Parks of Sarek and Stor Sjöfallet, on the other hand, are dominated by the towering peaks of the Scandinavian mountains and separated by deep, trough-shaped valleys and mighty rivers. The wild, alpine Arctic mountains and flat high plains of Stora Sjöfallet support very little vegetation. Bare boulders, snowfields, and glaciers dominate the landscape and it is only the depths of the valleys that are populated by primeval forests and birch woods.

Sarek National Park, with more than 200 peaks rising to over 5,900ft (1,800m), is extremely inaccessible. Six of Sweden's highest mountains are located here, along with some 100 glaciers. Sarek National Park's main artery is the Rapaätno River, one of Europe's most breathtaking water landscapes, which sweeps along the broad, majestic, U-shaped Rapadalen valley.

Ultimate, inaccessible wilderness

The green water from around 30 melted glaciers roars down into the valley in the raging torrents of the Rapaätno River. The river valley is carpeted with an almost impenetrable thicket of mountain birch, osier, and other vegetation. Nevertheless, only a few plant species actually manage to survive here. However, an unusual variety of wildlife compensates for the paucity of plant species. Bears, wolverine, lynx, and moose remain virtually undisturbed by man. Sarek is indeed one of the world's most re-

mote wild places, with no trails or accommodation facilities for visitors.

Abisko National Park, on the other hand, provides much easier access to Lapland's bleak beauty. Situated in a broad valley in one of Sweden's sunniest regions, it is sheltered by high mountains to the south and west, while the large expanse of Lake Torneträsk sparkles to the north. Just before the mighty Abiskojokka River empties into the lake, it forces its way through a canyon 65ft (20m) deep, whose steep cliff walls document Lapland's geological history. From the summit of Mount Njulla, accessible by cable car, there are simply breathtaking views across the tundra and the lake.

The shores of Lake Torneträsk are covered with dense coniferous forest. In the background, low hills form part of the tundra landscape (above)

Reindeer are an integral part of traditional Saami culture (below, right) Every autumn, the tundra bursts into a blaze of color (below, center)

A tiny, round church is one of the more unusual features of Padjelanta National Park (below, left)

EUROPE

Vivid mountain landscape

France's Luberon region has evolved over the centuries

Getting there:
By rail: express train to Avignon, then regional bus connections. By road: A7 from the north, A8 from the south, Aix-en-Provence exit to Pertuis. Airports at Marseille and Avignon

Where to stay:
Wide choice of hotels, guesthouses, country villas, and farmhouses; campsites

Climate:
Sun shines 300 days a year. Hot summers and mild winters

Main attractions:
Hiking trails: botanical trail in the Massif des Cèdres (Cedar forest); ochres trail near Roussillon with ochre quarries.
Places to visit: Apt; Lourmarin with visit to Albert Camus' grave and house; Village des Bories (open-air museum); Buoux fortress

"Rustrel Colorado" is the French name for the spectacular limestone cliffs of the Grand Luberon (above)

Pont Julien near Apt is one of the Luberon's oldest cultural sites (below, center)

Vineyards and castle ruins are reminders of the Luberon's turbulent past (below, left and right)

The mountain landscape of the Luberon, the very epitome of Provence, is a myriad of colors including fields of vivid purple lavender, mighty forests in varying hues of green, bright red and orange ochre cliffs, and dazzling white limestone hills. The rugged mountain chain is situated to the east of Avignon, rising over 3,300ft (1,000m) in places and stretching for some 35 miles (55km) between Manosque to Cavaillon. Its highest peak is the Mourre Nègre, which rises to 3,692ft (1,125m). Picturesque villages cling precariously to craggy cliffs while regimented lines of vines and stony limestone fields occupy the slopes leading up to deserted high plateaus. To the north, the mountains descend gently into the Calavon Valley and the plains of Carpentras.

This stunningly beautiful and often mysterious terrain forms part of the Luberon Nature Park, which extends over an area of 640 square miles (1,650km2). It was established to protect not only a unique natural landscape, but also a region with a cultural history in which man and nature have co-existed in mutually influential and adaptive relationships dating back some 1,000 years. Even though the old, traditional farming methods that were geared to fit the peculiarities of the climate, local soils, and mountainous terrain are now just a distant memory in many places, Luberon farmers still practice these traditional farming methods in order to preserve the indigenous plant and animal life.

Early farming practices have created an open landscape. If the growth of constantly sprouting trees and shrubs were not kept down by grazing sheep, many species of plants and animals would lose one of their last sanctuaries.

Grand and Petit Luberon

Situated between the Alps and the Mediterranean, the Luberon is exposed to two climatic systems. The northern and southern flanks of the mountain chain are exposed to the sun and wind, and temperatures fluctuate dramatically due to the differences in altitude between the deeply hollowed out valleys and the high plateaus, producing an astonishing diversity of habitats, which have experienced both help and hindrance at the hands of man.

The Combe de Lourmarin bisects the mountains of Bonnieux and Lourmarin, dividing the mountain chain into the Petit Luberon in the west and the Grand Luberon to the east. The deep ravines, steep cliffs, and dramatic river valleys of the Petit Luberon (Little Luberon) have produced a picturesque landscape of rugged mountains and constitute a refuge for many endangered bird species, such as Bonelli's eagle, the Egyptian vulture, the snake buzzard, and owls. Wild boar and Europe's largest lizards are also found here. The plateau heights support dense Mediterranean garigue vegetation, a dry, sparse landscape of macchia bushes, chestnut oaks, palms, and juniper, interspersed with a variety of herbs including thyme, rosemary, and lavender.

Steep limestone cliffs

Situated between Bonnieux and Cheval Blanc is Europe's largest plantation of Atlas cedars, covering an area of four square miles (ten square kilometers). These trees were introduced from North Africa in 1862 and first planted in the vicinity of Bonnieux village.

Another unforgettable sight are the distinctive ochre-colored cliffs near Roussillon. This unusual rock formation is remarkable for its coloring, which covers virtually the whole spectrum of glowing reds and yellows. Ochre is a mixture of sand and clay. The iron oxide, or rust as it is commonly known, contained within the ochre gives the cliffs their striking hue.

The Grand Luberon is characterized by dazzling, white, limestone crags rising from steep, rocky cliffs. This part of the mountain region is older than its western counterpart. Over the centuries, wind and weather have eroded these mountains to form smoothly rounded hills. Meadows carpet the hilltops and dense woodland clings to the hillsides.

EUROPE

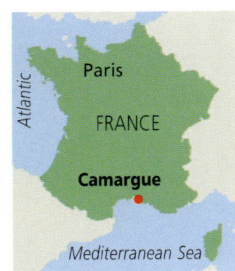

The land of pink flamingos

The Camargue region in the Rhône delta, a paradise for wild horses and migrating birds, is France's best-known national park

Getting there:
From Arles on Route D35 east of the delta to Salin-de-Giraud, or on Route N570 on the western side of the Camargue to Les-Saints-Maries-de-la-Mer

Where to stay:
Les-Saints-Maries-de-la-Mer is a tourist resort with a wide choice of accommodation

Climate:
Mediterranean climate

Main attractions:
Hiking along the three trails known as "Flamingo Way," "Salt Way," or "Rice Way." Horseback riding on Camargue horses. Bird watching. Places to visit: Arles, St-Gilles, Aigues-Mortes

The amphibious conditions of the Rhône delta resulting from the combination of freshwater, sea, and mud have, over hundreds of years, produced one of Europe's most fascinating, yet most fragile, ecosystems. The Camargue is the alluvial land between the two arms of the Rhône river as it flows into the sea. The 330 square miles (850km2) of land, one of the world's most important wetlands, consist of a spectacular mosaic of lagoons, marshes, ponds, dunes, and beaches, together with an extensive area of steppe landscape that is home to the incomparable, semi-wild Camargue horses. At the heart of the delta is the Lagune Vaccarès, covering an area of 23 square miles (60km2). This body of water is pivotal to the Camargue's entire irrigation system, acting as a water treatment plant for the agricultual drainage water that collects here. Periodic Mediterranean storms whip up the water surface, ensuring the lagoon is always well supplied with oxygen and that micro-organisms are able to convert every last nutrient. This large-scale biological production not only supports 40,000 flamingos, the largest colony of these birds in the Mediterranean, but also countless coots, ducks, snipe, and gulls.

The Camargue is a land of extremes. Very few plants can tolerate its harsh environment and the continual see-sawing between the dry salt desert conditions that prevail during the summer months and the widespread flooding that occurs in winter. The extensive marshes and steppes are primarily populated by saltwort, while dwarf eelgrass is the predominant vegetation in the lagoons. Trees and bushes are uncommon, growing in just a few small pockets on higher ground in the north, mainly as riverine woodland along the banks of the Rhône. A few wind-battered trees also manage to survive on the ancient sand dunes south of Vaccarès. The landscape is dotted with occasional juniper bushes, some of which are said to be more than 500 years old.

The transition zone between freshwater and saltwater

A different situation altogether prevails with regard to the animal life. The Camargue wilderness is in fact home to over 600 species of animal, not to mention 356 varieties of bird, millions of which arrive here in spring and autumn to rest and feed before continuing their journey. Autumn is the ideal time to see virtually every kind of European wader and, during the winter months, these flooded plains are home to 13 different species of duck. The Camargue is a breeding-ground for eight species of heron, terns, and of course the wonderful pink flamingo. The 35 square miles (90km2) of freshwater and saltwater marshes and the 58 square miles (150km2) of freshwater and saltwater ponds virtually dry up during the summer, but in autumn and winter they provide a source of food for bitterns, mallard, and wagtails.

The flat salt pans, dried in summer and flooded in winter, are overgrown with saltwort, the main diet of the Camargue horses. In spring, they are invaded by wading birds, such as snipe, redshanks, and black-winged stilts.

Most of the mammals, such as rodents, foxes, and wild boar, tend to avoid the open terrain, preferring instead the wooded areas in the southern part of the delta.

On the Mediterranean side, a 12 1/2 mile (20km) long dike protects the Camargue from the onslaught of the waves. Further west, the dunes perform the same function. To prevent the wind from dispersing the sand, wooden boardwalks have been installed to protect this habitat, which supports a unique collection of vegetation including marram grass, devil's grass, spurge, and narcissi.

Saline pans behind the dikes

The lagoons behind the dikes, surrounded by dunes, are used primarily for salt extraction. The Salin-de-Giraud salt extraction works, covering 43 square miles (110km2), produces around one million tons of salt per year. The Camargue is the product of man's relentless struggle against the river and the sea. It is certainly not the wild, untamed landscape it is often claimed to be. The first dike was completed in 1859 to protect the region from flooding. Ten years later, dikes were also built along the Rhône River to enable farmers to plant extensive vineyards which could be irrigated with fresh water. Meanwhile, rice-growing has replaced wine-growing to a large extent.

In spring, autumn and winter, vast expanses of the Rhône estuary are underwater. The Camargue as twilight falls (left)

The semi-wild Camargue horses, which roam the river delta in herds, are one of Europe's rarer species of wildlife (above, right)

The elegant pink flamingos are a stunning spectacle. The Camargue boasts Europe's largest colony of these birds (center)

Some parts of the delta are still used as agricultural land (below, right)

EUROPE

In the shelter of the dunes

The shifting dunes of Doñana National Park in southern Spain are a paradise for bird life

Getting there:
Cadiz and Seville airports. Bus service from Seville to Centro del Acebuche by the Park not far from Matalascañas. By boat from Sanlúcar de Barrameda

Where to stay:
Hotels; guesthouses; chalets; apartments. Camping available in Huelva and Matalascañas

Climate:
Warm summers and mild winters

Main attractions:
Bird watching; walks along the beach from Matalascañas

Special tips:
Core zones are only accessible as part of a guided tour accompanied by a park ranger. Advance booking required for bus tours. One to two miles of trails are suitable for wheelchairs.

On the rare days when the wind is still and the sea becalmed, light bounces off the Atlantic like the reflection off a mirror, illuminating the gently undulating white dunes along the coast in its dazzling glare. Along this stretch of coastline, known as "Costa de la Luz" because of this intense luminosity, lies Spain's Doñana National Park.

This Park, situated at the mouth of the Rio Guadalquivir, was established to protect Europe's largest complex of shifting dunes and is exceptional in that the landscape combines such a variety of different ecosystems, ranging from dunes, lagoons, and cork oak forests to marshland. This nature reserve with a core zone of around 190 square miles (500km2) is also an international biosphere reserve and, as one of Europe's largest and most significant wetland areas, has been awarded world heritage site status.

Just beyond the last houses of Matalascañas, a handful of wooden posts mark the boundaries of the National Park. To the west of this seaside resort, there are over 20 miles (35km) of unspoiled sandy beaches, strewn with shells. The gathering of shells, or "coquinas," for use in traditional handicrafts is one of the few human activities permitted within the heart of the Park. The tough young men of the area fish the coquinas out of the cold Atlantic Ocean, while the older men sort the catch according to size and variety. The quantity of the catch is restricted. Each "coquinero" is only permitted to take a maximum of 18lb (8kg) of shells home per day.

Along the freshwater lagoons

A belt of dunes, about half a mile wide and reaching 100ft (30m) high in places, stretches along the beach. The Atlantic winds drive the grains of sand relentlessly before them, pushing these "dunas móviles," or shifting dunes, away from the shore at the rate of 6–15ft (2–5m) a year. The seaward side of the dunes is swept bare and plants find it virtually impossible to gain a foothold. On the landward side, however, hollows supporting plant growth gradually fill with sand, causing any trees and vegetation there to die off. The dead vegetation eventually decomposes to provide the organic material needed to support the next generation of trees, which will spring up here in 50 to 100 years' time once the dune has passed over the area.

Wooden walkways lead across dry, sandy heath land and stable dunes to the pine forests and freshwater lagoons of the hinterland. Here are several thatched hides, from which the abundant bird life can be observed all year round, an absolute paradise for the large numbers of visiting birdwatchers. Doñana Park boasts no less than 365 different species of birds. Traveling further inland, the pine forests give way to dense, shrubby vegetation including cistus and juniper, known as Vera. This Mediterranean steppe region is home to several rare birds of prey, such as the booted eagle, Imperial eagle, and snake buzzard. Adjoining this shrubby landscape are groves of cork oak, behind which are the wet marshlands of the Marismas. These extend about 135 square miles (350km2) to the natural boundary of the Rio Guadalquivir.

Storks in trees

During the winter months, the marshes are ankle or even knee-deep in water, a veritable paradise for millions of water birds including the purple gallinule, which is seldom seen elsewhere. More than 150 species of birds observed in and around Doñana National Park breed in these marshes, some of the most spectacular being perhaps the dense colonies of nesting herons.

In addition to the resident birds, around 150 migrants also break their journey here en route to and from Africa. December and January witness the arrival of more than 600,000 birds eager to feast on the rich pickings of the Marismas wetlands. For some species, like the wild geese, this area is the most important wintering site in Europe. Storks also nest here. The skies above the aptly named "stork hill" on the eastern edge of the National Park are filled with dozens of circling storks. The marshes dry out in springtime, leaving only barren, dry vegetation in their wake and the trees are densely packed with breeding pairs. Only the Lucios, the small ponds, still retain a little brackish water at the end of a hot summer.

Where the Guadalquivir flows into the sea, numerous freshwater lagoons provide an ideal habitat for several rare bird species (above, right)

In the hinterland, pine forests give way to a steppe-like landscape (below, left)

A rare sight among the large numbers of birds is the peacock, seen here displaying its plumage (below, right)

EUROPE

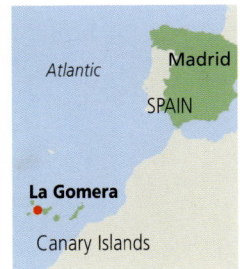

In the lee of the mild Atlantic trade winds

The cool, moist climate on the Canary Island of Gomera has produced extensive evergreen laurel forests

Getting there:
To Reina Sofia Tenerife Sur airport on Tenerife or by ferry from Cadiz to Tenerife. From Tenerife, take a high-speed ferry to La Gomera. The Park can be reached along a mountain road

Where to stay:
Holiday Island has a wide choice of accommodation. Package tours

Climate:
Mediterranean climate with no extreme temperature fluctuations. Fair amount of rain in winter

Main attractions:
Hikes; guided tours; Garajonay summit

Terraced steps on the slopes of Fortaleza Table Mountain on Gomera (right)

View from Gomera across to Tenerife (center, above)

Gran Rey Valley (below, center)

The root systems of Gomera's mighty eucalyptus trees are an impressive sight (above)

On a raft made from inflated goatskins, Jonay sailed across the 22 mile (35km) channel every day to meet in secret with Princess Gara, whose parents strongly opposed any marriage between their daughter and this peasant boy. He crossed the channel between Tenerife and La Gomera, the home of his beloved, until the lovers were discovered by villagers, whereupon they fled to the highest point on the island and speared each other with lances made of laurel wood.

It is from this legend that Mount Garajonay derives its name. On a clear day, its 4,880ft (1,487m) high summit provides magnificent panoramic vistas across the glittering blue Atlantic Ocean and the other Canary Islands of El Hierro, La Palma, Tenerife, and Gran Canaria. The densely forested heights of the rest of the island unfold beneath it. The wooded vegetation occupying the drier southwestern and southeastern flanks consists mainly of sweet-willow and tree heather or brier, which can grow to over 50ft (15m) in height. Because of its high silicic acid content, the roots of a briar tree will not burn. Brier wood is therefore frequently used to make pipes.

The northern and northeastern mountain slopes are covered by laurel forest whose trees bear large, robust, shiny, dark green leaves, just like those used in ancient times to make the victor's crown.

Jungle of ferns

The National Park was established in 1981 and is now a designated world heritage site. Almost three-quarters of its area of 15 square miles (40km2) are covered with laurel forest.

Walking through this evergreen forest on a hot day is a delightful experience. The air is moist and pleasantly cool. Even at the height of summer, the leaves are constantly dripping with moisture. There are no streams or waterfalls bubbling beside the trails, but every now and then the forest opens up into a clearing, where enough light penetrates to allow various rare flowers to grow, such as Tabaiba spurge with its profusion of yellow flowers, or the white rockrose and orange bellflower. In other places, the forest floor is covered with tall ferns which form an impenetrable jungle. Surrounded by 65ft (20m) high tree trunks, thickly covered with moss and festooned with long strands of old man's beard dangling from gnarled branches, it is easy to imagine oneself in the middle of an enchanted forest. All the more so when dense veils of mist swirl between the trees, assuming mysterious, gnome or elf-like shapes.

When the clouds build up

This lush, green vegetation in an otherwise a dry region is entirely due to the northeast trade winds. These Atlantic trade winds bring a constant supply of rainfall to the northern and northeastern slopes of La Gomera. As the rain-bearing clouds collide with these slopes, they deposit their moisture in the form of drizzle or wet mists. This natural phenomenon is crucial for the island's water supply since most of its drinking water is acquired in this way.

Of the 450 species of plants on La Gomera, several are indigenous, including various tree species such as Canary Mahogany, Canary Ebony, and the Tilo tree. Similarly, several species of fauna are also exclusive to this island. During the Tertiary period, laurel forests were widespread throughout large areas of North Africa and Southeast Europe. The climatic changes induced by the Ice Age, followed much later by man's influence in the form of forest clearance, have almost completely eliminated them. The rainforest in Garajonay National Park represents one of the greatest surviving remnants of continuous laurel forest in the world — a living fossil.

The rocks beneath this primeval forest also date back to the Tertiary period. Five to 15 millions years ago, volcanic eruptions spewed basalt and ash to the earth's surface, which was deposited in horizontal layers. Later, streams of hot lava burned their way through these basalt strata and ash fields.

EUROPE

The laurel forests of Madeira

The laurisilva covering the island's northern slopes is protected within a national park

Getting there:
International airport at Funchal. Package holiday destination. The laurisilva forests can only be accessed on foot

Where to stay:
Madeira is a popular holiday island with a wide choice of accommodation

Climate:
Average January temperature 61°F (16°C), rising to 70°F (21°C) in July. Warmer in the south, with frequent rainfall

Main attractions:
Walks through the laurisilva forests and along the "levadas," or canals; botanical garden; Funchal Ecological Park; Ribeiro Frio and Queimadas forest parks

Special tips:
Some sections of the Park are closed to visitors

Rearing up out of the Atlantic some 370 miles (600km) off the coast of Morocco is the volcanic island of Madeira and its three satellite islands. Like the Canary Islands, Cape Verde Islands, and the Azores, Madeira is part of the Macaronesian island group. These islands still support what is left of a habitat that evolved between 20 and 2 million years ago, long before the great Ice Ages of the Tertiary period.

In the days when the earth's climate was warmer and wetter than it is now, vast forests of laurel, or laurisilva, blanketed large tracts of southern Europe and north Africa. When the last Ice Age laid its cold mantle over the continents, most of this type of woodland was killed off. The Macaronesian islands with their own distinct Atlantic climate are the only place that these laurel forests have managed to survive until the present day. While the smaller, neighboring islands support nothing more than a few sparse remnants of this unique type of forest, Madeira itself is still generously populated by laurisilva. The northern slopes of all its ancient volcanic mountains, the entire northern half of the island, its deep valleys, and inaccessible gorges are all still covered with dense laurel forests. Ninety percent of the area is thought to be original forest, untouched by human influence.

On Madeira, the laurisilva forms a lush green belt of vegetation around the mountain slopes between altitudes of 990–4,290ft (300–1,300m). The areas are similar to tropical rain forest areas because the northeast trade winds are constantly driving moist sea air onto the islands, hitting the north-facing slopes and forming rain clouds over the course of the day.

Water, water everywhere

Inevitably, the discovery of this densely wooded island in 1419 by Joćo Gonćalves Zarco Madeira, a Portuguese navigator, soon led to vast numbers of hardwood trees being felled to provide timber for the ship-building industry. On top of this, large tracts of forest were burned in order to make room for sugar-cane plantations.

Despite these depredations, around 80 square miles (200km2) of irreplaceable forest has managed to survive. A nature reserve and designated world heritage site now protects 60 square miles (150km2) of this unique forest, an area equivalent to 16 percent of the island.

Wherever you are in the laurisilva, there is water: running, gurgling, and flowing down into the valleys from the mountain uplands, or

tumbling over scores of spectacular waterfalls. The laurisilva forests also have a key role to play with regard to the island's water supply. On the one hand, they preserve the humus layer, thereby ensuring the ground's capacity to filter and store water. Furthermore, the forest prevents the topsoil from being washed away. Without the stabilizing force of the forest, rainwater would flow straight down the resulting bare mountainsides and drain straight into the sea.

Early settlers on Madeira devised and built an extremely clever system of canals along the mountain slopes, catching the valuable water deposited in the northern part of the island and channeling it down into the fields in the south. Footpaths run alongside

these so-called "levadas," enabling present-day visitors to experience Madeira's remarkable scenery first hand and to penetrate deep into the rainforest itself.

The dense, leafy canopy on these wet, northern slopes is most commonly populated by the Azores laurel, tilo tree, and Canary mahogany. Some of these specimens are 500-year-old giants and their trunks are frequently thickly overgrown with mosses and lichens, likewise endemic to the region. The forest floor is home to ancient ferns, which evolved some 20 million years ago and have become extinct elsewhere. The drier, southern slopes support a variety of trees including Canary ebony, tea trees, and olives.

Paradise for ornithologists

More than 150 plant species thrive in these laurel forests. Although many are also present on the other Macaronesian islands, 66 varieties are endemic to Madeira. These include the Madeiran blueberry and a species of tree heather that can top 20ft (6m) in height, as well as numerous orchids such as the large-leaved rattlesnake plantain.

In sharp contrast to the profusion of plant life, animal life on Madeira is relatively scarce, though no less diverse. The altogether 500 or so species of fauna consist mainly of invertebrates, insects, and spiders.

The profusion of bird life, including species such as sparrow hawks, swifts, Madeira chaffinches, and the rare Cape Verde petrel, attracts many birdwatchers to the island — often to the detriment of the birds themselves. Consequently, there are only 20 to 30 breeding pairs of the seriously endangered, soft-plumaged petrel left in these misty, mountain forests. Additionally, the breeding pattern of the species is not particularly fecund. The female lays only one, single egg after successfully pairing. During the breeding season, these nocturnal birds now have to be protected from overly intrusive birdwatchers.

Madeira's damp marine climate has helped the gnarled laurel trees in this unique primeval forest to survive the ages. They thrive only in damp conditions (above)

View across the laurel-covered mountain slopes on Madeira's northern coast where the valleys are often veiled in mist (left)

EUROPE

A kaleidoscope of colors

The Lüneberg Heath and Südheide Nature Park in northern Germany are ancient cultural landscapes

Getting there:
Via the Hamburg-Hanover Autobahn. Train and bus links to Schneverdinge, Soltau, Celle, Bergen

Where to stay:
Hotels, rural inns, and holiday parks

Climate:
Moderate climate with continental influences

Main attractions:
Wilsede with its museum and 16th-century farmhouses; Undeloh and its Magdalena Chapel; Totengrund

Special tips:
Vehicles prohibited in the nature parks

The Lüneberg Heath, measuring 2,780 square miles (7,200km2), is a unique area of man-made heath land situated in the lowlands of northern Germany between the two major cities of Hamburg and Hanover. It is the last remnant of the landscape that once stretched all the way from Denmark to Belgium, encompassing the entire Geest region of northern Germany. When the last Ice Age glaciers retreated northwards 10,000 years ago, this predominantly flat landscape was covered with dense forest.

The first settlers arrived around 5,000 years ago during the Bronze Age and began farming the land. Their livestock grazed on the young saplings and the forest receded in many places for lack of fresh growth.

Large tracts of forest were also felled for firewood. The settlers hit upon a new method of enriching the poor-quality, sandy soil. It became known as "heather farming." They cleared away the thin surface layer of humus along with its sparse covering of vegetation and scattered it in the cattle sheds. They then fertilized their fields with the resulting mixture of soil and livestock dung. This method of soil enrichment, known as "plaggen," was an early method of manuring to improve soil quality and was common practice on the Lüneberg Heath until the nineteenth century. In order to maintain sufficient supplies of humus for their fields, farmers needed to retain a reservoir of heath land that was ten times larger than their arable acreage. The exposed sand was often blown by the wind into sand dunes. During the nineteenth century, this method of farming became uneconomical and many farmers lost their farms.

Forest began to regain a foothold in unused areas.

Thousands of years of human intervention in the natural environment have played a key role in shaping this unique landscape. Many plants and animals have successfully adapted to life in this habitat and found a niche here. The region includes wide expanses of savannah-style plains, with broad grassy areas, crystal-clear streams, silent moorland, forests, and heaths.

Common heather and bell heather

The heath vegetation consists predominantly of common heather and cranberries, with bell heather replacing common heather wherever the soil conditions are wetter. Other varieties of vegetation thriving here include various grasses, lichen, and moss, dotted with occasional juniper bushes and common broom. The rare bog asphodel, marsh gentian, and heath pinks can also be found here.

It is also a good place for observing rare birds, such as great gray shrikes, black storks, woodlarks, nightjars, whinchats, and stonechats. Adders and smooth snakes, which have disappeared elsewhere, can be seen slithering over the sandy ground among the heather. The most significant mammals found on the Lüneberg Heath, however, are the horned moorland sheep. Without moorland sheep, there would no longer be any heath left. This small, modest sheep is believed to have been introduced during the Bronze Age and is descended from the Mouflon, a tough breed of mountain sheep found in Corsica and Sardinia. It is also related to the Gotland sheep, which was introduced to that Baltic island around 3,000 BC. The majority of today's moorland sheep were crossed with another breed during the 1970s. These cross-breeds differ from their pure-bred ancestors because the females no longer have horns.

The advent of modern farming methods and commercial conifer plantations around the turn of the twentieth century threatened to destroy a thousand-year-old natural ecosystem. Around 1904, nature conservationists decided to try and preserve the landscape, using traditional, if not cost-effective, methods of farming. Thanks to them there are still flocks of moorland sheep grazing peacefully among the juniper and broom. The process of "plaggen," i.e. the heavy task of removing the top layer of humus, is now accomplished by machines.

Protected heath

The Lüneberg Heath is rich in reminders of earlier human settlement, ranging from Bronze Age barrows, ancient tracks, and boundary markings to thatched farmhouses, originating in the sixteenth and seventeenth centuries.

Two nature reserves have been established to protect what is left of this once vast landscape: the Lüneberg Heath Nature Park, covering around 90 square miles (230km^2) between Lüneberg and Hamburg, and the Südheide Nature Park, extending nearly 200 square miles (500km^2), between Munster and Celle.

In late summer, when the heather is in full bloom, the landscape is a mass of brilliant purple. The stunning colors are as unusual as the rest of the heath vegetation: Juniper bushes (below, left) thrive well on sandy soil and the silver birch is also a typical feature of heath vegetation (above, right)

Shepherds move their flocks of moorland sheep around, whatever the season (below)

EUROPE

Primeval forest setting

Berchtesgaden National Park is Germany's oldest nature conservation area

Getting there:
Train links with Berchtesgaden and Bad Reichenhall. Bus services to both places. By car along the A8 highway to Bad Reichenhall exit, then on the B20 to Berchtesgaden

Where to stay:
All categories of guesthouse and hotel, as well as self-catering apartments, in all the surrounding villages

Climate:
A good deal of rain, especially at higher altitudes. Frequent thunderstorms in summer. Average annual temperatures in the valley 43°–46°F (6°–8°C), in the high mountains 36°–39°F (2°–4°C)

Main attractions:
Königsee and Obersee lakes. Hikes on Mount Watzmann.

Towards the end of the nineteenth century, Berchtesgaden decided to follow the example of Yellowstone National Park in the United States and place the flora and fauna within this alpine region under protection. The decision came almost too late for many species, however, as by then entire areas of ancient mountain forest had already been felled. Giant larches had been used to build wooden walkways around Lake Starnberger, magnificent firs were used as firewood to heat ovens, and aromatic arolla pines had been fashioned into wood paneling to decorate expensive villas. Approximately one-third of the alpine forest had already vanished in the Berchtesgaden region as a direct result of felling, forest clearance, karstification, and a drop in the altitude of the tree line due to climatic influences.

By the dawn of the twentieth century, the damage to wildlife was also irreversible. While inordinately large populations of chamois, red deer, and roe-deer populations had been deliberately bred on the traditional hunting grounds of Bavarian kings, any other wild animals regarded as dangerous or useless to the hunting fraternity were mercilessly slaughtered. The last bear was killed in 1835 near Ruhpolding; the last wolf in 1836 on the Steinernes Meer Mountain. The last bearded vulture was blasted out of the sky in 1855 by a smug marksman in the Wimbachtal Valley, although a harmless carrion eater would have been completely uneatable. The last surviving lynx was also killed around the same time.

Alpine flowers for festival decorations

Following lengthy discussion, conservationists succeeded in 1910 in getting 20,500 acres (8,300 hectares) of land around the Königsee Lake and part of the Watzmann Mountain designated as the "Berchtesgaden Plant Protection Area." A vast number of rare alpine flowers had already been "harvested" from this same area to decorate the tables of elegant hotels for various festivals. These flower displays consisted of edelweiss, for example, alpine roses, Christmas roses, lady's slipper, and other types of orchid.

This protection area later paved the way for other conservation areas and in 1978, the Berchtesgaden National Park was established, covering an area of 80 square miles (210km^2). Since then, there have been systematic attempts to preserve these last pockets of alpine wilderness and encourage the remaining woodland, mostly state-owned forests, to return to a natural development process. The forests have been left mainly to their own devices and tree-felling, removal of dead wood, clearance work are not allowed. Only occasional attempts to encourage mono cultures of natural species, in order to give the forest a helping hand with its recovery and return to mixed alpine woodland, are permitted. At the same time, the amount of game in the forest is being reduced to a manageable level, thereby considerably limiting the

amount of damage caused by wild game.

The last remnants of the ancient forest that once covered the entire Alps right up to the tree line are mostly located off the main tourist track. On Mount Rotofen (4,490ft/1,369m) in the Latten Mountains and in the Gamskendl region near Reichenhall, there are still ancient stands of firs, spruce, and beech. The Untersberg Mountain and Reiteralm on the lower slopes of the Mühlsturzhörner mountains are also home to larch and beech trees, which are several hundred years old. In Wimbachgrieß, an ancient forest of dwarf pine has survived intact, and on the Hochkalter (8,555ft/2,607m) are remnants of an ancient spruce and larch forest.

Wilderness around St. Bartholomä

Natural areas of forest, which have gradually regained the character of ancient woodland now that commercial forest management has ceased, can be reached either via the main hiking trails traversing the National Park or by boat. The Königsee peninsula with its pilgrimage church of St. Bartholomä is situated right on the fringes of this wilderness area of mixed alpine forest. The shores of the Obersee Lake are populated by ancient mountain maple and spruce completely covered with moss and ferns. A few dead trees, which are now bare of needles, have tipped into the lake and from a distance resemble gigantic fish skeletons. Species of plants growing beneath these trees include alpine honeysuckle, red-berried elder, spindle, and dog rose. Yellow globe-flowers and blue alpine clematis bloom long into the autumn.

Nature is slowly regaining the upper hand in the National Park, as the ancient forest re-establishes itself. Previously managed forest is reverting to its natural state, but bears, lynx, and wolves are unlikely ever to return to their old haunts. Only the bearded vulture has returned to circle above these mountains after an absence of over 150 years. These birds are visitors from the Rauriser Valley in neighboring Austria, where conservationists are hoping they will settle again.

Looking down on the Königsee nestling at the foot of the Watzman massif (above)

The stunning beauty of the lake glimpsed through the breaks in the trees (left)

EUROPE

Eerie forest wilderness

The Bavarian Forest and Bohemian Forest National Parks, situated on both sides of the German-Czech frontier, form a conservation area for some rare sphagnum bogs and for the remnants of the great Central European primeval forests

Getting there:
Rail links to Zwiesel, Spiegelau, and Grafenau in the vicinity of the National Park. By car via the A3 Autobahn, Hengersberg junction, then along the B 85 to Grafena. The National Park area can be reached via the B 11 from Deggendorf and the B 12 from Passau

Where to stay:
Varied and plentiful accommodations available in private houses, bed and breakfast establishments, and smaller hotels. More expensive accommodation available in the "Hotel Sonnenhof" near Grafenau

Climate:
Frequent rainfall. Cold winters, moderately warm summers

Main attractions:
Ancient forest areas near the Czech frontier. Well-marked hiking trails, to the Lake Rachel and Arbers region among others

Special tips:
Trips into Sumava National Park (Bohemian Forest) in the Czech Republic can be arranged

Roklanské jezero, with its dark, brooding waters, is surrounded by legend. Superstition has it that the lake is the gateway to the netherworld (above, left)

Over the past few years, lynx have re-established themselves in these protected forest areas. (below, right)

For centuries, smugglers, quartz seekers, and treasure hunters have found this hilly region, extending along the border between Bavaria and Bohemia, a wild and frightening place. This great expanse of primeval forest in the heart of Europe stretches over an endless landscape of rolling hills and ridges. It is singularly lacking in properly defined tracks — an eerie environment, inhabited by wolves and wildcats, where it is all too easy to lose one's way and perish. Even the 19th century novelist, Adalbert Stifter (1805-1868), who grew up in the region, still regarded this forest wilderness as a dangerously alien and hostile landscape.

Even now, as we enter the third millennium, the Bavarian and Bohemian Forests, which straddle the German-Czech frontier, still constitute the largest continuous forest region in central Europe. This once menacing ancient forest, however, has long since been forced to make room for cultivated plantations of fast-growing spruce. Only a few pockets of ancient woodlands have managed to survive, tucked away in parts of the German and Czech reserves. These primeval forest areas are one of the main attractions of the Bavarian Forest National Park, established in 1969 and the first of its kind in Germany. Many of the hikers, visiting the National Park, head for the 90 acres (36 hectares) of ancient forest around the Mittelsteig lodge, south of Bayerisch Eisenstein, where spruce, fir, and beech trees as high as church towers surround the isolated village of Zwieslerwaldhaus. After receiving special protected forest status in 1763, this woodland no longer had to sacrifice its trees to the axe. If its trees succumbed at all, it was to old age, parasites, damage caused by wild animals, or lightning storms. Some dead trees manage to remain upright for many decades, providing a home for woodpeckers, pygmy owls, and dormice before they finally rot and break down completely.

A forest of old-timers

High up on the Grosser Falkenstein (4,315ft/1,315m) and in Sumava National Park in the Bohemian Forest across the border, tall mountain spruce, beeches, mountain maples, fir, and ash trees can be found growing on steep precipices, jutting out from beneath rocky outcrops, or leaning out over rushing mountain streams. These trees, some of which are 300 to 400 years old, were not planted by any human hand, but are survivors of the original primeval forest. Some of these old-timers have reached 130ft (40m) in height, their massive root systems resembling pythons, gripping rocky promontories in a stranglehold. The surrounding rocks are covered with brimstone-yellow sulfur lichen, while the stream itself plunges into the Höllbach gorge below.

This German-Czech frontier area abounds in legend, and this lake (Roklanské jezero) is no exception. It lies at an altitude of around 3,300ft (1,000m) and was left behind by the retreating Ice Age glaciers. It is now surrounded by ancient forest, comprising trees over 500 years old whose mighty crowns tower over the younger competition. This primeval lake is consequently so well sheltered that scarcely a breath of wind ruffles its surface. The water appears either blue or black in color, depending on atmospheric conditions, making the lake appear strangely devoid of life.

Steinberg hiking area

While less eerie, the Steinberg hiking territory between Weidhütte and Glashütte is nevertheless a perfect setting for games of trappers and Indians. Situated in the heart of an tranquil forest is a 650ft (200m) high knoll, furrowed with narrow ravines, dotted with strange-looking gneiss boulders, and populated with spruce, fir, and beech trees, all several hundred years old. From these splendid natural viewpoints, one can look out over a sea of treetops to Mount Lusen (4,500ft/1,373m) on the German-Czech frontier, where the Bavarian Forest merges imperceptibly into the Bohemian Forest.

EUROPE

Krakonoš's icy kingdom

The Krkonoše Mountains on the Czech-Polish border are sublime

Getting there:
The main highway between Prague and Wroclaw bisects the Park near Nachod. Rail connections between Prague, Göritz, and Wroclaw

Where to stay:
Wide choice of hotels; mountain cabins also available

Climate:
Mean annual temperature 32°–43° F (0–6°C). Damp changeable climate. Snow to a depth of three to ten feet (one to three meters) in winter

Main attractions:
Source of the Elbe; Sněžka summit; Adrspach cliffs; Bozkov dolomite caves; waterfalls; castles and fortresses; walking and riding

Special tips:
High risk of avalanches from January to March

On the eastern fringes of Central Europe surrounded by the Sudeten mountains lies an insular area of Arctic and Alpine ecosystems, known as the Krkonoše Mountains, Along the ridges of this 4,300ft (1,300m) high mountain massif are the kind of ecosystems that are otherwise only found some 620 miles (1,000km) away in Scandinavia, the Alps, or even Great Britain. The loftiest peaks of the Krkonoše Mountains support an alpine vegetation zone consisting of grasses and lichen that bear a strong resemblance to those found in Arctic tundra regions. Even cloudberries are found here, a plant more typically found in Scandinavian fjäll landscapes. During the colder periods of the earth's history, these Mountains formed an important bridge between the northern tundra and the alpine ecosystems typical of the northern Alps, amalgamating a variety of species from completely different ecosystems.

The unique ecological features of the Krkonoše Mountains are protected by two National Parks. The highest peak in the region rises to 5,256ft (1,602m) and is known as "Sněžka." One of the Parks includes the steep slopes situated on the Polish side of the frontier while the other, on the Czech side, comprises mountain ridges and elongated valleys that drop gently down into the hilly landscape of Podkrkonošska Pahorkatina. Together, these Parks cover an area of around 230 square miles (600km2) and are a significant international biosphere reserve, preserving a natural landscape that man has influenced, often to nature's detriment, for the past 800 years.

The Black Triangle

The Krkonoše Mountains are a region of extensive mixed woodland and dense undergrowth. The beech forests that once covered the valleys up to a height of around 2,650ft (800m) have been replaced with dark, sunless plantations of solid fir, although a few remnants of this magnificent deciduous woodland still survive in a few river valleys. In areas where cleared patches of forest have been reclaimed by nature, a rich diversity of new and colorful flora has evolved including orchids, sedges, spring snowflake, and crocus.

The higher elevations 2,600–3,900ft (800–1,200m), once covered with mixed coniferous forest have been replaced by solid fir plantations. Wide tracts of the forested land have all but died off. The Krkonoše Mountains lies within the so-called Black Triangle, in range of major German, Czech, and Polish industrial centers. Emissions from lignite power stations have polluted the soil to such an extent that the trees have been poisoned. Even though air quality has improved drastically since the 1990s, the forests are still dying.

Even so, some fascinating ecological niches still exist in this mountainous region. The summer meadows are carpeted with a brilliant display of flowers including yellow pansies, arnica, and rare species of gentian and campanula, while alpine blue lettuce and various types of butterbur grow beside the clear, babbling brooks.

Remnants of surviving tundra

In the Krkonoše Mountains, above the tree line at the fairly low altitude of 3,900ft (1,200m) a few leftover areas of Ice-Age tundra still survive, sporting occasional stands of knee pine often containing trees up to 100 years old. The hollows are filled with sub-arctic peat bogs. The places where this knee pine was once burned away to make room for new pastures are now populated by tough matgrass, which is intolerant of other vegetation.

The region's main ecological treasures, however, are the so-called "cirques." These basin-shaped hollows nestling below the mountain ridges were scoured out by melting Ice-Age glaciers as they flowed down into lower-lying valleys. A spectacularly varied and colorful collection of flora has been preserved over a relatively small area, boasting every species found in the Riesengebirge. The cirques are known as "Krakonoš's Garden" (*Krakonosova zahradka*, after a mountain sprite), "Schustler's Garden" (*Schustlerova zahradka*), or the "Devil's Garden" (*Čertova zahradka*).

Sněžka is the highest peak in the mountains (above)

Icy winds and heavy frosts produce picturesque snow scenery in winter (below, right)

Mountain cabins provide inviting stopping-off places in summer (below, left)

The Czech name for the Riesengebirge reserve is Krkonossky National Park (below, center)

EUROPE

High in the Carpathian mountains

Tatras National Park in Slovakia and Poland provides a refuge for wild animals

Getting there:
Good rail and road connections from Zakopane. Airports at Krakow and Poprad

Where to stay:
Wide choice of all types of accommodation

Climate:
Sunny weather in September and October. In January-February, warm in the uplands, cold in the valleys

Main attractions:
Sucha Bela gorge; bird and wildlife watching

Special tips:
Some trails only open from July 1 to October 30

The High Tatras, which stretch for 16 miles (25km) along the border between Slovakia and Poland, are Europe's smallest mountain range. They do, however, have the distinction of being the highest mountains of the 750 mile (1,200km) long Carpathian chain, with 20 peaks reaching upwards of 8,250ft (2,500m) in height. The highest of these is Gerlachovsky Stit, which rises to a height of 8,710ft (2,655m). This mighty ridge of gray granite, running from west to east, forms the frontier between Slovakia and Poland. Numerous steep, secondary ridges branch out from the main ridge, inset by deeply carved valleys. The views from the summits offer stunning vistas across this untamed and dramatic mountain scenery. This incomparable landscape of mountains, valleys, and basins — including the romantically wild Sucha Bela gorge, equipped with walkways for the benefit of tourists — is unmistakably the work of Ice Age glaciers. These ice fields also left behind 130 or so tarns. Tarns, or water-filled basins in the hollow of a cirque, can descend to depths of 165ft (50m) or more and are filled with crystal clear water that shimmers dark blue or green in the sunlight.

Dense, silent forests of evergreen pine cover the steep slopes of the Tatras. Up to 5,100ft (1,550m) they consist mainly of spruce and fir, interspersed with a scattering of mountain maple. At higher elevations, these are joined by occasional specimens of stone pine with their characteristic, contorted trunks. The subalpine or dwarf-tree zone up to 6,100ft (1,850m) is dominated by gnarled mountain pines. Above the tree line, the terrain is carpeted with alpine meadows, which burst into a dazzling display of flowers in spring and summer.

Remote mountain landscapes

The forests of the Tatras are like an island refuge, providing a home to various relicts from the Ice Ages, such as ring ouzels and three-toed woodpeckers. Other rare species, such as the lesser spotted eagle, peregrine falcon, hazel hen, capercaillie, and black grouse, have also found an undisturbed refuge here amid these vast mountain forests.

This unique and largely inaccessible mountain landscape likewise represents a safe sanctuary for European pine martens, wild cats, wolves, and lynx. Even brown bears are fairly common here. Most of the time these shy creatures avoid human settlements and trails, but now and then they have been known to rummage through the garbage cans in the local villages.

The high alpine grasslands, pastures, and barren, rocky terrain are home to the Tatras chamois, emblem of the High Tatras National Park. They are preyed upon by lynx, which regularly emerge from the forests to hunt for their next meal. This type of chamois has remained completely isolated since the last Ice Age and has evolved into a separate species of its own. The Tatras marmot, whose whistle is a familiar sound to mountain hikers, is indigenous to the area.

Paradise for tourists

The steep, rugged rock formations surrounding the summits above the mountain meadows and pastures may at first glance appear deceptively devoid of life. These craggy heights nevertheless provide an important nesting site for golden eagles, wall creepers, and alpine accenters, which remain well hidden and scarcely visible among the rocks. Hugging the scree slopes and nestled amongst the clefts and cracks of dry limestone veins are a number of different varieties of flora, including mountain avens and glacier carnations, all relicts from the Ice Age. Rare plants such as the willow-leaved gentian, Tatras larkspur, turk's cap lily, and edelweiss also manage to survive in this inhospitable rocky terrain.

Otters frequent the banks of rushing mountain streams and the numerous waterfalls, constantly on the look-out for shoals of huch, brown trout, and grayling.

The peaks of the High Tatras tower high above the surrounding landscape (above, right)

This mountain region is dotted with scores of picturesque tarns (bottom right)

The hiking trails are punctuated with mountain chalets such as the one shown here

EUROPE

A forest undisturbed for almost 500 years

The National Parks straddling the border between Poland and Belarus provide a sanctuary for the European bison

Getting there:
Poland: by road from Bialystok to Bialowieski with access into the Park. Belarus: by road from Brest to Kamenets, from where it is 12 miles (20km) to the Park

Where to stay:
Poland: a few hotels in Bialystok, but numerous private rooms. Belarus: 3 hotels and 4 guesthouses in Kamenets

Climate:
January: 25°F (-4°C); July 64°F (18°C). Rarely more than 50 to 60 days of snow

Main attractions:
Hiking trails; carriage trips; museums; outdoor enclosures. Poland: trip by narrow-gauge railway; nature trails

Special tips:
Most areas of the Parks are inaccessible, except in the company of a licensed guide, either on foot or in a horse-drawn carriage. On the Polish side, visitors restricted to groups of 25. Several nature trails

Europe's last truly ancient forest, which has remained virtually undisturbed for hundreds of years, straddles the border between Poland and Belarus not far from Bialowieski in Poland and Kamenets in Belarus. The forest, which is both a world heritage site and a significant biosphere reserve, covers an area of approximately 565 square miles (1,460km^2), 225 (580) of which lie in Poland and the remaining 340 (880) in Belarus. Right in the midst of this great forest area are the inaccessible National Parks of Bialowieski in Poland and Belovezhskaya Pusha in Belarus.

This vast forest could easily serve as the setting for ancient legends and fairytales. Not a single tree has been felled or any undergrowth cleared for several decades. Even diseased trees are left in peace and any dead wood remains where it has fallen. For centuries now, the forest has been left to renew itself at its own pace. By 1541, the Russian section had already been declared a hunting reserve in order to protect Europe's largest wild animal, the European bison. Strict regulations were introduced in 1557 to control forest exploitation, although tree felling had never figured significantly as the forest was simply too wet and inaccessible.

From 1598 on, only Polish kings were permitted to hunt here, a privilege shared by Russian tsars and tsarinas in 1795. All this changed during the German occupation in World War I when arrangements were made to start felling the forest. The German occupying force even built a special railway for transporting the logs out of the region. During the occupation, the forest ended up sacrificing six-and-a-half million cubic yards (five million cubic meters) of timber as well as its last herd of bison. After this episode, it was once again left to its own devices.

On the watershed

Despite its seemingly infinite vastness, this ancient forest situated on the watershed between the Baltic and the Black Sea is, in fact, only a remnant of what was once a continental forest zone linking the Russian tundra with the Black Sea steppes and the Baltic with the Mediterranean. This explains why some species, which are more likely to be found in southern Europe, are just as much at home here as northern species. Many of the ancient tree trunks are thick with fungi and lichens, indicating an extremely diverse natural history.

On the Belarus side, biologists have recorded 900 flowering plants, while in Poland 630 have been identified, including 26 tree varieties. Spruce reach a height of up to 165ft (50m), oak, ash, and lime trees reach 130ft (40m) or more. Many of these trees are over 500 years old with trunks around 6 1/2ft (2m) thick. The varying soil types and moisture levels have produced 20 different types of woodland, covering 90 percent of the area in Belarus. These consist mainly of mixed stands of oak, lime, and hornbeam, of pines and spruces, or of a combination of deciduous trees and pines. There are also two distinct populations of bush vegetation, including the hazels bordering the marshland, as well as 13 different bog and meadow habitats. Many of the plants common to this region are endangered species elsewhere in Europe.

Black storks, cranes, and owls

The forest is surprisingly light and bright, having rather less in the way of undergrowth than one might imagine. An extremely rich variety of animal life thrives in the unique and unspoiled sanctuary which it provides, allowing virtually every European species its own niche. In addition to the 8,000 or so different species of insect that have been identified in the region, the trees and bushes are home to well over 200 different varieties of birds, 120 of which also breed here. These include large numbers of rare black storks, cranes, and many species of owl.

Elk, red deer, roe deer, wolves, martens, badgers, beavers, and otters rank among the most common of the 55 mammals indigenous to the area, but the most significant species found in these Parks are, without doubt, the two impressive herds of free-roaming European bison. Separated by a six-feet-high, barbed wire fence, a 250-strong herd of these animals exists on the Belarus side of the border, while another herd of around 300 animals lives in the Polish National Park. These are the last of their kind, and it is thanks to the fact that their forest habitat has remained undisturbed that their numbers have recovered since World War I. These herds come from a pool of just 52 zoo animals, 5 of which were selected in 1929 as the basis for a breeding program to begin the return of these animals to the wild.

The inaccessible forests of Poland's Bialowieski National Park and Belarus's Belovezhskaya Pusha are home to many ancient, giant trees. The deep forest harbors some 550 bison, living either side of the boundary fence (above and left)

Access to the shores of the numerous lakes is barred by piles of dead wood

EUROPE

The plains of the Puszta

Hortobágy National Park, in Hungary, preserves a cultural landscape that has produced a unique set of natural habitats

Getting there:
Highway 33 to Hortobágy. Rail links between Debrecen and Füzesabony. Visitor access to the Park by horse, carriage, cycle, or by foot.

Where to stay:
Luxury and middle-range hotels in Hortobágy

Climate:
Moderate continental climate with severe winter and warm summers. Windy

Main attractions:
Bird-watching; walks along nature trails; riding; cycling; shepherd's museum

Special tips:
Much of the Park is closed to visitors

Beneath the vast skies of eastern Hungary, the Hortobágy *puszta*, or "plains," form a table, stretching across an apparently endless expanse of grassland between the Tisza River and the town of Debrecen. Currently 290 square miles (750km2) of this unique cultural landscape are under protection and the region has also been designated an international biosphere reserve. Its marshes and lakes are among the world's most significant wetlands. The Park consists of a mosaic of canals, marshes, moors, fishponds, and forests — an endless expanse of continuous wetland, relieved only by occasional patches of grassy terrain on higher ground and a few stands of woodland.

This fascinating landscape is the product of hundreds of years of agricultural and domestic livestock farming and has given rise to a variety of unique natural habitats. The low-lying areas were once the floodplains of the River Tisza, which punctually burst its banks twice a year. It was thickly forested and its lowest-lying sections consisted of impassable marshland. The Tisza River meandered its way in a series of broad curves right across this area. During the Middle Ages, the forest was cleared and a thriving farming community began to flourish on this fertile soil, which provided a livelihood for the inhabitants of the 50 or so villages that the Puszta once comprised. Remnants of some of the loveliest woodland ever to thrive on these flood plains are still seen near Ároktõ and Tiszacsege. Islands located in the midst of these open waters support mixed woodland consisting of oak, ash, and elm, while poplars and willows grow on the wooded peninsulas.

When the farmers moved away

The farming community left the area during the fifteenth century when the country was under Turkish rule and the grasslands were left as grazing ground for native Nonius horses, Hungarian gray cattle, and the famous Racka sheep with their long, curly horns.

This breed of sheep was much sought after for its meat throughout medieval Europe. The shepherds drove their herds into Western Europe, Poland, and Turkey, in order to sell them.

In 1846, efforts got underway to tame the Tisza River and canalize it. The damp pastures dried out and the land dried up. It was not until irrigation canals were introduced much later that the plains became agriculturally viable again. Nowadays the grasslands are home to grazing animals such as cattle and semi-wild herds of horses, which roam the steppes accompanied by shepherds wearing traditional costume.

Although these animals no longer have a great deal of economic significance, they nevertheless play a major role in preserving this immensely important habitat with its great diversity of rare flora and fauna. They are also key factors in ensuring the genetic continuation of traditional breeds of domestic animal, in pre-

serving Hungary's traditional forms of land use and animal breeding, and in serving, not least, as a tourist attraction. By the end of the Second World War, this breed of gray cattle had all but vanished. Fortunately, it has been possible to build up the herds again, thanks to modern breeding methods and material from gene pools.

Plans for reclaiming the dried up, saline grasslands had been under consideration since the nineteenth century, but it was not until 1915 that prisoners-of-war began building the first fishponds. Over the years, this collection of ponds has become the largest artificially created system of fishponds in the world, extending over an area of 23 square miles (60km2). They are fed by water from the Tisza River, channeled to them via a network of canals.

Unspoiled landscape

Only 10 of the original 17 fishponds are still in use. The banks of the abandoned ponds, like other areas of open water, have become overgrown with dense reeds and reed mace, while white and yellow water-lilies, floating hearts, and water nuts bloom in profusion across the surface of the water. The surrounding reed-beds are home to bearded reedlings, water rail, and small coots. This relatively untouched steppe and wetland landscape is also one of the main refuges and last retreats for numerous rare birds, including several species of heron such as the gray heron, purple heron, and great white heron. It is home to egrets, cormorants, black storks, and several types of geese and also boasts the largest colony of rare spoonbills in central Europe, numbering around 250 breeding pairs.

Many relatively uncommon warblers also breed here, including sedge warblers and tamarisk warblers. Hortobágy is also home to a population of 3,500 great bustards, the biggest of all steppe birds, while staker falcons, imperial eagles, and ospreys circle majestically in the skies above.

The draw-well has become the symbol of the Puszta (left)

Horse racing was once one of the major pastimes of Puszta dwellers (above)

Large parts of this conservation area are still inaccessible

EUROPE

The underwater kingdom of the Kornati islands

Off the coast of Dalmatia, a national park preserves the underwater life around the Kornati Islands

Getting there:
Only accessible by boat. Day trips from Vodice, Biograd, and Zadar

Where to stay:
300 guesthouses on different islands. Camping not permitted

Climate:
Mediterranean climate. The moist, warm, Jugo winds off the sea often bring rain; the Bora wind off the mainland usually brings good weather

Main attractions:
The 6th-century Toreta Tower near Tarac; ruins of an Illyrian settlement near Pedinka; Roman fish vivarium on Piskera

Special tips:
Only one food store near Piskali. Provisions available from local fishing boats during the summer

One of the Mediterranean's richest underwater kingdoms is hidden beneath the azure blue waters of the Adriatic Sea off the coast of Croatia. It is home to sea scorpions, gilthead sea bream, great shoals of other Mediterranean fish and dolphins. Lying approximately 9 miles (15km) off the Dalmatian coast within Kornati National Park, it is an area popular with divers.

Extending over 115 square miles (300km2), this cluster of 140 small, closely-packed islands, shallows, and reefs forms a unique landscape, not found anywhere else along the Mediterranean coast. Eighty-nine of the islands lie within the National Park, named after the main island of Kornati, which covers 12½ square miles (32.5km²). There are two main groups of deeply fissured, rugged limestone islands strung out over a length of 15½ miles (25km) along the coast. The islands of Pasman, Vrgada, and Murter form the boundary of this 8-mile (13km) wide archipelago on the mainland side, extending as far as Dugi Otok Island in the northwest and the Zirije Islands in the southeast.

Wave action, tides, and constant sea winds have, over thousands of years, eaten away at what was once a single, continuous plate of soft limestone to create this unique labyrinth of channels and rocks. Wherever you look, steep cliffs rear up out of the sea, such as the sheer, 260ft (80m) high cliff near Klobucar. Local residents call these cliffs "crowns," from which the Kornati Islands presumably derive their name (kruna = corona). Breakers have cut deep furrows and clefts into these rocky islands and, along the coast of Mona, the sea has carved deep rocky overhangs around the base of the island.

Remains of ancient cisterns

These islands have examples of numerous other fascinating geological formations: for instance, the multi-colored geological strata visible on Kornat, with their intricate patterns of concentric circles. The southern end of the main island, measuring 660–990ft (200–300m) across and over 4 miles (7km) long, also has its hidden treasures, namely a single huge boulder towering 360ft (109m) in height and known as the "Opat."

The Kornati Islands were covered in forest until the Romans started felling trees to use in ship-building, thereby robbing the islands of their green vegetation. The Romans also deepened the shallow straits between the islands of Kornat and Dugi Otok by six feet to allow big ships to pass through. Near Mala Proversa, ruins of ancient rainwater cisterns and a vivarium, in which fish were kept to provide fresh food for sailors, testify to the presence of these early settlers.

During winter, the Kornati Islands are uninhabited. They are owned by a number of families, most of which reside on Murter. The archipelago only comes to life in summer when tourists converge on the 300 or so guest cabins and the owners come to tend the olives groves thriving on some of the islands. The olive groves are interspersed with grasses and bushy brome-grass and the steep slopes are home to patches of Dubrovnik centaury, a protected species that is only found in the Kornati Islands. Dubrovnik centaury is the original form of the yellow centaury commonly found in garden rockeries.

The islands provide grazing for a few sheep, which favor the ancient patches of meadow surrounded by natural stone walls. The skies are home to herring gulls and birds of prey, circling over these largely barren, dry, and dusty islands.

A world of algae

The most precious of the region's natural treasures lies mainly underwater, as three-quarters of this National Park of 86 square miles (224km2) protects a submarine environment. The water is so clear and still that sunlight filters down to depths of 260ft (80m). The labyrinth of stones, crevices, and caves is home to at least 436 species of maritime plants and algae, including 222 types of red algae alone. Nearer to the shore are mats of algae, consisting of 72 species of brown and 51 species of green algae. This nutritious environment is home to 300 different animal species, including sponges, cave-dwelling creatures, crabs, invertebrates, echinoderms, and other varieties of tunicates.

The vast labyrinth of caves shelters huge numbers of fish as well as octopi waiting for their next meal. Schools of dolphin are often seen out in the open sea. Since fishing is completely prohibited in the area, this National Park area provides a safe habitat for altogether 65 species of fish. The open waters are consequently populated by large numbers of striped barbel, dentex and gilthead sea bream, drumfish, large and small scorpion fish, brown wrasse, and even sea eels. The shallow, sandy bays are a perfect starting-point for snorkeling expeditions to explore this fascinating underwater kingdom.

Settlements like the village of Vrulje are rare in the Kornati Islands. Note the typical stone walls, parceling up the land (above)

Evening across the Bay of Telascica (below)

EUROPE

Wolves of the south

Abruzzo National Park is a sanctuary for brown bears and Apennine wolves

Getting there:
Not far from the highway between Rome/Naples and Bari. Bus services from Rome, Naples, and Avezzano to Pescasseroli. Railway station in Avezzano

Where to stay:
Abruzzo National Park is a popular tourist center. There is a wide choice of accommodation in the small mountain villages

Climate:
Mediterranean climate; cool at higher altitudes with snow in winter

Main attractions:
Hiking; European black pine forest; Mancino Castle and viewpoint overlooking Pescasseroli from Trail BN1; Lake Vivo; Barrea

When Abruzzo National Park was established in southern Italy, it represented the last hope for Italy's brown bears, the Abruzzo chamois, and the Apennine wolf. Brown bears once roamed all over the Central Apennines, from the Alps to Abruzzo. New settlements and forest clearance to make way for fields in central Italy meant that the bears' natural habitat dwindled proportionately. By 1500, they had already become restricted to the North Italian Alps and the Abruzzo region of southern Italy.

Four hundred years later, the two populations had shrunk to fewer than 100 animals and were on the verge of extinction. Most of the surviving bears in the Abruzzo occupied an area of just two square miles (five square kilometers) within the royal hunting grounds, where they remained safe from persecution by local farmers and shepherds. In 1923, when the National Park was created, this small area formed the heart of what is now a national reserve covering 170 square miles (440km2) between Salerno and Barletta in central Italy.

The Park preserves a rugged, harsh mountain landscape, with summits rising on either side of the Sangro River valley to heights of 6,600ft (2,000m) and more. It is separated by narrow ravines and broad valleys and dotted with a handful of picturesque villages.

Black pine forests

Two-thirds of this breathtakingly beautiful mountain region is covered with deep, dense forest, consisting mainly of beech, interspersed with plane trees, maples, and a species of sorbus or mountain ash trees. Silent forests of solid beech line the Cervara Valley, while Villetta Barrea, another lateral valley, is home to a wonderful, dark forest of European black pine, a habitat now very much a rarity in Europe. Above 6,300ft (1,900m), the only trees that grow are mountain firs and, above the tree line, bushes and shrubs struggle to survive on the bare, inhospitable scree and rocky ground.

This terrain nevertheless supports well over 200 different plant varieties, which have remained largely unaffected by the traditional farming that in and around the five villages in the Park. On the contrary: it is the farmers sending their goats and sheep into the upper pastures to graze during the summer and wintering them in the valleys each year that has resulted in the stunning variety of flowers that bloom each spring and summer to carpet the meadows with a dazzling display of color. Some of the flora species are now quite rare: for example, the lady's slipper orchid, a striking species that only blooms properly once every two years or so.

Shy brown bears

It was some time before farmers and shepherds could bring themselves to accept the brown bears as fellow inhabitants of the region. After all, these awesome predators, weighing some 440lb (200kg), would occasionally make off with one of their goats or sheep. The situation was eased to some extent by the National Park authorities offering compensation payments in the event of any losses incurred as a result of wild animal damage. Hikers are unlikely to catch a glimpse of this shy creature, but will frequently come across rocks that have been rolled aside, a sure indication of a bear having passed that way in its search for worms and insects

Not only has this unique National Park provided a sanctuary for 100 or so Abruzzo bears, it also represents a refuge for the Apennine wolves, which teetered on the brink of extinction a few decades ago. Their numbers have since swelled to such an extent in this forested mountain region that they are now found right across the Apennines as far as the Southern Alps.

The Abruzzo chamois once faced a fate similar to that of the bears. Though related to the Alpine species, the Abruzzo chamois is an individual species in its own right. The National Park is home to the sole surviving herd, now numbering over 1,000 animals.

Panoramic view of the Sangro river valley that bisects the National Park (above)

Lago Montagne Spaccata on the fringes of the Park is a popular attraction for visitors (below, left)

The village of Anversa degli Abruzzi, 6 miles (10km) to the north of the Park, is regarded as the gateway to this nature reserve (below, center)

The harsh winter climate and strong winds have left many trees misshapen

ASIA

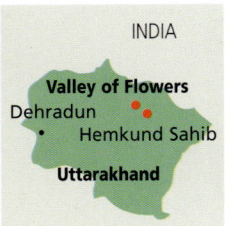

The Valley of Flowers

Hundreds of wildflower species bloom in this paradisical glen

State capital:
Uttarakhand, Dehradun 200 mi./320 km

Convenient access:
Road to Govindghat, air to Dehradun, rail to Haridwar

Accommodation:
Budget at Gangharia

Best season:
April to October, snowbound in winter

Also worth seeing:
Badrinath Temple, ski slopes of Auli

At least some of Frank Sydney Smythe's weariness must have vanished when he walked into the valley of the Pushpawati stream, on the trudge back from the arduous first ascent of Mount Kamet 25,446 ft. (7,756 m). What lay before the mountaineer-writer-photographer and his fellow climbers, the legendary Eric Shipton, and R.L. Holdworth, was a wondrous vista of blooms that inspired him to christen his discovery the "Valley of Flowers." That was in 1931, and more than 75 years later the name still holds; in 1982 it was suffixed with "National Park." Over this period, the once exclusive domain of nomadic shepherds set deep in the high reaches of the western Himalayas has attracted many visitors. One of the earliest was the Englishwoman Margaret Lague, a lover of flowers, drawn by the stories of its botanical profusion. While reaching out to pluck one, she slipped off a rock and died, to be buried in the midst of the meadows. Today her tombstone is the only permanent structure in the Valley. It says, "I will lift mine eyes unto the hills from whence cometh my strength."

Brahma kamal, the king of Himalayan flowers

What makes the Valley special is that it is just 6 miles (10 km) long and 1 mile (2 km) wide (though the Park encloses 54 miles (87.5 km) of surrounding area). The unusual abundance in such a small area is due to its location at the junction of a major Himalayan transition zone: besides being sandwiched by the extreme eastern edge of the Zanskar and the Greater Himalayan ranges, in the north and south, respectively, it is also the meeting place of eastern and western Himalayan flora. The Pushpawati, joined by streams and waterfalls along the way, runs its length. From April to October, climatic and environmental dynamics change on a monthly basis, leading to the birth and decline of over 300 varieties of flora. The season begins with the slow melting of glaciers, which moisten the slumbering soil. Soon, new flowers begin to emerge, multiply and blossom in a rich riot of colours, smells, shapes and sizes. Rhododendrons are one of the first to appear, followed by sweet-smelling blue primulas, irises and snow-white anemones, two-flower violets, bal-

sams, marsh orchids and thymus. July brings geraniums, pendicularis, morinas, potentillas and blue poppies, some of them lasting up to September. Other vivid bloomers are golden-yellow grandiflora during August-September, wild roses and colonies of forget-me-nots. Out of crevices at awkward angles protrude the revered brahma kamal, a member of the daisy family. The king of Himalayan flowers is used as an offering in hill temples, and also as a balm for bruises and cuts. While the surrounding mountains are obscured during most of the season, a perfectly clear view of the snow-clad heights—Gauri Parbat 22,043 ft. (6,719 m) is the tallest finial within the Park, the lower end of which is at 10,662 ft. (3,250 m)—opens up post monsoon. As winter closes in, the flowers begin to turn brown and peter out until woken

once again by spring. Supported by the fiesta of flowers is obviously a large and diverse population of butterflies, but there is bigger Himalayan fauna too: tahr, bharal (blue sheep), red fox, seraw and black bear.

The Valley is still not within easy reach. A 9-mile (15 km) trek or pony ride from Govindghat 2,716 ft. (1,828 m) winds up a steep cobbled pathway amidst mountains covered with oaks, silver birches and pines. Small food stalls along the path provide relief, for it also leads to Hemkund Sahib, a much revered pilgrimage site for Sikhs. At Gangharia, a ramshackle village where the first day's walk ends, the route bifurcates, one leading into the Valley of Flowers and the other towards Hemkund.

Hemkund Sahib, higher up in the mountains

Four steep miles (7 km) up from Gangharia, the second trail brings one up to the 14,763 ft. (4,500 m)-high Lokpal Lake, on the banks of which is the shrine. In a verse in the autobiographical Bichittar Natak, it is suggested by Guru Gobind Singh, the 10th and last Sikh Guru, that in a previous life he practiced spiritual discipline by the side of the Lake, an episode now consecrated by a pentagonal-roofed gurudwara. A small temple nearby is dedicated to Laxmana, the brother of Lord Rama, who is said to have per-formed austerities here as well. Visitors arriving at Hemkund after the laborious hike are served tumblers of steaming hot, sweet tea by gurudwara sevaks (volunteer workers). Devotees consider it customary to take a dip in the ice-cold glacial lake over which a wispy mist usually hangs, periodically lifting to reveal the reflection of the seven surrounding mountain peaks in the crystal clear waters.

Left: Hemkund Sahib, the highest gurudwara in the world, was first consecrated in 1936 with the Holy Book of the Sikhs being placed in a small structure. The current hexagonal structure is designed to bear the weight of heavy snowfall, besides representing an upturned brahma lotus placed by the Creator on the spot where the Guru meditated. Above: Sweeping view of the Valley of Flowers.

ASIA

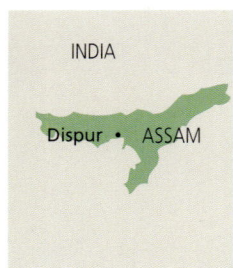

Plantations for the perfect brew

Assam's tea gardens produce strong and smooth teas

State and capital:
Assam, Dispur

Convenient access:
Road to individual tea estates, air to Guwahati, Jorhat, Dibrugarh, Tezpur, also rail (except to Tezpur)

Accommodation:
Budget to high-end in main towns

Best season:
November to March

Also worth seeing:
Annual winter Tea Festival at Jorhat (dates vary), Kaziranga and other wildlife reserves

Darjeeling tea from West Bengal may have the fragrance and flavors, but it is actually the plantations of Assam—the world's single largest tea-growing region—which produce the traditional full-bodied Indian tea. Thousands of neatly serried and clipped, undulating lush green fields, marked with light and shade-facilitating trees, and picturesque red-roofed factories and bungalows are ensconced between the snow-covered eastern Himalayan ranges and the thickly forested hills of the north-eastern states of Nagaland, Manipur, Meghalaya and Mizoram. Spread out over the year, rainfall is plentiful here and the soil has good drainage qualities. In the south flows the Brahmaputra, contributing its waters to the cause. Assam tea is categorized as the first and the second flushes. While the former has a fresh, rich aroma, the second flush produces the more famous "tippy teas," essentially black tea with gold tips, which creates a sweet and smooth brew. This black tea is far different in taste and color from the green tea made in China.

Bushes became big business

It all began in the early 1820s, when the Scottish brothers Robert and Charles Alexander Bruce established contacts with the Singhpo tribe, reputed to grow a hitherto unknown species of tea. It was only after a decade that they succeeded in having their discovery certified as tea but events moved fast thereon. British commercial and strategic interests encouraged planters to carve out estates from the dense forests and, by 1862, there were 160 tea gardens in Assam owned by 62 companies. George Williamson, founder of Williamson Magor; Maniram Dewan, the prime minister of the last Ahom king and the first Indian to grow tea on a commercial basis in Assam; Hanuman Bux Kanoi, the largest individual tea producer in India; and later B.M. Khaitan and the Tata Tea Company were to become legends in the tea industry. In those early years, sensing opportunity, intrepid Marwari traders were gravitating from faraway Rajputana, indelibly soaking their destinies in the brown beverage. The saying went that "the Marwari can plough a trail where even bullock carts cannot," as the dense north eastern forests. Disease and non-existent infrastructure were no deterrent for one of India's most enterprising communities. Eventually, Marwaris were to buy out most British companies and today most of the tea industry is controlled by Marwari families.

Right: The leaf and bud of the robust, malty Assam tea, enjoyed particularly well with milk.

Life at the tea estates

The lifestyle of the burra (big) sahib—as tea estate managers are still known—revolves around their burra bungalows. Though the occupation may have lost its earlier romance, the latter survive as edifices of old-world graciousness. Built in the 1930s, the sprawling colonial constructions boast up to eight bedrooms, separate kitchen wings, several acres of lawns planted with magnolia, Indian lilac, frangipani, plumaria and other scented blooms, besides a formidable retinue of domestic help. There is also the world of the tea

taster, comparable to his Scotch-sampling counterparts. Existing in well-lit but sun-shaded rooms, it demands an accurate analysis of sips from as many as 1,000 porcelain cups of different brews in a day. Out in the fields, the tea-pluckers are generally women, deft fingered to tweak, break and pluck the single leaf and the bud, which makes the best golden and flowering Orange Pekoes. Pruning is usually the task of trained and experienced men, who trim the tea bushes into shape with their long iron blades.

Much of India's well-known wildlife dwells in the vicinity of the luxuriant hill estates of Assam. Virgin natural rainforest in all its hues of green is visible all around and some of the finest mountain vistas and remains of colonial history—clubs, cobbled streets and snooker—endure here. You can ride horse-back through the gardens as the old planters did, or walk through on the lines between the bushes, or on the roads, or wade through the bushes themselves, as the sunlight filters through.

Above: Assam's 800 organized tea gardens produce around 10 million pounds of tea. Women comprise close to half of the total labor force. They are descendants of tribes like the Oraon from Orissa and Jharkhand, the Sonthals from Bengal, and others from Central India, who were brought in by British planters.

ASIA

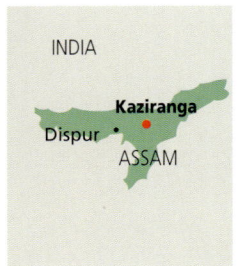

State and capital:
Assam, Dispur
155 mi. (250 km)

Convenient access:
Road to Kaziranga, air to Jorhat and Guwahati, rail to Guwahati

Accommodation:
Budget to mid-range

Best season:
November to March
Also worth seeing: Nearby tea plantations, Karbi and Mising tribal villages

Stronghold of the one-horned rhino

The big beast thrives on the wet savannah grasslands of Kaziranga National Park

E.P. Gee, the famous conservationist closely associated with Kaziranga in its early years, wrote in its visitors' book of an elephant-back foray into the jungles, "Twice charged by rhino, and the elephants each time bolted for some distance." Some months later, he recalls, other visitors wrote in the same book, "Rather disappointing. Charged only by the Forest Department!" This is one of the stories of Kaziranga, now a World Heritage Site, illustrating how it developed from a place of swamps, leeches and malaria, not accessible to even elephants, where its prize species, the Indian one-horned rhinoceros, would, unused to being disturbed by any other being, respond aggressively to intruders. And then, when the sanctuary opened to public in 1938, the "armored" beasts soon became accustomed to outsiders, allowing themselves to be watched as they grazed or wallowed in slushy mud. Another interesting anecdote preceding this one goes back to 1904, when Lady Curzon, wife of the then British Viceroy to India, hoping to see rhinos had to be satisfied with only a few hoof prints because the animal had been so mindlessly hunted that only "a few dozen" remained. Disappointed, she convinced her husband to have the forests declared as reserved and closed to hunting. The biggest story, however, is undoubtedly of the fierce battle that has been fought since then by several generations of Indian and British forest officers, and conservationists, to bring the Kaziranga rhino back from the edge of decimation. About 122 anti-poaching camps are now scattered throughout the 166 square miles (430 km²) of swamps, thickets, floodplain wetlands and forest that make up the National Park. Today, with its rhino numbers standing at about 1,700—genetically, the most viable population anywhere—the Park is considered one of the most successful conservation efforts in the world.

Whereas other parks of India are better known for the big striped cat, at Kaziranga its density, at about 17 per 39 square miles (100 km²), is highest. Yet Kaziranga is known best for its rhinoceros, not just because they are not found anywhere in India outside its north-eastern region but also because the park terrain allows for easy viewing. Unfortunately, rhinos have something that makes them coveted by man; their horn is still in high demand in the illegal market where it is sold mainly for use in Chinese traditional medicine and ornamental accessories. The horn, between 8 and 24 inches (20-60 cm) long, is not strictly a horn as it consists of a mass of tightly compressed hair placed above the nose.

Home of India's only ape

Kaziranga is divided into four ranges. The eastern woodlands interspersed with grassland and waterbodies constitute the Agoratoli range, while at the centre is the Kohora range. The western Baguri range has the highest rhinoceros density and Burhapahar, the fourth range, covers the first additional area attached to the Park. Wet savannah grasslands, which cover about 70 percent of the Park comprise tall grasses, mostly reeds, bulrushes and elephant grass. The dominant force, which shapes the Park is the monsoon, when the Brahmaputra floods low-lying grasslands for several weeks, sometimes months, causing animals to migrate to higher ground. Amongst over 52 mammalian species recorded in the area are the rare Gangetic dolphin, Chinese pangolin, hog-badger, and the tail-devoid hoolock gibbon. The latter, India's only ape, is called the musical animal. Others like the hog deer, sloth bear, jungle cats, otters, capped langurs, wild boar and jackals are more common. Thirty-nine reptiles make the list, including the gharial and the Assam roofed turtle. Both the reticulated and rock pythons occur here.

A few 100 Bengal floricans

Rich in avian fauna, the Park's different habitat zones host over 250 local and 100 migratory species. At small lakes, locally called *bheels*, are found pelicans and the increasingly rare greater adjutant storks. The grasslands are prime raptor country; the oriental honey buzzard, Pallas's fishing eagle and Himalayan griffon are usually seen. But most well known of Kaziranga's winged denizen is the

Bengal florican, of which only 400 still survive.

Located in northeastern India on the floodplain of the Brahmaputra River, the wildernesses of Kaziranga are home to the Indian "Big Five": the elephant, wild buffalo, tiger, swamp deer and rhino, of which the Park identifies most with the latter. Rhinos are solitary animals with a lifespan of about 40 years. Often weighing considerably over two tons, approximately 5.5 ft. tall at the shoulder and about 11 ft. in length, they have no natural enemies except opportunistic tigers preying on the occasional calf.

ASIA

Park of pachyderms

Elephants rule over Periyar's rich tract of rainforest

State and capital:
Kerala, Thiruvananthapuram 166 mi. (267 km)

Convenient access:
Road to Park, air, rail to Ernakulam, Thiruvananthapuram

Accommodation:
Budget to high-end

Best season:
September to May

Also worth visiting:
Ancient temples of Mangaladevi and Sabarimala, in the Park's buffer zone

Ex-poachers persuaded into the fold of conservation are Periyar's forest guards and guides, and former sandalwood smugglers are their counter-parts in the adjacent farmlands of mango, jasmine, sunflower and tamarind, nestled in the lee of the Periyar Hills. Because of the integration of these one-time marauders of this South Indian wilderness, Periyar Tiger Reserve is considered one of the biggest success stories of conservation in India.

Periyar's birth pangs took place in the late 19th century when the British constructed a dam across the river of the same name, in the princely state of Travancore (now south eastern Kerala), to create a storage reservoir. The dam created a huge, 10-square-mile (26 km^2) lake, and over time the environs around the lake developed bountiful wildlife and woodlands. Eighty years later the area was notified as one of the 27 Tiger Reserves in the country and, in 1982, a core area of about 135 square miles (350 km^2) became Periyar National Park. Today, the large watery expanse of the lake and the forests around it teem with game, and despite the chugging engines of ferries and boats, it is common to spot a variety of animals, especially herds of elephants.

Tracking wildlife on foot

Though the Park is one of the homes of the tiger in India, chances of spotting the elusive cat are slim. Elephants numbering over 900, however, cannot easily keep their presence under wraps, and Periyar, also known as Thekkady after a nearby village, is particularly renowned for sightings of the lumbering beasts. Besides from bamboo rafts, they can be tracked on foot. In fact, Periyar is one of the very few Parks, rich in big game, where escorted walks are allowed. Here, the insightful knowledge of the area and its habitat gathered by the guides through years of stalking wildlife opens up exciting dimensions of the forest. Usually overnight forays covering 12-22 miles (20-35 km), these stomps through sticky bogs and leech infested country are worth it for the invariable trysts with elephants and gaur (bison), the Park's second largest animal. At Gavi, in the buffer zone, one often comes face to face with the former, as they break and chew bamboo grass, and amble past the forest rest house. Usually seen are also sambar, the largest of the Indian deer, and the barking deer, while less common are the Nilgiri tahr, an animal endemic to this part of the country, which roam the high meadows, and lion-tailed macaques, who restrict themselves to the dense forest canopies. Three types of squirrels, the giant Malabar, large and Travancore squirrels—the last rarely glimpsed—inhabit the Reserve, and the great pied hornbill rules for sheer

Protruding tree trunks help boatmen navigate the lake

size Periyar's 320 species of birds, of which many are peculiar to this part of the Western Ghats. Periyar literally flutters with butterflies. About 160 counted species include the Travancore evening brown, a rarity, which was till recently thought to be extinct. The list of 45 types of snakes features some of India's most venomous: king cobra, cobra, Russell's viper, pit viper, krait and the striped coral snake.

2,000 kinds of flowering plants

Surrounded by dense spice plantations and set in the midst of the typical blue-green hills of this region, Periyar boasts of one of the richest tracts of rainforests in the Western Ghats. Marshes proliferate the lower regions, while open grasslands and sholas, from where many small rivulets and streams emerge, dominate the higher, salubrious reaches. Between them, they harbor 2,000 kinds of flowering plants. A particularly interesting walk traverses the ridge, which overlooks the sprawling plains. Towards the west, a 3,937-ft.-high (1,200 m) high plateau drops steeply to the Park's lowest level, the 328 ft. (100 m) deep valley of the Pamba River. And above it all stands Kottamalai, at 6,624 (2,019 m), Periyar's highest pinnacle.

The Asian elephant is one of three elephant species of the world. One of its four sub species is the Indian elephant. It is distinguishable from its African cousin by a smaller ear size. Measuring between 6.5-13 ft. at the shoulder, it is also smaller in height, has a more arched back, and two forehead bulges.

ASIA

Blue-green river amid labyrinthine ravines

The Chambal Wildlife Sanctuary was once the lair of bandits

State and capital:
Uttar Pradesh (Lucknow), Madhya Pradesh (Bhopal), Rajasthan (Jaipur)

Convenient access:
Road (via Agra, UP), air, rail to Agra

Accommodation:
Budget to luxury at Agra, mid-range at Jarar (near Sanctuary)

Best season:
November to March

Also worth seeing:
Agra 60 mi. (97 km) NW of Sanctuary jetty, Bateshwar temples 15 mi. (25 km) N

Bordering the meandering Chambal River, sometimes for 6 miles (10 km) on each side, is a unique system of shallow, scrub-forested ravines created by centuries of soil erosion. These unstable formations crumble, shift, change shape and reform every year with the rise and ebb of flood waters. It is a bewildering maze, very easy to get lost in. For long, this jigsaw of mud hillocks was used by dacoits (bandits) to melt away from the fumbling arm of law without a trace. The fearsome brigands are much dwindled now, leaving the beautiful river to its natural, wild denizens, and allowing it to emerge out of obscurity on to India's wildlife map.

Flowing from the Vindhyachal Mountains of Central India, the Chambal is India's only major north-flowing stream. Its initial content, myth says, came from the blood of cows sacrificed by a king to please the gods and ask them to bestow him supremacy over his rivals. Alarmed by the ruler's ambitions, the priestly class reacted by cursing him and the crimson effluence he had created, and it is a result of this, it is said, that no temple towns have ever come up on the banks. Peering though, into the cyan translucence (sometimes transparence) of the waters, it is hard to find traces of the king's misjudged sacrifice. For the Chambal is certainly one of Indian plains' least polluted and pristine rivers.

Aggressive crocodiles, gamboling otters

The Chambal Wildlife Sanctuary covers 249 miles (400 km) of the Chambal River, from Kota, through its confluence with the Yamuna, extending 25 miles (40 km) further along the Yamuna itself, up to its confluence with the Sind at Panchnada. Two big predators, the freshwater crocodile and the gharial reign over this aquamarine kingdom. In the 1970s, with the gharial population of India severely endangered, the valley's fluvial habitat was demarcated to attempt a recovery. Almost 1,500 of these reptiles and a few crocodiles were reared and released into the river. With adequate protection, they thrived, and today, the Chambal is one of their strong bastions. Though it is easy to mistake a motionless, long, thin-snouted gharial for a piece of driftwood, both species can be spotted basking on the sandbanks. Appearing deceptively sluggish and unobservant, they speedily slither into the water on being disturbed. Some of the crocodiles are massive, and are known to make grabbing assaults on unwary humans or cattle which stray into their territory. The Chambal also hosts smooth-coated otters seen gamboling in groups, at least eight kinds of tortoises that tumble off into the water from rocks like dislodged stones as the boat passes by, and 30 varieties of fish. Besides these, a prized species of the Sanctuary is the acutely threatened Gangetic dolphin, which makes its presence felt occasionally by fleeting surface rolls on the deeper stretches.

Refuge of skimmers

However, more than for its healthy stock of reptiles and mammals, the Chambal is known for its 250 species of resident and migratory birds. Though the biggest avian draw here is a colony of Indian skimmers, a bird whose numbers have been observed to be on the wane, cruising down on the boat one also runs into masses of cormorants, bar-headed geese, gulls, ruddy shelducks, pintails and pochards taking off, wheeling and flying low over the turquoise blue expanse of the rippling river.

A gharial basking on a sandbank.

Right: Take-out point of the river safari; the ravines extend outward from the far bank.

Top right: Camels are commonly domesticated in this arid region.

Top left: Indian skimmers, Chambal's prize avian species.

ASIA

Where a million turtles nest

Bhitarkanika, breeding ground for the Olive Ridley turtle

State and capital:
Orissa, Bhubaneshwar 75 mi. (120 km)

Convenient access:
Road to Bhitarkanika, rail to Bhadrak, air to Bhubaneshwar. Boat into sanctuary

Accommodation:
Budget

Best season:
March to July, September to November

Also worth seeing:
Kendrapara, Cuttack, Konark

In Oriya *bhitar* means "interior," and *kanika* is that which is "extraordinarily beautiful." The description holds for this wildlife sanctuary located on the coast of the Bay of Bengal, between Paradip and Chandipur, at the estuarine confluence of the Brahmini, Baitarani and Dhamara Rivers, in the state of Orissa. Bhitarkanika and its adjoining 22-mile (35 km) long Gahirmatha Beach are a unique habitat to some of the rare and endangered wild creatures of the world.

Bhitarkanika extends over an area of about 308 square miles (800 km²), 147 miles (380 km) of which is forest while the rest consists of mud flats, mangroves, islands and marshes. Bhitarkanika National Park, declared in 1998, has an area of about 54 square miles (140 km²). It was created from the core of the Bhitarkanika Wildlife Sanctuary, designated in 1975. The Gahirmatha Marine Wildlife Sanctuary, which binds Bhitarkanika Wildlife Sanctuary to the east, was created in September 1997 and encompasses Gahirmatha Beach and an adjacent portion of the Bay of Bengal.

Bhitarkanika is one of the largest contiguous patches of mangrove forest in the country, representing the Indo-Malayan mangrove community. Though home to 55 of India's 58 known mangrove species, two species, kanika sundari and bana lembu (local names), both exclusive to Bhitarkanika, are predominant. Other species include kalban or bada bani, baniya, kala bani, hental and rai. Numerous kinds of grasses and herbs are also found here, and a variety of wild rice found on the tidal mud flats have been used to develop several saline and flood resistant varieties of rice.

Bhitarkanika Wildlife Sanctuary harbours nearly 700 saltwater crocodiles making it one of India's largest single population of the reptile. A large ongoing breeding and conservation programme for these amphibious animals ensures that the population is growing. Additionally, five species of amphibians, nine kinds of lizards, 18 species of snakes and seven types of turtles, including the Olive Ridley, hawksbill, leather-backs and Bibron's soft-shelled turtle are part of the Bhitarkanika repertoire.

Three mass nesting sites along the beaches

Arguably, Bhitarkanika's most famous animal is the Olive Ridley, approximately a million of which nest here annually. Homing in from as far as the southern Pacific Ocean, they lay almost 84 million eggs, making these beaches the world's largest nest for this long-distance swimmer. Such nesting occurs in only three other locations in the world—two beaches along the Costa Rica coast, and one in Mexico. Conservation began in this area only after the discovery of the Gahirmatha breeding ground in 1974. In 1981, a second mass nesting at the Devi River mouth was discovered, and in 1994, a third at the mouth of the Rushikulya River, both south of Gahirmatha. As a result, Bhitarkanika was designated a Ramsar Wetland of international importance. However, despite it being a protected area, the turtles continue to be under threat from predating animals, poachers and the nets of fishing trawlers plying illegally during the breeding season. Habitat depletion and the pressures exerted by increasing local human population and economic develop-ment are other contributing factors.

Over 200 species of birds, including eight varieties of king-fishers, are found in this wetland. With more than 20,000 birds ranging across 11 species, it happens to be one of the country's largest heronries. Bar-headed geese, grey pelicans, ruddy shelducks and whistling teal are regular visitors.

Boats take you through the creeks and rivers that meander through the Park.

Facing page: An Olive Ridley turtle crawls out of the sea on Gahirmatha beach to lay eggs. Such mass nesting occurs in only three other locations in the world: two beaches along the Costa Rica coast, and one in Mexico. The turtle is a globally endangered species.

ASIA

Roar of the Asiatic lion
The "pride" of Gir National Park

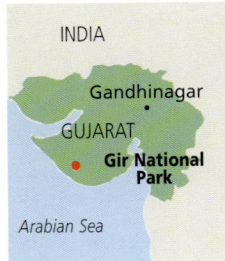

State and capital:
Gujarat, Ahmedabad 249 mi./400 km

Convenient access:
Road to Junagadh, air to Ahmedabad, Rajkot, rail to Junagadh

Accommodation:
Budget to high-end
Best season: November to March

Also worth seeing:
Junagadh Fort and caves, 26 mi. (42 km) NW, old Portuguese town of Diu, 68 mi. (110 km) SW

At the foothills of the Girnar mountain stands what is possibly the world's first decree for the conservation of wildlife. It is an edict, carved in stone, dating back to the third century BC in the name of Emperor Ashoka, who on seeing the ravages of a fierce battle fought by him in present day Orissa turned to the teachings of the Buddha and came to believe that all life was sacred and worth protecting. Spreading out from these hills, which appear as blue shadows from the scrubby flatlands of the Park, the Gir jungle of south-western Saurashtra was once so thick and lush and surrounded by streams that horses had difficulty in passing through. Now, the corridors that linked the forest are lost and they exist as two smaller, separate jungles. In these jungles live the last wild lions outside the African continent.

Asiatic lions once roamed from Central India to Arabia and Persia, even as far as Greece, but coveted as a hunter's prized trophy, were nearly wiped out. The Nawabs of Junagadh, in whose domain the Gir jungles lay, organized hunts for the largest, most handsome beasts with the heaviest manes for British Viceroys and officials, and their own favored friends. Yet, to their credit, it was the Nawab himself, on the urgings of Lord Curzon—'The preservation of fauna and flora is more important than the preservation of any of the great monuments which after all were fashioned by man and can be recreated at a price. The present generation owes it to its successors to restore the only species of a large mammal lost in the plains of India in historical times. Failure to do so would not be forgiven by the judgment of history—who put a ban on the hunting. By this time only a dozen or so individuals survived. But protected across the National Park area of 545 square miles (1,412 km^2), they have come back strongly and today Gir is home to about 300 lions. In fact, the point has been reached where the forest can support no more of the big beasts and the government is trying to set up another sanctuary to relocate some of the population.

Pastoral Maldharis coexist with wildlife

Apart from its lions, Gir has 300 leopards, making this the largest concentration of big cats in any national park of India. On their menu are sambar and spotted deer, nilgai antelope, chousingha (the world's only four-horned antelope), chinkara (Indian gazelle) and wild boar. Jackal, striped hyena, jungle cat, rusty-spotted cat, langur, porcupine, and the black-naped Indian hare represent the smaller mammals. The marsh crocodile is one of the 40 species of reptiles and amphibians, and the checklist of birds numbers 250. All these can be sighted in jeeps provided by

the forest department; the deciduous vegetation, interspersed with large patches of grasslands, is conducive to long pleasant drives through thick forest cover. Gir's trees are mostly broad leaved and evergreen, giving the area cool shade and moisture content. Of the six well-designated routes in the Park, the longest one is 19 miles (31 km).

Coexisting with the galaxy of animals, in settlements called nesses, are Hindu and Muslim pastoral people called Maldharis. One comes across them, while driving through the Park, wearing traditional clothes, colorful turbans and earrings, and carrying huge lathis (sticks) to protect their buffaloes, cattle, camels, sheep and goats from wild animals. Also settled in the vicinity of Gir are the Siddis of African origin, who first came here many years ago as mercenaries, slaves and labor, some rising to become generals and rulers in their own right. Today their villages are famous with visitors for lively dances and performances.

Left: Spotted deer are a favourite prey for the lions.
Facing page & above: Asiatic lions, a subspecies that split from their African cousins perhaps 100,000 years ago, hang on today to an impossibly small slice of their former domain. The entire Gir population, originating from the common gene pool of a handful of animals that survived in these forests, is highly vulnerable to epidemics.

ASIA

Birdwatchers' destination

Keoladeo Ghana National Park resounds with the call of over 400 bird species

State and capital:
Rajasthan, Jaipur
111 mi./179 km

Convenient access:
Road to Keoladeo, air to Agra, Delhi, rail to Bharatpur

Accommodation:
Budget to high-end

Best season:
Year round

Also worth seeing:
Bharatpur fort, 3 mi. (5 km) NW, Deeg, 25 mi. (41 km) NW, Mathura, 27 mi. (43 km) NE, Agra, 37 mi. (60 km) E

At the confluence of Gambhir and Banganga Rivers in the Bharatpur district of Rajasthan lies, arguably, the best wetland bird sanctuary in India. The Keoladeo Ghana National Park (also known simply as Bharatpur), a UNESCO World Heritage and Ramsar Site, is famous for its fish-eating birds (heronry), cranes and thousands of other mig-rants, including waterfowl, waders, passerines, ducks and raptors, that visit it during winter.

For birdwatchers around the world, a trip to this sanctuary is a pilgrimage of sorts. The National Park, with its shallow marshes, scrub jungle, greenwoods, and golden grassland, plays host to over 400 species of birds—about as many as in the entire United Kingdom. Many of the IUCN (International Union for the Conservation of Nature and Natural Resources) endangered species can be spotted at Bharatpur.

The origin of Bharatpur is linked with the ancient kingdom of Matsya Desh, which finds mention in the Mahabharata. Year after year, a natural depression spread over a considerable area, trapping rainwater and wildfowl homed in. The local maharaja identified it as a waterfowl hunting preserve, and it became the site of regular carnage committed by royals and the colonial elite. In the early part of the 20th century, more than 5,000 birds fell victim to guns during a single shoot in Lord Linglithgow's honour, a record etched on sandstone pla-ques near the Keoladeo Temple. Hunting was banned in 1971, thanks to the efforts of the legendary ornithologist Salim Ali.

Prime heronry of the world

One can explore the Park on foot, by bicycle or by a rickshaw; the rickshaw pullers have evolved as bird guides and are excellent sources of bird-related trivia. The birding area lies on either side of the four-kilometre-long road running straight through the park to the Keoladeo Temple. The Mansarovar and Hansarovar marshes and swamps constitute one of the most important heronries of the world, and it was for this that Keoladeo was notified a World Heritage Site. Thirteen species of heronry (herons, storks and cormorants) nest here in thousands. Post monsoon and in early winter, the Park resounds with the cacophony of storks, cormorants, herons and their voracious chicks. Openbills, egrets, night herons, grey herons, black-headed ibis, darters and cormorants jostle for space on the kikar (a species of acacia) trees. Water levels permitting, one can hire a boat for a closer look at bird families. The raptor cast includes steppe, imperial, tawny,

Right: About one third of the Park's area is made up of shallow lakes fed by streams and rainwater—if the water is high enough, usually in the monsoon, which is the main time for breeding, boats are a good way to explore. Besides birds one can see monitor lizards, water snakes and turtles. In a single day, it is not uncommon to spot as many as 100 species of birds by boat and land.

Above: The black necked stork is one of Keoladeo's stork species which include the black, white, painted and open-bill storks.

cranes in the hope that they would instinctively migrate. Additionally, to build up the crane population within the Park, birds were released into Keoladeo. However, except for the fact that the introduced cranes survived successfully, the project did not yield the desired results. Since then very few Siberian cranes have flown into Keoladeo over the years.

Recently, the spotlight has turned onto another winged visitor—the sociable plover. In India, Bharatpur is the only wintering ground of the rare bird, which flies in from Kazakhstan and the bordering regions of Russia. With a reported population of only 200 breeding pairs in the world, this species is on the verge of extinction. Around 22 plovers were spotted in 2004 at Bharatpur, but in 2006 sightings had plunged to not more than a dozen.

Apart from birds, Keoladeo has five and seven species of lizards and turtles, respectively. Of the 13 types of resident snakes, the most famous are the big rock pythons that can be seen soaking the winter sun at the various "Python Points." Neelgai antelope, sambar deer and wild boar are the big mammals, and the porcupine one of the smaller ones.

greater, lesser-spotted and crested serpent eagles, Eurasian hobby, shikra and kestrel, their cries echoing down as they glide the sky.

Rare visitors from North and Central Asia

Until the recent past, the most celebrated visitors to the Park have been the Siberian cranes, migrants to India for more than 30 years. Keoladeo was the only wintering site in India for this bird, which travels more than 3,728 miles (6,000 km) from its summer homeland. While in 1984-85, 41 birds made it to Keoladeo, this figure had drastically fallen to two by 2001, prompting the setting up of the "Save the Crane Project" jointly by the Governments of India and Russia, the International Crane Foundation and the Wild Bird Society of Japan. Cranes bred in captivity were released amongst the existing Siberian

Left: A sleeping trio of barred jungle owl chicks. Other owls found in Bharatpur are the barn owl, oriental scops owl, collared scops owl, Eurasian eagle owl, dusky eagle owl, brown fish owl, mottled wood owl, spotted owlet, brown hawk owl and the short-eared owl.

ASIA

Kingdom of the Bengal tiger

The Sundarbans mangrove forest surrounding the vast Ganges and Brahmaputra river delta is a haven for wildlife

Getting there:
By car, bus, or boat from Dhaka. Airport near Jessore

Where to stay:
Accommodation available at Hiron Point in Mongla Port

Climate:
June/July: 99°–108°F (37°–42°C); December/January: 48°–84°F (9°–29°C). Monsoon season from June to October

Main attractions:
Wildlife watching at Hiron Point, Katka, and Tin Kona Island. Fishing village at Dubjar Char

Special tips:
Guided package tours available from Dhaka between October to March

In southern Bangladesh, three main rivers, the Ganges, Brahmaputra, and Meghna, along with their thousands of tributaries, canals, and creeks, converge over an area of 31,000 square miles (80,000km^2) to form the world's largest river delta. The western section of the delta emptying into the Bay of Bengal is called "the Sundarbans," an inhospitable landscape of mangrove swamps, islands and a few dunes thrown up by the wind and tides. The Sundarbans extend over an area of 3,900 square miles (10,000km^2) and extend across the border into India. On the Bangladeshi side, 2,300 square miles (6,000km2) of this area are preserved as a wildlife sanctuary and natural heritage site, while 500 square miles (1,300km^2) are situated over the border in India.

Twice a day, the tides in the Bay of Bengal inundate the countless, shallow waterways, some of which are a mile wide, while others are just narrow tidal creeks. They wash the sand from the rivers and deposit it in sandbanks wherever tributaries flow into the sea. Once these sandbanks have reached the high-water level, the strong, south-westerly monsoon winds begin whipping them into dunes. This creates fresh mudflats that eventually become islands supporting salt grass vegetation. Wind and water are constantly altering the blurred lines between land and sea, a pattern representative of the eternal cycle of growth and decay in nature.

A dense jungle of mangroves covers this landscape of land and water. The almost impenetrable maze of root systems holds the soil together on hundreds of islands. The mangroves form a mosaic of shore and tidal forests, some of which are no taller than bush height, while others consist of high trees with light leaf canopies. In other places, some emergent species live with their roots in saltwater or freshwater. Palm trees grow on some of the younger mud flats. So far, biologists have identified 334 plant species from 245 different families — a most unusual diversity of fundamentally different species.

Rescue cabins in the trees

The Sundarbans are a last refuge for numerous animals. Even so, no less than five out of a total of some fifty species of mammal have completely vanished from certain areas: for example the Java rhinoceros, water buffalo, certain types of deer, and gaur wild cattle.

The Sundarbans are, however, home to the largest population of magnificent royal Bengal tigers now left in the wild. Around 300 of these majestic, nearly 10ft (3m) long, big cats still roam the dense forests. They are regarded here as man-eaters and the local inhabitants, who live mainly on houseboats, live in fear of them. Wood gatherers and honey collectors, who empty the beehives in the mangrove swamps in April and May, build emergency cabins for themselves high up in the trees so they can take refuge if a tiger gets too close. Even so, people get attacked and killed by tigers every year, although how these big cats in the Sundarbans ever acquired a taste for human flesh is a mystery. The fact that over the years these waterways carried many human corpses out to sea in the wake of a flood disaster may well have played a role.

Between land and water

Three other, smaller members of the cat family also roam the jungle here: leopards, fishing cats, and jungle cats are at home in the region. The Axis deer with its wonderful markings and wild boar are the Bengal tigers' favorite prey. Ganges River dolphins are also found in some of the larger waterways. While lacking the characteristic back fin, they just have a hump or protuberance with a small point instead. They frequently swim and hunt in a line. They hold larger prey above water and shake it to death.

The profusion of bird life here is spectacular. The air is filled with fluttering wings and twittering while some species just quietly search for food in the still waters beneath the comparatively light canopy of trees. So far, 315 different species have been identified, including 95 types of moor hen, 38 birds of prey, and 9 different varieties of kingfisher. Magnificent sea eagles are particularly easy to spot with their brilliant white underbellies.

Because their root systems grow upward, mangrove trees in the swamp retain a foothold in the waterlogged mud (above)

The Sundarbans' villages are under constant threat from flooding (left)

ASIA

Kanas Nature Reserve, Xinjiang

A magical place of extraordinary beauty

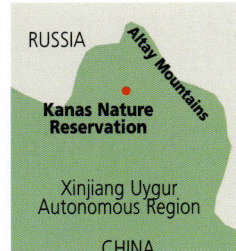

Location:
Kanas is located to the north of Burqin county of Xinjiang, 94 miles (150km) away from the town center. Kanas Lake is an alpine lake deep in the forests of the Altay Mountains.

Climate:
There is a fairly long winter, lasting seven months, and a warm spring and fall, but there is effectively no summer. July is the hottest month, with an average temperature of 60.6°F (15.9°C). The annual average temperature is 31.64°F (–0.2°C).

Special interest:
Kanas is a state-level nature reserve and a state geological park. It is China's only extension of the Siberian Taiga Forest and the place of origin of the biggest tributary of the Ertix River, part of the river system of the Arctic Ocean.

Main attractions:
Kanas Lake, Kanas Country Villa, Crouching Dragon Bay, Moon Bay, and villages of the Tuwa tribe.

Western China has, for ages, possessed a powerful mystique. From the biography of Faxian to *The Journey to the West* by the monk Xuan Zhuang, the quest to learn more about the west has never been quenched. The west recalls to us such familiar terms as the 36 mysterious kingdoms, the ancient Silk Road, the girls of the vanished ancient city of Loulan, Luobupo Lake, and so on. We cannot help feeling excited by the unique landscape of the west, featuring desolate deserts and ironclad troops on horseback. However, the remoteness and wilderness are only partially true of the west in its real sense. The other side of the west is gentle and graceful with oases, as is evidenced by Kanas Lake.

Kanas means "the lake in the valleys" in Mongolian. The surface of the lake is 4396 ft (1340m) above sea level and the deepest place in the lake reaches 618 ft (188.5m). The whole Kanas Nature Reserve covers an area of 2158 square miles (5588 square kilometers).

The scenery around the lake is quite extraordinary, featuring undulating ice-capped peaks, lush forests, luxuriant grasslands, flowers in bright colors, and butterflies flapping around. Kanas, the only Palaearctic Euro-Siberian wildlife region in China, abounds in precious tree species such as Siberian larch, Korean pine, dragon spruce, firs, and birches. Many of the flora and fauna species found here are the only ones in Xinjiang or even in the whole country. With forests linking up with grasslands – crisscrossing rivers, lakes, ravines, and gullies – the natural reserve offers not only a feast for the eyes but also great historical and cultural value for sightseeing, nature preservation, and scientific research.

In Kanas Country Villa, there are luxuriant grasslands and a bridge that extends to the heart of the lake. Standing on the bridge, visitors can marvel at the view around the lake and the morning mist shrouding the mountains in foggy grandeur. Visitors can also enjoy fishing along the railings or take a cruise on the lake.

On the way from the county seat of Burqin to Kanas lies the Crouching Dragon Bay. It is also known as Guodi Lake (meaning lake in the shape of the bottom of a pan). Dense forests, blooming flowers, and meadows in lush green can be found around the lake. A huge rock sits in the middle of a stream that flows into the lake, giving rise to waves that lap against it, with foam drifting and swirling. A log bridge spans the east and west ends of the lake near the lake's outlet. To the north of the bridge is the lake, as limpid as a mirror, while to the south the surging Kanas River roars on its way down its course.

Along the Kanas River and two-thirds of a mile (1 km) north of Crouching Dragon Bay is Blue Moon Bay, among the valleys. Like a prismatic gem in the Kanas River, the water in Blue Moon Bay changes along with the Kanas Lake. It is said that bare footprints were left in the lake by Chang'e in her legendary flight to the moon. Blue Moon Bay, graceful and tranquil, is an emblem of the Kanas Nature Reserve.

The Tuwa tribe is an ancient ethnic group that has lived near Kanas Lake for almost four hundred years, subsisting mainly by herding and hunting. Brave and strong, the Tuwa people are talented in riding horses, skiing, singing, and dancing. Their traditional way of living and customs have been preserved. Their log houses are scattered all over, forming several villages with small bridges across the gurgling streams. Cooking smoke arises and the aroma of milk wine permeates the air. The ancient Tuwa villages remain as mysterious as Kanas Lake.

The enchanting scenery of fall at Kanas Lake (right)

Kazakh herdsmen living in Kanas

ASIA

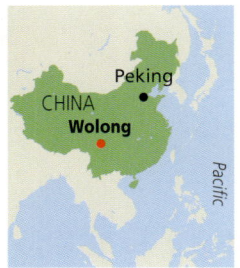

The pandas have all the bamboo they need

Wolong National Park, on the eastern flanks of the Himalayas, is China's foremost protected area for pandas

Getting there:
By road or regular bus service from Chengdu (airport) to Sawan. Tours arranged by specialist travel organizations

Where to stay:
Hotels in Sawan; private accommodation also available

Climate:
Mild mountain climate; frequent mists and rain

Main attractions:
Panda breeding station at Wuyipeng (former research station); panda museum; mountain hiking (Wuyipeng is the starting-point for several trails); birdwatching

Special tips:
Hiking trails often impassable after heavy rainfall

On the eastern flanks of the Himalayas, surrounded by giant mountains towering to heights in excess of 16,500ft (5,000m), is the last main sanctuary of the Giant Panda, a species of bear currently teetering on the brink of extinction. Wolong National Park, which extends across an area of 770 square miles (2,000km2), lies 145 miles (230km) northwest of Chengdu in the Chinese province of Sichuan. It is here that the Quinhai mountain plateau, itself part of the Qionglai mountain range, drops abruptly down to the broad, flat Sichuan basin, situated at an altitude of around 4,100ft (1,250m).

Wolong National Park borders the banks of the Pitiao River as it carves its way between steep mountain slopes and deeply incised valleys. The surrounding mountain giants tower to heights of 16,500ft (5,000m) and more. Even the Balang Shan Pass is 15,100ft (4,600m) above sea level, a twisting road of hair-pin bends winding its way up the river valley from Dujiangyan via Sawan.

Surrounding the reserve is a landscape of gnarled larch trees, dense rhododendron bushes, impenetrable bamboo thickets, and swirling rain clouds – scenery that could be straight out of a delicate Chinese silk painting. The Park represents an ecological oasis amid a desert of deforested and denuded mountain slopes. Yet this conservation area boasts one of the richest biodiversities in the world, combining both high alpine vegetation and tropical plant life. The higher altitudes are naturally subject to a variability of factors governed by weather, sun radiation and air pressure, which in turn have produced a variety of vegetation zones supporting several different habitats.

Biologists have so far identified more than 1,500 different plant species, including 16 varieties of rhododendron, 59 species of mammal and 155 different bird types, which attract large numbers of bird watchers from all over the world each year.

Around 100 species of flora have additional significance as medicinal plants, a valuable resource of which it is hoped better use can be made in future. The root of the fritillary can be used as a remedy for heart and circulatory problems. Extracts of Gastrodia, a type of orchid, are beneficial in improving brain function in stroke victims and one special type of fungus is said to be effective in increasing energy and boosting the immune system.

Persecuted by poachers

Needless to say, Wolong National Park, which is also a significant international biosphere reserve, revolves almost entirely around the Giant Panda. Nearly ten percent of all wild pandas live in these mountains. Protecting the pandas means preserving their habitat as well as the dense thickets of the bamboo which are the staple of the panda's diet.

It is somewhat ironic that, after this protection zone was established in 1987, far more panda habitats were destroyed within the Park than outside it. More and more forested areas are being cleared by the valley dwellers for farmland and poachers continue to hunt the panda for its fur. For this reason, the intricate network of trails, often extremely steep in places, is regularly patrolled by heavily armed members of the People's Police.

Solitary creatures of the forest

Scientists disagreed for a long time as to whether pandas were in fact bears at all. For although they look like bears, with the exception of their black-and-white fur and distinctive black eye-patches, many aspects of their behavior are quite different. For instance, these mammals, which stand 5ft (1.5m) tall and can weigh over 350lb (160kg), do not hibernate. Nor do they need to, since bamboo is evergreen and plentiful all year round — provided it does not suddenly bloom, as it does once every 30 to 80 years, causing it to die off across large areas. In the past, the pandas could migrate to other areas if this eventuality arose, but increased human settlement of the region, road building and deforestation have cut them off from other feeding areas further away and, as a consequence, many of them have starved to death.

Pandas are solitary creatures; they mate only every two years. The female remains fertile for a very brief period of just a few hours in spring, rearing only one of her offspring, and even this is likely to fall prey to snow leopards or eagles. Pandas consequently have a very low reproductive rate, which is the main reason why they require such stringent protective measures.

Affection in the panda forest: two pandas exchanging a kiss while climbing a tree (right)

Pandas are vegetarians, with their primary diet consisting of evergreen bamboo. A bear seated on a rock makes himself comfortable at meal time

ASIA

The land of dragons

Giant lizards find their refuge on Komodo Island, in Indonesia's National Park

Getting there:
Flights from Bali and overland buses to Bima (East Sumbawa) and Labuan Bajo (West Flores). Ferries to Komodo from Sape on Sumbawa and Labuan Bajo on Flores

Where to stay:
Simple bungalows, rooms, and a restaurant at the Loh Liang ranger station, otherwise very basic accommodation in rangers' cabins

Climate:
Best time to travel is during the dry season from May to October, when temperatures are around 90°F (32°C)

Main attractions:
Scuba diving; guided walks

Special tips:
Do heed any travel warnings

The barren, grass-covered hills of Komodo rise gently above the choppy, blue-white waters of the Sape Straits between the Indonesian islands of Sumbawa and Flores. Here and there, a slender lontar palm tree reaches skyward and mist-shrouded forests are visible higher up the mountain slopes. The coastline alternates between sheer rock faces dropping abruptly away to the sea and tranquil bays featuring small, sandy beaches or dense mangrove vegetation.

Komodo is the largest island within the National Park bearing the same name. The reserve also includes Komodo's smaller sister islands, Rinca and Padar, as well as numerous tiny islands and the entire marine world off Flores in the eastern Sape Straits. Most visitors come here to see the legendary giant monitor lizards or to dive in one of the world's most fascinating underwater reserves.

Unpredictable predators

Komodo's main attraction is without doubt the giant monitor lizards, known as Komodo dragons. They can grow to almost 10ft (3m) in length and are the biggest, if not the longest, of their kind. Despite their fearsome reputation, they no longer eat human beings. Yet Komodo dragons are still unpredictable, like all wild animals. However, knowledgeable and experienced park guides can lead the visitor within an arm's length of these prehistoric-looking creatures, which spend most of the day sun-bathing or wandering through the savannah, their long tongues darting in and out in search of prey.

The oras, as they are known locally, are primarily carrion-eaters. Their sense of smell is so acute that they can detect decomposing flesh from a distance of 6 miles (10km). Thanks to their Jacobson's organ, a sensory detector in the roof of their mouth, they are able to smell by sticking out their forked tongue. Thus they are constantly "scenting" the air with this sensitive organ, which flickers in and out continually.

If they cannot find any carrion, as is often the case, they will resort to goats, wild boar, horses, or even water buffalo. An untreated bite from a giant monitor lizard can lead to death within days, if not hours. The saliva contains bacteria which infects its victim with a deadly septicemia. This creature with its ancient origins developed over 4 million years ago from the "varinides" family that was indigenous to Asia 25-40 million years ago. Today, there are only around 2,900 of these giant lizards left on Komodo, 900 on Rinca, and fewer than 100 on Gili Motong, as well as a few in the western corner of Flores Island, which is also part of the National Park. Their numbers have remained quite stable since the Sultan of Bima designated them a protected species in 1915. The huge migration of people from other Indonesian islands to this conservation area has meant, however, that an increasing number of the animals on which the giant lizard preys are being poached.

Wildlife from two continents

Meanwhile, the National Park is more than just a habitat for Komodo dragons. Komodo, like the rest of Indonesia, is a transition zone between the Australian and Eurasian animal kingdoms. Consequently, the resulting wildlife population is a mixture of mammals, such as sambars, wild boar, macaques and civet cats of Asiatic origin, and various reptiles and birds, such as scrub fowl and sulfur-crested cockatoos, from Australia.

The number of different species is small because the islands are situated in one of the driest regions of Indonesia. For eight months of the year

there is little or no rain at all. Only during the monsoon period between November and March do the small, mist-covered, tropical forests on the mountain heights receive occasional, hefty downpours unleashed by low-lying clouds.

The underwater world, however, constitutes two-thirds of the National Park area. Divers in these waters will encounter a myriad of colors and a breathtaking variety of life in and around the coral reefs, the mangrove swamps and seaweed forests, as well as in the smooth, calm bays. Naturalists have identified 1,000 species of fish, 260 reef-forming corals and 70 varieties of sponge. Furthermore, at least 14 species of whale, dolphin, and turtle have also made their home here.

Underwater, a similar collision of two different worlds is taking place. Coming from the Indian Ocean, cold, nutrient-rich, deep water from Antarctica rises up, encountering a warm, tropical stream from the Flores Sea. Strong tidal currents and whirlpools also help oxygenate the water making the seas between Sumbawa and Flores some of the richest marine environments in the world.

A Komodo dragon can grow up to 10ft (3m) in length. The giant lizard is predatory, but does not deserve its reputation as a man-eater (above)

View over the Komodo Sound to Rinca (below, left)

Australian birds have become resident here along the shores of the National Park (below, right)

ASIA

Walkways over the jungle

Taman Negara National Park, in Malaysia, provides access into the jungle

Getting there:
By car, taxi, or bus from Kuala Lumpur (daily or park shuttle service) to Kuala Tembling. From there, by jungle boat to the Kuala Tahan visitors' center

Where to stay:
Park guesthouse with dormitories and several well-equipped chalets with bathrooms and air-conditioning. Simple fishermen's huts on the opposite side of the river and outside the park boundary. Wide choice of hotels also available outside the Park. Adventure camping sites and tree-houses in idyllic locations, but with no facilities. Camping equipment hire available

Climate:
Tropical heat and humidity throughout the year

Main attractions:
Jungle treks; boat trip; "canopy walk"; a night in an observation hide; guided night safaris

Special tips:
Getting around the Park is only possible by boat or on foot. Catering facilities available in the Kuala Tahan visitors' center

Centrally situated on the Malayan Peninsula is one of the most untouched tropical jungles in the world, which has been carefully developed to accommodate visitors. Covering an area of 1,677 square miles (4,343km2), Taman Negara National Park is situated between the Banjaran Timur mountains in the east and the Banjaran Titiwangsa chain in the west. These warm, humid forests consist of high plateaus and green valleys interspersed with clear, unpolluted streams. Here and there, the peaks of majestic mountains emerge above the lush, green canopy. This virgin jungle has remained undisturbed for over 130 million years — despite the Ice Age and other geological calamities. At the northwestern end of the Park, Gunung Tahan, Malaysia's highest mountain rises 7,175ft (2,187m) above the jungle greenery. It can only be reached after a four to five-day trek through unmarked lowland rainforest, which becomes shrouded in mist at higher altitudes. Good mountaineering skills are essential for anyone intending to ascend its precipitous rock faces.

Up the Tahan River

Although it is quick and easy to reach its boundaries, the Park is not accessible by road or path. The Taman Negara Resort visitor center, the starting-point for all the treks and boat trips, can only be reached after a several-hour boat trip from Kuala Tembling up the Tahan River. After just a few miles, the last of the huts on the river bank disappears from sight and the mighty green jungle starts pressing in toward the river. Tree branches reach across the water, thick lianas hanging from their limbs. Dead tree trunks, sometimes barely above water level, have to be circumnavigated.

After approximately 40 miles (60km) the jungle clears, revealing boats and rafts along the shore and, perched above the bank, the buildings of the Taman Negara Resort, a unique hotel complex in the heart of the jungle.

Near the visitor center, a nature trail comprising a 1,640ft (500m) long "canopy walk" leads through the forest. It consists of a system of rope bridges, suspended 100ft (30m) above ground, which wind through the jungle canopy. The trunks and branches of these giant old trees form the basis for a natural habitat that supports the rich diversity of life found in every tropical rainforest. Here you will find plants growing on other plants. These have achieved a sensitive balance within a complicated system of interdependence. Butterflies and other insects pollinate the flowers and utilize the remains of plants. Birds build their nests here and monkeys use the flat branches as nurseries for their young. The aerial walkway is not just a tourist attraction, but is also used by scientists investigating the various factors that interact with one another within the complicated jungle ecosystem.

The cacophony of sound within the rainforest is incredible. From dawn to dusk, 250 different varieties of birds try to outdo each other with their songs, all to the underlying accompaniment of the shrill chirping of

innumerable cicadas and the croaking of rare species of frogs. This is frequently interspersed with the shrieks of gibbon monkeys.

Treehouses in the branches

Several marked trails lead into the jungle from the visitors' center. Some of these can be followed for several days. The further they get from the resort, the lonelier they become, not to mention the more difficult to follow. Tree houses or hides have been built up in the branches in many places along the routes. These can provide basic shelter for the night, as well as being an ideal observation hide for watching the animals. The larger mammals, such as elephants, tigers, leopards, bears, rhinoceros, and tapirs are rarely spotted. They are very shy and remain perfectly camouflaged by the jungle.

A 5-mile (8km) trail follows the Sungai Tahan River and leads up to the magnificent Lata Berkoh Cascades, whose cool, crystal-clear waters plunge via a roaring, foaming waterfall into the valley below. The water has carved out pools in the rock, a tempting spot for a refreshing bath.

In the north of the National Park are some karst caves, lying deep within the limestone cliffs. Some of these contain impressive, if somewhat faded, cave paintings – reminders that this area has been inhabited since prehistoric times. Small bats populate many of the caves. Hundreds of thousands of them hang from the ceilings of these hidden habitations which reek with the overpowering odor of bat guano.

The walls of the jungle crowd in along the river's edge. The National Park is only accessible by water (above)

Floral splendor in the rainforest (left)

NORTH AMERICA

The mammoth trees of America

They grow up to 442 feet high and live for a few thousand years

Route
From Los Angeles over interstate 5 to Bakersfield, Highway 99 and 63 to Visalia, Highway 198 through to the Sequoia National Park. Total surface area 135 square miles (350 km).

Best time
June through to September (the park is closed during the winter)

Accommodation
Giant Forest Lodge, Grant Grove Lodge, motels in Three Rivers

Also worth seeing
Kings Canyon National Park (northern neighbor to the Sequoia NP), Yosemite Park 124 mi. (200 km to the north)

It was fur hunters who claimed in the middle of the last century to have seen conifers in California, with trunks as thick as an elephant. They swore that they had actually seen these trees with their own eyes and that it was the God's honest truth. The trees were on the western steeps of the Sierra Nevada. They should have kept their mouths shut! Because their story quickly reached the ears of the lumberjacks and complete rows of these mammoth trees, the largest and oldest plants on the earth, were chopped down.

The Californian mammoth trees, called by botanists *Sequoiadendron giganteum*, pertain to the morass cypress sort and can reach heights of upto 442 ft. (135 m). Some of the mammoth trees in the Sierra Nevada were as old as 3,000 to 4,000 years when they were axed and their wood was used to make dance floors or bowling lanes. Two especially large trees were auctioned in order to exhibit their trunks as world wonders.

That these mammoth trees can be seen in Southern California today is thanks to the work of a few men, who in 1890 against the will of the timber industry founded the Sequoia National Park corporation. The Giant Forest Area with a mammoth tree forest, became the show piece of the nature reservation to the north of Los Angeles. This is the place where the Monachi indians brought the cattle breeder Hale Tharp in 1858. He moved into a burnt out Sequoia trunk, bought a piece of ground and then despite offers of large sums of money refused to sell the ground, until the state took over the Giant Forest to make a nature reservation.

An especially exciting hiking route, the Congress Trail, runs through the middle of this the world's largest mammoth tree forest. At an easy pace, wandering between the trees, the hike takes two hours. And the trees are just as they were once described by the trappers, as high as church steeples and as thick as elephants. One of the trees is named after Cherokee indian chief "Chief Sequoyah." Other giant trunks have been given the names of prominent politicians and generals from American history.

A mammoth tree of especially large dimensions is called the General Sherman Tree, after the famous army leader during the civil war of 1861-1865, who with his troops was of decisive importance for the final victory of the northern states against the southern, confederate, states. The celebrated "Largest Living Thing" Sequoia is 2500 to 3000 years old and is 275 ft. (83.8 m) high. The diameter of the trunk at the bottom is 102 ft. (31 m), the diameter is 36 ft. (11 m). The volume of the trunk is 1,943 yd³ and its weight is thought to be around 1256 tons.

Trees of similar dimensions can be found in two neighboring nature parks. In the Kings Canyon Park is the Sequoia General Grant, a southern general. The General Grant is 267 ft. (81.5 m) high and at the base the trunk's diameter is 107 ft. (32.8 m). In the Yosemite National Park you can admire the Grizzly Giant. Not far from this tree is the "tunnel tree." The tree fell in 1968 and to attract the tourists, a tunnel, big enough to allow a stagecoach to ride through, was drilled through its trunk.

The largest trees in the Sequoia National Park are between 2500 and 3000 years old and higher than 262 ft. (80 m). Mammoth trees do not usually die of old age, but die when the roots can no longer support the more than 100-ton heavy trunks or they are destroyed in forest fires.

NORTH AMERICA

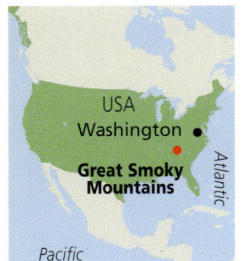

The mists clear slowly in the valleys

Great Smoky Mountains National Park is a haven for animals

Getting there:
Nearest airports: Charlotte, North Carolina, and Knoxville, Tennessee. Interstate Highways 40 and 75

Where to stay:
All categories of hotel available outside the Park; caravan parks; camping sites; Le Conte Lodge, a mountain cabin (open to the public March-November)

Climate:
Fairly unsettled weather with warm, humid summers and mild winters

Main attractions:
Clingmans Dome, Charlie's Bunion viewpoint, Mountain Farm Museum, Roaring Fork Motor Nature Trail

Indian Summer in the Smoky Mountains: The sensational colors of the mixed woodland in all its autumn glory are one of the National Park's unforgettable sights (right)

View of the peaks in the Appalachian Chain. The landscape owes its name to the fine mists clinging to the valleys (below)

Waterfalls accompany the rivers on their way down into the valley (above)

A delicate blue mist fills the valleys intersecting the 6,600ft (2,000m) high mountains and cloaking the dense forests in a mysterious veil. It takes the morning sun a long time to disperse these mists, which give the Great Smoky Mountains its name. This National Park, measuring 815 square miles (2,110km2), is situated along the border between North Carolina and Tennessee. It is an internationally designated biosphere reserve and world heritage site established to protect the central part of what is, geologically speaking, one of the oldest mountain ranges in the world with an ecosystem which owes its unique diversity to the last Ice Age.

Great Smoky Mountains National Park encompasses some of the highest peaks in the Appalachian Chain: Clingmans Dome, Mount Guyot, Collins, LeConte, and Keohart. None of these is lower than 5,900ft (1,800m). The best view over these incredibly beautiful, dark green mountains and steep, dark valleys is from the observation tower on Clingmans Dome. This is also the best spot for observing the amazing sunsets. Clingmans Dome rises 6,645ft (2,025m) in height and is the highest mountain in the Park.

The Appalachian Chain, which stretches some 1,600 miles (2,570km) southwest from the Gaspé Peninsula in Quebec, Canada to the Gulf coastal plain in Alabama, was formed 200 to 300 million years ago when two continental plates collided. Over the millions of years, rain, wind, frost and rivers sculpted the round, softly sloping mountains we see today out of once rugged peaks.

Five different types of forest

The vast ice shield that covered North America during the Ice Age did not manage to get past this mighty chain of mountains. The Appalachians were the last refuge for plants and animals whose original habitat was much further north. The resulting combination of species from both northern and southern regions has produced and preserved a unique a diversity of flora and fauna in this area.

The Smoky Mountains support a variety of habitats whose varied elevations determine a whole range of climatic zones. Several areas that experience heavy precipitation classify as rainforest.

All these factors have contributed to an astonishing diversity of undisturbed flora and fauna within the Park. A total of 1,500 flowering plants, including 130 species of trees, as well as an estimated 2,200 spore-producing plants, such as ferns, mosses, lichen, and algae, form the basis of a complex food chain.

The valleys and mountain slopes support five different types of forest. Campbell Overlook, a couple of miles beyond Sugarlands Visitor Center, provides the visitor with an incredible panoramic view of all five.

Stunning display of colors

At elevations of more than 4,600ft (1,400m), the forest resembles woodland in the northern North American state of Maine or near Quebec in Canada. Forests of red spruce, at its colorful best above 5,250ft (1,600m), cap the highest peaks in the Park, while the middle elevations around 3,300ft (1,000m) are dominated by various northern hardwoods, such as sugar maple, beech, and yellow birch, which resemble those species found throughout New England. In autumn, these forests are ablaze with color, producing a sensational display of brilliant reds, browns, and oranges, thrown into relief by occasional fir trees.

The drier ridges and peripheral areas around the Park tend to be populated by pine and oak. These areas often dry out because the ground is unable to retain water despite plentiful rainfall. Forest fires are consequently regarded as an inevitable part of the environment and, in their own way, play an integral part in the regeneration of this type of woodland. Forest management now includes controlled burning of selected areas in order to prevent unintentional forest fires from threatening lives and destroying property.

The harsher environment surrounding the river banks in these mist-covered valleys supports hemlock forest, while the warmer valleys sustain a diverse mix of lush woodland, including poplars, maple, birch, and dogwood, which remain green even when the forests higher up the mountains are aflame with their festive autumn colors.

NORTH AMERICA

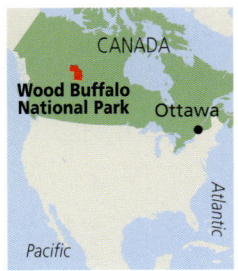

A haven for whooping cranes and buffalo

Canada's Wood Buffalo National Park is home to several species of animal that once teetered on the brink of extinction

Getting there:
Highway 5 between Hay River, Pine Point, and Fort Smith leads through the northeastern corner of the Park. Airports at Hay River, Pine Point, and Fort Smith

Where to stay:
Camping grounds and hotels in Hay River and Fort Smith

Climate:
January: -13°F (-25°C), July: 61°F (16°C). An average of 40 thunderstorms each summer

Main attractions:
Wildlife watching; canoeing trips; numerous hiking trails; Peace Point; Northern Lights in winter

Special tips:
Roads in the National Park closed from November to April

In 1830, around 40 to 60 million bison still roamed the plains of North America. That was before the great slaughter, a tactic employed by the American Army to quell the Indian uprisings, began. Hunters, hired to kill the buffalo, not only benefited from the sale of buffalo meat, but also received a cash reward for each buffalo killed. By 1898, less than 1,000 of these ancient animals remained, some in Yellowstone Park and Northern Alberta, as well as 709 on a farm in Montana. Robbed of their main source of food, many Indian tribes also starved to death as a direct consequence of the buffalo's disappearance.

In 1906, the Canadian government purchased a breeding herd of buffalo in Montana and successfully returned them to the wild in Alberta, the area where Wood Buffalo National Park is now located. There, they interbred with some indigenous wood buffalo that had managed to survive, with the result that there are no longer any pure-bred animals of either buffalo species. These crossbreeds continue to be rather susceptible to disease. During the 1960s, however, a small, pure-bred herd of wood bison was discovered in a remote part of the Park and transported to Elk Island, where their numbers are gradually increasing.

Unique natural saline meadows

Wood Buffalo National Park, established in 1922 specifically to protect the buffalo, covers an area of 17,500 square miles (45,000km2). Today, 5,000 bison, the largest bison herd in the world, are once more roaming freely across the tundra.

This vast Park is so remotely situated that very few visitors make their way here. It spans three different landscapes, each with its own individual natural wonders.

Along its southern and western boundaries are the Caribou and Birch high plateaus, lying 1,650ft (500m) above sea level, in which numerous rivers have carved long, deep ravines out of the soft substrata. An abundance of fossils, the petrified remains of long extinct plant and animal life, has been exposed on the edges of the escarpment. These elevated plains are covered with typical polar tundra, consisting of firs and lichen.

The largest section of the National Park is the Alberta Plateau, part of the Canadian Shield, which terminates at the Slave River and continues as a vast, lowland plain. Springs, which surface where the lowlands run up against the edge of the Shield, are rich in mineral salts. During the dry season these are deposited over a salt pan of almost 100 square miles (250km2). These natural saline meadows, an unusual feature in North America, are home to numerous salt-tolerating plants, which are otherwise found exclusively in coastal regions.

Water from Lake Claire

The plateau is an extensive wilderness of innumerable woods and mighty, meandering rivers, countless lakes and endless marshes. It is a karst landscape, peppered with numerous subterranean rivers which have hollowed out huge underground caves. When the roof of one of these caves collapses, great sinkholes are created, often with a small lake shimmering at the bottom of it. The fish that live in these lakes make their way here via subterranean streams, which connect with the rivers.

Situated in the southeast of the Park surrounding Lake Claire is the world's largest inland freshwater delta where the rivers Peace, Athabasca, Slave, and Birch converge. The mud deposited by these rivers has created a wetland area extending over 1,700 square miles (4,500km2), comprising marshes, grasslands, and forest. The delta forms a vast nesting area and refuge for millions of water birds, as well as a spawning ground for fish. It is also one of the last breeding grounds for the endangered whooping crane.

Surrounded by a seemingly endless expanse of forest, two rivers converge in the Peace-Athabasca delta (above, right)

To the south, numerous tributaries empty into a huge wetland area (below, right)

Pelicans nest on islands in Slave River (top, right)

Arrow grass is found in northern sections of the Park

More than 5,000 bison roam the land freely once more (below, right)

SOUTH AMERICA

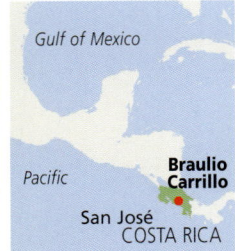

A gondola ride through the rainforest canopy

Braulio Carrillo is Costa Rica's largest National Park – its jungle environment is home to the legendary quetzal birds

Getting there:
From San José follow the Guápiles Highway No. 32 towards Limón, 12 miles (20km) to the main ranger station at Zurquí or 26 miles (42km) to the Puesto Carrillo station. Various bus connections from San José along these routes to Guápiles, Siquirres, or Limón

Where to stay:
A full range of accommodation is available in San José. Camping is permitted within the National Park, but it is recommended that you consult a ranger.

Climate:
The weather does not vary a great deal. March and April tend to be a little drier, but showers can be expected in the afternoon. Depending on altitude, the temperatures range from 79°F (26°C) to 32°F (0°C).

Main attractions:
Barva volcano and its crater lake (accessible on foot or in a four-wheel drive vehicle); walk from the Barva crater to La Selva biological station (4 days); trip on the "Rainforest Aerial Tram"

The National Park provides a protected area for around 195 square miles (500km2) of rainforest. Fifty years ago, jungle still covered 75 percent of the country.

Aerial view over the rainforest (right)

Looking up into the tree canopy (left)

About 12 miles (20km) from San José along Highway 32 in the direction of Limón, just beyond the Zurquí tunnel, civilization comes to an abrupt end. This busy highway cuts through the middle of a wild volcanic mountain landscape and is surrounded on either side by untouched rainforest wreathed in mists.

Braulio Carrillo National Park, the largest in Costa Rica, is situated a mere 30-minute car journey from the heart of the nation's capital and is consequently the country's most easily accessible nature paradise. This does not mean, however, that you are likely to encounter other visitors and hikers at every step.

Extending over an area of some 180 square miles (470km2), the Park is, in fact, so vast that there are frequent cases of visitors, native Costa Ricans and tourists alike, losing themselves amidst the dense forest and rugged, mountainous terrain.

The entire Park is really a vast jumble of massive, often heavily eroded volcanoes, which have lain extinct for many centuries. Over the years, an impenetrable, and so far untouched, primary forest has established itself over the area. The dramatic differences in altitude, the multitude of rivers running through narrow gorges, and the numerous rushing waterfalls have created a complex and varied environmental system. The often precipitous mountainous slopes are clothed in dense, emerald-green, tropical rainforest, consisting of tree ferns, numerous species of palms, lianas, and plants

that have entwined themselves in the branches of trees beneath the forest canopy. Colorful orchids and heliconias provide bright splashes of color amid the depths of the forest. Like most jungle environments, Braulio Carrillo is first and foremost a haven for birds. All 400-500 species of birds indigenous to Costa Rica are found here, including large numbers of humming-birds as well as quetzals, the sacred bird of the ancient Mayas, with their iridescent plumage. The females of the species, shimmering in shades of bright red, sapphire blue, and emerald green, measure only 13in (35 cm) while the male birds with their resplendent long tails can be over 39in (1m) long. Despite their vivid coloring, they are so well adapted to their jungle environment that it requires a well-trained eye to spot them among the profusion of plants. Their call song is unmistakable, however. Killing a quetzal was strictly forbidden by the Mayas and these birds are still regarded as a symbol of freedom and independence throughout present-day Central America. From the three ranger stations, there are numerous trails leading off into the mountain and jungle regions. Even during the dry season from the end of December to April, these trails are usually wet and slippery. Each of them allows viewing of the tree canopy high above, thickly festooned with its colonies of plants as well as glimpses of crystal clear mountain streams, cascading over waterfalls into deep gorges below.

Starting from Guápiles

The Barva volcano rises majestically in the northwestern corner of the National Park. A road, as well as a hiking trail, leads from Puesto Barva station to the small lake, situated at an altitude of approximately 9,500ft (2,900m) in the crater of the volcano.

One particular attraction is a trip on the aerial tramway, which carries you up through the different levels of the rainforest. It runs along the eastern boundary of the Park, not far from the village of Guápiles. The ride in an open gondola ascends through two levels of the tree canopy, first crossing over a valley and then climbing a small mountain.

SOUTH AMERICA

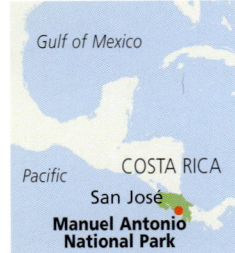

The jungle and the coast

Backing onto the beaches of Costa Rica is Manuel Antonio National Park, an area abounding in wildlife

Getting there:
By bus from San José (direct or via Quepos). By car: Panamericana from San José, with a good access road to the park

Where to stay:
The area is a popular holiday resort, with accommodation ranging from tourist class to exclusive hotels with their own reserves. Simple cabins provide peaceful retreats off the beaten track

Climate:
Hot and humid all year round with cooling sea breezes. Dry season from December to April

Main attractions:
Jardín GAIA wildlife refuge and rehabilitation center for breeding endangered species in captivity and releasing them into the wild; Espadilla Sur and Manuel Antonio beaches with a circuit around the Punta Catedral; various sporting activities

Special tips:
Only 600 visitors admitted to the Park per day

Covering an area of just two-and-three-quarter square miles (seven square kilometers), Manuel Antonio National Park is the country's smallest and most popular National Park. This is hardly surprising, considering its unique location right on the shores of the Pacific next to some of Costa Rica's most beautiful beaches, just over 4 miles (7km) south of Quepos and a mere stone's throw from the resort hotels, beach bars, and nightclubs. It is such a popular destination for tourists staying at the nearby resorts that the park authorities restrict the number of visitors to 600 per day to avoid disturbing the animals.

Surrounded by fields and pastureland, the National Park represents an oasis of natural green wilderness and peaceful tranquility which sustains a fast-growing tourist industry. The mountains overlooking the ocean form a backdrop to the perfect, white sandy beaches of Espadilla Sur, Manuel Antonio, Escondido, and Playita. The National Park also encompasses 12 small islands, lying off the coast. Although most of these islands have little vegetation, they are important nesting sites for seabirds, such as the rare white-bellied booby.

Punta Catedral, whose densely forested cliffs rise to 236ft (72m), was once an off-shore island itself. Ocean currents gradually deposited enough sand between the island and the coast to form a narrow land-bridge, linking it to the sandy crescent beaches of Espadilla Sur and Manuel Antonio, two of the National Park's most popular beaches.

Monkeys cavort in the canopy

To enter the Park, one has to wade across the mouth of a shallow creek. Normally, the water is only ankle-deep, but during the rainy season the water level can rise to 5ft (1.5m). Beyond the stream, numerous hiking trails meander through the cool, shady forest. From the hills, there are spectacular views through the jungle greenery to the turquoise expanse of the Pacific Ocean, where migrating dolphins and whales can sometimes be spotted.

The main attraction of this National Park, however, is its abundance and variety of wildlife, which visitors can experience at close quarters. The animals have become so accustomed to humans that they permit close-up encounters.

The most conspicuous inhabitants of the park are undoubtedly its butterflies, its wealth of bird life, and the large, colorful land crabs. There are 109 species of mammals and 184 varieties of birds jostling for space in the Park's three main habitats: primary forest, secondary forest, and the mangroves. The tidal basins off the coast are home to 10 types of sponge, 19 species of coral, 24 types of crustaceans, 17 different algae, and 78 species of fish. During the dry season, when the seawater is at its clearest, this underwater world is best explored by snorkeling off the cliffs separating the two main beaches, or in the tidal basins just off-shore.

High up in the forest canopy above the hiking trails are large numbers of monkeys, chattering noisily and performing their acrobatics. Most common are the capuchin and howler monkeys, but troops of up to 30 red-backed squirrel monkeys can also be seen swinging through the branches in search of insects and fruits. Manuel Antonio National Park is one of just two areas in Costa Rica where this endangered species still survives. The red-backed squirrel monkey is the smallest of the four species of monkey indigenous to Costa Rica and the only one with a non-prehensile tail.

Sanctuary for sloths

Every so often, you will come across three-toed sloths draped over tree branches, doing full justice to their name. These animals too have become relatively rare everywhere else. These fascinating creatures move very slowly and eat exclusively plants. The low energy content of their leafy diet is the reason for their slow metabolism. Although their diet includes the leaves of more than 100 different trees and creepers, they have a particular preference for the foliage of the cecropia tree, a type of mulberry tree. The cecropia tree is a distant relative of the cannabis plant and breadfruit tree. It is a pioneer species in secondary tropical forests, easily identifiable by its large, palm-shaped leaves and smooth trunk characterized by distinctive bark rings.

The area's designation as a National Park was regarded as a conservation victory by the local population along this stretch of the coast. Although the land had long been under private ownership, local residents had always enjoyed free access to the beaches. A North American purchased the land in 1968 and proceeded, violating all local regulations, to fence off the whole area, even erecting heavy gates. The local population retaliated with vandalism. After the local legislative authority finally won and insisted that the path to the beach be kept open, the property passed into the hands of a Frenchman, who planned to turn the region into a tourist center. Before he could do so, however, the land was appropriated by the government in 1972 and declared a National Park.

Enclosed by lush jungle vegetation, the sand banks of Espadilla Beach connect an off-shore island with the mainland (above)

Twelve offshore islands also form part of the National Park (below)

SOUTH AMERICA

The land of ancient lizards

Ten million years ago, primeval fauna evolved in the Galapagos archipelago

Getting there:
Daily flights from Quito and Guayaquil to Baltra, less frequently to San Cristóbal

Where to stay:
On cruise ships, all categories of hotel available on San Cristóbal and Santa Cruz

Climate:
Daytime temperatures around 86°F (30°C) from January to May, otherwise around 82°F (28°C)

Main attractions:
All trails offer spectacular views of the archipelago's wildlife

Special tips:
Ban on any imports of fresh food

The brilliant plumage of the frigate bird (top)

A small population of red marine iguanas, the last of their kind, has survived on the Galapagos Islands

Lonesome George is the sole surviving member of his species. Around 80 years old and weighing 200lb (90kg), he is in the prime of his life. When he dies, it will mark the end of the line for his race, leaving only 11 of the original 14 species of tortoise that were once endemic to the Galapagos Islands. He was discovered quite unexpectedly in 1971 on Pinta Island and currently enjoys the protection of the Charles Darwin Research Station on Santa Cruz Island. It is from giant land tortoises like George that this archipelago, situated in the middle of the Pacific and straddling the equator 620 miles (1000km) off the coast of Ecuador, derives its name. Far removed from the nearest continent, these barren and rugged lava islands that are dotted with numerous shield volcanoes rising over 5,500ft (1,700m) in height have developed a unique ecosystem of flora and fauna over the course of millions of years. The entire archipelago belongs to Ecuador and, as a designated National Park, is a protected area.

Just one single pregnant tortoise, which turned up here 10 million years ago, was enough to start a unique evolutionary process.

The volcanic island on which the original tortoise was washed up has long since sunk back into the ocean. The Galapagos Islands lie directly over a so-called "hot spot," a hole in the earth's crust from which hot lava bubbles up from the earth's core. It erupts through the plate, forming volcanic cones. While the ocean floor has been shifting toward South America over millions of years, the old islands have been sinking into the sea, with fresh ones constantly forming over the hot spot.

EspaÉola in the eastern part of the archipelago, dating back 3,300,000 years, is the oldest island, while the islands of Fernandina and Isabela to the west are a mere 700,000 years old and still volcanically active.

Tortoises and finches

Around the same time that the pregnant tortoise came ashore on these distant islands, a storm must have also carried a flock of finches to the same area. These birds have evolved into the famous Darwin Finches, which can be grouped into 13 sub-species. Each group has its own specific niche in the food chain.

The ground finch with its stout, strong beak can crush tough seeds, while the warbler finch's pincer-like beak is designed for catching insects. The woodpecker finch even uses a tool: it probes insect larvae out of tree bark with a cactus spine. The most unusual species, however, must surely be the vampire finch, which pecks open the flesh on the heads of seabirds and dines on their blood. The victims do not seem unduly concerned by this procedure.

Large predators never found their way to the Galapagos, with the result that the indigenous animals know no fear of each other. Even the numerous sea lions and fur seals show little concern when curious snorkellers swim around them in the crystal-clear waters of the Pacific. Nor do the hun-

dreds of prehistoric-looking miniature dragons—land lizards and marine iguanas—sunbathing on the bare, black lava rocks seem to notice when their larger neighbors enjoy a friendly nibble at their long tails. They are unafraid of humans as well as seabirds, thousands of which colonize the rugged cliffs that drop steeply away to the sea. The seabird population includes flamingos, blue-footed boobies, frigate birds, flightless cormorants and even small penguins, which like to cool off in damp, lava caves.

Treeless crater landscape

The central lowlands are arid and barren, the only vegetation being thorn bushes and cacti growing on turf. A transition zone at higher elevations is covered by forest consisting mainly of guava trees and pisonnia, a "four o'clock" plant with white or yellow, and occasionally red or pink-tinged, flowers which do not open until late afternoon. The forest above this transition zone is very damp and often shrouded in mist. The vegetation here, consisting predominantly of 6 1/2 –13ft (2–4m) high trees, is much lusher, with dense undergrowth. Finally, the treeless upland zone around the crater supports only lichen and mosses.

These islands were probably first discovered in the 15th century by the Inca ruler Tupac Yupanqui. The first documented discovery, however, was by the Bishop of Panama, Tomás de Berlanga, whose ship ended up here in 1535 after being blown off course during a storm.

When Charles Darwin, the famous naturalist, visited these islands in 1835 at the age of 26, they provided him with inspiration for the ground-breaking ideas that later revolutionized existing biological theories on the origin of the species.

View across the rocky Isla Bartolomé to James Island, beyond (above)

Two individual forms of the same species, adapted to different living conditions: Marine iguanas (above, left) Land iguanas (below, left)

SOUTH AMERICA

Paradise for sea lions

Paracas National Park in Peru safeguards huge colonies of sea lions along its Pacific coast

Getting there:
Airport at Pisco. From Lima, a 150-mile (240km) drive along the Panamerican Highway. A number of tracks are accessible to vehicles within the National Park itself

Where to stay:
Several hotels in Pisco; camping permitted

Climate:
Typical desert climate, with temperatures in excess of 86°F (30°C). Frequent strong winds ("Paracas Winds") and little rainfall

Main attractions:
"La Catedral" rock formation at Paracas; motorboat excursions to the Islas Ballestas islands; bird-, seal-, and dolphin-watching trips; El Candelabro "Nazca lines"

Special tips:
Landing not permitted on the islands. Viewing from the boat only

Paracas, on the Peruvian coast, is plagued by perpetual, strong, and searing winds. Scarcely anything thrives in this semi-arid region at the foot of the Cordilleras near the town of Pisco. The barrenness of the land stands in stark contrast to the astonishing diversity of life found in the ocean. This marine abundance was once a source of immense wealth to the region's early inhabitants and later settlers.

The constant trade winds and the Humboldt current swirling northward just off the coast stir up oxygen and nutrient-rich seawater from the depths of the Pacific, propelling it to the surface. Despite being 12-14°F (10-11°C) colder than the water in the surrounding open ocean, it nevertheless supports a huge population of algae and micro-organisms, providing plentiful supplies of food to nourish the prodigious shoals of fish that live off the Peruvian coast and making it one of the richest fishing grounds in the world.

For thousands of years, this superabundance of fish, particularly shoal varieties like anchovy and sardine, has inevitably attracted millions upon millions of sea birds to the area, first and foremost among them the cormorant. On the wind and wave-battered rocky islands lying off the coast, there are such vast colonies of these birds that their droppings accumulate as the recognized resource of guano, used all over the world as a natural fertilizer. Until the beginning of the twentieth century, these guano deposits were being blindly excavated without the slightest regard for the birds' breeding season. The population of guano producers has consequently declined, but so too has the demand for guano following the invention of artificial fertilizers. Nowadays, guano is harvested from the Chinchas Islands by a handful of individuals who appear to be inured to its reek. English sailing ships also used to anchor in the area to collect their cargo of guano for transport to Europe and North America.

Resting-place for migrant birds

A little to the south are the Paracas Peninsula and the Islas Ballestas, now comprising a national reserve which protects spectacular colonies of sea birds as well as considerable numbers of sea lions. Each year, the reserve also provides a refuge for dozens of species of migrating birds that choose the area to break their long, exhausting journey. Biologists have identified more than 200 varieties of birdlife, including pelicans, the rare blue-footed booby, Peruvian booby, and red-legged and Bigua cormorants. For some birds, such as the Humboldt

penguin, flamingo, and Andean condor, the National Park represents a final refuge.

In 1804, Alexander von Humboldt, the German explorer, returned to Europe with samples of the remarkable guano, known as "Huanu" in the Inca tongue of Quechua. As a result, guano became highly sought after as a natural nitrogen and phosphorous-rich fertilizer, destined to revolutionize agriculture. A lively trade in this organic substance quickly developed. Peruvian guano from the Chinchas Islands became the world's first commercial fertilizer.

It was not, however, harvested with the same degree of concern for the environment displayed by the Incas in their day. Ruthless exploitation soon caused problems and it was not until 1909 that the "Compania Administradora del Guano" was founded in Lima, charged with the specific purpose of safeguarding the existing bird population and ensuring their protection. The organization simultaneously aimed at achieving a long-term increase in annual guano production. By then, however, the bottom had already more or less dropped out of the guano market.

The nature reserve, two-thirds of which comprises the marine environment off the coast, covers an overall area of around 1,300 square miles (3,350km2) along the Pacific coast. The ocean and sea bed are home to toothed whales, seals, sea otters, turtles, and countless varieties of fish and invertebrates, not to mention the rare ratfish. Scientists have recorded a total of 19 species of mammal, 52 varieties of fish and six types of reptile in the National Park.

Barren coastal desert

The original varieties of Peruvian coastal flora have survived largely intact throughout the ages. Although most of the landscape consists of arid desert, dotted here and there with occasional grassy tussocks, the transition zone leading to the mountain tops supports some drought-resistant species of cacti, occasional bushy thickets of which occur on elevated areas and in a few places prone to moist mists.

The coast itself comprises a unique habitat supporting various types of grasses found in the brackish and salt marsh areas. These were once of great significance to the Nasca Indians, long before the advent of the Incas. Domestic items and clothes made from such grasses were unearthed from burial grounds discovered on Paracas in 1927 by the archeologist Julio C. Tello. The mummified remains found in these graves, along with tools, weapons, jewelry, and even food items, were wrapped in finely woven grave cloths – the fabric and enduring colors of which are still a source of wonder to scientists. Some of these items are on display in the Anthropological and Archeological Museum in Lima.

Water temperatures off the cliffs of Paracas are colder than in the open ocean. The resulting abundance of fish makes this inhospitable cliff landscape a paradise for migrating birds (above)

The area is home to huge colonies of sea lions – clearly at ease in these cold waters (left)

NOMINATED 7 for the new wonders

SOUTH AMERICA

Paradise in the swamps

Pantanal, in northwestern Brazil, protects a rich diversity of tropical landscapes and is a veritable Garden of Eden

Getting there:
Flight from São Paulo to Cuiaba; by hire car to Poconé and Jofre, where boats and horses can be hired

Where to stay:
On ranches, or "fazendas," although several months' advance booking is required

Climate:
Best time to visit is between April/May and September, when the climate is dry and hot. Rainy season from November to March

Main attractions:
A paradise for biologists and ornithologists. Piranha fishing; monkey watching

Special tips:
Substantial areas of the Pantanal can only be reached by boat or on horseback

The dark, leafy canopy of the dense riverine forest echoes with a cacophony of birdsong and the fluttering and flapping of wings. The swampy river is full of floating dead tree trunks, wading waterfowl, water birds, and jumping fish. These are the immediate, unforgettable first impressions of Brazil's Pantanal region, the world's most spectacular marsh area with its unparalleled biodiversity. It is hardly surprising that Brazilians call it the "Garden of Eden." Innumerable lakes and rivers, evergreen tropical rainforests, dry woodland, savannahs, and watery lagoons provide a range of habitats unequalled anywhere else in the world for many endangered species of animal and plant life. Not only do the Pantanal forests provide rich hunting grounds for jaguars, but the region is also a protected paradise for tapirs, giant monitor lizards, spectacled alligators, and countless species of waders.

Eighty percent of the Pantanal, a region comprising 54,000 square miles (140,000km2) of dense primeval jungle and dry steppe lands, lie in Brazil and extend into Bolivia and Paraguay beyond. The area is a marshy floodplain surrounded by mountains, with a single runoff to the south. From October to March, when rainfall is heaviest, the mighty Paraguai River and its many tributaries, including the São Lourenso, Cuiaba, Taquari, Miranda, Negro, and Aquidaduana, burst their banks and form a vast marsh, ten times bigger than the Everglades in Florida.

The largest volume of water comes from the forests in the north, flowing down the Cuiaba tributary and emptying into this extensive wetland landscape. It discharges water into the Paraguai at the rate of 17,000 cubic feet (480m3) per second, so much that the river is obliged to create fresh channels for itself. Two-thirds of the Pantanal basin is submerged during the rainy period. In May, the floods recede, leaving behind a thick layer of sand, plant, and animal material. This silt makes a nutrient-rich, natural fertilizer.

Three ecological zones

The Pantanal can be divided into three ecological zones, depending on water quantity and water levels. In the Alto Pantanal area, the water remains up to 20in (0.5m) deep for two to three months, while the Medio Pantanal is inundated for three to four months at a time. In the lower-lying Baixo Pantanal region, on the other hand, the water levels reach depths of 10–13ft (3–4m) during the rainy season.

The abrupt change from a dry to wet landscape is one of the reasons for the huge diversity of flora, which has only just begun to be explored. The terrain here comprises a gently undulating steppe landscape as well as paspalum grasslands. To the west, jojoba and jobo woodland stretch alongside permanently wet, green regions comprising riverine forest, with trees reaching 33–60ft (10–18m) in height and dense thickets of plant vegetation. The river tributaries contain floating islands of tangled reed roots known as "camalotes" and are dotted here and there with groups of assorted tropical palms.

The wildlife is equally abundant. Scientists have so far identified 80 different species of mammal, approximately 650 bird varieties, 50 types of reptile, and around 400 kinds of fish.

Above all, this tropical, watery refuge is paradise for a profusion of birds. One of the most famous of these is the Jabirú, or "Tuiuiú" as it is known locally. This is Latin-America's representative of the stork family. Standing up to 5ft (1.5m) tall, with a wingspan of almost 8ft (2.5m), it is one of the largest birds in the world. It is the only stork in the world with entirely white plumage. The green forests are populated by 26 different species of parrot alone, includ-

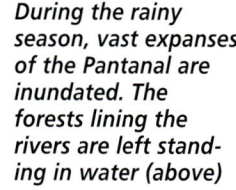

ing the world's largest parrot, the hyacinth macaw, measuring an incredible 39in (1m) in length. These extremely shy, blue-feathered parrots only live in one type of tree and an estimated 3,000 of magnificent them reside in the forests of Pantanal.

Refuge for waterfowl

The Pantanal also provides a perfect refuge for various species of heron, ibis and duck, while the wetlands provide a temporary home to huge flocks of waders and waterfowl from North America, which winter in the Pantanal.

Although large areas are inaccessible to man, the region is increasingly under threat. A significant proportion of the area, first developed during the early eighteenth century by Luso Brazilians in search of gold and slaves, is now cultivated for soybeans and sugar cane. Unfortunately, farming methods also include the use of fertilizers and pesticides, which are just as damaging to the wetlands as the few remaining pockets of gold and diamond mining.

Luckily, large expanses of the Pantanal have been acquired, however, by private purchasers and added to the 73 square miles (190km2) of National Park conservation area that protects the unparalleled beauty of these wetlands.

During the rainy season, vast expanses of the Pantanal are inundated. The forests lining the rivers are left standing in water (above)

The marshlands provide a rich source of food for storks and herons, even during the dry season (opposite)

The abundant wildlife includes the stork-like Jabirú (center, left) and caiman alligators (below, left)

251

AFRICA

Where lions laze in trees

The scenic landscapes of Queen Elizabeth National Park in Uganda are a paradise for wildlife

Getting there:
Five to six hours by car from Kampala, on mostly metaled road; landing strips for light aircraft in Kasese and near Mweya Safari Lodge; bus connections from Kampala and within the region

Where to stay:
Luxury lodges; a simple guesthouse in Mweya belonging to the Research Institute for Ecology; several camp sites

Climate:
Best to visit after the rainy season in October–November and March–April

Queen Elizabeth National Park is a popular reserve, being regarded as one of the jewels in Uganda's ecological crown. It lies nestled in one of the most beautiful landscapes in East Africa, the West African Rift Valley. The Rwenzori Mountain rises 16,400ft (5,000m) on its northern boundary. To the northeast, the Park is almost completely surrounded by the marshy, wet hinterland of Lake George while the southeastern portion is characterized by savannah and forest extending as far as the Congo border on the shores of Lake Edward. The Kazinga Canal, which connects the two lakes, splits the Park into a northern and southern sector.

Grassy savannah, open bush, tracts of forest, rainforest, marshland, lakes, streams, and to the north of the Kazinga Canal, a bizarre crater landscape, provide distinctly different habitats that support an extraordinary diversity of flora and fauna. It is hardly surprising that the Park is on UNESCO's list of the world's major biosphere reserves and Lake George is on RAMSAR's list of primary wetland ecosystems.

Home of the hippo

Since Uganda's independence, many national parks and lakes have changed their names several times. For many years, Queen Elizabeth National Park was known as Rwenzori National Park, before reverting to its former, royal, colonial name. Both names are current, however, which can lead to confusion with the more recently established Rwenzori Mountain National Park, a reserve that only protects the high mountains on the border with the Congo.

Queen Elizabeth National Park is home to about 100 species of mammal and 606 varieties of birds. The Kazinga Canal boasts the largest concentration of hippos on earth. A boat trip will bring you face to face with hundreds of them, jostling for a position among the papyrus along the banks, snorting noisily or yawning hugely. And there are always the elephants that congregate here to drink and bathe.

A boat trip is an ideal and comfortable means of observing the animals at close quarters and it is certainly the best way to see the numerous birds in their individual habitats of open water, marshy riverbanks, or dense forest: black bee-eaters, shoebill storks, over eleven different species of kingfisher, falcons, and whole colonies of pelicans and cormorants.

Lake George, north of the two other lakes, is actually a landscape where open water, permanent marshland, marsh vegetation, swamp, grassland, and forest merge imperceptibly with one another. This shallow lake averages a depth of 8ft (2.4m) and is 13ft (4m) at its deepest point.

Storybook jungle

In the middle of the vast, dry savannah on the Park's northwest boundary is the Kyambura gorge. It is somewhat surprising to encounter here a dense, lush, verdant green jungle, of the kind you read about in storybooks, with a dense canopy and thick lianas dangling down to the forest floor. It is home to several families of chimpanzees, which chatter and crash about excitedly in the treetop branches.

Elephant, buffalo, giraffe, and bushbock graze peacefully among the waving grasslands, which are also home to Uganda's very own signature animal, the deer-like cob antelope with its amazingly long, coiled, S-shaped horns.

Naturally enough, the predatory leopards, hyenas and lions are never far behind. The lions occupy the southern part of the Park and exhibit a rather unusual behavioral characteristic, namely a penchant for tree-climbing. They drape their bodies along a branch and lie dozing with all four paws dangling. Such behavior is unique to these "tree-climbing lions," as they are known locally, and is not found in lion populations elsewhere.

Tourists are few and far between in this region as the Park's tourist and administrative center is situated on Mweya Peninsula, which juts out into Lake Edward and lies on the far side of the Kazinga Canal. Some distance north of here, the terrain becomes a lunar landscape punctuated by numerous volcanic craters. Many of these are now crystal-clear lakes, attracting attract thousands of flamingos.

Queen Elizabeth National Park is just beginning to recover from the depredations of civil war. The poachers have been driven out, thereby guaranteeing the animals' protection from further persecution. In fact, the Park seems to have become something of a sanctuary for elephants, which find their way here from the neighboring Congo where they are still hunted by poachers.

Dried-up lake in Queen Elizabeth National Park, situated in the west of Africa's Great Rift Valley (above)

Several large groups of baboons populate one particular area of the Park (left)

AFRICA

Where the White Nile thunders

Murchison Park in Uganda is a paradise for hippos and giraffes

Getting there:
By ordinary vehicle to the Park, which will provide you with four-wheel-drive vehicles. Five hours from Kampala, along partly paved roads. Landing strips at Paraa and Rabongo for light aircraft

Where to stay:
Several lodges in all price categories; the historic, luxury lodge of Sarova Paraa, situated right by the waterfall; several camping sites

Climate:
Pleasant all year round, does not exceed 84°F (29°C).

Best time to visit:
January to March (low season)

Main attractions:
Murchison Falls; Nile boat trip; Buligi Peninsula circuit; Rabongo rainforest

Bisecting Uganda's biggest nature reserve from east to west, the White Nile River, (also known as the Victoria Nile), flows through the center of Murchison Falls National Park and empties into Lake Albert. Before reaching this lake, however, it drops in a sequence of spectacular cascades and waterfalls into the East African Rift Valley. At the Falls, the Nile forces its way through a 20ft (6m) wide cleft in the rocks and plunges 140ft (43m) with a deafening roar and a great cloud of spray into two more sets of rapids before eventually ending up in a foaming pool. For the final 20 miles (30km) or so of its journey, the broadening river flows sedately towards the lake, rippling gently. This waterfall, also known as the Kabarega or Kabalega Falls, is by far the most spectacular to be found anywhere along the entire 4,185 miles (6,735km) length of the Nile. The water thunders down into the gorge at a rate of 66,000–132,000 gallons (300,000–600,000 liters) per second. The resulting curtain of spray forms a huge, dense cloud of mist between the rocky cliffs, which appear to tremble under the sheer weight of water. The most impressive view of the waterfall is undoubtedly from the top, looking down over the plummeting torrent of foaming water to the calmer, lower stretch of river in the distance, winding its way around sand banks and small wooded islands. A path leads from the top of the Falls all the way down to the swirling pool at the base of the waterfall. From here, there are fascinating views of the foaming waters rushing into the narrow ravine.

Hippos all the way

Over the course of a boat trip from the Falls to Lake Albert, every bay seems to be filled with hippos in their hundreds, snorting and blowing as they wallow in the water while, in their midst, huge crocodiles bask on the sand banks. When the first Europeans explored the Nile during the mid-nineteenth century, the whole river teemed with these armored reptiles. However, they have since retreated to escape the intrusions of man and motor boats and now only inhabit the more remote, upper reaches of the Nile. Its well-stocked waters provide them with an abundant supply of giant fish, such as the Lake Albert or Nile perch, which can grow to around 7ft (2m) in length and weigh 440lb (200kg). The varied landscape of the Rift Valley supports a wide range of different habitats and consequently a rich diversity of animal and plant life. Dense, primeval rainforest covers the higher terrain in the southwest. The Rabongo rainforest south of the cascades is home to various species of primate, including several families of chimpanzees.

To the north, on the far side of the river, the landscape unfolds into gentle, rolling savannah, interspersed with occasional Borassus palms. Vast herds of buffalo, antelope, waterbuck, bushbuck, and reedbuck make their way through the long waving grass which camouflages the lion following hot on their heels.

Breathtaking bird life

The shores of the Nile River, the vital artery traversing Murchison Park's 1,480 square miles (3,840km2), are a natural magnet for numerous groups of elephants. Majestic and dignified Rothschild giraffes patrol the forest perimeter, stripping the occasional leaf and fresh shoots from the treetops.

The main focus of interest in Murchison Park, however, is the bird life, a major attraction for ornithologists and amateur bird lovers alike. Seldom can so many varieties of African birds be observed in such close proximity to one another. Around 450 different species have been identified in the Park. Egyptian geese, pelicans, hornbills, and cormorants are usually seen along the broad sweep of the river below the waterfall, conducting their courtship rituals along the bank while keeping an eye out for likely prey.

Giraffes regard the riverine woodland along the Nile, as well as the palm-studded savannah, as their personal pantry (opposite)

With its foaming torrents, the river is the region's main life-giving artery

AFRICA

Land of the Masai

Kenya's Masai Mara game reserve is home to the largest herds of animals anywhere

Getting there:
Main road route via Narok, approximately five hours by car from Nairobi. Two daily flights from Wilson Airport in Nairobi to Narok. Four landing strips for light aircraft in the Park

Where to stay:
A choice of lodges in all price ranges. Around 25 camp sites in the reserve — not all are shown on maps

Climate:
Cooler, dry season from July to October. Temperatures rarely rise above 86°F (30°C) and seldom fall below 59°F (15°C)

Main attractions:
The great migration of wildebeest, zebra, and antelope. Hot-air balloon trips. Masai village near Narok

Special tips:
A local driver/guide recommended, especially if driving off-track. Night driving not permitted

Vultures feeding off animal carcasses (below, left)

The rainy season transforms the savannah into paradise. Vast numbers of zebra migrate to this area from the south (top right)

Many hoofed animals, including huge herds of wildebeest, visit Masai Mara park (center)

The herds of zebra and antelope must cross great rivers like Sand River, where cheetahs, crocodiles, and other predators lie in wait for a meal on the shore (opposite)

Many seasoned safari travelers, travel writers, documentary film makers, and researchers refer to Masai Mara as one of their favorite landscapes in East Africa. The vast expanse of sky above the open savannah, the immense amount of game, and the annual migration of huge herds of gnu, zebra, and antelope entice them back time and time again. Many people also come to see the Masai themselves, the warrior nomads who have roamed these plains since the seventeenth century — not as hunters, but as herdsmen, killing wild animals only in self defense.

The Masai people still dress in traditional red robes and proudly carry traditional weapons: a spear, bow and arrows. Their lifestyle is linked so closely with the savannah and its game and so rooted in the soil that they are the only tribe permitted to graze their herds of goats and cattle within the confines of this national reserve. Nowadays, the Masai's actual dwellings, consisting of round, brown huts made of clay and cow dung, lie outside the boundaries of the reserve. As a defense against lions, cheetahs, and leopards, a family's group of huts is ringed by a high thorn fence. Each village comprises several groups of huts encircled in this way, as well as cattle enclosures similarly protected by a ring of thorn bushes.

Prey and predators

The Masai Mara is a vast savannah of gently rising hills, scattered woodland, and occasional acacia trees. Its vital arteries are the Mara and Talek Rivers, which supply the area with water all year round. To the south, the hilly terrain unfolds into the vast, virtually endless plains of the Serengeti in Tanzania. On the western boundary, the high plateau of the Oloololo Escarpment towers looms on the horizon. Throughout the year, the base of this mountain is a popular gathering place for large numbers of animals, especially zebras and antelopes as well as their predators.

Herds of wildebeest frequent the lush grasslands and scattered acacia woodlands along the Mara River, while the rhinos, including the rare black rhino, prefer the privacy of the thick vegetation found eastwards in the sandy Ngama Hills. The vast central plains, interspersed with a few scattered bushes and boulders, are the best place to see the "big nine" of African game: buffalo, elephants, leopards, lions, rhinos, cheetahs, zebras, giraffes, and hippos.

A trek to the Mara River

In April, the rains arrive and the parched savannah is transformed into a fertile, green paradise. This is the signal for the start of one of nature's most breathtaking spectacles. Millions of wildebeest and other hoofed animals begin their journey from the seemingly endless vastness of Tanzania's Serengeti plains to Masai Mara. They are followed by 7,000 giraffes and 1,000 elephants, trailed of course by the savannah's own predators, 3,000 lions, along with leopards, cheetahs, hyenas, and jackals. Around the end of July and beginning of August, the migration crosses the Mara River whose shores provide the setting for some of nature's most dramatically breathtaking, if somewhat gruesome, scenes. Crocodiles lie in wait ready to fall upon their prey as they try to cross the river. Lions, cheetahs, hyenas, and jackals pounce on any animal that shows the slightest hesitation at the dark, swirling river water or staggers out on the other side, weak from its exertions. By the time these enormous herds reach Masai Mara, some of them will have covered around 620 miles (1,000km) on their hazardous journey. They will be joined by another 100,000 wildebeest, which migrate here from the Loita Mountains in the east.

AFRICA

The red soil of the savannah

Tsavo National Park, in southern Kenya, is one of East Africa's most spectacular wildlife sanctuaries

Getting there:
Two-hour car trip from Mombasa; three hours from Nairobi. Six landing strips for light aircraft in the south of the National Park; 13 in the north.

Where to stay:
Lodges and tents to suit all budgets and tastes

Climate:
Warm all year round. Best time to travel is during either of the dry seasons in January (high season, around 86°F/30°C) or June to September (around 82°F/28°C)

Main attractions:
Herds of elephants and other wild animals; Mzima Springs; Lugard's Falls; Crocodile's Point; Yatta Plateau

View from one of the lodges across the red earth of the savannah to the Chyulu Mountains in the distance (above)

While elephants congregate during the dry season around the few water holes (below, right), marabous gather in the tree-tops of the savannah's gnarled trees (below, left)

The story of the two man-eating lions of Tsavo is still a prominent part of local folklore. In 1898, or so the story goes, they killed 135 laborers working on the railway line between Mombasa and Lake Victoria. Aside from the fact that it was actually "only" 28 men, there was something very distinctive about the appearance of these two male lions: they had no manes.

Lions like this still live in Tsavo National Park in southern Kenya, an area half the size of the Netherlands. While it is usual for two or three male lions to be in charge of a pride of six females, Tsavo lions will not countenance rivals and have even bigger harems, numbering around eight lionesses. Biologists believe that they possess more sex hormones than others of their species in the rest of Africa, which explains their aggressiveness and lack of mane, the lion equivalent of baldness.

The Park is bisected by the Nairobi-Mombasa highway and railway line, splitting it into a west and east section. The endless expanse of savannah in Tsavo East with its thorn-bush vegetation still evokes the atmosphere of an untamed Africa. The only landmark rising abruptly from these flat plains is Mudanda Rock, a miniature replica of Ayers Rock in Australia.

The water hole attracts large numbers of wild animals at its base. Hundreds of elephant, buffalo, and hyena congregate here during the dry season. From its summit, there are panoramic views for miles, right across to the mountains in the east as far as Kilimanjaro and across the plains to the west, dotted here and there with green strips of forest along the shores of rivers and streams, helping to break the monotony of the landscape.

Elephants and their uses

The Galana River with its dense growth of palm trees along its banks is home to a large number of hippopotamuses and giant Nile crocodiles. Its source is 375 miles (600km) away in the mountains of Mount Kenia, from where it flows straight across Tsavo East before emptying into the Indian Ocean under the new name of the Sabaki River. The best place to observe the river wildlife is from Crocodiles' Point and from beneath the magnificent Lugard's Falls, where the Galana thrusts its way through a narrow gap in the rocks in a series of rapids.

At the start of the rainy seasons in March and October, things start happening in the soil of the Aruba plains to the east of Voi. Dung beetles, or tumblebugs, measuring 2 inches (5cm) across, start emerging from their holes in the ground in search of elephants, whose dung they roll into tiny pellets. They begin mating after just three weeks and the females disappear back into the ground, where they excavate holes the size of a shoebox and fill them with the dung pellets in which they have wrapped their eggs.

Tsavo West is much smaller, but its landscape is much more diverse thanks to its mountains, volcanoes, rivers, and water holes. Baobab trees are plentiful, but make it more difficult to get close to the animals.

Along its eastern border is the Yatta Plateau. It is 180 miles (290km) in length, making it one of the longest lava flows in the world. It originated as a lava flow from the Chaimu Crater just over 200 years ago. It is intersected by trails leading up to viewpoints offering incomparable vistas over the bright red soil that is typical of this broad expanse of African bush savannah.

Oasis in the steppes

This soil is also responsible for the coloring of the famous pink elephants, which are a common sight in Tsavo West. The animals "spray" themselves liberally with this red laterite dust, which acts both as a sunscreen and keeps irritating insects at bay.

The jewel of the Park is undoubtedly the Mzima Springs, where crystal clear water bubbles up out of volcanic rock in the middle of a bone-dry steppe landscape, creating a fertile oasis of abundant life in the barren wilderness. Each day, 40 million gallons (190 million liters) of water that percolates through the porous lava in the Chyulu Hills 25 miles (40km) away and flows from a subterranean river into three large lava basins. These springs also supply drinking water to Mombasa by pipeline.

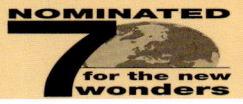

AFRICA

A land of lush grass

The Serengeti's vast savannah is some of the best grazing grassland in Africa, making it a paradise for big game

Getting there:
By car via Arusha. Regional airports in Moshi and Arusha, with several landing strips in the Serengeti

Where to stay:
Comfortable lodges available in the Serengeti. Camping is also permitted

Climate:
Temperatures warm, but pleasant all year round, thanks to the higher elevation. Rainy seasons: October–November and April–June

Main attractions:
Guided safaris

Special tips:
Many roads are temporarily impassable after heavy rainfall

Storm over the Serengeti (right)

The tall, dense grass of the savannah provides predators like the lion (below) and the cheetah (below, right) with ideal hunting grounds

Unperturbed by their presence, elephants congregate around the water holes during the dry season (center)

Who can possibly resist the magic of the Serengeti plains, whose vast sea of grass waves gently in the breeze beneath the hot, African sun? The animals integral to this awe-inspiring scene have no boundaries or frontiers. They obey only the call of the wild.

The habitat that has survived in the Serengeti is one of the oldest ecosystems on earth. Together with the neighboring Ngorongoro Reserve to the east and the Masai Mara Park in Kenya, it forms one of the largest, intact migration areas for hoofed animals anywhere in the world.

When the brief rainy season in October and November turns the steppes green with fresh growth, it is the signal for 1,500,000 gnus and hundreds of thousands of zebras and gazelles to begin their great migration. They descend from the northern hills and drop down into the Serengeti Plains in the southeast. They are driven by a primeval instinct, which overcomes any familial bonds. If a calf can no longer follow its mother, it is simply left behind, an easy meal for lions, cheetahs, and jackals.

The return journey

After the heavy rainfall between April and June, the main wet season, the herds set off return home by different routes. Nothing, not even deep gorges or crocodiles lurking in the rivers, can distract them from their chosen route home. Humans also pose hidden dangers. Not only do the animals' migratory routes involve crossing state frontiers, but they can also lead the animals away from the safety of the reserves.

Since time immemorial, man has shared the savannah with animals. Over three million years ago, as evidence discovered in Ngorongoro reserve has testified, this part of the world formed the cradle of mankind. Today, the proud Masai continue to drive their herds freely across the plains of the savannah. They are the only people permitted to graze their cattle within the Park.

When Ngorongoro's now dormant volcanoes erupted two to four million years ago, they ejected lava and ash far and wide across the area now known as the Serengeti Plains. Salts contained within this debris seeped into the earth, forming an impermeable, rock-hard layer no more than 39in (1m) below the surface. It is too hard for even the toughest tree roots to penetrate, which is why the Serengeti remains virtually treeless.

Subterranean saline barrier

This very same salt barrier creates perfect growing conditions for the various grasses, ensuring that any rainwater remains close to the surface, promoting the growth of luscious pasture for all the grazing animals. What is more, the animals themselves actually help regenerate this lush grassland by feeding on it. The shorter they crop the grass, the quicker it grows and the more moisture it contains.

The frequently dried-up riverbeds are lined with strips of riverine woodland, providing unique and rare habitats within the Serengeti. These rivers fill up so much during the two rainy seasons that enough water is retained in the ground over the dry months to support this dense woodland with its own microclimate.

Strange-shaped rocks

This microclimate is home to numerous orchids peeping out of the lush greenery. Climbing plants entwine themselves around the trees, enveloping them and creating a perfect habitat for the innumerable insects that populate the forest floor and tree canopy, including great swarms of stalk-eyed flies. The prolific bird population includes osprey, mouse birds, bee-eaters, and owls.

Up above in the canopy, colobus monkeys and shy bush babies frolic from branch to branch. On the forest floor, African monitor lizards, measuring from 39–78in (1–2m) in length, forage for food or lie sleeping in the undergrowth. Elephants, buffalo, hyenas, and lions come seeking the cool shade of the forest.

The Grumeti and Mara Rivers, which almost never run dry, are home to the mighty hippos which stand up to their necks in water and, during the dry season, amicably jostle giant crocodiles for space in the dwindling, greenish waters of the shrinking water holes.

The vast plains are interspersed with the bizarre shapes of rocks, silhouetted against the skyline. The water table in the vicinity of these rocky outcrops is usually higher than out on the open savannah.

AFRICA

The cradle of civilization

Ngorongoro Crater provides lush grazing for big game

Getting there:
By car from Arusha; airfield for chartered flights near the lodges and camping sites.

Where to stay:
Comfortable lodges on the rim of the crater, as well as camp sites. Equally comfortable, more modestly priced, lodges on private farms outside the reserve

Climate:
Rainy seasons are November-December and April-May. Pleasantly warm throughout the year, but lodges on the crater rim can be quite cool at night

Main attractions:
Panorama over the crater; Olduvai gorge; Bomas, a typical Masai village

When a volcano dies, the whole lava cone collapses inward, leaving behind what is known as a caldera, a ring wall encircling a flat area at the bottom of the volcano. This is how the Ngorongoro Crater originated in northeast Tanzania, to the west of the Kilimanjaro massif. It may not be the world's largest volcanic crater, but it has the distinction of being the largest to have so well withstood the passage of millions of years.

There is a simply breathtaking panoramic view from the rim of the crater across the 12-mile (20km) wide valley basin with its steep, wooded slopes. Its real treasure, however, lies nearly 2,000ft (600m) lower on the floor of the caldera. Its 100 square miles (260km2) have become home to one of the most fascinating concentrations of African big game. Its lush, short grass provides a rich supply of fodder for a permanent population of 25,000 animals. Herds of ungulates including gnus, zebras, gazelles, buffalo, eland, and hartebeest graze here, drifting from one water hole to another. Hippopotamuses inhabit the marshy areas. Lions, leopards, and cheetahs have an abundant choice of prey.

Ngorongoro Crater offers the visitor a unique opportunity to catch sight of one of the 20 to 30 black rhinos, a species that has been almost wiped out in Africa by poachers. Nowhere else can one see so many lions in such a compact area. Five prides, numbering altogether 100 or so animals, have divided up the crater floor into individual territories, each with its own small lake.

Constant changes

Many visitors are surprised by the fact that the elephants that regularly descend into the crater are all males. The herds of cow elephants and their young apparently baulk at making the steep descent and strenuous climb back up, preferring to remain around the forested rim of the crater.

One of the highlights of the Ngorongoro Crater's bird life is the spectacular sight of vast flocks of pink flamingos, which sometimes fly in from the nearby soda lake.

When the great migration season gets underway, herds of zebra, gazelle, and gnu leave the crater to join the procession of animals heading for the adjacent Serengeti. When drought strikes, transforming the fertile crater basin into a dust-blown savannah, many animals seek greener pastures in the mountainous areas beyond the crater. If a mighty deluge of rain occurs, causing the lakes and marshes in the valley to flood, they return. Consequently, the face of the Ngorongoro Crater changes from month to month and year to year.

The Masai also graze their herds of cattle in Ngorongoro. No one knows precisely how many of these nomadic people pass through the country; there are possibly 25,000, or even 40,000. They migrated here some 200 years ago and have virtually become part of the landscape of the Ngorongoro mountains.

Fossil footprints

Man is believed to have originated in this area some 3,600,000 years ago. The volcanoes were still active when an upright, humanoid creature left a clear footprint in a soft lava field near Laetoli, not far from the Ngorongoro Crater.

Even more corroborating evidence was discovered in the Olduvai Gorge. This gash in the solidified lava forms a ravine nearly 300ft (90m) deep, which runs for about 30 miles (50km) towards the Serengeti.

The first discovery was made by the German entomologist, Kattwinkel, who came across the bones of a long extinct, three-toed species of horse whilst searching for new species of butterfly and took them back to Germany with him. When Louis Leakey, a Kenyan-born archaeologist, saw the bones in Berlin, it prompted him to organize an expedition in 1931 to research the discovery more closely. His wife, Mary Leakey, found the 1,750,000-year-old remains of a hominid, Australopithecus boisei, in the Olduvai gorge in 1959. Australopithecus boisei is nicknamed "Nutcracker man" because of his extremely powerful jaw. The gorge has since yielded the remains of 50 specimens of prehistoric and early man, including homo habilis, who bears strong similarities to us today.

Herds of gnu and zebra grazing in perfect harmony on the pastures of Ngorongoro Crater (above)

The big game within the crater includes the rhinoceros, which finds ample fodder here to rear its young (opposite)

After the rains, some lakes in the marshes of the crater basin retain their water for a long time, providing an ideal source of water for numerous animals (left)

AFRICA

Forest giraffes of the Congo

The Okapi Reserve in the central African rainforest is home to many rare species of wildlife

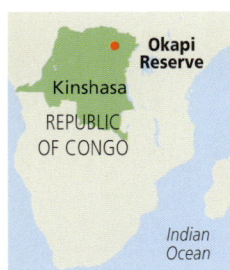

Getting there:
Private car rental from Bunia or Isiro, but very poor roads. It is recommended that travel and trekking be arranged through authorized agencies

Where to stay:
Basic accommodation available

Climate:
Hot and humid all year round: 75°F–88°F (24°C–31°C). Dry season: December–March

Main attractions:
Treks through the Park; okapi breeding station; taking part in a traditional pygmy hunting expedition

Special tips:
Heed any travel warnings, as Ituri is still considered a particularly unsafe area

Okapis are extremely shy creatures which require a tropical rainforest habitat where the ground is firm and dry

In the northeastern corner of the Democratic Republic of Congo between the Ituri and Nepoko Rivers lies the Ituri rainforest, which has flourished here for well over one million years. This region remains largely unexplored and no doubt still harbors many secrets. One of its best kept ones came to light only recently. In the beginning of the twentieth century, the world's biologists thought they knew about every kind of African big game that existed. In 1901, however, during a visit to a pygmy settlement, a British colonial official noticed two skulls and a complete animal skin that he was unable to identify. He sent the latter to London, where experts established that it was from a member of the giraffe family. It was another six years before European eyes rested for the first time on a living example of this species: an okapi calf.

The most striking characteristic of the okapi is the horizontal white striping on its hindquarters and haunches. The rest of its coat is a glossy, dark chestnut brown and its head, sporting small, backward sloping, furry horns, is gray. In contrast to its savannah cousin, this forest giraffe, with its short legs and short neck, stands just shoulder-high at 5–5 1/2ft (1.5–1.7m). What it does have in common with its taller relatives, however, is its 16in (40cm) long tongue, which it uses to strip the leaves and fruit off trees.

Okapis are exceptionally timid animals, living exclusively in the depths of the rainforest in the northeastern part of the Congo where the forest floor is firm and dry.

There are around 30,000 of these animals in the wild, 5,000 of these in the Okapi reserve. This conservation area covers approximately 5,400 square miles (14,000km2) and, in turn, comprises around one-fifth of the Ituri rainforest.

Hunted by poachers

The reserve was originally established as the logical accompaniment to a breeding station set up in 1952 in Epulu to supply zoos all over the world with captive-bred okapis. Okapis also became a popular gift given to foreign heads of state on official visits.

Since then, the reserve itself has come under threat and, along with all conservation areas in the Congo, now features on UNESCO's list of endangered nature parks. During the civil war of 1997–1999, the forests of central Africa served as popular hiding places for the rebel armies, who hunted local game to excess. In their wake followed an influx of gold and coltan (columbite-tantalite) prospectors from the neighboring, densely populated region around Kisangani, who constructed dams, cut down areas of forest for fields, and poached the animals.

Following the ceasefire in 1999, however, many international organizations have become actively involved in supporting local authorities' efforts to regain control over the reserve and help Nature reclaim her own.

The Ituri rainforest can still spring a few more surprises, however. The Congo is one of 25 countries with the highest rate of endemism and the greatest diversity of species. Around 15 percent of all plant and animal species are exclusive to this region. One such example is the African mouse deer that, despite any resemblance to a piglet, is, in fact, a species of deer. It inhabits the wetter areas of the forest close to rivers and streams. Biologists have identified 52 different kinds of mammals, including giant ground pangolin, African crested porcupine, rare species of meerkat, and red colobus monkeys, as well as more species of Duiker, a deer-sized antelope with short horns, than are found anywhere else in the world.

Rare Congo peafowl

Among the profusion of birds was one that persistently eluded detection by the white man. It was not until 1935 that a visiting ornithologist came across the feathers of an unknown type in a pygmy elder's headdress. This bird turned out to be the Congo peafowl, for which a new zoological family had to be created. Not only does this violet and green bird have all the characteristics of a peacock, it also has those of a guinea fowl.

So far, 329 different types of bird have been recorded in the Ituri rainforest, including long-tailed hawks, plumed guinea fowl, black guinea fowl, and various species of rail.

AFRICA

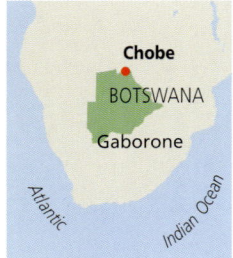

Where elephants roam the streets

Chobe National Park, in northern Botswana, is home to the largest elephant herds on earth

Getting there:
Local airfield in Kasane. By car via Kasane, Maun, or four-wheel drive vehicle via Ngoma Bridge (Caprivi/Namibia). There are no service facilities between Kasane and Maun. Four-wheel drive vehicles are essential in the Park, and it is advisable to travel with two vehicles

Where to stay:
Lodges available throughout the Park in various price categories, plus several camp sites with toilet and shower facilities. Booking several months in advance is essential

Climate:
Best time to travel is April to August, when the climate is fairly pleasant and the animals remain close to the water holes. Wet season starts in November, when it is hot and humid and the roads are often impassable

Main attractions:
Boat trips on Chobe River, Linyanti Swamps, and Savuti marshes in the Mababe Depression

Special tips:
Exceptionally good infrastructure

Chobe National Park boasts a variety of different habitats. The Savuti marshes are currently dried up (above, right)

Hippos live happily alongside crocodiles in Chobe's waterways (below, right)

Rock pictures in Allen's Camp reveal the artistic skills of early inhabitants

Almost no other national park in southern Africa can boast an abundance of wildlife to compare with that found in Chobe National Park in northern Botswana. This reserve is particularly noted for its huge elephant population, numbering over 70,000, and it is not uncommon to come across herds of 100 or more animals. Sometimes, these gray giants can even be seen wandering inquisitively through the provincial town of Kasane and its nearby encampments.

These elephants form part of what is probably the largest single concentration of this mammal left in Africa, a population estimated at around 120,000 extending over the whole of northern Botswana as well as northwest Zimbabwe. Their numbers have gradually increased from just a few thousand animals that survived the extensive poaching prevalent during the civil wars in the 1970s and 1980s. The Chobe elephants are migratory. During the dry season, they move north where they congregate around the Chobe and Linyati Rivers. During the rainy season, they return to the lowlands in the southeastern part of the National Park, traveling approximately 125 miles (200km) each year.

Although the Chobe elephants are among the largest in Africa, their tusks are very brittle and often in a lamentable state. It is rare to find an animal with a good, strong pair of tusks.

A trip by riverboat

It is not just the elephants that make Chobe National Park so special, however. Visitors find the magnificent African landscape equally enthralling. This area covering 4,000 square miles (10,000km2) of African soil is characterized by four distinctly different ecosystems and supports an astonishing variety of different habitats. In the extreme northeast around the Chobe River is the Serondela region with its lush plains and dense forests, while the hot, dry savanna nestles between the fertile Savuti marshes in the southwest and the Linyanti swamps in the southeast.

If you want to experience something really special, it is worth taking a boat trip on the Chobe River to observe the teeming wildlife. Herds of elephant can be seen trampling the banks, while hippopotamuses wallow and snort in the muddy shallows, surveyed by crocodiles lying in wait for their prey. Otters can be glimpsed darting into the undergrowth, while large herds of buffalo, giraffe, antelope, and zebra warily lower their heads to drink, knowing that lions, cheetahs, and hyenas are not far away.

In the far northwestern corner of the reserve lies the virtually forgotten and seldom visited Linyanti Swamp, which covers an area of nearly 350 square miles (900km^2) adjacent to the river after which it is named. It flows into Lake Liambezi, at which point it becomes the Chobe River. During the dry season, animals such as elephant, buffalo, and zebra congregate here. The trees and vegetation along the riverbank are filled with an overwhelming cacophony of sound from large numbers of birds sporting a dazzling array of colors. Even the pelican, a rarity elsewhere, can be seen here.

A network of waterways

The Mababe Depression to the south of the Park is all that remains of a large lake that once covered the whole of northern Botswana. These flat and inhospitable Savuti lowland marshes are mainly frequented by elephants, but lions, wild dogs, and hyenas are also regular visitors. It is rare nowadays to see herds of impalas, gnus, buffalo, zebras, and antelope occurring in vast numbers. The three main rivers of southern Africa — the Okavango, Chobe, and Zambezi — are in fact closely interlinked. The Selinda Spillway connects the Okavango via the Linyanti and Chobe Rivers with the Zambezi. The spillway branches off eastwards at the start of the Okavango Delta, forming a link with the Linyanti Swamp in Chobe National Park. When the Okavango Delta is flooded, a small amount of water also flows along this channel into the Linyanti Swamp, the Chobe River, and into the Zambezi. When water levels are low, the swamp empties again.

AFRICA

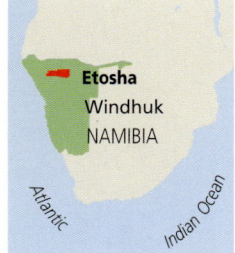

Spectacle of the salt flats

The wildlife of Etosha National Park, in northern Namibia, has survived despite numerous onslaughts

Getting there:
310 miles (500km) of tarmac road from Windhuk. Nearest local airport in Tsumeb, landing strips for light aircraft near the camps. Bus and rail connections

Where to stay:
Three camps offering hotel, bungalows, and campground, each situated a day's journey — 45 miles (70 km) — apart

Climate:
Best time to visit is during the dry season between May and October, when temperatures rarely exceed 86°F (30°C). Extremely hot in December/January

Main attractions:
Water holes at Okaukuejo, Halali, and Namutoni

Special tips:
Enclosed vehicles only. Do not get out of your vehicle

The harsh glare of white salt stretching as far as the eye can see. Dust, heat, and burning sun. The Etosha salt pan in northern Namibia may well seem one of the most inhospitable places on earth to humans, yet it is nevertheless home to 114 mammals and around 340 species of birds. Even some endangered species like the black rhino and sable antelope have found a refuge here.

The central pan itself occupies an area of 1,850 square miles (4,800km2) at the heart of Etosha National Park, which in turn extends over some 8,500 square miles (22,000km2) and supports one of the largest concentrations of African game, including lions, elephants, giraffes, antelope, zebras, and springbok. Cheetahs and leopards can also be glimpsed occasionally, although they prefer to remain hidden in the thick grass. The diversity of bird life reaches a peak during the rainy season, when flocks of flamingos and vast numbers of wading birds fly in from afar to join the vulture, hawks and eagles.

At one time, Etosha National Park covered nearly 40,000 square miles (100,000km2) and was the largest national park in the world. Under South Africa's apartheid regime, however, the Park was reduced in 1967 to well under a quarter of its original size as part of the government's homeland policy.

Twelve million years ago, the Etosha salt pan began as a lake bed, fed by the Kunene River as it flowed southward from Angola and filled this large depression with its waters. Later, the river altered course, turned westward, and discharged its waters straight into the Atlantic Ocean. The water evaporated, the lake dried up, and all that remained was the salt pan. During the rainy season, however, a number of otherwise dried-up rivers, which follow an almost parallel course down from Angola in the north, channel so much water into the area that large parts of the Etosha Pan can be waist-deep in water.

Inhospitable saline soil

Plants do not grow in this saline soil. Only in places where the ground remains damp is there evidence of some algae and bacteria, which cast a green sheen over this salty desert. Grass, rushes, and a few stunted trees may be found on the low-lying islets, which are only submerged when water levels are high.

Beyond the rim of the salt pan is the savannah with its low-growing scrubby vegetation, which in turn gives way to the fertile soil of the extensive grasslands, providing abundant fodder for gnus, zebras, and springboks. In the western sector of the Park, where the soil is brackish and chalky, the sparse vegetation consists mainly of savannah thornscrub. To the east, however, is a savannah populated by gnarled mopane trees, figs, and date palms. A mixed dry forest of camel thorn palms and purple pod cluster leaf trees covers the northern sector.

The entire Park is surrounded by a strong, 10ft (3m) high electric fence intended to keep the animals in and poachers out. This inevitably disrupts the natural annual migration cycle of the herds but artificial routes have been created to replace them. Water is fed through pipes to the numerous watering holes in the park and the flow is turned on and off at certain times to encourage the herds to migrate.

When gravel roads were first built to accommodate visitors to the Park, it almost caused a disaster. The quarries from which the gravel was extracted filled up with water in which salts dissolved. This produced a perfect breeding ground for the baccillae that cause anthrax. Because of the particular susceptibility of many herbivores to this disease, the hartebeest population dropped in just 30 years by 90 percent and the number of zebras fell from 15,000 to a mere 5,000. The Etosha lions, however, remained immune and their numbers rapidly increased.

Sick lions — elsewhere

In contrast to other Africa game reserves, the big cats of Etosha are free of the FIV virus, the big cat equivalent of the HIV virus in humans. As a result, Etosha lions are often relocated to build up numbers in other wildlife parks. In the Kruger National Park, 83 percent of the big cats are affected by FIV and the figure is 79 percent in the Serengeti.

In order to avoid disturbing the animals and upsetting the natural balance, a special protected area for endangered species has been established in Otjovasandu in the western section. Around 20 percent of Etosha National Park is open to visitors—more than enough, certainly, to enable a close encounter with Africa's animals in this magnificent natural setting.

A herd of springbok congregating at a water hole (below, left)

Just a few months later, the same spot is overgrown with dried grasses (above)

A herd of zebra visit another watering hole (center, left); gemsbok, whose horns can grow to over 39in (1m) in length, graze on the dried grasses of the savannah (below, left)

AFRICA

The greatest game reserve

South Africa's Kruger National Park becomes Limpopo Park

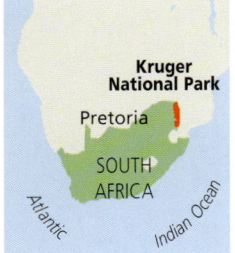

Getting there:
Daily flights from Johannesburg to Hoedspruit; private charter flights also available to Timbavati in Kruger Park. Excellent roads from Johannesburg and Harare

Where to stay:
Wide choice of accommodation in South Africa; camping and luxury lodges available in Zimbabwe and Mozambique outside the park boundaries

Climate:
Warm all year round. Best game-watching season is during the dry months from October to March, although veldt temperatures are often very high at this time

Main attractions:
Site of the Iron Age palace of Thulamela; ruins at Pafuri and around Mpumalanga. Guided wilderness hiking trails in Kruger Park (book well in advance!)

Special tips:
Heed any travel warnings in respect of Mozambique and Zimbabwe

View from a hill looking down into the Olifant River Valley, which traverses Kruger National Park from west to east (opposite, top)

Lions, leopards, and the distinctively spotted puma are the most dangerous predators of the savannah. They prey mainly on antelope and other ruminants (below, left and right)

South Africa once had plans to erect electric fences around its borders to keep illegal immigrants out of the country, but now even the simple wire fence constructions separating Mozambique, Zimbabwe, and South Africa are being dismantled to accommodate what will be the largest nature reserve in the world.

This new reserve, the Great Limpopo Transfrontier National Park, extends over the triangle where the three countries meet and straddles the Limpopo River, which forms the border between South Africa and its two northern neighbors. This enormous park, an amalgamation of the former Kruger National Park in South Africa, Limpopo, Zinave, and Banhine in Mozambique, and Gonarezhou in Zimbabwe, already encompasses an area of 13,500 square miles (35,000km2). This will expand in time, as more and more areas are placed under protection, and will eventually comprise around 38,600 square miles (100,000km2) of territory, an area far larger than Portugal.

In this way, a rich diversity of African habitats will be united under the aegis of a single reserve, ranging from the dry, flat savannah terrain of Kruger National Park, the wet, humid landscapes and lakes of Mozambique, to the spectacular sandstone cliffs of Gonarezhou. The new arrangement will be a blessing for the former Kruger National Park, enabling it to better accommodate some of its elephants and other grazing animals, which have multiplied to such an extent that they are in danger of destroying the very habitat on which their survival depends. They will now find a new home north of the Limpopo River, along with hundreds of zebras, blue wildebeest, impalas, and other low veldt animals from the Kruger National Park's savannah plains. Sixteen years of civil war in Mozambique and Zimbabwe, not to mention the great drought during the 1980s, have brought many species of large mammals there to the verge of extinction.

Lost cultures

Limpopo National Park is not only designed to protect Africa's animals, but also intended to safeguard the ancient cultures of the Shangaan-speaking tribal communities of Makuleke in South Africa, the Shingwedzi and Limpopo peoples of Mozambique, and the Sengwe and Chiredzi tribes of Zimbabwe. Visitors have the opportunity to experience unfamiliar cultures, observe their tribal dances and handicrafts, and even learn something about the skills of traditional healers.

There is a great deal of evidence to suggest that the land within this triangle of countries has been inhabited since the Stone Age. Some of its earliest inhabitants were the San, who left a legacy of wall paintings in the sandstone caves. They were followed over the course of about 800 years by the Bantu and by the time the first Europeans arrived in the early sixteenth century, some remarkably civilized cultures had developed here, the impressive ruins of which can still be seen today.

Kruger National Park, as it was formerly known, offers the ultimate in Safari tourism. The "Big Five" African game animals can be spotted with relative ease. Buffalo, lions, elephants, rhinoceros, and leopards have become accustomed to the safari vehicles, ferrying tourists along the approximately 3,100 miles (5,000km) of well-built roads that criss-cross the flat, dry plains of the savannah. Cheetahs, giraffes, hippos, and herds of different species of antelope also seem unperturbed by this attention.

Dramatic cliff formations in the savannah

Despite the highly developed tourist infrastructure of Kruger Park, its network of roads, rest camps, and lodges still comprise only 3 percent of its overall area. The remainder belongs to nature. In addition, there are a number of large, privately owned game reserves bordering the Park, offering a high concentration of African big game combined with luxurious accommodation and even so-called "eco safaris," on which guests can accompany experienced biologists, vets, and rangers on their patrols. Less well-known is Gonarezhou National Park, a little gem among Africa's nature reserves situated in the remote northwestern section of Limpopo

Park. Gonarezhou National Park encompasses dramatic rock formations such as Chilojo Cliff, which is visible from a distance of 30 miles (50km), rearing up out of the vast expanse of untouched savannah grasslands and magnificent baobab forests. The elephants in this region are the largest and heaviest anywhere in Africa. Since very few visitors find their way here, many of the park's trails are overgrown or have been swallowed up by the sea of savannah grassland.

Here too, civil war and drought have left their scars on the land. By the mid-1990s, however, when the park re-opened after the ravages of war, the elephant population had recovered to such an extent that 750 animals could be transferred to other parks.

Visitors to this region, which covers an area of just 2,000 square miles (5,000km2), will be entranced by the great sense of peace and tranquility that reigns here, far away from the well-trodden tourist track.

AFRICA

Island of exotic plants

Unique tree ferns and orchids inhabit the misty rain forests of Réunion Island, in the Indian Ocean

Getting there:
Regular flights from Paris, numerous flights between Mauritius, South Africa, Madagascar, the Seychelles, the Comoro Islands and Kenya

Where to stay:
All categories of hotel, book well in advance for July and August. Some very comfortable cabin accommodation available in the hinterland.

Climate:
Best time to travel is between May and October (around 21°C), the rest of the year temperatures are around 82°F (28°C) with a lot of rain and occasional tropical cyclones

Main attractions:
Point de la Table volcano nature trail. Waterfalls: Voile de la Mariée (Bride's Veil), Ravine Blanche, Ravine de Caverne, and Ravine Mazarin in the Cirques des Salazie. Trail through the Cirque de Mafate. Climb the Piton de la Fournaise

Tropical rainforest covers vast sections of the island. View of the Grand Bassin gorge and mountain chain (opposite)

The steep banks of the Bassin des Aigrettes (top)

The Piton de la Fournaise volcano is one of the island's highest elevations (8,235ft/2,510m). This photo shows the view across the caldera to the summit and the "Formica Leio" crater (center)

Réunion's forests are home to many species of chameleon

Réunion is the youngest and highest of the three Mascarene Islands. They owe their existence to the Piton des Neiges volcano, which formed two to three million years ago, rising to a height of 23,000ft (7,000m) above sea-level. Reaching a height of 10,069ft (3,069m), it is the highest mountain on the Mascarenes.

Just over one million years ago, another volcano emerged on its southeastern flank, the Piton de la Fournaise, which remains active to this day and shifts a little further southeast with every eruption.

Erosion of the mountain massif around the old, extinct volcano in the center of the island has meanwhile produced spectacular rock formations. Grouped around it and resembling steep-sided amphitheatres are three former volcanic basins, the Cirques Cilaos, Mafate, and Salazie. Each covers an area of around 40 square miles (100km2) and is composed of hills, mountains, and ridges, debris from the collapsed volcanic shield. The entire island is a protected area.

Temperate climate

Very few people in mainland France are familiar with France's southernmost Département. Even fewer are aware of its spectacular natural wonders although, admittedly, the island does not have much in the way of dream beaches. Its wildly rugged, dramatic mountains, mighty gorges, countless waterfalls, and dense jungle interior amply compensate for the shortcomings of its coastline.

Although Réunion is situated in the tropics, the climate remains relatively cool with temperatures hovering around 70°F (21°C) between April and October and 82°F (28°C) during the summer months. In the mountains, temperatures can drop as low as 54°F (12°C). The southeast trade winds deposit a good deal of rain on the island's southern and eastern slopes during the cool season, promoting luxuriant growth in the dense, verdant rainforests that are home to numerous tree ferns and over 100 types of orchid.

The brown mountain landscape on the western side of the island receives little precipitation. Consequently, savannah plants dominate here, including palms and agaves. Like other remote islands, Réunion Island has a large number of indigenous species. Long ago, seeds carried here from Mauritius, Africa, and India by wind, rain, or birds evolved into individual species unique to the island. The mountain tamarind, a species of mimosa found primarily on the high plateaus of the caldera that can grow more than 80ft (25m) in height, is one example.

However, the island's fauna is relatively limited. Early in the seventeenth century, the first Europeans to set foot on the island hunted many animals to extinction. The first settlers encountered only two kinds of mammal, both of which have since disappeared: dugongs and bats. All the giant tortoises, which provided a welcome source of food on long sea journeys, have also disappeared. Ships' rats took care of the rest, decimating many endemic species of lizards and geckos. The ones seen today darting about on house walls were mainly introduced from Madagascar and India, together with a species of chameleon from Java that is sometimes found around the Grand Étang lakes.

It was the birds that coped best with the invasion of domestic animals, colonial plants, and pests. Of the 36 indigenous bird varieties, 9 are unique to the Mascarene Islands, including the Mauritius cuckoo, the Mauritius falcon, and the cardinal with its brilliant red plumage.

Hiking into adventure

The legendary dodo, a large, flightless bird with a hooked beak, has long been extinct. It was first documented in 1598 and last seen in 1662 on two of the small islands off Mauritius.

Along the exciting trails within the three volcanic basins, you will frequently encounter huge spiders' webs, spanning up to 65ft² (6m²), with a large orange and black silk spider, a member of the nephilia family, measuring up to 4 inches (10 cm) across, lying in wait for its prey right in the center.

AUSTRALIA

An Aboriginal paradise

Fraser Island is the world's largest sand island, providing a unique habitat for rare plants and bird life

Getting there:
Frequent ferries and passenger ships operate daily from Hervey Bay or Inskip Point. Suitable only for four-wheel drive vehicles

Where to stay:
All categories of hotel, cabin, and holiday home; campsites of varying standards; off-site camping also available

Climate:
Maritime, sub-tropical climate, 72°–82°F (22–28°C) in December, 57°–70°F (14–21°C) in July. Wettest months: January to March

Activities and attractions:
Bushwalking along forest tracks and nature trails; Central Station at Wanggoolba Creek; Stonetood shifting dune

Special tips:
Beware of dingoes (Australian wild dogs) Do not bathe in the sea: there may be sharks, not to mention the extremely poisonous box jellyfish during the rainy season. Take all litter back to the mainland

Fraser Island is famed for its deep, clear lakes, one of which is Lake KcKiney (above)

Petrified sand formations are among the island's main attractions (below, left) as well as the luxuriant ferns found in Fraser Island's rainforests (below, right)

Endless white beaches that are the stuff of dreams, flanked by jagged multi-colored sandstone cliffs. Vast, enchanted rainforests surviving on ancient dunes. Crystal-clear lakes and babbling brooks winding romantically through the forest. This is Fraser Island, situated off Australia's central eastern coast.

The aborigines have always referred to it as "K'gan," or paradise. Numerous piles of shells, fish traps, encampments, and scarred trees whose bark was used to build canoes are all reminders of the fact that this island has been inhabited by the Butchella people for at least 5,000 years.

The first European settlers found the island too barren to warrant further exploration. James Cook sailed past it between May 18 and 20, 1770, but Mathew Flinders, the navigator, set foot on the beach here in 1802 although he, too, had ignored it some four years previously.

Nowadays, Fraser Island is a dream destination for nature lovers and seekers of solitude. Measuring over 80 miles (130km) in length, there is plenty of room on the island for everyone – providing they have their own four-wheel drive, as there are no roads, only rough forest tracks that you are not allowed to leave and 75-Mile-Beach on the Pacific seaboard that provides a lonely "highway" link along the beach to the northern end of the island.

Rainforest on sand

Fraser Island is the world's largest sand island, sporting the only sub-tropical rainforest to survive on infertile sand while also managing to provide a lush habitat for 600 different species of plants. Unusual varieties, such as the Angiopteris fern, which boasts the largest fronds of any fern, seem to prosper here. Unlike other plants, its fronds are not kept upright by tissue structure, but by high water pressure in its capillaries.

For over 700,000 years, rain has been washing sand down from the mountains of eastern Australia and into the ocean. Strong currents then carry it northwards where it accumulates in reefs. Indian Head, an imposing sandstone cliff in the north of the island, was formed in this way. From this vantage point, the view stretches far across the white beaches, the sea of dunes, and the sand hills crowned with green vegetation. Over the millennia, these have grown to heights of up to 800ft (240m) and chart the area's geographical history.

The sand along the coast can shimmer in 72 different hues. The most impressive composition occurs along a 22 mile (35km) stretch of shore, north of Happy Valley. Yet further north, beyond the wreck of the "Maheno" passenger steamer that ran aground in 1935 on its final voyage to the scrap yard, are the uniquely colored rock formations known as "The Cathedral."

Glittering amid the dense green lushness of the tropical rainforest are some 200 crystal-clear, azure-blue lakes and ponds, a tempting prospect for the would-be bather. So pure are they that only very few organisms can find any form of nutrition in them. One creature that has adapted in order to survive in these slightly acidic lakes is the endangered "acid frog," not to mention the Lake Bowarrady turtles.

The water in 40 of these lakes has the consistency of tea, however. Over the course of 300,000 years, leaves and dead plant material have accumulated on the lake beds, effectively sealing them. There are very few such lakes on the planet and Fraser Island boasts half of them.

The other crystal-clear lakes are either fed by the huge reservoir of fresh water beneath the island, or else a shifting dune has blocked off the usual soak away for rain. Clear, cool streams radiate from these lakes like arteries across the rainforest. Wanggoolba Creek, for example, has channeled out a white sandy bed for itself, winding through the dense rainforest from Central Station to the mainland side of the island.

Where the dunes are too high to sustain rainforest, vast eucalyptus forests flourish. Where the soil is even poorer, these, in turn, give way to the type of forests typically found on sandy soil, consisting primarily of kauri spruces and araucarias.

These forests and shores provide food and a haven for over 230 species of bird, as well as numerous birds of passage that stop to rest here on their journey to Siberia. Fraser Island boasts one of the largest and most varied bird populations in all Australia.

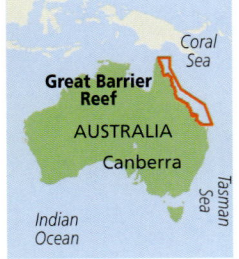

AUSTRALIA

The beauty of the coral

The Great Barrier Reef extends for more than 1,200 miles (2,000km) off the coast of northeast Australia

Getting there:
By ship or light aircraft to the islands; most reefs accessible by boat

Where to stay:
There are 20 luxury-class island hotels and a wide range of accommodation on the mainland. Onboard ship accommodation available near Seetörns

Climate:
Air temperature 75–86°F (24–30°C) in January, 64–75°F (18–24°C) in July

Main attractions:
Numerous opportunities for visiting the islands and reefs in combination with water sport activities. Flights and cruises available to more remote parts of the Great Barrier Reef. Islands: Great Keppel (hiking trails); Bedarra (rainforest); Dunk (artists' colony); Lizard and Hinchinbrook (rock paintings)

Special tips:
Utmost heed should be paid to warnings by tour guides and diving instructors regarding dangerous sea creatures

The largest single structure ever created by living creatures lies almost totally underwater. The full extent of its glory and its sheer size can really only be appreciated properly from space, as seen by the Space Shuttle. The Great Barrier Reef, the largest coral reef of all time, stretches over 1,200 miles (2,000km) along the flat continental shelf off Australia's northeastern coast, at a distance of 10–100 miles (16–160km) from the mainland.

The Reef is one of nature's greatest achievements and the architects of this magnificent edifice are tiny coral polyps whose finely chiseled, calcareous skeletons form the framework of the structure, "cemented" together by microscopic coral algae and moss animalcules. Reef-forming corals require sun and warmth due to their close, symbiotic relationship with zooxanthella algae, which need light to survive. The polyps waft nutrient-rich water toward the algae, which in turn ensure that the polyps have the right chemical environment to absorb the large amounts of calcium they need for healthy growth. Consequently, a coral colony always grows towards the light when the water level rises. New layers are constantly being added as each new generation of coral builds on the skeletal remains of the previous generation.

Water temperature is critical

The 2,900 coral reefs and islands, which now fall under the aegis of the 135,000 square miles (350,000km2) of protected area that is the Great Barrier Reef National Park, were all formed in this way. Seven hundred and sixty of these reefs have developed in a circular pattern, often encircling former continental islands. When the continental shelf rose slightly, it lifted 300 of them above the water level. In addition, there are 618 true continental islands, which once formed part of the Australian mainland and are now overgrown with dense rainforest.

Geologically speaking, the Great Barrier Reef is relatively young, its origins dating back a mere 500,000 years. Its present structure is only 8,000–10,000 years old. When the

sea settled down to its present level 6,500 years ago, the corals stopped growing upwards. The first examples of coral reef on earth were formed 500 million years ago. The species that populate today's reefs began their successful colonization just 250,000 years ago.

The symbiotic relationship that exists between the zooxanthella algae and the reef-building corals is extremely sensitive to environmental changes, e.g., water temperature. Conditions in the southwest Pacific are theoretically perfect as temperatures hardly vary from around 82°F (28°C) throughout the year. If the temperature does rise above 86°F (30°C) however, the brightly colored algae abandon their host, depriving the reef of its colorful splendor and leaving a white, calcareous structure in their wake. Over the past few years, global water temperatures have already risen by 1°F and some areas have already witnessed an increasing trend in temperatures exceeding the critical 86°F (30°C) threshold. Even the Great Barrier Reef has seen its algae disappear temporarily from the corals. So far, these creatures have always managed to recover and re-es-

The majority of the 2,900 coral reefs in the Great Barrier Reef lie just below the surface (main photo)

Only 44 of the reefs have accumulated enough sand and soil above sea level to support vegetation (below, left)

Yellow soft coral is just one of the 400 species found in this marine National Park (below, right)

Waving fronds of algae form a perfect background for the brilliant colors of the anemone fish (center, right)

tablish their equilibrium with the help of cold ocean currents which serve to cool down the water temperatures. The Great Barrier Reef, the greatest reef in the world, is still one of the healthiest.

Over the years, marine biologists have watched with concern as swarms of starfish occasionally besiege coral reefs. As a result of their frenzied feeding and clumsy movements, which break off pieces of coral, it is not uncommon for them to eat their way through entire reefs, destroying them in the process.

Nowadays, we know that this is simply part of the natural ecosystem of the Great Barrier Reef and that the starfish actually preserve the diversity of the reef by eating their way through the faster-growing species of coral, which would otherwise end up monopolizing these shallow waters.

400 species of coral

Coral reefs are among the most diverse ecosystems on earth. The Great Barrier Reef is no exception. More than 400 different varieties of coral have been identified on the Reef, which also supports countless other creatures. The Barrier Reef is home to altogether 1,500 species of fish, 4,000 mollusks, more than 200 types of bird — 40 of them seabirds — 20 sea snakes, and six species of turtle. There is also a large population of dugong sea cows, which are very rare elsewhere, not to mention approximately 30 different species of whale, dolphin, and porpoise that regularly visit the Reef.

AUSTRALIA

The Southern fjords

Mount Cook and Fjordland National Parks, in New Zealand, cover much of South Island

Getting there:
Between Invercargill and Haast, Highway 6 passes all Te Wahipounamu's National Parks. Daily bus services. Airports at Invercargill and Mount Cook

Where to stay:
Mainly middle-range hotels, youth hostels, and campsites in towns along Highway 6

Climate:
Cool to moderate climate. January: 66°F (19°C), rising to over 86°F (30°C) in the valleys. July: average temperatures of 34°F (1.3°C), occasionally dropping to 14°F (-10°C). Temperatures drop as the altitude increases. Westland Park is one of the wettest places on earth

Main attractions:
Hikes along well-marked trails; Mount Cook; Sutherland Falls; Kea Point (viewpoint); Hooker Valley; mountain climbing and glacier trekking; scenic flights

Special tips:
The National Parks are not easily accessible and only to visitors on foot. It is necessary to book several weeks in advance to walk some of the trails as only a limited number of hikers are permitted at any one time

Te Wahipounamu is a dramatically beautiful landscape of high mountains and fjords in the southwest of New Zealand. From remote beaches on the wild, jagged coastline bordering the shores of the Tasman Sea to the grandeur of the rugged, glacier-clad mountains of the Southern Alps, the two National Parks preserve a unique, almost untouched, natural landscape with a large diversity of habitats. The scenery has been shaped by various periods of glaciations spanning hundreds of thousands of years.

Steep, forested slopes plunge into deep, impenetrable gorges. Dense rainforests occupy the low-lying areas and the coastal region is studded with an abundance of tranquil, shimmering lakes and inlets. It is a land of dramatic contrasts and its 10,000 square miles (26,000km2) have now been designated a world heritage site, encompassing not only Westland, Mount Cook, Fjordland, and Mount Aspiring National Parks, but also 36 additional conservation areas in southwestern New Zealand.

This nature park is situated in one of the most seismically active regions of the world. Southeast New Zealand lies precisely above the spot where the Pacific and Indo-Australian plates collide. The resulting mountains are the product of five million years of geological movements combined with the effects of the glaciers that have carved out deep valleys between the mountains. Westland and Mount Cook National Parks together boast 28 of the 29 peaks in New Zealand that exceed 9,900ft (3,000) meters. At 12,350ft (3,764m), Mount Cook is New Zealand's highest mountain. The force of the breakers, which have rolled in unchecked from the Southern Ocean since prehistoric times, has created some dramatic coastal scenery with steep, bizarrely shaped cliffs, innumerable rocky outcrops, and sheer rock walls.

Three-feet-high tussock grasslands

The most spectacular coastal scenery was created as a result of land being thrust up from the sea and forming numerous terraces, tiered one above the other. The lowest level supports mixed woodland, while the middle band is dominated by mountain beech and yew. Approaching 2,000ft (600m), the terrain becomes shrub landscape.

The rich diversity of habitats, ranging from rainforest to grasslands, shrub land, and broad-leaved woodland is due largely to the dramatic differences in altitude and temperature between east and west. Colorful flower meadows carpet the mountaintops between the tree level and snow line.

Large mountain daisies and Mount Cook lilies, the largest buttercup in the world, grow in the shelter of the three-feet-high tussock grass.

Its remote location has spared Te Wahipounamu any significant human interference and preserved it as a key habitat for many indigenous species. Around 50,000 fur seals now congregate in colonies along the coastline. These mammals were once hunted so ruthlessly by Europeans that by the end of the nineteenth century, the species had almost been wiped out.

The bird life here is also outstanding. The National Park is home to a large proportion of New Zealand's forest birds with many of the 170 varieties exclusive to this region.

The one and only mountain parrot

Above the tree line, the *kea* can be found hopping among the tussocks of grass, apparently finding the effort of flying against the blustery mountain winds too arduous to contemplate. These crow-sized birds with their dull, olive-green plumage are the only mountain parrot to be found anywhere in the world. They are extremely curious and will rummage through people's belongings at campsites, even having been known to make off with small items of equipment such as cameras.

The flightless Takahe is a rare and endangered species of rail with blue-green foliage and a red, curved bill. The Park's coastline is also the sole habitat of the 20in (50cm) tall Victoria penguin with between 1,000 and 2,000 breeding pairs occupying the coastal cliffs. In contrast to the rest of New Zealand, the numerous lakes and fjords in this region are a veritable paradise for fish. Seventeen species occur here, many of which are rarely found elsewhere in New Zealand, for example the giant Kokopu, a species of pike popular with anglers that is frequently found in Te Wahipounamu's rivers and lakes.

The picturesque Lake Pukakai lies at the foot of 12,350ft (3,764m) high Mount Cook, New Zealand's tallest mountain (above)

The twin peaks of Mount Tasman and Mount Cook dominate the mountain scenery of South Island (below, left)

EUROPE

Sanctuary from the Stone Age

Stonehenge is Europe's most important prehistoric edifice

Route:
7.5 mi. (12 km) north of Salisbury (train). From London over the M 3/A 303 approx. 186 mi. (300 km)

Opening times:
Limited, can not be specified

Best period:
Summer solstice (June 21st Druid gathering)

Also worth seeing:
Stone ring at Avebury, 15.5 mi. (25 km) north, Europe's biggest historic building

It looks as if a Titan race tried to build a temple from the giant heavy rocks and were not able to finish it. The giant rocks now stand on the flat heather landscape of Southern English county of Wiltshire, 7.5 mi. (12 km) north of the town Salisbury, in a secretive circle and set the riddle for the visitors as to what the actual meaning is of the stones. One thing is certain: Stonehenge, as the monument is called, is the most important prehistoric building in Europe.

The archaeologists now think that they know a few things about the stones. About 5,000 years ago, people from the start of the stone age placed the stones here in a 3370-foot (113 m) diameter circle. Around the circle is a bank with parallel grooves and the entrance was marked with boulders. It is thought that the builders wanted to build a holy area or a ritual meeting place. Possibly they paid homage to the sun in the circle, as did many earlier cultures, and considered the sun to be a god who created life.

Approximately a thousand years later, presumably in the early Bronze Age, the first monoliths were placed, long, square 26-ton sandstone blocks. They built a ring of rock pillars, which were approximately four and a half metres high and on the tops of which stones were placed lengthways and linked together. Over the centuries more and more monoliths were placed, until in the 16th or 17th century a temple building had been built. This is what archaeologists suspect, on the basis of remains and computer simulations.

At the final completion - as it was at that time - Stonehenge consisted of two circles of stone, the already mentioned outer circle and a small circle in the center. Further in the center were five "gateways" placed in a hoof shape. The gateways were built from three stones chipped from rocks, so-called trilithons, which stick out above everything else, and can still be seen at Stonehenge today. In the center of the edifice is a single, the most highest stone, an "altar stone," which is in turn surrounded by a number of smaller stones in a semi-circle. The edifice was probably not only directed towards the sun, but also to other celestial bodies.

Most of the stones which were used, must have come from quite a distance from Stonehenge. Geological research has showed that the stones come from Preseli Hills Pembroke in west Wales, which is 186 mi. (300 km) from Stonehenge. The 33-foot (10 m) long rock pieces were probably rolled on tree trunks over land and transported across water on rafts - possibly over the Avon, which flows quite close to Stonehenge. The problem of placing the heavy roof stones onto the standing stones, was solved by the unknown builders with the help of wooden constructions and a special lifting technique.

It was not until the 17th century that people began to study the history of Stonehenge, which means something to the effect of "hanging

TRACES OF CIVILIZATION

stones." At that time the archaeologist Aubrey discovered 56 graves containing human bones and charcoal rests in the inner bank. Who is buried here, is today still as unclear as many other aspects of the stone temple. From approximately a thousand so-called monolith edifices found in Europe in stone circles, menhirs and dolmen graves and that have withstood the centuries, Stonehenge will without a doubt remain the most mysterious.

Sandstone blocks from Wales weighing up to 26 tons were used to build Stonehenge. The blocks were placed perpendicular and linked with roof stones to form gateway structures.

EUROPE

The Lascaux Caves' Stone-Age drawings

Galloping horses, deer, ibexes and buffalos inhabit the rock walls and show the animal world from then.

Route
Clermont-Ferrand-Perigueux to Le Jardin-St. Lazare E 70/N 89, then on the D 704 6 mi. (10 km) to Montignac

Opening times
Lascaux II: daily July through to August 9:30 am-7:30 pm. Fewer visitors are allowed in in the summer: advisable to purchase tickets in advance

Also worth seeing:
Grottes de la cave 28 mi. (45 km) southwest, Grotte du Pech Merle 75 mi. (120 km) southwest.

The 17-year-old Marcel Ravidat and three friends fell upon a secret. A woman farmer from Lascaux in the French province of Dordogne, had told the pupils of a peculiar hole. They noticed it when they wanted to bury their dead donkey under a fallen silver spruce. The spruce seem to be deep in the ground. The boys took matches and an oil lamp with them, whistled the terrier Robot, and went in search of treasure. They found the hole under some wood close to the river Vezere. The dog jumped in the hole and Marcel followed. A little while later the ground caved in under them and swallowed the three of them. At the bottom of the hole the shocked friends saw a match light up and heard Marcel calling them to come to him. And so they walked further downwards. Together they found their way by feeling their way along the walls of a dark tunnel and after a while they reached a five metre high room. In the flickering light of the oil lamp they discovered something quite remarkable: between the horns of two bulls a red horse had been painted on the rock wall. This room, which was 49 by 33 ft. (15 x 10 m) was later called the "Bull room."

People as dolls

Abbot Henri Breuil, France's expert on cave drawings, who had been called-in by the teacher of the boys, immediately realized that this was a very big discovery: in the small room the boys had stumbled across the largest collect of drawings from the Stone Age that had ever been found. Two tunnels lead from the room to lower parts of the cave, which entered into larger areas with dome like ceilings. The cave was a total of 459 feet (140 m) long. Some of the walls had so many drawings on them of color-

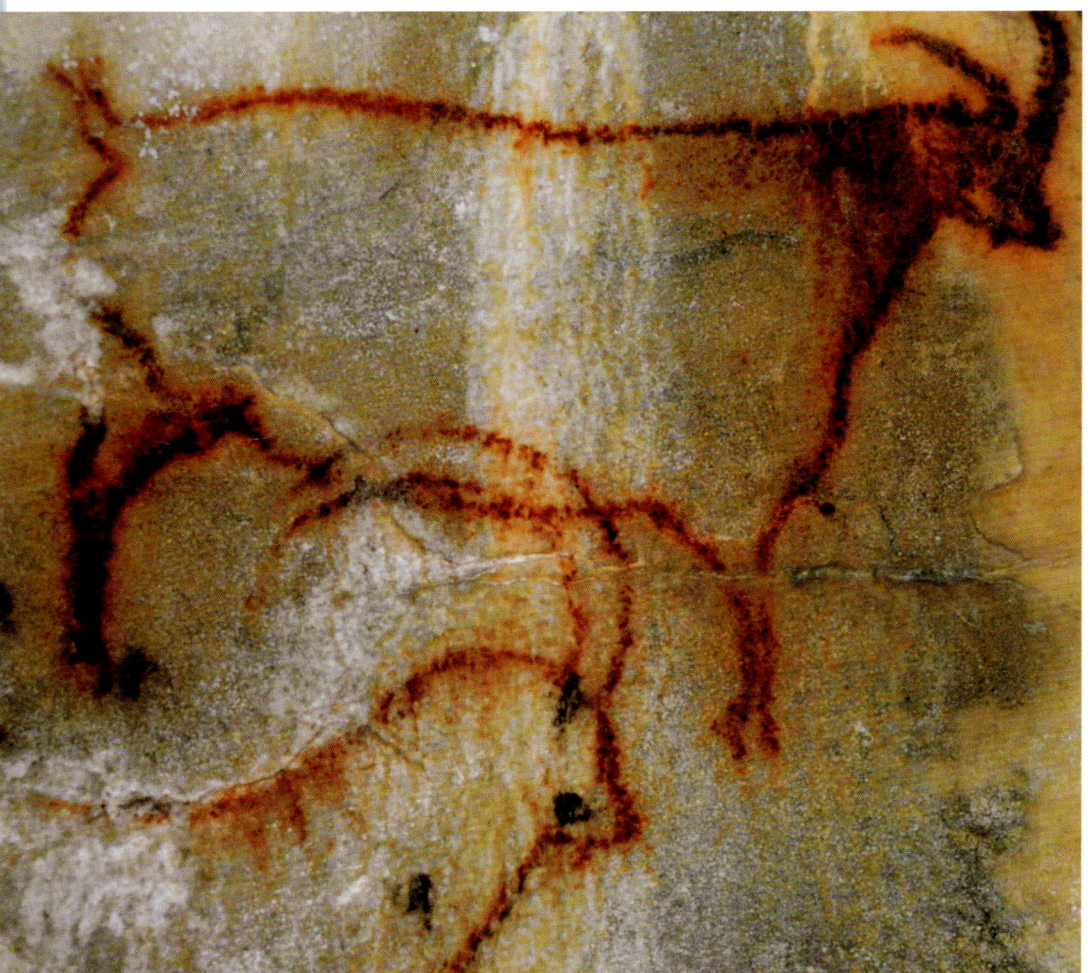

20,000-year-old cave paintings - ibexes along with illustrations of footprints.

ful illustrations of animals, that the drawings overlapped. In total amazement the Abbot studied the galloping horses, deer with detailed antlers, 49 foot (15 m) long bulls, ibexes and buffalo - the most of which were painted in ochre, red or black. Between all these animals there was only one person drawn. He was not realistically drawn as the animals, but looked more like he had been drawn by a child. As a child's doll he lies at the bottom, arms stretched, and there under drawn in the same still life way a bird on a branch, with a buffalo drawn above and a running rhinoceros under.

Abbot Henri Breuil thought the paintings to be about 18,000 years

old. This estimated proved to be very close. Modern research placed them at 15,000 years old. At that time, what is now Germany was an ice plateau. The south of France on the other hand was a prairie with a small amount of trees. Horses, buffalos, reindeer and thick skinned rhinoceroses inhabited the area. The hunters from the Stone Age knew how to kill with spears with stone points. Why they made the cave paintings is still today a riddle and is the topic of many a fierce discussion. Did the Michelangelos of that time want to enforce their success at the hunt, as was always thought? But in a lot of the rooms there are no drawings of reindeer, the most important catch of the hunt. Or maybe they are mystical perceptions, of which we do not know the meaning and the caves are holy places for ceremonies?

After the find in Lascaux, wall paintings were discovered in other caves. Especially in the valley of Vezere and in the Dordogne, in the region of the Perigord, down by the Rhine, at the foot of the Pyrenees and the Cantabrian mountains. The last location that was found was on the coast by Marseille, where the cave entrance is 118 feet (36 m) under water. It was thought that prehistoric man was not capably of such creativity.

The danger of the colors fading

The discovery of Lascaux was not made known to the public until a few years later. This was due to the fact, that at the time of the discovery there was a war going on. Germany had just occupied France. It was the summer of 1940. It was not until eight years later that the find was made known. Visitors visited the cave in their hundreds. A road was built to make the cave more accessible. To protect the paintings from the exhalation of the visitors, hermetically closing doors and a climate regulator was put in. Despite these precautionary measures, the colors in these prehistoric paintings began to fade.

Never before had present-day man seen so many paintings from the ice age as in the caves of Lascaux. As well as bison, illustrations of giant bulls, horses and cat-like predators decorated the long-concealed cave of Dordogne.

EUROPE

Floating monasteries

In Thessaly, Greek monks found peace on the mountains of Metéora

Route:
236 mi. (380 km) northwest of Athens, 124 mi. (200 km) southwest of Thassaloniki, E 75 to Larissa, N 6 to Kalambáka.

Best time:
May to June, September-October

Accommodation:
Hotel Amalia, Kalambák 2 mi. (3 km) from monastery

Further points of interest:
Témbli valley, 62 mi. (100 km) east. Mountain village Makrinitsa, 75 mi. (120 km) east in the Pilion mountains.

Nowadays, monks live in the Russanú (left) and Hagia Triada Mountain Monasteries (right) again, and tourists can visit them.

In Greek the word "metéoros" refers to the trajectory of a meteor, to floating between heaven and earth. High in the sky, far above the earth, we find the famous Metéora monasteries of Greece. Monks built them on the mountain tops that tower some 984 ft. (300 m) above the Pinios river. When dusk covers the valley and the sun has almost disappeared, or when the morning mist still hovers over the peaks, the monasteries float amidst veils of gossamer white.

As early as the ninth century the hermits felt attracted by the landscape of mountain peaks in the northwest of Thessaly. The grottoes at the foot of the mountains offered them adequate shelter and made undisturbed meditation possible. With ladders some of them climbed to niches in the sandstone, somewhat higher up, cast the ladder away, fasted and sought the nearness of God by self-castigation and ecstasy.

Servic campaigns in the early 14th century against Byzantine Thessaly probably prompted the construction of the first settlements and monasteries on the almost inaccessible rock plateaus and mountain peaks. Using ropes or ladders lashed together, the builders brought their materials to the site. Later, monks made nets of rope to hoist both workers and materials aloft in large baskets.

No admission for women

One of the first Metéora monasteries, Agios Stéfanos, was established in 1332 by Byzantine emperor Andronicus III. After Thessaly was conquered in 1340 by the Serves – orthodox Christians like the monks – building activities increased rapidly. Abbot Athanasius, named after the Athos mountain, and nine fellow believers started in 1356 to wall the largest and highest mountain monastery Metamorphosis on the Platos Lithos, the Broad Stone. The most prominent monk of the fraternity was Servic dauphin John. Like everyone else in the monastery he too, had to observe stern rules, especially the strict injunction forbidding woman in the cloister. If they came to offer food it could not be accepted, even if starvation were the result.

During the long Turkish rule, which began in 1420, large and small monasteries kept being added. In 1438 monks built the small monastery Hagai Triada on a narrow plateau with sheer walls. The red sandstone structure against the background of the dark rock is pleasing to the eye. One gets to the building and the fresco-decorated chapel via a steep stairway hewn from the rock – the route taken by thieves in 1979 when they made off with valuable icons.

In the 16th century the number of picturesque Metéora monasteries had grown to 26. The Turks levied high taxes and appropriated land on behalf of Greek refugees from Asia Minor. Ultimately this weakened the monastery economy to the point that many of them had to be abandoned and became derelict. During the 19th century only seven of them were still inhabited. During World War II monastic life halted almost completely. Thessaly became a battle field, first because of the advance and retreat of German troops, later because of the civil war between communists and anti-communists.

Halfway into the 1960s monks took up residence in the monasteries again, at least in those that had not been damaged beyond repair. Meanwhile, almost seven are now fully in use, one of them exclusively by nuns. Abbots are not opposed to tourism and for the community it has even become the major source of income. To enhance accessibility additional approaches were built.

Also, the abbots are not nearly as dismissive regarding women as they were in former ages. Women are permitted to visit the monasteries, on condition that long skirts cover their legs.

EUROPE

The cliffs of Cinque Terre

The rocky coastal cliffs of Liguria have retained their own natural rhythm of life despite the many summer visitors

Getting there:
The regional railway from Montorosso passes through all five villages. Verona-La Spezia-Genoa Highway

Where to stay:
Cinque Terre is a very popular tourist resort with a wide choice of accommodation

Climate:
Mediterranean climate: June/July 86°F (30°C); November/December rarely drops below 50°F (10°C)

Main attractions:
The five coastal villages; coastal footpath; Roman port of Porto Venere at the mouth of the Gulf of La Spezia; San Pietro church on the Arpaia heights; trips to the islands

Special tips:
Car access not impossible, but inadvisable in view of the extremely narrow, steeply twisting streets. Very few parking facilities. Better to use electric buses

A 10 mile (15km) stretch of coastline runs between Punta Mesco in the north and Cala di Montenegro in the south, encompassing an area of around 15 square miles (39km2) along Italy's Ligurian coast. Cinque Terre, a designated world heritage site, offers a unique coastal landscape, which man has been trying to shape for centuries. Cinque Terre takes its name from the five villages of Montorosso al Mar, Vernazza, Corniglia, Manarola, and Riomaggiore.

This breathtaking mountainous scenery of multi-colored sandstone was formed over 25 million years ago during the Tertiary period. Wind and rain have gouged deep valleys, sheer cliffs, and scores of little bays and promontories out of the soft rock. The area is unsuitable for major roads or settlements as the slopes are much too precipitous. The houses in these five villages are huddled tightly together, clinging to the sheer rocks, or perched on the crest of mountain summits. Over the centuries, farming families have turned the mountainsides into a spectacular succession of tiered terraces, some of which are no more than a yard wide. The soil needed to grow olive trees and cultivate vineyards had to be brought in from far away. To create each square yard/meter of cultivatable land, approximately one cubic yard/meter of sandstone was required to build a one-yard/meter length of dry stone wall, 20in (50cm) wide and often over 61/2ft (2m) high.

Wines worthy of princely palates

At 330–495ft (100–150m) above sea level, the terraces become so narrow that laboring among the vines is a grueling task. It is these higher altitudes, however, that produce the best grapes, which are used in the production of the internationally renowned and highly desirable Sciacchetra wine. Even back in the Middle Ages, the wines of Corniglia and Vernazza enjoyed an outstanding reputation. Not only were they greatly prized in Rome itself, but by the late Middle Ages were also being supplied to the princely courts of France and England.

For hundreds of years, these five villages could only be reached from the sea or by narrow paths twisting steeply up the cliff face. When the railway reached Cinque Terre in the late nineteenth century, many impoverished farm workers seized the opportunity to abandon the area and move to La Spezia. More and more land was left uncultivated and the dry stone walls, built with so much effort, disintegrated, causing whole terraces to fall away. Mediterranean vegetation was quick to reclaim the abandoned terraces. Maritime pines and chestnut oaks quickly gained a foothold and the soil filling these sandstone terraces, brought in at such great pains to increase the cultivatable area, became overgrown with arbutus, tree heathers, and broom.

Meanwhile, the unique character of this coastline has been recognized and efforts are underway to preserve it. Crumbling terraces are being rebuilt and, thanks to the incentive of state support, many farmers are returning to traditional wine-growing methods in the region.

Wildlife has never stood much of a chance in this terrain. Only wild boars trample paths through the dense woodland that has taken over the higher ground in these sandstone mountains. Hikers frequently mistake these wild boar paths for proper trails, following them until they end up well and truly lost.

One footpath, leading along the coast from Montorosso al Mar to Riomaggiore, offers breathtaking and magnificent views across the terraces, villages and far out to sea. Parts of the trail have been carved precariously out of the rock face while the cliffs fall away in a sheer drop to the sea.

Three offshore islands

Just opposite Porto Venere to the southeast are the three picturesque islands of Palmaria, Tino, and Tinetto. Palmaria is the closest to the mainland. Rising to a height of 610ft (186m), it is a popular destination for locals and tourists alike. Tino is a military base and only open to visitors on September 13, the Festival of the Holy Venerio. The body of this saint is said to have lain on the spot where the ruins of San Venerio monastery now stand. Tinetto is only 120 square yards (100m2) in size, but nevertheless once boasted a double-naved church and monastery. The ruins of the church, the oratory, and the monks' cells are well preserved.

Magical colors: The village of Vernazza perches on a rocky promontory surrounded by water (above)

Halfway up the cliff, a path leads from one village to the next (below, left)

Montorosso is the Italian name for these rocks lying just off the coast (below, right)

EUROPE

The fertile valleys of the Monti Lattari mountains

The Amalfi coast, with its picturesque hillside villages, boasts some of Italy's most spectacular natural scenery

Getting there:
Airport at Capodichino/Naples. Good road links

Where to stay:
Well-developed tourist resorts

Climate:
Mediterranean

Main attractions:
Pompeii; Herculaneum; Duomo di Sant'Andrea in Amalfi; numerous churches and cultural monuments

Special tips:
Photography is not permitted in some churches and museums

Amalfitana became famous in the nineteenth century as a rather exclusive tourist resort. It is along the Costiera Amalfitana coastal highway, which hugs the coastline high above the sea (left and below, right)

The Costiera Amalfitana is probably the most scenic coastal road in all of Italy. The gentle, green hills of the Monti Lattari, literally "Milk Mountains," extend between the Sorrento peninsula and the coast of Amalfi further south. These mountain slopes run down to a wildly romantic stretch of coastline, dotted with small holiday resorts, many of which appear to be clinging to the steep rock faces in a series of terraces. The villages are surrounded by extensive olive plantations and vineyards, their rich harvest of fruit shimmering with a silver sheen in the autumn sunlight. All this visual beauty is heightened by the all-pervading perfume of citrus trees, for which the Amalfi coast is so famous.

Dense chestnut forests still grow in many areas along the coast, interspersed with cypress, cedars, and dense thickets of almost impenetrable Macchia scrub. These are all that is left of a forest that once covered large areas of the peninsula. Over the past few centuries, much of it has been felled to make room for the cultivation of citrus fruits, nuts, and vineyards. The high plateau up in the hinterland is now used mainly as grazing land. In many places along the coast, indigenous shore vegetation has been forced to give way to major new building projects. Even so, a few native plants can still be found here, including rock samphire and a species of bird's foot trefoil.

World heritage site

As in many parts of Italy, wild animals suffer greatly from hunting. Birds especially, particularly the huge numbers of migrants, tend to be the main victims. Larger mammals are no longer found in the region, although occasionally lone birds of prey, including buzzards or falcons, may be seen riding the thermals above these steep cliffs. The rocks, which heat up during the day and give off their store of warmth at night, provide a perfect habitat for lizards and snakes, harmless as well as poisonous. Scorpions also lurk under some of the stones.

The Amalfi landscape has been affected by man and it is for this reason that the peninsula has been awarded world heritage status. It is situated within a region of major geological activity, most powerfully illustrated by the presence of Mount Vesuvius, which rises to a height of 4,190ft (1,277m) north of the Amalfi coast. This is one of the world's most thoroughly researched volcanoes and Europe's most active continental volcano. Like Mount Stromboli, it is a stratovolcano, built up of sheets of lava and ash with just one central chimney.

Here, along the western coast of Italy, the lower parts of the South Apennine chain are below sea level. A grid-like network of active volcanic rents in the earth's crust have determined the coastal landform, from which the Sorrento peninsula rises in the form of a mountain ridge extending out to the Isle of Capri.

Volcanic rumblings

Deep within the earth, there are still unmistakable rumblings of volcanic activity along a fault line running through the Bay of Naples. The town of Pompeii at the foot of Vesuvius became tragically famous after being buried in ash and destroyed during an eruption on August 24, AD 79. The excavations at "Pompeii Scavi" offer the visitor a remarkable, though uncomfortably real, glimpse of Roman life at the time of the eruption.

The ancient volcanic rock, now covering the original rocks that once rose from the sea bed, forms the bedrock for the chain of famous coastal towns which have sprung up all along the Amalfi coast: Positano, Praiano, Furore, Amalfi, Ravello, Minori, Maiori, and Cetara.

The small Italian town of Amalfi on the Gulf of Salerno was originally built in AD 320 by soldiers of the Roman Emperor Constantinus after they were transferred here from Melphe on the Adriatic coast. During the tenth century, the town became one of the most powerful maritime republics in Italy, rivaling Genoa, Pisa, and Venice as a naval power in trade with the Orient. Amalfi's maritime code, the so-called "Tavola Amalfitana," or "Table of Amalfi," regulated shipping throughout the entire Mediterranean region and was still recognized until well into the sixteenth century.

ASIA

Petra: rock city of the Nabatean kings

Burial chambers and temples of a lost nation

Route
Via the "Kings Road" 174 mi. (280 km) south of Amman, 81 mi. (130 km) north of Aqaba (buses from both cities)

Best time
May – June, September – November

Accommodation
Petra Forum hotel

Other points of interest
Pass Siq al-Barid ("Little Petra"), 5 mi. (8 km) north; former Knights of the Cross fortress Shaubak, 25 mi. (40 km) north.

Suspicious Bedouins in the Petra valley, 50 miles (80 km) south of the Dead Sea, kept their eyes on a traveller in Eastern garb who called himself Ibrahim ibn Abadallah al-Schami and claimed that he was on pilgrimage to Moses' brother Aaron's grave. The stranger spoke excellent Arabic, but his Swiss-German was better still. Without the Muslim camouflage, Swiss orientalist Johann Ludwig Burckhardt would not have succeeded. In August 1812 he was the first European to reach, via an ancient caravan route, the fascinating ruined city in what today we call the kingdom of Jordan.

Via Burckhardt, the West was informed of the former capital of the Nabateans. In the second century BC these nomads had settled in a mountain-enclosed plateau, accessed only by way of a narrow pass. Over the next three hundred years, Petra (Greek for "rock") developed into a centre of trade at the crossroads of various caravan routes. In that period were created numerous monumental structures and burial chambers were hewn in the rocky face of the settlement, about 528 mi. (850 m) above sea level. Art historians view the sculpture-like style as a symbiosis of Eastern and Hellenistic art.

Well-preserved tombs

Burckhardt gained no more than a superficial impression of all this. Suspicion among genuine Muslims grew and he was forced to leave quickly. Soon afterwards, however, British, French, American, German and, later, Arabic archaeologists followed, in search of Nabatean history, whose culture already declined early in the second century after Christ, when the Romans occupied the rock city and turned it into the citadel for Arabia province.

Among the well-preserved buildings from Nabatean days is the temple Qasr el-Bint Fira'un ("fortress of Pharaoh's daughter") with its 75-foot (23 m) high walls. Built at the beginning of our calendar, the temple was dedicated to the high god Dhushara and his mother el-'Uzza. An altar, measuring 39 by 39 feet (12 by 12 m), in front of the temple, was probably used for fire rites and animal sacrifices. Archaeologists named a second imposing structure the "Lions Claws Temple" after the inscriptions on excavated columns.

Especially well preserved and renovated are the beautiful facades and the temple-like tombs cut into the rock at the edge of Petra. The craftsmanship of these anonymous stonecutters, whose labors exposed many-colored layers of sandstone, demand the greatest respect.

Artistically most successful is the red facade of el-Khazne, the "treasure house," in which Bedouins at some time vainly searched for the legendary "Pharaoh treasure." The entrance to floor level consists of six pillars with Corinthian capitals. At the upper level there is a circular rock pavilion housing a statue of the Egyptian goddess Isis. Additional sculptures include Amazons, lions, Nabatean goddesses and Greek mythological figures. The consensus is that this marvellous example of rock building is the burial chamber of one of the latest Nabatean kings.

In contrast to the days of Burckhardt, strangers today need not disguise themselves in order to visit the holy places, the rock graves, the beautiful gates and the rock-hewn Petra theatre. The city behind the narrow pass, Siq, has been a tourist attraction for some time now.

Entry to the rock graves. For the burial chambers of their kings, the Nabatean cut temple-like façades and sculptures into the rock.

The entrance to one of the most beautiful rock temples, held up by high pillars. The legendary "Pharaoh treasure" caused Bedouins to search in vain the vaults behind.

Master works of anonymous stonecutters.

ASIA

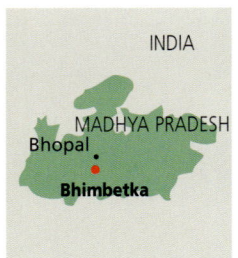

Mesolithic petroglyphs
Bhimbetka's primeval paintings

State and capital:
Madhya Pradesh, Bhopal 28 mi./45 km

Convenient access:
Road to Bhimbetka, air, rail to Bhopal

Accommodation:
Budget to luxury in Bhopal

Best season:
November to March

Also worth seeing:
Mosques of Bhopal, Bhojeshwar Temple, 17 mi./28 km NW

On a train journey in 1958 to Bhopal in Madhya Pradesh, archaeologist V.S. Wakankar made an immediate note of what would have seemed to be mere rock formations to the untrained eye but were, in fact, rock shelters and caves in the distant hills. Returning to the site, armed with a professional team and tools, Wakankar found almost 600 natural dwellings, once occupied from the Paleolithic era onwards. Although this was a momentous discovery on its own, it turned out to be an exceptional one when paintings were discovered in the caves dating back to over thousands of years, made by those who had once resided in them. The earliest paintings reflecting a primitive, hunting-gathering way of life, can be traced back to the early stages of the Mesolithic period (about 12,000 years ago). Following this is art created when a sedentary, agricultural culture was in place, and thereafter come the pictures clearly made during the historical period.

Surrounded by the Vindhya and Satpura Hills, Bhimbetka is tucked into a dense forest of sal and teak, with craggy overhanging rocks and dried leaves for ground cover. Branches extend from knotted trees, the sound of gushing water mixes with the sound of wind whooshing through the caves, some of whose interiors have smooth surfaces in a variety of textures suggesting that they once might have been under water. The setting is primeval and the area's richness in wildlife has led it to be declared a wildlife sanctuary.

Scenes from everyday life in a variety of colors

The selection of 15-odd caves easily accessible via a concrete path bear myriad painted tales of hunters and their game, men and their families, childbirth, rites, rituals and ceremonies, warriors and chiefs. The figures of animals are well etched while those of humans are like typical line drawings of young children. Hunters wear head dresses and ornaments, children are shown playing and running, women grinding and preparing food, musicians playing drums and families getting together for honey collection and sacred rituals. Animals seem to be a favorite theme with the artists: there is a whole array of wildlife ranging from bigger beasts like elephants, tigers and bison, as on the "Zoo Rock," to smaller fauna like deer, rabbits, fish, frogs, lizards, peacocks and other birds. Domestic animals are in plenty too and include grazing buffaloes.

The paintings are simple yet convey movement and fluidity. The emotional impact of the scene comes through by using insightful techniques. For instance, in trying to convey fear, the size of the wild animal, as it tears after a petrified hunter, is greatly exaggerated. The fact that various hues of red, green, yellow and white still survive is partly because the drawings are often tucked away in niches and deep recesses, and also due to the remarkable durability of the paint. Crushed hematite (iron oxide) was used to procure red while green was derived from chalcedony. These powders were possibly mixed with some kind of resin or gum from trees, vegetable dyes, roots and animal fat to impart long lasting as well as waterproof qualities. Fanned twigs combined with animal hair must have served as brushes. At times, one can discern that the same surface has been used as the palette for different artists at different periods.

Some paintings showing horses ridden by men evidently belong to a later date, as the advent of the horse into India is believed to have been after the prehistoric period.

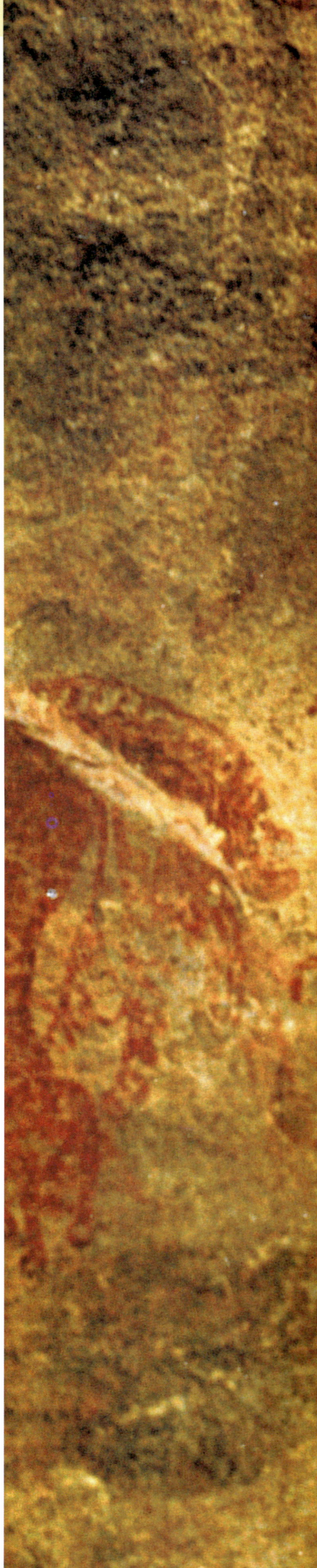

ASIA

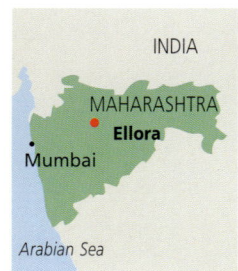

Ellora's grand grottoes
The finale of rock-cut architecture

State and capital:
Maharashtra, Mumbai 256 mi./412 km

Convenient access:
Road to Ellora, air, rail to Aurangabad

Accommodation:
Budget to high-end

Best season:
October to March

Also worth seeing:
Bibi ka Makbara in Aurangabad, 15 mi. (24 km) SE, ruins of Daulatabad, 9 mi. (15 km) SE

Lower left: A stone panel shows the abduction of Sita by Ravana, from the Hindu epic Ramayana.
Lower right: Ellora caves are more carved than constructed.
Facing page: Artisans chiselled the last detail of the Kailashanatha Temple, planned as per the principles of Vastushastra, the ancient Hindu treatise on architecture.

Formerly known as Elapura, Ellora lay on the thriving trade routes between Ujjain and the west coast, in the time of the Rashtrakuta and the Western Chalukya dynasties, between the seventh to the ninth century. Essentially, Ellora is a 1.2 mile (2 km) basalt escarpment, chiselled into 34 caves of Buddhist, Hindu and Jain affiliation. Prosperous merchants and nobles, kings, determined clergy and an active laity sustained three centuries of rock excavation to make Ellora's grand grottoes. This was the time when Hinduism was crystallizing into an orthodox Puranic pantheon governed by Brahmanical ritual, and Buddhism was on the wane. Preceding Gupta and Pallava dynasties had seen the emergence of stone architecture and formal Hindu temples. The Ellora caves mark the glorious finale of rock-cut architecture in India. Temples of the ensuing centuries were not to be sited on dramatic or somewhat isolated rocky ridges such as at Ajanta and Ellora.

The Ellora caves fall into three distinct groups and are numbered from the left. The Buddhist caves (1–12) date from the Chalukyan period. The first nine resemble viharas (monasteries) and are filled with images of the Buddha, Boddhisattvas and related figures. Cave 10, named for Vishwakarma, the celestial architect, contains a teaching Buddha image before a votive stupa, within an imposing *chaitya* (stupa) hall.

Hewn around the same time, the Hindu caves (13–29) are the highpoint of Ellora's aesthetic development, carrying forward Pallavan rock-art tradition from Mammallapuram with intense, detailed renditions of mythological scenes. Cave 16 is somewhat a misnomer, as the magnificent Kailashanatha Temple is hewn free of the surrounding cliffs, in an unparalleled feat of Herculean stonework. The Jain caves (30–34) date from the last phase of Ellora, around the ninth century, and are simpler than the others. The finest in the group is Cave 32, also called Indra Sabha, a monolithic shrine with carvings of elephants, lions and tirthankaras.

The gigantic Kailashanatha Temple

Now a UNESCO World Heritage Site, this mammoth complex was commissioned by the Rashtrakuta King Krishna I in the eighth century. A deep rectangular trench was dug in the cliff, isolating a block of stone over 98 ft. (30 m) high and 197 ft. (60 m) wide. Working patiently from top down, masons displaced approximately three million cubic feet (85,000 m³) of rock to create a multi-layered structure with columns, halls and spires; in effect, a peninsular version of Mount Kailasha, the abode of Shiva in the lofty Himalayas.

A rock-cut wall and entrance way screen the Temple. Once through the monumental gateway, the sheer scale of the conceiver's vision is overwhelming. A 25-ft. (7.6 m)-high plinth raises the structure out of the yawning pit. From this plinth emerges the flat-roofed mandapa, seemingly supported on 16 richly carved columns in groups of four. Two gigantic pillars and two elephants appear in the foreground, while a larger than life Nandi bull stands guard in a tall, graceful pavilion. The main shrine is surmounted by two towers. It was once covered in white gesso plaster to emulate the snow-capped peaks of Kailasha, and the temple friezes painted in polychrome colours. Subsidiary shrines, chapels and galleries exist in the side walls, and a perambulatory path scooped out of the surrounding cliff face.

The exterior walls of the complex are richly decorated with niches, pilasters, windows and cornices as well as images of deities, amorous couples, animals and other motifs. On the east of the Nandi shrine is a relief depicting a 10-armed Shiva, watched by his consort Parvati, destroying the demon Andhaksura. Another large, dramatic relief shows Ravana shaking Mount Kailasha, much to the fright of attendants, animals and sundry maidens. Even Parvati appears distraught and leans towards her Lord, while an unperturbed Shiva uses his big toe to subdue the multi-armed and multi-headed demon.

ASIA

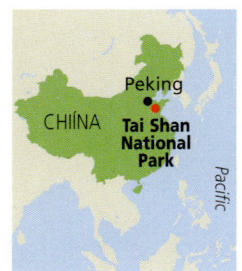

Getting there:
Good road, bus, and rail links to Tai Shan. Airport at Jinan

Where to stay:
All categories of hotel available in Tai Shan and Jinan

Climate:
Moderately warm climate. Occasional frost on the Tai summit

Main attractions:
Eastern route good for cultural sites (up 6,000 plus steps); western route better for natural scenery. Trip on one of the three cable cars; helicopter round trip

The sacred mountain

Tai Shan National Park combines sacred sites with unspoiled nature

The most important of China's five sacred mountains rises dramatically and steeply out of the plains in China's eastern province of Shandong. Wu Tai Shan mountain rises to a height of 5,070ft (1,545m), making it the highest summit in the Tai Shan massif. This mountain region is situated to the north of the city of Tai'an, and is regarded as one of the cradles of Chinese culture. It would seem that this mountain was already drawing prehistoric man under its spell 400,000 years ago. During the Neolithic period, it became the focus of two cultures, namely the Dawenkou on its northern flank and the Longshan on its southern side. Thousands of years later, these evolved into the rival states of Qi in the north and Lu in the south. Between 475 and 221 BC, Qi went so far as to erect a 310-mile (500km) wall to protect this sacred mountain from hostile forces. Ruins of this early precursor of the Great Wall of China can still be seen to this day.

Tai Shan Mountain forms the focus for a number of different faiths that have been associated with Taoism and Buddhism for the past 2,000 years. It is regarded as the center of Yang, the positive masculine principle, and the well-spring of life. Indeed, the mountain has become a deity in itself.

From the Qin dynasty (221–206 BC) to the Qing dynasty (1644–1911), every Emperor of China has climbed this holy mountain to offer a sacrifice to the gods. More than 20 groups of buildings and over 2,200 memorials and stone carvings still exist, a powerful testimony to the spiritual significance of Wu Tai Shan.

Granite and gneiss

The most important edifice is the Dai Temple at the foot of the mountain. This was built between 221 BC and AD 220 during the Qin and Han dynasties. During the Tang and Sang dynasties (AD 618–1279) the buildings were substantially extended. Tiangung Hall, the main building, rivals both Taihe Hall in Beijing's Imperial Palace and Dacheng Hall in the Confucian Temple of Qufu, ranking as one of China's largest palace-style buildings.

These cultural sites are in perfect harmony with the impressive diversity of nature. The sacred stature of the mountain has made it virtually inviolable and its original ecosystems have therefore survived intact. Extending to nearly 100 square miles (250km2), the Park now protects Tai Shan's treasures as an area of natural and cultural heritage.

Geologically speaking, the Tai Shan massif is the oldest and most significant geological fold in eastern China. The spectacular, towering rock formations of granite and gneiss were formed 170–200 million years ago. Rich fossil layers on its northern flanks contain clear evidence of petrified remains of long extinct plants and animals.

Thousand-year-old trees

Around 80 percent of the nature reserve and cultural park is covered with a remarkable diversity of dense vegetation. There has so far been very little research carried out on the different habitats in this region. So far, 1,000 plant species have been identified, including 433 tree varieties. Some individual trees are extremely ancient and steeped in legend: the Han dynasty cypress trees were planted by Emperor Wu Di 2,100 years ago, and the Tang, or scholars' tree, has been growing here for the past 1,300 years.

The forests are home to around 200 species of animal, not counting the 122 different types of birds fluttering around in the treetops and from rock to the rock, although biologists as yet know very little about these populations. Rivers situated at altitudes of around 1,000–2,600ft (300–800m) support a species of fish known as the Common Chramuija, a carp that grows to more than 15in (40cm) in length and was regarded as a culinary delicacy during the Qing dynasty.

Two main routes lead up to the summit of Tai Shan. The western trail passes through virtually untamed and unspoilt natural scenery. The route is lined with magnificent fir trees and numerous waterfalls. From Tianwaicun, it leads up to Zhontianmen Gate, passing through a number of scenic sights, with picturesque names such as "Black Dragon Pool," the "Bridge of Longevity," and "Fan Crags."

The eastern trail is better known for the cultural sights. A series of 6,293 steps climbs from Hongmen to Nantianmen Gate, passing the Hongmen Palace, the Wanxian building, Doumu Palace, Jingshi Gorge and the Zhongtian Gate en route.

The 1,000-year-old trees are one of the National Park's most spectacular sights (above)

This holy mountain accommodates more than 20 temples on its slopes (below, left)

A bordered pathway consisting of 6,293 stone steps climbs up to the Nantianmen Gate

ASIA

Dunhuang Mogao Grottoes, Gansu

A rarity of far more than one thousand years

Location:
Located at the extreme west of the Hexi corridor, the junction of Gansu, Qinghai, and Xinjiang, and enclosed by desert. The Danghe River originating in Qilian Mountains is the river of its life. People call it the Oasis of the Gobi.

Climate:
The climate is dry, and there is a great difference in temperature between day and night. Rainfull is low, and there is plenty of sunshine. This is a typical continental arid climate.

Special interest:
Mogao Grottoes, or Dunhuang Grottoes, are the biggest in China. Most of the murals depict religious stories, but there are some relating to customs, farming, hunting, and festivals. The sculptures and paintings are so fine that they are recognized to be world treasures of religious art.

Main attractions:
Mogao Grottoes, Echo Sand Mountain, Crescent Moon Stream, West Thousand Buddha Cave, Yulin Grottoes, West Hill Buddha Cave, and many more.

An external scene at the Dunhuang Mogao Grottoes (left)

The Big Buddha Temple at Mogao Grottoes (below, right)

When in Dunhuang, the first thing you see is a vast sea of yellow. It is so yellow all over that if you looked down from an airplane, you would have a sense of despair. The yellow is so vast, so massive, so quiet and so confident, that it almost makes you breathless. No other colors, no other signs of life can be seen. Occasionally, there are anomalous white lines on the sand that seem to be ancient dried up lakes. Or you may see some fine curved lines left by the wind. Here we see only the footsteps of nature. Two thousand years ago, there used to be a prosperous oasis, there were riotous routes full of caravans, silk products, official documents and swords and spears, and performances of secular dances and songs and religious chanting. Now all are submerged in the boundless sand. All the music and prosperity, trades and diplomacy, wars and campaigns, were so vulnerable, so flimsy, in the face of the vast yellow, with the eternal shadows left over on the Dunhuang stone walls.

The Echo Sand Mountain is to the southeast of Dunhuang city, with precipices at its east end. People began to dig caves here in 366 AD, and it became prosperous during the Sui and Tang dynasties. It seems a giant engineering enterprise, regardless of age and dynasty. From East Jin and West Jin until the Yuan dynasty, people worked on it continuously. Take Mogao Grottoes as an example. Here seven hundred caves, three thousand statues, and huge murals stretching 48,450 square feet (4500 square meters) were left behind. In Chinese terms, the murals would extend 60 li if laid out one after another. What they depict is mostly related to religion and mythology, and includes stories about Buddha, fairytales, scenes showing the conversion of worshipers, and so on. Others include paintings showing spirits, animals, landscapes and buildings, and social life at different times in history, as well as different artistic features. We can find out something about the demise of the North Wei Dynasty, the gentle Sui dynasty, the magnificent Tang dynasty, the serene Five dynasties, and the elegant Song dynasty. On visiting the caves, you feel as if you are experiencing the vicissitudes of history. The narration of the stories is three dimensional and chronological. Dunhuang is an accumulation of generation after generation. History is active here. These dark and cold caves are in full bloom because of the art they reveal.

According to one book, in Chinese *Dunhuang* means "the thriving earth." This book was written in the Han dynasty, but the definition was proved only after two thousand years had passed, namely, at the end of the Qing dynasty. It seems that all the chisels, all the strokes of brushes, and the long, long time were just preparations for that evening, in the summer of 1900.

Wang Yuanlu was a native of Macheng in Hubei province. At first he enlisted in the army, and then he became a Taoist. In 1897 he made a journey to Dunhuang, where he stopped to build Taoist temples. He hired a poor local man named Yangguo as his secretary to copy some Taoist scriptures to sell to passersby and those who were on pilgrimage. One day, Yangguo was sitting in the passage of Cave No.16 smoking. He began to knock off the ash on the wall behind him, and he suddenly realized that there seemed to be an echo from the wall. A hidden cave, maybe? People still remember the day this happened: May 25th, 1900. With the fall of an ax, the riddle was finally solved, and it caused a sensation throughout the world.

Now we turn back to 1035, in the Song dynasty. Then Dunhuang was on the route to the famous Silk Road, a strategic point, and the scene of constant battles. When a riot of the West Xia broke out and spread to Dunhuang, the monks here decided to flee from the disaster. Before leaving, they sealed in Cave No. 16 the scriptures, documents, embroideries, and paintings that it was not possible for them to carry with them. The monks never came back. All the treasures were safe for eight hundred years.

They are treasures, some 50,000 pieces of them, from several different dynasties. But to the wretched Taoist Wang, they were worth just a few coins. They were scattered all over the world. Only some four thousand rolls of them are left in Beijing Library.

The great calamity made Dunhuang world famous, but today in Echo Sand Mountain, we can still hear bitter weeping.

ASIA

Longmen Grottoes, Henan

Extending along cliffs on either side

Location:
The grottoes are located to the south of Luoyang, 8 miles (13km) from Luoyang city.

Climate:
This area is in the transitional band from the south subtropical border to North Temperate Zone, there being a clear contrast in temperature between the four seasons.

Special interest:
One of the great treasure troves of stone carving art in China, the grottoes are listed by UNESCO as a World Heritage site.

Main attractions:
Grand Vairocana Statue, Guyang Cave, Binyang Cave, Lotus Cave, Stone Grottos Cave, and so on.

Buddhas at the Longmen Grottoes in Luoyang (above)

Groups of "Grand Vairocana" stone grottoes (below, right)

The poet Bai Juyi once said, "Among all the landscapes in Luoyang city, Longmen is the best." He settled down in Xiangshan, facing Longmen, in his later years and was buried there. Maybe he was fascinated by the beauty and mystery of the Grand Vairocana Buddha.

Longmen is the natural gate to the south of Luoyang. Here cliffs tower aloft, with the green Yi River flowing between them. Sculptors began to work here after the emperor of the North Wei moved his capital to Luoyang, and continued right through the successive dynasties of East Wei, West Wei, North Qi, Sui, Tang, and North Song. Their day-to-day work left on the mountain precipices nearly 110,000 stone Buddhist images and 2800 stone tablets, together with about 70 Buddhist pagodas. The caves they dug and the niches they constructed are concentrated like beehives. They stretch for about half a mile (1 km) on the west bank of the Yi River. Longmen Grottoes is one of three places in China to see magnificent grottoes. The statues, carved in different periods, are varied both in appearance and in style. These Buddhist images produced by anonymous ancient artists have now become an important source for those who want to carry out research into ancient Chinese art. The elegant statues, the green hills, and the blue waters harmonize in one scenic spot what may be termed Longmen landscape, and are the most important of Luoyang's eight scenic areas. Longmen Grottoes offer examples of the religious art produced under the political influence of the ancient powers of China. They feature a royal style owing to the fact that two imperial houses, the Wei and the Tang, took the lead in sculpture. The starting and stopping of individual structures usually reflects the political situation of the time.

The Grand Vairocana niche is the biggest open niche in the Longmen Grottoes and displays some extraordinary representatives of the stone sculpture of the Tang dynasty. After you climb up the steep steps, the Grand Vairocana Buddha appears before you. She is 56 ft (17.14 m) high. She has a plump face, and from under arched eyebrows her merciful and supremely beautiful eyes gaze out. Her long earlobes hang down, and with her kind, serene, and inscrutable smile she shows her divine wisdom, her unrivalled experience in judging, and her constant care for the human world. From any angle you will feel she is looking at you. You will be greatly moved, and will perhaps suddenly think of the broad mind of the Buddha – "to deliver all living creatures from torment." This figure is the eastern Venus. Anyone who stands before her for the first time will be enchanted by her elegant face, beautiful eyes, and stately and generous manner. What she presents is a confident smile that never repulsed foreign cultures in the heyday of the Tang dynasty. It is said that the statue was modeled after Empress Wu Zetian. According to the Account of the Grand Vairocana Niche Project, printed in the tenth year of Kaiyuan of the Tang dynasty, Empress Wu Zetian once made a contribution of 20,000 guan for the project, from her savings for cosmetics. On each side of the Grand Vairocana, there are two disciples, two bodhisattvas, two heavenly kings, and two guards, all vivid and impressive, and all manifesting the eternal appeal of art.

There are many other caves that were dug in the North Wei dynasty – such as Guyang Cave, Binyang Middle Cave, Lotus Cave, Stone Grottos Temple, among others. The main ones are Guyang Cave, Binyang Middle Cave, and Stone Grottoes Temple. Of these, Guyang Cave holds groups of stone images of imperial nobility and ministers, reflecting the historical fact that the whole country worshiped the Buddha. All the grotesque and versatile sculptures are the record of a Gandhara Buddhist artistic style, and also of a site where there was a merger of traditional culture and foreign civilizations, for Indian stone carving techniques was passed into Luoyang. The colorfully painted Apsaras – some flying freely between moving clouds, some holding sacrificial fruits or dispersing flower rain in the sky – are forever vivid in their expression and graceful in their movement. The famous "Longmen 20 Articles" is an outstanding representative of North Wei stone tablet calligraphy. There are 19 articles in the form of stone tablets in this cave. The calligraphy of the inscriptions is extremely majestic and rigorous. These are all national treasures.

Here the tourist can appreciate the art of stone carving, and become aware of the inclusivity and profundity of the Chinese Buddhist culture. There is also the opportunity to find out about such things as the politics, economy, and social conditions. A large number of objects of historical value that relate to religion, fine arts, calligraphy, music, dresses, medicine, architecture, and many other areas are displayed here and there modestly, so that the visitor may feel as if he is in a museum.

ASIA

Yungang Grottoes, Shanxi

A treasure trove of stone sculpture

Location:
The Yungang Grottoes are situated at the foot of Wuzhou Mountain, 10 miles (16 km) west of Datong on the loess plateau.

Climate:
In this area there is a weather pattern of cold winters and cool summers, with a big difference in temperatures between day and night. The two best seasons to visit are spring and summer.

Special interest:
The grottoes date back some 1500 years to the Northern Wei dynasty. In the existing 53 grottoes, which stretch about two thirds of a mile (1km) from east to west, there are 5100 or so statues. Grottoes Nos. 16–20 are the earliest, the giant statue of Buddha in the open at Grotto No. 20 being the representative work of Yungang. Noted as one of the four most famous grottoes in China, this particular one is of very high artistic merit.

Main attractions:
Giant Buddha at Grotto No. 20, Grottoes Nos. 5 and 6, and Grottoes Nos. 16–20.

Located 10 miles (16km) west of the city of Datong in Shanxi province, the Yungang Grottoes became a famous tourist attraction in the 1980s. The image of Buddha in the twentieth grotto has already become popular, and is available in pictures and souvenir albums, and on postage stamps. The big statues in the grottoes are known as a landmark scene, while small statues behind the big ones – ignored by many – attract the attention of the discerning visitor, especially those in the fifth and sixth grottoes.

The statues covering the cliff catch your eye upon entering. The most representative grotto is No. 6, which features the story of the spreading of Buddhism, together with Buddha, Bodhisattvas, arhats, and flying Apsaras.

Also known as the "Grotto of Sakyamuni," it is dominated by a huge square pillar some 49 ft (15m) high. The 20-odd statues on the four sides of the pillar depict scenes from the life of Sakyamuni, from his birth to his attainment of nirvana.

In the Chinese-style pavilion, some of the figures play flutes, others play stringed instruments. Still others invite reclining men to have more to drink. Above these are two figures sitting hand in hand, who are presumably talking lovingly to each other.

Groups of standing or kneeling Bodhisattvas and arhats are reminiscent of sculptures in ancient India, Greece, and Egypt.

The stone statues of Buddha in the Gown style are characteristic of Chinese images of Buddha. Those in other styles are foreign, even western. According to The Chinese History of Art by Wang Xun and The Cambridge Introduction to the History of Art by Susan Woodford, et al., both the Chinese and the western-style sculptures are equally impressive, despite their different techniques and clothing.

The atmosphere of Grotto No. 12 is enlivened by statues of flying Apsaras that dance on the ceiling and walls. Of these, perhaps the most captivating is a group carved on the northern wall. One Apsaras is known as the "Chinese Venus."

With a history of 1500 years, the Yungang Grottoes were first built in the Northern Wei dynasty (386–534 AD). The whole area extends about two thirds of a mile (1km) from east to west. The existing 53 grottoes are home to an amazing total of more than 5100 stone statues.

Historians of Buddhism regard the grottoes as a treasure trove. The Northern Wei dynasty is an important period during which Buddhism was fairly popular, and instrumental in the emperors' rule of the country.

In a word, the Yungang Grottoes are both a scenic spot and a valuable historical resource.

One of the stone statues of Buddha at Yungang Grottoes (right)

The stone statue of "Buddhism Guanyin with One Thousand Hands" in Yungang Grottoes (left)

ASIA

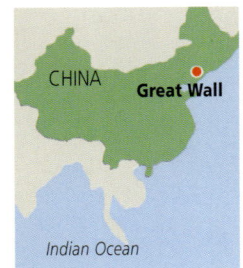

The amazing Chinese wall

For over 2,000 years, the Chinese built the world's largest line of defense

Route:
From Beijing by train and tourist coaches (from Qianmen near the Mao-Mausoleum) to Badaling; Buses to Mutianyu, 53-60 miles (85-95 km) northwest

Best time:
September-October

Further points of interest:
Valley of 13 Mingh graves, 31 miles (50 km) north of Beijing, Imperial palace

Among all that mankind has wrought in the course of the ages, the Chinese Wall, 4,051 miles (6,520 km) in length, has demanded the greatest number of laborers and the vastest amount of material. According to American astronauts, from the moon the naked eye can identify only the Wall, nothing else. Even in places where the Great Wall is in decay, it looks, in the words of French writer André Malraux, "a still extant prehistoric dragon winding his body over the hills."

It would be wrong to think of the wall as an uninterrupted Chinese bulwark against the rest of the world. Essentially, it was built to ward off attacks from the north. And in addition to the main line of defence, which extends from the Turkestan steppe 2,144 miles (3,450 km) eastward to the shores of the Yellow Sea, there are numerous walls parallel to the outer boundary or sheltering specific areas. Seen from the moon, the wall looks like a big scrawl.

Protection against marauders

The first sections of the line were built in the north of China, ages prior to our calendar. They were meant to defend the peasants in the fertile plains of Central China against nomadic tribes, frequent invaders of the South in search of pasture for their cattle. The truly great work of the Wall was started in the 3rd century BC during the reign of Qin Shi Huangdi, the "First Emperor of China." Legend says that the ruler, so advised by one of his wizards, had a man by the name of Wan executed at the foot of the wall because only in this way completion of the construction was assured.

Certainly true is that construction, which continued well into the 17th century, claimed the lives of hundreds of thousands. The work traversed mountains and valleys. Building materials had to be transported in scorching heat and freezing cold – 20-pound bricks, hewn rock and enormous numbers of field rock as filler of the up to 30 foot (9 m) high and 26 foot (8 m) wide wall construction. It is said that in the days of the First Emperor some 300,000 soldiers and 500,000 peasants convicted to forced labor were involved in the project. In later ages, the 1.8 million farmers worked temporarily alongside the harshly punished convicts.

But even this enormous army of laborers would have been unsuccessful if not guided by the inventiveness and organizational talent of the leadership in each period of construction, mostly military officers. If no natural stone was available, bricks and panes were made locally. In loamy areas that was the material worked with, in the Gobi desert coolies filled the wall with sand, pebbles, twigs of tamarisk and rushes. Where the Wall crossed white water and deltas, construction had to be very meticulous.

Every 328 to 656 feet (100-200 m) a watchtower was placed, a total along the entire wall of almost 20,000. Smoke signals or flags would announce the approach of the enemy, so that the troops would be in place. On the paved walls they could move more quickly than the enemy in the terrain. Soldiers' barracks and fortresses in strategic locations increased boundary protection. Still, the enemy could not always be repulsed. In spite of the Wall, the fearsome Mongolian warlord Genghis Khan and his horsemen successfully invaded China in 1211.

This largest defense system in the world, which took about 2000 years of construction, is mostly kept preserved. Time and again it safeguarded the peace for long periods of time and became a symbol of national unity. Naturally, the Wall inspired poets like Ho Chifang, who in 1934 has a traveller utter the lyrical description: "The Wall is like a long column of galloping horses that, just as they reared their necks and neighed, turned to stone."

If the Wall was meant to ward off strangers, it now achieves the precise opposite. As prime attraction of China, it draws enormous numbers of tourists. Especially on the section northwest of Beijing the Wall is

crowded by a mass of people, the likes of which was formerly seen only on New York's Broadway, the Champ Elysées in Paris or the Kurfürstendamm in Berlin.

Traversing mountains, deserts and grainfields, the Great Wall constitutes China's snake-like line of defense against attacks from the north. Chinese emperors would at times deploy up to 1.8 million peasants for forced labor. Hundreds of thousands did not survive.

NORTH AMERICA

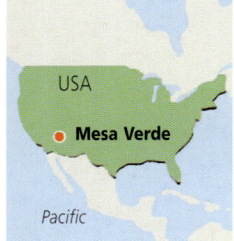

The cliff dwellings of Mesa Verde

In Colorado, ancient cave villages were discovered

Route:
Closest regional airport: Cortez-Montezuma. Arrival via US 160 Durango-Cortez

Best time:
May through to October (Visitor center is closed during the winter)

Accommodation:
Far View Motor Lodge (only in the summer)

Also worth seeing:
Monument Valley, Arches National Park (Utah)

On a clear December morning in 1888, Richard Wetherill and his father Charlie Mason rode over the wild landscape of "Mesa Verde" in the south west of Colorado. The two farmers were searching for strayed cattle. The "green table" as the Spanish call the flourishing mountain, rose abruptly 1,968 feet (600 m) out of the flat land and formed a plateau, 32 times 15 miles (24 km) big and 7,545 feet (2,300 m) above sea level. Over millions of years deep splits had been formed in the sandstone and in the mountain walls niches had formed cliff protuberances and caves. The two farmers ascended the steep canyon and looked straight into a giant oval cave - lit by the morning sun - and discovered a ghost town which seemed to float. They had discovered Cliff Palace.

According to the myths of the Navajo indians, this inaccessible area was once inhabited by a high cultural civilization. The Navajo's settled in this area in the 16th century, and found villages still intact, without any trace of the original dwellers. They called them "Anasazi," "they who were here before us." The archaeologists also use this name when referring to this tribe of Pueblo Indians.

For 600 hundred years long the cliff dwellings remained empty and not one Spanish or American had ever seen them. But in the same year Wetherill found two other large settlements. After this, many gold diggers stormed Mesa Verde. More and more of these rare villages were being discovered, plundered and ramshackled. Riches were not found, only skeletons wrapped in mats and everyday articles of use. In 1906 the government declared this area a national park and stopped the vandalism.

In the years since the chance discovery, archaeologists have traced the Anasazi and their history as far back as to their prehistoric tribes. In the 6th century A.D. the Anasazi formed village communities and built close together terrace houses with several floors. The houses, which were sculptured from the sand stone, were fixed to the steep canyons' walls, or were built in the caves or in the inaccessible stream valleys. Entry was only possible via a ladder which went through an opening in the roof. When danger was nearby, the ladder was immediately pulled in through the roof opening - the houses were antique burglar proof penthouses. By each house were usually several large round buildings, which were sunk halfway in the ground and were used for religious ceremonies.

The thinly populated area was probably quite heavily populated in earlier times. According to the last scientific estimation, there were more than 50,000 Anasazi-Pueblo indians in the New Mexico and Arizona region. Still today not all the ruins have been registered, never mind explored. Very little is known about the inhabitants. They grew corn, beans and pumpkins. They kept turkeys and used dogs for pack animals and food. From cotton they weaved fine fabrics, their ceramics were decorated with black and white designs, and they made double baskets which they lavishly decorated. Dug-out canals and artificial ponds supplied drinking water for about 16 villages in the area. They apparently lived a peaceful existence. Nowhere have the archaeologists found any traces of battle, oppression, slavery or violence.

At the end of the 13th century, the Anasazi indians left their settlements and disappeared. The reason for this remained a mystery for a long time. These days the reason is thought to be known: from 1274 through to 1299, there was a terrible drought.

Hidden in an oval rock opening lies Cliff Palace (photo left and below). This primal town of the Anasazi indians is considered to be the most important evidence of a pre-Columbian culture. The circular kivas were used for religious ceremonies. Today there are still many mountain villages to be found between New Mexico and Arizona, which have not yet been scientifically explored. Drawings were found in some of the caves. However, the drawings were made much later: the horse, on which the archer is sitting, was made after the introduction of the horse in the New World by the Spanish.

SOUTH AMERICA

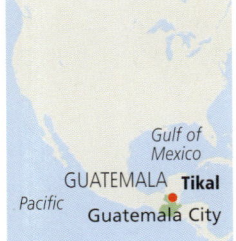

Ruined rainforest city of the Mayas

Tikal National Park holds the remnants of Mayan civilization

Getting there:
Daily flights and bus connections from Guatemala City, Cancun and Belize. Shuttle buses to the park

Where to stay:
3 hotels and one campsite in the grounds around the Tikal ruins, as well as a wide selection of sites in El Remate, Flores and Santa Elena

Climate:
Humid and warm all year round, with temperatures around 25°C. Dry season between November and May

Main attractions:
Hikes along jungle trails following ancient Maya paths, Tikal ruins, panoramic views from Temple IV

Special tips:
It is advisable to visit the National Park in groups and only in the company of a guide

Towering above the dense green tree canopy of the tropical rain forest, the largest of its kind in Central America, are the gray stone peaks of the pyramids, mysterious remnants of a civilization which suddenly collapsed a thousand years ago. Tikal was the center of Mayan culture, which evolved here around 900 B.C. and reached its peak between 700 and 800 A.D. Indiscriminate exploitation of the environment led to an ecological crisis, as a result of which man disappeared and the rainforest emerged triumphant, burying the last traces of his madness under its green canopy.

Today, these ruins form an integral part of this fascinating rain forest and one of the main attractions for the visitor. In the thousand years that have elapsed since the collapse of the Maya civilization, an unparalleled ecosystem has developed in this area. Tikal National Park, which covers an area of 358 miles (576km2) is both a natural and cultural world heritage site. It is also the core area of the Maya Biosphere Reserve, which covers 6,214 miles (10,000km2) and also includes the San Miguel La Palotada wetlands, an area of almost 311 miles (500km2). Altogether, this conservation area comprises around 137 miles (200km2) of continuous tropical rain forest – the largest of its kind in Central America.

Over 300 species of trees

Tikal's Temple IV, known as the "Temple of the Two-Headed Snake," is 213ft (65m) high and the view from its summit provides an unforgettable panoramic view over the forest canopy, dotted here and there with the pointed tips of the gray stone pyramids peeping through the trees. If you can get here early enough, the sight of the blood-red morning sun rising slowly in the tropical sky is a breathtaking experience. Far below, in the quiet of the jungle, the visitor is enveloped in a blanket of wet humidity. It generally rains for approximately 150 days of the year, but the porous limestone floor does not retain the water. Instead, it constantly circulates within the delicate equilibrium of this rainforest ecosystem between the thin layer of humus on the forest floor and the canopy formed by the giant trees.

Three hundred different species of trees have been identified so far, including cedar, mahogany, palm, strangler fig and ceiba, Guatemala's national tree, also known as the kapok tree. Because of its spreading crown, which can extend 164ft (50m) across, the Mayas often planted it in the squares between the temple buildings to provide a source of shade. In the rainforest, it supports a little ecosystem all of its own. The crevices in its grayish-pink bark and branches are home to numerous orchids, ferns, cacti and bromeliads. Iguanas and other reptiles rest on its branches soaking up the few rays of sun which manage to filter through the leaf canopy.

Monkeys chatter noisily among the trees

The National Park is home to 54 species of mammal, an opportunity for the visitor to enjoy a close encounter with life in the jungle. The tapirs, white-tailed deer, armadillos, giant and lesser anteaters and three-toed sloths, dangling lazily from the branches, are stalked by predators such as pumas, ocelots and jaguars. And the ubiquitous monkeys, mainly howler and spider monkeys, are everywhere, chattering and leaping about in the treetops.

Small American crocodiles lie in wait for prey along the banks of the numerous rivers. Six genera of turtles rustle about in the riverbank vegetation, as do 38 different varieties of snakes, including the poisonous coral snake.

Ruins of a Maya temple, rearing up through the rainforest canopy in Tikal National Park (left)

The ruins of the Maya temple complex of "Acropolis" (above, left)

Two crumbling temple towers peep through the wide expanse of rainforest canopy (opposite)

SOUTH AMERICA

Floating islands of reeds

Lake Titicaca National Park is home to members of the Uro community, who depend on the lake for their livelihood

Getting there:
Regular flights from Lima to Juliaca, followed by a one-hour bus journey to Puno

Where to stay:
All categories of accommodation available in Puno and around Lake Titicaca, as well as on some of the islands

Climate:
May to October sunny, with little rain; daytime temperatures up to 77°F (25°C), night temperatures around 32°F (0°C)

Main attractions:
Boat trip through the reserve; the floating Uro island dwellings; the islands of Taquile and Amantani

Lake Titicaca is the world's highest navigable freshwater lake (above)

Totora reeds provide all the Uro Indians' essential needs. They use reeds to build their floating island dwellings (below, center), their ships are built of reeds (below, left), and reeds harvested from the shore are transported into the hinterland to be used as building material (below, right)

Despite being regarded as an inferior race by the Incas, the Uros managed to survive invasions by would-be conquerors and even emerged intact from years of Spanish colonial rule. They are one of the oldest Indian peoples anywhere in America. Although their younger descendents have mixed with other Aymará tribes in the Lake Titicaca mountain region over the past 50 years, they have continued to uphold the traditions of their forefathers. Present-day Uros still live, as their ancestors did thousands of years ago, on floating islands in the middle of Lake Titicaca. There are more than 40 of these islands, artistically crafted from totora reeds, floating in the marshy wetlands of the Peruvian sector of Titicaca National Reserve at the northwestern end of the lake. The area is a mere 15-minute boat ride away from the bustling tourist city of Puno.

This national reserve was established in 1978 and covers an area more than 140 square miles (360km2). It is included on RAMSAR's list of the world's main wetland areas. The largest section, comprising an area of around 115 square miles (300km2), encompasses the Bay of Puno with its individual pockets of densely growing totora reeds. The Ramis sector, centering on the area around Huancané and extending about 7 1/2 miles (12km) inland, was established to protect a large expanse of reed bed. The dominant emergent species here is totora, but 12 other sub-species of this flat, flexible-stemmed water plant are also present. This remote, inhospitable region, which nevertheless boasts a significant biodiversity, does not attract many visitors. Its indigenous plants and animals are consequently left largely undisturbed.

Floating houses

The Uro Indians' existence revolves entirely around the totora reed. Not only is it used as a building material for their dwellings, boats and islands, but it also provides a useful source of food. Each family occupies its own individual island which consists of a large quantity of individual woven mats which are tied together and anchored to the lake bed. Soil is collected from the shores of the lake and spread across the island in thin layers to create island gardens for growing root crops such as potatoes and yuccas.

Lake Titicaca, measuring around 3,200 square miles (8,300km2) and situated 12,500 ft (3,812m) above sea level, is the highest navigable lake on earth. It occupies the gap between two Andean mountain ranges. The lake is 460–590ft (140-180m) deep at its center, suddenly falling away to a depth of 920ft (280m) along the Peruvian-Bolivian border.

The fluctuating water table

Although 25 rivers discharge into Lake Titicaca, most of its water is derived directly from rainfall. Ninety-five percent of it evaporates as steam. The small Desagüadero River channels about 5 percent of Lake Titicaca's water into to Lake Poopó. During the Inca occupation, the lake was considerably larger than it is today. One thousand years ago, the Tihuanaco temple complex, now a distance of around 12 1/2 miles (20km) inland from the lake, stood right on the lake shore. It is unlikely, however, that the lake will ever dry up.

It seems that the water levels undergo short-term fluctuations over the course of a year as well as regular, long-term changes over centuries.

Lake Titicaca is home to 14 different varieties of fish in the lake. Many of these have become endangered since the introduction of rainbow trout into the lake in 1939. These fish, which can reach lengths of 24in (60cm), have driven out virtually every other species and have become the most popular fish dish on the Indios menu. The only other species, which are still relatively common, are the Andean carp and a large species of catfish.

Another delicacy forming part of the Uros' diet is the giant, eyeless, Titicaca toad, which can also reach 24in (60cm) in length and lives on the lake bed. It is one of 18 species of amphibians residing in the lake.

SOUTH AMERICA

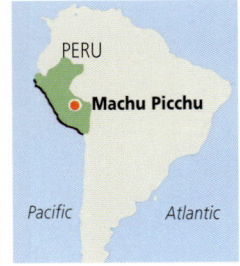

Forgotten Machu Picchu

The old Inca settlement in the Peruvian Andes was discovered in 1911

Route:
Flight from Lima to Cuzco, train to Machu Picchu

Best time:
June through to October

Also worth seeing:
Ruins from the Sacsayhuaman Inca settlement near Cuzco

On the east side of the Peruvian Andes, where the mountain river Urubamba flows to meet the nearby Amazon basin, the American Hiram Bingham made on July 24, 1911 the most important discovery of his career, whilst searching for relics from the Inca culture which was destroyed by the Spanish conquerors in the 16th century. After climbing a high steep mountain wall in one of the river bends, the young Yale University history professor, together with his two native guides, finally reached at about 7,545 feet (2,300 m) above sea level a mountain path surrounded by large rocks, which was not visible from the valley and whose entrance had been blocked due to an earthquake many years before. Numerous green-covered walls and high tiered terraces hinted, that there was once a large city here.

In the center of the temple complex

Bingham christened his discovery Machu Picchu, which means "Old Top" in the Quechua indian language. Later research showed that it was an old Inca settlement, which had been deliberately built in an inaccessible place to escape from the plundering Conquistadors. Although they were only 75 miles (120 km) northwest of the Inca capital Cuzco, which had been conquered by the Spanish. In the following years, archaeologists uncovered the overgrown temple and palace, whose walls were from the magnificent granite blocks.

In the center of the settlement place was the temple complex, where at the highest point is a terrace, hacked out of granite, which leads upwards via a spiral stairway chopped from the rock. The archaeologists identified the monolithen as a so-called Intihuatana, the sacred stone of the Incas, "which captures the sun." Similar rock buildings, which served as a sort of sun dial, were the centre of a sun cult in the Inca realm.

Not too far away from Intihuatana, three well-preserved walls from a Sun temple were found with an altar made from three blocks of rock. Another important construction in the palace quarter is the Torreón, a half round tower with sacrifice altar, under which is a pit, which Bingham called the "Kings' Mausoleum." 142 skeletons were found close by, mainly women, maybe Ajillas, as the girls who were called who had been specially selected for the sun cult. Other simply constructed districts were obviously inhabited by soldiers and workers. A flat open area, now called Plaza Principal, was probably used as a meeting place for festivities, such as the celebration of the winter solstice.

Hundreds of tiered terraces which lead upwards to the actual city center, were used to grow vegetables. Potatoes, corn and various vegetables were grown in the small fields, which were surrounded by the rock walls. The soil was thought to of been brought up from the 1,640 feet (500 m) Urbamba valley below. Calculations show that the mountain fields produced enough food for about 10,000 people.

On a mountain path hidden so well by rocks that the Conquistadors did not find it, the Incas built their mountain settlement, Machu Picchu. Stairways and sanctuaries were chopped, just as the "Kings' Mausoleum," bottom left in the photo, out of rocks. Other buildings were built without using cement from stone, which were made to exactly the right size. (bottom right)

SOUTH AMERICA

The mysterious giant pictures in Nazca

Why were they etched in the desert 1,500 years ago?

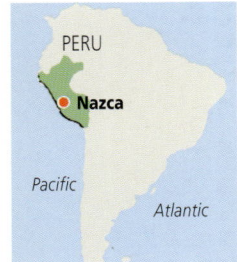

Route:
Route flight to Nazca; car or bus from Lima 280 miles (450 km) up the Panamericana to the south.

Best time:
Best time December through to April

Accommodation:
Hotel La Borda, Panamericana km 278 miles (447 km)

Also worth seeing:
Puerto de Lomas beaches

Secret grooves etched by unknown hands in the desert terrain pertain to the biggest archaeological mystery in South America. They were made about 1500 years ago in a 193-square-mile (500 km²) surface between the present towns of Nazca and Ica in the south of Peru. Some of the grooves run straight through the pampas landscape, others form enormous patterns on the high planes and steep hills, which from the ground cannot to be viewed or shown. Only when viewed from a plane do the grooves come together to form huge drawings.

Animals of enormous dimensions

The American cultural historian Paul Kosok first discovered the geometrical pictures in 1939 during an exploration flight.

His observations inspired the German mathematician Maria Reiche to devote her life to researching the patterns in the desert. She discovered that the approximately 8-inch (20 cm) deep and at least 3$\frac{1}{3}$ foot (1 m) wide recesses in yellow sand, once freed of the red desert soil, became more clearer than ever before. This is how the scientists were able to expose a drawing of a condor with a cross section of 394 feet (120 m), so that photos could be taken of it from in the air. Other pictures later exposed were of a spider with 131-foot (40 m) legs and giant contours of people, monkeys, fish, cacti and flowers.

Most of these etchings consist of a single line, which run a few hundred yards, or sometimes even miles through the desert. That the drawings, which include circles, squares and spirals, have lasted for more than 1500 years, is thanks to their geographical location. There is very little rainfall in the Pampa de las Figuras between Nazca and Ica, and the terrain is protected against sandstorms by the coastal mountain range in the west and by spurs of the Andes in the east.

What stands out in all of the drawings is not only the accuracy with which they have been etched in the ground, but also the artistic styling. Similar designs of the same high aesthetic level can be found on the ceramic objects of the Nazca culture, which flourished between the 4th and 9th century in South Peru. It is therefore certain that the Nazca artists drew the pictures.

Illustrations from astronomy

How the Peruvians, from before the Inca time, were able to make drawings they could not oversee in the desert soil, remains a mystery.

What is certain is that they definitely used ropes to draw the straight lines and circles. There is no clear explanation of the meaning of these giant figures. Most of the scientists agree, that they are astronomical illustrations. Maria Reiche believes that it has to do with "an account of old cosmic observations." This is because one of the grooves she discovered leads straight to the place where the sun sets in the southern hemisphere during the solstice in June. Also other, not entirely parallel lines show the different setting points where in our calender years 300 through to 650, the sun set during the solstice. Even knowing all this the pictures remain a mystery. Especially, the answer to the cultural definition is still a mystery today. This gives the people with plenty of imagination a lot of freedom, such as for example the Swiss writer Erich van Däniken, who believes that the giant Nazca desert pictures are signals and landing strips for aliens.

Most of the drawings drawn 1,500 years ago in the Nazca desert (below) by unknown artists can only be seen from an airplane. The right etching represents a bird.

SOUTH AMERICA

Prehistoric treasure chamber

Capivara National Park, in Brazil, contains some of South America's earliest cave paintings

Getting there:
Flight connections to Petrolina in the Piauí, Bahia, and Pernambuco Triangle. By four-wheel-drive vehicle to São Raimundo Nonato

Where to stay:
Basic hotel accommodation in São Raimundo Nonato

Climate:
Warm tropical climate

Main attractions:
Museu do Homem Americano in São Raimundo Nonato; caves: Boqueirao da Pedra Furada and Toca do Baixão da Vaca; more caves in Serra das Confusões National Park 60 miles (100km) away

Special tips:
Special permission required to visit the caves, and only with a guide

Until now, historians thought that man first crossed the Bering Straits to North America some 60,000 to 20,000 years ago, reaching South America a little more than 13,000 years ago. But the history of how South America was first settled will be re-written if the dating of prehistoric finds in Capivara National Park in northern Brazil proves to be conclusive. Some unique and extremely artistic cave paintings have been discovered in numerous caves in the province of Piauí. They have also found what may possibly be a place where early man used to make fire approximately 48,000 years ago.

Piauí is situated between the Amazon Basin and the Atlantic, where the climate is dry except for occasional torrential showers that descend upon the varied landscape. Most of the area is covered by bush and cactus landscape known as the Caatinga. To the east of the Bom Jesus da Guergeia Mountains lies the Cerrado, an increasingly rare landscape of tree savannah. This region is home to a wide diversity of wildlife, once a useful source of food to the region's early inhabitants.

Impressive canyons

This warm landscape with its relatively sparse forests and scenic beauty is a fascinating region. Spectacular canyons with sheer sandstone walls in a myriad of different hues, dotted with isolated, majestic rock pinnacles and arches, exhibit different colors of rock strata, testifying to the landscape's geological history.

The area is a significant sanctuary for some increasingly rare and special animals, such as America's largest bat, the "vampyrum spectrum," otherwise known as the large leaf-nosed or vampire bat. These nocturnal mammals have a wingspan of three feet. Despite their somewhat malignant appearance, they pose no threat to humans. The Park also boasts numerous types of parrot, snake, giant armadillo, giant anteater, jaguar, and puma, all of which are on the endangered species list.

The large number of natural caves in the white sandstone mountains of Capivara provided a haven for South America's earliest inhabitants. Some of the caves have been gouged out and extended, their walls decorated with wonderfully intricate rock drawings depicting hunting scenes and people dancing or giving birth. There are more than 400 such sites providing considerable insight into these peoples' everyday lives.

Rock drawings in reds and browns

The most famous and grandest gallery of rock art is located in the rock shelter known as Toca do Boqueirão da Pedra Furada, literally the "rock of many holes." The reddish-brown paintings depict various animals as well as men wearing typical feather headdresses. Another important archeological site is located at Toca do Baixão da Vaca, an overhanging sandstone rock 375ft (114m) long. A total of 749 individual examples of rock art have survived here.

For the most part, these prehistoric artists used nature's own materials to lend color to their drawings, such as red hematite (iron oxide), yellow geothite, white plaster or kaolin, and their black was derived from burnt organic material such as bones or charcoal. They even used blue, a color seldom seen in cave paintings, to depict a deer.

The subject matter of these incredible rock paintings can be split into two different cultural strands or traditions. On the one hand, the Nordeste tradition, during the period from 12,000 to 6,000 BC, focused mainly on narrative rock illustrations, depicting scenes of animals and people presented singly or in groups. The later Agreste tradition dating from 8,000 to 3,000 BC was characterized, on the other hand, by peculiar lines and geometric patterns that some researchers have interpreted as an early form of script or code whose meaning has been lost in the mists of time.

Prehistoric animals

The animals depicted in these early paintings illustrate the fauna that once populated this magical landscape in the Maranhão Paraiba Basin of Brazil: emus, armadillos, panthers, alligators, fish, a variety of birds, and apes, which to this day still guard these caves and can often be glimpsed during walks through this mountainous landscape.

Weather, wind, and water have sculpted remarkable rock formations out of the soft sandstone of the National Park (above)

This rocky karst landscape is typical of some parts of Piauí Province (below, left)

Caves within the National Park contain prehistoric animal paintings, some 14000 years old, illustrating the wildlife of the time (below, right)

AUSTRALIA

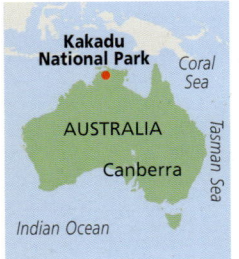

The Aboriginal world recorded in rock art

Kakadu National Park, in northern Australia, has saved many animals from extinction

Getting there:
Good road to Jabiru from Darwin, along the Arnhem Highway, or from Katherine via the Kakadu Highway. Airports in Darwin, landing strip at Jabiru

Where to stay:
Middle category hotels and simple accommodation available in Jabiru, Kakadu Resort, and Cooinda. Several campsites

Climate:
Dry season is April-May to September with temperatures around 90°F (32°C). October to December around 99°F (37°C). Downpours and thunderstorms. Rainy season January to March/April, around 91°F (33°C)

Main attractions:
Jim Jim Waterfall and Twin Falls, Yellow Water Billabong. Warradjan Aboriginal culture center near Cooinda. Rock drawings at Ubirr, Nourlangie. Nawurlandja Lookout viewpoint

Special tips:
Some of the Park's roads are flooded during the rainy season and there are few gas stations

The Aborigines carved the outlines of human figures into soft rock near Ubirr — these drawings are some of the oldest carvings in the world (opposite)

View from Obiri Rock onto the Magela Floodplains (below, left)

One of the premier wildlife sightings within the National Park is the rare monitor lizard (above, left)

There are very few regions that undergo so many seasonal changes over the course of a year as the Kakadu National Park in northern Australia. Situated 75 miles (120km) east of Darwin, this 7,700 square mile (20,000km2) Park extends 125 miles (200km) inland from the coast of Van Diemen Gulf. One third of it belongs to the Gagudju and Jabiluka Aborigines, who have leased it to the Australian park authorities. It is not only an outstanding natural heritage site, but also contains around 7,000 sites documenting the long history and culture of the Aborigine people.

More than 90 per cent of the annual rainfall occurs during the tropical monsoon season between November and April. Several times a day, torrential downpours batter the landscape. Violent thunderstorms unleash their fury over a bizarre landscape of cliffs and boulders, while howling tropical cyclones whip up the rivers, causing the flood waters to rise higher and higher each day and to leave large tracts of the floodplains under water. The landscape explodes into life and is suddenly carpeted with green plants, while water lilies burst into bloom on the vast expanses of water. Crocodiles are now in their element, while snakes and small lizards are forced to seek refuge on floating islands of vegetation.

Characteristic "X-ray style" art

The rainy season is followed by a period of almost no rainfall at all between May and October, with drought transforming most of the region into a desert in which temperatures frequently hit 108°F (42°C). The rivers dry up and all that remain are a few shallow freshwater puddles, the last refuge for one particular species of fish, which is specially adapted to enable it to survive the dry season.

In the east of the Park, the huge escarpment of the Arnhem Plateau, which gradually rises over a distance of 300 miles (500km) from 100–1,100ft (30–330m) in height, terminates abruptly. It is composed of a hard sandstone layer, millions of years old, overlying an older, softer rock, which has been eroded over the course of the different geological periods to create numerous caverns and rocky overhangs beneath the sandstone. Over the last 18,000 years, these rock walls have been filled with Aboriginal paintings, depicting this people's myths and stories. There are lifelike pictures of crocodiles, long extinct Tasmanian wolves, figures wearing elaborate headdresses, and characters from Aboriginal mythology. A typical feature of these rock drawings is the "X-ray" style of art, in which they are painted, for example, with the skeletons of fish showing through. Many of these drawings are some of the oldest examples of rock and cave art in the world. Deep sinkholes and narrow crevices have formed in places where the roofs of subterranean caves have collapsed. At the bottom of these, miniature habitats have evolved, each one supporting its own uniquely individual flora and fauna. Many of the creatures that form part of these miniature ecosystems are relicts of earlier geological periods that have somehow managed to survive in these enclaves.

Lizards and vipers

A few, small, monsoon forests also manage to survive at the bottom of these ravines, even during the dry season. Sheltering deep within the caves are Australian ghost vampire bats, one of altogether 64 species of mammal. There is a much greater diversity of reptiles, the 128 varieties including several rare species such as death adders, frilled lizards, and green and snake-necked turtles.

Photography credits

Pp. 10-11 **upper and lower right**, Schapowalow-Thiele; **lower left**, Schapowalow/Pratt-Pries. 12-13 **top**, Ragnar Sigurdsson/Tony Stone; **all bottom photographs**, Klaus D. Francke/Bilderberg. 14-15 **upper left**, picture-alliance/dpa/Mauri Rautkari; **upper right**, picture-alliance/dpa/Hannu Vallas; **lower right**, picture-alliance/dpa/Mauri Rautkari. 16-17 **all photographs**, Schapowalow/Pratt-Pries. 18-19 **top**, Georg Jung; **bottom**, Wolfgang Kunz/Bilderberg. 20-21 **lower left**, Schapowalow/Scholz, **upper and lower right**, Schapowalow/Huber. 22-23 **upper right**, Schapowalow/Komine; **lower left**, Schapowalow/Landschack; **lower right**, Schapowalow/Schröder; 24-25 **top**, Etienne Poupinet/Bilderberg; **lower left**, Klaus Bossemeyer/Bilderberg; **lower right**, Klaus D. Francke/Bilderberg. 26-27, Roli collection. 28-29, Ashok Dilwali. 32-33 **top**, Schapowalow/Huber, **right and lower left**, Schapowalow/Atlantide (MB). 40-41 **all photographs**, Bilderberg/Milan Horacek. 42-43 **top**, Wolfgang Volz/Bilderberg, **all bottom photographs**, Rainer Drexel/Bilderberg. 44-45 **lower left**, Schapowalow/Reichelt; **upper right**, Schapowalow/JBE; **lower right**, Schapowalow/Scholz. 46-47 **upper left**, Schapowalow/Larkins; **upper right**, Schapowalow/Fuhrmann; **lower left**, Schapowalow/Kölsch; **lower middle**, Schapowalow/Wolf; **lower right**, Schapowalow/Aspect. 48-49 **right and upper left**, Peter Ginter/Bilderberg; **lower left**, Eberhard Grames/Bilderberg. 50-51 **top**, Florian Wagner/Bilderberg; **lower left**, Eberhard Grames/Bilderberg; **lower right**, Ellerbrock & Schafft/Bilderberg. 52-53 **all photographs**, Arne Nicolaisen. 54-55 **upper right, lower left, and lower middle**, Schapowalow/Atlantide (SA); **lower right**, Schapowalow/Doormann. 56-57 **top**, Rainer Drexel/Bilderberg; **lower left**, Gert Wagner/Bilderberg; **lower right**, C. Boisvieu/Bilderberg. 58-59 **top**, John Lamb/Tony Stone; **bottom**, Till Leeser//Bilderberg. 60-61 **all photos**, Schapowalow/Pratt-Pries. 62-63 **upper right and bottom**, picture-alliance/ZB/Matthias Hiekel; **lower left**, picture-alliance/gms/Tourismusverband Sächsische Schweiz/Frank Richter. 64-65 **lower left**, Schapowalow/Geiersperger; **upper right**, Schapowalow/Kirsch; **lower right**, Schapowalow/Mader. 66-67 **all photos**, Schapowalow/Thiele. 68-69 **upper right and lower left**, Schapowalow/Schröder; **lower right**, Schapowalow/Doormann. 70-71 **top**, R. Kendrick/Aurora/Bilderberg; **bottom**, Dinodia/Bilderberg. 72-73 **all photos**, Corbis. 74-75 **upper right and bottom**, Schapowalow/Heaton; **lower left**, Schapowalow/JBE. 90-91 **top**, picture-alliance/dpa/ Scanfot Thinvold; **upper left**, Bilderberg/Wolfgang Fuchs; **lower left**, picture-alliance/dpa/Paul van Gaalen; **lower right**, picture-alliance/dpa/Winfried Wisniewski. 92-93 **top**, Schapowalow/Dr. Harten; **lower left**, Schapowalow/Heaton, **lower middle**, Schapowalow/Lossen; **lower right**, Schapowalow/Messerschmidt. 94-95 **top** Schapowalow/Heaton; **bottom**, Schapowalow/Scholz. 96-97 **all photos**, Schapowalow-Huber. 98-99 **all photos**, Arne Nicolaisen. 100-101 **all photos**, Schapowalow/Atlantide (GC). 102-103 **upper right**, Schapowalow/Atlantide (GC); **lower left**, Schapowalow/Art of Nature; **lower middle**, Schapowalow/K. Scholz; **lower right**, Schapowalow/K. Scholz, Photo Library/Bilderberg. 106-107 **all photos**, Schapowalow/Huber. 108-109 **upper left**, Schapowalow/Pratt-Pries; **upper right**, Schapowalow/K. Scholz; **lower right**, Schapowalow/Brooke. 110-111 **upper right**, Schapowalow/Aspect, **right and lower left**, Schapowalow/Aspect; **lower middle**, Schapowalow/Pratt-Pries. 112-113 **left**, Schapowalow/Gierig; **upper right**, Schapowalow/Gierig; **right middle and bottom**, Schapowalow/Aspect. 114-115 **upper left and lower right**, Klaus Bossemeyer/Bilderberg; **upper right**, W. Allgöwer/Transglobe; **lower left**, Milan Horacek/Bilderberg. 116-117 **upper left**, Schapowalow/Weisser; **upper right**, Schapowalow/Böker; **lower right**, Schapowalow/de Vrée. 118-119 **upper right**, Schapowalow/Nebe; **lower left**, Schapowalow/Koserowsky; **lower right**, Schapowalow/Backhaus. 120-121 **upper right**, Schapowalow/de Vrée; **middle left**, Schapowalow/Huber; **lower left**, Schapowalow/Messerschmidt; **lower right**, Schapowalow/Mader. 122-123 **upper right and bottom** Schapowalow/Nebe; **lower left**, Schapowalow/K. Scholz. 124-125 **upper right and left**, Schapowalow/Dr. Nowak; **top middle**, Schapowalow/Atlantide (GC); **lower right**, Schapowalow/Huber. 126-127 **all photos**, picture-alliance/dpa/RIA Nowosti. 128-129 **all photos**, Schapowalow/Lensch. 130-131 **upper right and bottom**, Klaus D. Francke/Bilderberg; **lower left**, Klaus Bossemeyer/Bilderberg. 132-133 **all photos**, Amrit P. Singh/wildphotos.com. 134-135 **left**, Sharatchandra Yanglem; **right**, Corbis. 136-137 **all photos**, Nirad Grover. 138-139 **all photos**, Nirad Grover. 140-141 **left**, Dinodia; **right**, Nirad Grover. 142-143 **all photos**, V. Muthuraman. 154-155 **left**, picture-alliance/dpa/Panasia; **right**, picture-alliance/dpa/Tomonori Otsuka. 156-157 **top**, Schapowalow/Moser; **bottom**, Schapowalow/Huber. 158-159 **left and upper right**, Schapowalow/Atlantide (SA); **lower right**, Schapowalow/Sander. 160-161 **top**, Schapowalow/Atlantide (GC); **lower left**, Schapowalow/v.d. Hecken, **lower middle**, Schapowalow/Fuhrmann; **lower right**, Schapowalow/Sander. 162-163 **all photos**, Rudolf Bauer/Transglobe. 164-165 **all photos**, Hackenberg/Silvestris. 166-167 **upper right and bottom**, picture-alliance/dpa/F. Hoogervorst; **lower left**, picture-alliance/dpa/Raimundo Valentim. 168-169 **top**, Schapowalow/Bernutz; **lower left**, Schapowalow/Rosenfeld; **lower right**, Schapowalow/Huber. 170-171 **upper right**, Schapowalow/Novak; **lower left**, Schapowalow/art of nature; **lower right**, Schapowalow/Scholz. 172-173 **all photos**, ABPL/Bilderberg. 174-175 **top**, Schapowalow/Thiele; **bottom**, Schapowalow/Pratt-Pries. 176-177 **upper right and bottom**, Schapowalow/Nebe; **lower left**, Schapowalow/Ponzio; **lower middle**, Schapowalow/Huber. 178-179 **all photos**, Bilderberg/Klaus Bossemeyer; 180-181 **upper right a lower middle**, Schapowalow/Gierig; **lower left**, Schapowalow/Fahn; **lower right**, picture-alliance/dpa/Jesper Sandström. 182-183 **all photos**, Schapowalow/Atlantide (GC). 184-185 **left, upper right, and lower right**, Schapowalow/Pratt-Pries; **lower left**, Schapowalow/Fuhrmann. 186-187 **upper left and lower right**, Schapowalow/Gessler; **upper right**, Schapowalow/Thiele. 188-189 **left and upper middle**, Schapowalow/Thiele; **upper right, middle, and bottom**, Schapowalow/Ambild. 190-191 **top**, Bilderberg/Klaus-D. Francke; **bottom**, Schapowalow/Klee. 192-193 **upper left**, Schapowalow/Dr. Nowak; **upper right**, Dr. Nowak; **lower right**, Schapowalow/Rakebrand. 194-195 **top**, Schapowalow/art of nature; **bottom**, Schapowalow/Huber. 196-197 **left**, Schapowalow/Huber; **right**, Schapowalow/Busert. 198-199 **upper left**, picture-alliance/gms/Czech Center for Tourism; **upper right**, picture-alliance/ZB/Transit/Christian Nowak; **left and lower right**, picture-alliance/dpa/_TK Saskia Bergová. 200-201 **upper left and lower right**, picture-alliance/Polska Agencja Interpress; **upper right**, picture-alliance/dpa/Göbel. 202-203 **upper left**, picture-alliance/dpa/Dick Klees; **lower left**, picture-alliance/dpa/Sari Gustaffson; **right**, picture-alliance/dpa/RIA Nowosti. 204-205 **upper left**, Schapowalow/Nebe; **upper right**, Schapowalow/Huber; **lower right**, Schapowalow/Johansson. 206-207 **top**, Schapowalow/Huber; **bottom**, Schapowalow/Bodo Müller. 208-209 **all photos**, Schapowalow/Atlantide (GC). 210-211 **left**, Dinodia; **right**, Schapowalow/Atlantide (GC). 212-213 **all photos**, Dinodia. 214-215 **all photos**, Dinodia. 216-217 **all photos**, Dinodia. 218-219 **all photos**, Nirad Grover. 220-221 **left**, Nirad Grover; **right**, P.C. Dheer. 222-223 **left and upper right**, Dinodia, **bottom**, Corbis. 224-225 **all photos**, Corbis. 226-227 **all photos**, Roli Collection. 230-231 **left**, picture-alliance/Okapia KG/Hans Reinhard; **right**, picture-alliance/dpa/Zhou Kang. 232-233 **all photos**, Schapowalow/Behrendt. 234-235 **all photos**, Schapowalow/Reichelt. 236-237 **left**, Bernd Jonkmanns/Bilderberg; **right**, Benelux Press/Bilderberg. 238-239 **all photos**, Schapowalow/Novak. 240-241 **all photos**, Schapowalow/Wood Buffalo National Park. 242-243 **all photos**, Schapowalow/Huber. 244-245 **top**, Schapowalow/Alantide (GC); **bottom**, Schapowalow/Beckert. 246-247 **left, middle, and upper right**, Schapowalow/Tolkmitt; **lower right**, Schapowalow/Ziegler. 248-249 **all photos**, Arne Nicolaisen. 250-251 **all photos**, Bilderberg/Michael Ende. 252-253 **all photos**, Schapowalow/Atlantide (GC). 254-255 **all photos**, Schapowalow/Atlantide (GC). 256-257 **all photos**, Schapowalow/Scholz. 258-259 **upper right and lower left**, Schapowalow/Huber; **upper left**, Schapowalow/Fahn. 260-261 **upper right**, Schapowalow/Atlantide (SA); **lower left**, Schapowalow/Aspect; **middle and lower right**, Schapowalow/Nebbia. 262-263 **upper right**, Schapowalow/Aspect; **lower left**, Schapowalow/Atlantide (SA); **lower right**, Schapowalow/Nebbia. 264-265 **all photos**, Schapowalow/Wende. 266-267 **all photos**, Schapowalow/Pratt-Pries. 268-269 **upper left**, Schapowalow/Jean; **upper right**, Schapowalow/Sperber; **middle right**, Schapowalow/K. Scholz; **lower right**, Schapowalow/ Nacivet. 270-271 **upper right**, Schapowalow/Ebel; **lower left**, Schapowalow/ Maetschke; **lower right**, Schapowalow/Huber. 272-273 **left**, Schapowalow/Röhrbein; **right and lower middle**, Schapowalow/Atlantide (MB); **upper right**, Schapowalow/Huber. 274-275 **all photos**, Schapowalow/Neuner. 276-277 **lower left and upper right**, Schapowalow/Heaton; **middle right and bottom**, Schapowalow/Kägi. 278-279 **top**, Schapowalow/Neuner; **bottom**, Schapowalow/Newton. 280-281 **top**, Florian Monheim/Architekton/Bilderberg; **bottom**, Till Leeser/Bilderberg. 282-283 **all photos**, Herman Meyer/Interfoto/Transglobe. 284-285 **upper left**, Klaus D. Francke/Bilderberg; **bottom and upper right**, Wolfgang Kunz/Bilderberg. 286-287 **upper right**, Schapowalow/Kirsch; **upper left**, Schapowalow /Atlantide (SA); **lower right**, Schapowalow/Cora. 288-289 **all photos**, Schapowalow/Atlantide (MB). 290-291 **all photos**, Andre Reiser/Bilderberg. 292-293 **all photos**, Nirad Grover. 294-295 **all photos**, Roli Collection. 296-297 **all photos**, Schapowalow/Huber. 304-305 **lower left**, Eberhard Grames/Bilderberg; **top**, Reinhart Wolf/Bilderberg. 306-307 **all photos**, Eberhard Grames/Bilderberg. 308-309 **left**, Schapowalow/Schulke; **upper right and bottom**, Schapowalow/Peters. 310-311 **upper right**, Schapowalow/Atlantide (MB); **left, middle, and lower right** Schapowalow/Dörig. 312-313 **top**, Renate v. Forster/Bilderberg; **right and lower left**, Rainer Drexel/Bilderberg. 314-315 **all photos**, Rainer Drexel/Bilderberg. 316-317 **all photos**, Bilderberg/Michael Ende. 318-319 **left**, Schapowalow/Rennings; **upper right**, Schapowalow/Sander; **lower right**, Schapowalow/Newton; 30-31, 34-35, 36-37, 38-39, 76-77, 78-79, 80-81, 82-83, 84-85, 86-87, 88-89, 144-145, 146-147, 148-149, 150-151, 152-153, 228-229, 298-299, 300-301, 302-303 Mei Sheng, Xiao Yun, Guo Youming, Liu Shizhao, Bian Zhiwu, Yang Ying, Li Yuqun, Chu Xiaoqin, Zhu Chunshu, Yan Xinfa, Niu Aihong, Yu Jianyin, Yuan Zhu, Zhang Ziqiang, Ren Jin, Miao Jun, Zhao Zhijun, Xue Yao, Dong Jiancheng, Wang Jigang, Zhang Qunxing, Liang Daming, and Liu Xiaotian.